PRENTICE-HALL HISTORY OF
THE AMERICAN PEOPLE SERIES

Leon Litwack, Editor

Published titles:

*THE GREAT CAMPAIGNS: REFORM AND
WAR IN AMERICA, 1900–1928*
Otis L. Graham, Jr.

*FROM THE REVOLUTION THROUGH THE AGE
OF JACKSON: INNOCENCE AND EMPIRE
IN THE YOUNG REPUBLIC*
John R. Howe

*RED, WHITE, AND BLACK:
THE PEOPLES OF EARLY AMERICA*
Gary B. Nash

Volumes on the following subjects are planned:

CIVIL WAR—RECONSTRUCTION
Eugene Genovese

THE GILDED AGE
Charles Glaab

RECENT AMERICA
James Kindregan

RED,
WHITE,
AND BLACK

PRENTICE-HALL, INC., ENGLEWOOD CLIFFS, NEW JERSEY

Gary B. Nash

University of California
Los Angeles

RED,
WHITE,
AND BLACK
The Peoples of
Early America

Library of Congress Cataloging in Publication Data

Nash, Gary B.
    Red, white, and black: the peoples of early
America.

    (Prentice-Hall history of the American people series)
    SUMMARY: A history text of America's colonial
period emphasizing the interaction of three cultures—
colonialists, Indians, and blacks.
    Includes bibliographical references.
    1. United States—History—Colonial period.
2. America—Discovery and exploration. [1. United
States—History—Colonial period. 2. America—
Discovery and exploration] I. Title.
E188.N37 1974   917.3′03′2   74–1003
ISBN 0–13–769810–0
ISBN 0–13–769802–X (pbk.)

"A people without history is like wind upon the buffalo grass"
Old Teton Sioux saying

Printed in the United States of America

10   9   8   7   6   5

PRENTICE-HALL INTERNATIONAL, INC., London
PRENTICE-HALL OF AUSTRALIA, PTY. LTD., Sydney
PRENTICE-HALL OF CANADA, LTD., Toronto
PRENTICE-HALL OF INDIA PRIVATE LIMITED, New Delhi
PRENTICE-HALL OF JAPAN, INC., Tokyo

FOR BROOKE, ROBIN,
JENNIFER, AND DAVID

contents

foreword

The uniqueness of this study is apparent at the very outset. Unlike the traditional approach to early American history, Gary Nash begins neither with the first English footholds at Plymouth Rock and Roanoke Island nor with Christopher Columbus's voyage, but some 20,000 years before Christ when the first Americans spread themselves over the continent. By the time the Europeans managed to find their way to the old "New World," a diversity of native cultures had existed for thousands of years. Challenging the ethnocentric focus of traditional history, Nash views the Europeanization of the New World as only one crucial stage in the evolution of colonial society. The history of the American people is not primarily the story of European settlers but the complex interaction of three major cultural groups—white, red, and black: "the story of a minority of Englishmen interacting with a majority of Iroquois, Delawares, Narragansetts, Pequots, Mohicans, Catawbas, Tuscaroras, Creeks, Cherokees, Choctaws, Ibos, Mandingos, Fulas, Yorubas, Ashantis, Germans, French, Spanish, Swedes, and Scotch-Irish." That the Europeans should have emerged as the dominant group was in large measure a tribute to their organizational skills, military know-how, and expertise in the arts of duplicity and repression.

When, in the 1630s, the hand of God sifted from among the English people a chosen company of men and directed them to this new Canaan, Peter Bulkeley, a Puritan clergyman, made his classic pronouncement that "we, the people of New England, are as a City set upon a hill, in the open view of all the earth, the eyes of the world are upon us, because we profess our selves to be a people in Covenant with God." Utopias, model societies, and wilderness Zions tend to breed a strange variety of man. Like most recent historians, Nash rejects the notion that the Puritans were the drab, colorless, humorless, sexually-inhibited creatures that could prompt Henry L. Mencken to define Puritanism as "the haunting fear that someone, somewhere, may be happy." But neither does he view the Puritans as immune to totalitarianism, intolerance, or violence. (This is not necessarily to suggest, as did one United States senator, that the Puritan and frontier traditions must bear some of the responsibility for the assassination of President John F. Kennedy.) Of course, as Nash demonstrates, New England did not remain the homogeneous society some of its founders had envisioned but evolved into a region where the spirit of commerce, speculation, and business distracted new generations from the righteous path to salvation. Rather than confine himself to internal politics and the often strange manifestations of religiosity, however, Nash examines with particular care how the Puritans interacted with the several Indian tribes who were initially in their midst. For the Puritans, after all, the Indian represented a substantial challenge, not only because he possessed the land they coveted but also because he appeared to be the very "counter-image of civilized man, thought to be lacking in what was most valued by the Puritans—civility, Christian piety, purposefulness, and the work ethic." For the Indians, on the other hand, the Puritan Commonwealth familiarized them with the white man's potential for deceit, arrogance, broken trust, and savagery. "It was deemed wiser," Nash writes, "to urge war against threatening Indians than to punish fellow Englishmen who had initiated the violence." That enormous sense of mission that pervaded the Puritans, and the felt need to protect their internal security from "the demons of the invisible world," victimized Quakers, heretics, fortune tellers, and Indians alike, though with varying degrees of ferocity.

The tragic story of Puritan-Indian relations, although comprising only a small portion of Gary Nash's treatment of European-Indian contact, illustrates the way in which he has chosen to view traditional subjects (like the Puritans) in a much broader perspective. Few, if any, general studies of early American historians devote as much attention as does

Red, White, and Black to the impact of the Indians and ethnic and cultural conflict. How Englishmen first perceived the Indians, the contradictory images that evolved out of their relationships, the initial expectations of the European settlers and the Indians, and the insatiable appetite of the white man for more territory and wealth provide the necessary background for examining the violence and brutality that ensued until the elimination of the Indian could be rationalized as the extinction of an inferior, cultureless, and savage people. English-Indian relations, as Nash demonstrates, differed from region to region; the ways in which the interior tribes—the Creeks, Cherokees, Iroquois, and others —interacted with the English colonists, for example, provide some strikingly different patterns from those which characterized Puritan New England. Although the coastal Indian cultures eventually lay shattered, Nash shows how the prolonged resistance of those tribes gave the interior Indian cultures the necessary time "to adapt to the European presence and to devise strategies of survival as the westward-moving frontier approached them." And he makes one other point quite explicit. Many of the early colonists had envisioned a virtuous society organized around concepts of "reciprocity, spirituality, and community." With the passage of time, and with the steady growth of the white population, however, "the only people in North America who were upholding these values, and organizing their society around them, were the people who were being driven from the land."

If the Indian provoked among white men a violent response to his presence and cultural differences, the African excited even greater antipathy among a people who had come to view blackness as the very incarnation of evil and ugliness and as synonymous with heathenism, savagery, and bestiality. In examining the origins of racism and slavery, Nash critically examines and synthesizes the most recent scholarship. The result of several centuries of experience with African labor in North America helped to sustain and reinforce the initial impressions of blacks and created what Nash rightfully terms one of the great paradoxes of American history. "In the land heralded for its freedom and individual opportunity the practice of slavery, unknown for centuries in the mother country, was reinstituted." While addressing himself to why this happened, Nash also examines the Afro-Americans as "active participants in the cultural process" and describes their response to enslavement. Viewing the Africans and their enslavers as "an encounter or interaction of two cultures," he suggests that "the acculturation of slaves involved not only adaptation to the death-dealing daily toll of the plantation but education in strategies of survival, resistance, and rebellion."

Throughout this volume, Nash focuses our attention on the "historically voiceless," not only the slaves and Indians but white indentured servants, involuntary white immigrants, and those who came to America with high hopes but remained in the lower stratum of white colonial society. Whatever the legend of American success and unlimited opportunity, Nash finds equally compelling the story of those who struggled and lost. Even as political democracy expanded in colonial society, economic democracy appeared to be waning. "An open society," Nash argues, "with ample opportunities in the eighteenth century for entrepreneurship and with relatively few restraints imposed by government, was leading, paradoxically, to a growing gulf between rich and poor and to a concentration of economic power in the hands of a thin upper layer of society. Culturally committed to a society in which the individual, and not the community, was the central concern, the white population of colonial America was transforming what they thought to be uniquely American into what was more and more resembling the European conditions that they had fled." Synthesizing the work of recent demographers, Nash finds that the steady growth of the population and economic developments resulted in a less even distribution of wealth, more social stratification, and a marked increase in propertylessness in virtually every community. If American society on the eve of the Revolution still remained a land of opportunity for most people, Nash reminds us that some one-fourth of the population was in bondage or had been evicted from their lands and that "the promise of American colonial society was intimately and unforgettably intertwined with the exploitation of African labor and Indian land."

To the reader expecting a traditional treatment of traditional subjects, this volume suggests an altogether different perspective and approach. But to say that this is an "uncommon" view of early American history is only to underscore the extent to which historians have defined that experience all too narrowly and provincially.

Leon F. Litwack

acknowledgments

The pages that follow began to take form in my mind three years ago when Alexander Saxton, Stephan Thernstrom, and I undertook to redesign the introductory course in American history at the University of California, Los Angeles. Our effort was directed at making American history more understandable to an ethnically, socially, and intellectually diverse undergraduate audience by studying it as the process of change that occurred as people of widely varying cultural backgrounds interacted over a period of four centuries. Although this does not sound like a startling innovation, I discovered that it required me to read broadly in areas that had largely escaped my notice during fifteen years of studying and teaching colonial American history—anthropology, ethnohistory, African history, and Latin American history. That they "escaped my notice" is to put the point obliquely, for one of the thrusts of this book is that we read, think, and write selectively and in ways that reflect our cultural biases. Nothing more than changing my "angle of vision" was required to make it apparent that early American history *could* become the early history of the American peoples only if I vastly widened the scope of my reading and thinking about the subject.

In the process of doing this and in the process of writing this book I have been informed, aided, corrected, inspired, and sustained in various degrees by Phillip Borden, Robert W. Griffith, Francis Jennings, George Phillips, Terence O. Ranger, Neal E. Salisbury, and Margaret Strobel, as well as by countless undergraduate and graduate students at the University of California, Los Angeles, whose insights and interest have helped me pursue this work.

Gary B. Nash

Introduction

"God is English." Thus John Aylmer, a pious English clergyman, exhorted his parishioners in 1558, attempting to fill them with piety and
patriotism.[1] That thought, though never so directly stated, has echoed
ever since through our history books. As school children, as college students, and as presumably informed citizens, most of us have been nur-
tured on what has passed for the greatest success story of human history,
the epic tale of how a proud, brave offshoot of the English-speaking people tried to reverse the laws of history by demonstrating what the human
spirit, liberated from the shackles of tradition, myth, and oppressive authority could do in a newly discovered corner of the earth. For most
Americans, colonial history begins with Sir Walter Raleigh and John
Smith and proceeds through John Winthrop and William Bradford to
Jonathan Edwards and Benjamin Franklin. It ends on the eve of the
Revolution with wilderness-conquering settlers preparing to pit themselves against an increasingly tyrannical mother country.

[1]Quoted in Carl Bridenbaugh, *Vexed and Troubled Englishmen, 1590–1642* (New
York: Oxford University Press, Inc., 1968), p. 13.

That this is ethnocentric history has been charged frequently and vociferously in the last decade, both by liberal white historians and by those whose citizenship is American but whose ancestral roots are in Africa, Asia, Mexico, or the native cultures of North America. Just as Eurocentrism made it difficult for the early colonizers and explorers to believe that a continental land mass as large as North America could exist between Europe and Asia—the known parts of the world for Europeans for many centuries—historians in this country have found it difficult to understand that the colonial period of our history is the story of a minority of Englishmen interacting with a majority of Iroquois, Delawares, Narragansetts, Pequots, Mahicans, Catawbas, Tuscaroras, Creeks, Cherokees, Choctaws, Ibos, Mandingos, Fulas, Yorubas, Ashantis, Germans, French, Spaniards, Swedes, and Scotch-Irish, to mention only some of the cultural strains present on the continent.

Recently, American historians, most of them educated in the post-World War II era, have tried to provide a corrective to the white-oriented, hero-worshipping history of the high school textbooks. But in the main their efforts have amounted to little more than a restocking of the pantheon of national heroes with new figures whose skin is not so pale. Thus pedestals are erected for Crispus Attucks, the half-Indian, half-black fisherman of Boston who fell first at the Boston massacre; for Eli Parker, the Seneca Indian general who helped the North win the Civil War and later served his friend, Ulysses Grant, when the latter attained the presidency; and for Caesar Chavez, the leader of the United Farm Workers, who has brought major gains to the Chicano agricultural workers of the country.

This kind of historical revisionism does not promise to serve us very well. No doubt the old mythology will be altered slightly by including new figures in the national drama. But is it a "new history" at all, if the revisionism consists primarily of turning a monochromatic cast of characters into a polychromatic one with the story line unchanged? Vine Deloria, Jr., an outspoken Indian leader, has charged that much of the "new" history still "takes a basic 'manifest destiny' white interpretation of history and lovingly plugs a few feathers, woolly heads, and sombreros into the famous events of American history."[2] What is revisionist about a history that still measures all events of our past in terms of the values of white society, that views American history through an Anglo-American perspective, and that regards Indians and Africans in the colonial period as inert masses whose fate was wholly determined by white settlers?

The pages that follow proceed from the belief that to cure the historical amnesia that has blotted out so much of our past we must look at

[2]Vine De Loria, Jr., *We Talk, You Listen: New Tribes, New Turf* (New York: The Macmillan Co., 1970), p. 39.

American history as the interaction of many peoples from a wide range of cultural backgrounds over a period of many centuries. For the "colonial period" of our history this means attempting to understand not only how Englishmen and other Europeans "discovered" North America and proceeded to transplant their culture there, but also how societies that had been in North America and Africa for thousands of years were actively and intimately involved in this process. Africans were not merely enslaved. Indians were not merely driven from the land. To include them in our history in this way, simply as victims of the more powerful Europeans, is no better than to exclude them altogther. It is to render voiceless, nameless, and faceless people who powerfully affected the course of our historical development as a nation.

Neither Indians nor Africans were merely masses of "primitive" people to be kneaded like dough according to the whim of the "superior" European culture. The Pequots and Narragansetts of southern New England, for example, were not only affected by Puritan culture but also responded to the arrival of Europeans in a variety of ways that made sense within the context of their cultures and their prior experience. It is as important to understand their perception of Europeans as it is to understand the European perception of them. Both perceptions led to decisions and actions, for both peoples were interested in serving their own needs. Benjamin Franklin put it well more than two hundred years ago. "Savages we call them," he wrote, "because their Manners differ from ours, which we think the Perfection of Civility; they think the same of theirs."[3]

Similarly, we are accustomed to studying how white Europeans devised a variety of ways for coping with the people whose land they were invading. But native peoples were simultaneously developing strategies for adapting to the presence of Europeans and for placing that presence in the service of their own needs. For more than two hundred years on the eastern edge of the continent, Europeans of various backgrounds intermingled with Indians of various tribal traditions in a process of political, economic, and cultural interaction. To think of Indians simply as victims of European aggression is to bury from sight the rich and instructive story of how Narragansetts, Iroquois, Delawares, Pamunkeys, Catawbas, Cherokees, Creeks, Yamasees and many other tribes, which had themselves been changing for centuries before Europeans touched foot on the continent, responded creatively and powerfully to the newcomers from across the ocean and in this way shaped the course of European settlement.

This book adopts a cultural approach to our early history. By this I mean that we will look at the land mass which Europeans called "North America" as a place where a number of different cultures converged dur-

[3]"Remarks Concerning the Savages of North America " (1784), in *The Writings of Benjamin Franklin*, ed. Albert H. Smyth (New York: The Macmillan Co., 1907), 10: 97.

ing a particular period of history—between about 1550 and 1750, to use European methods of measuring time. In the most general terms we can define these cultural groups as Indian, African, and European, though, as we will see, this oversimplification is in itself a Eurocentric device for classifying cultures. In other words, this book is not about colonial American history, as usually defined, but about the history of the *peoples* of eastern North America during the two centuries that proceeded the American Revolution.

Each of the three cultural groups was tremendously diverse. In their cultural characteristics Iroquois were as different from Natchez as Englishmen from Egyptians; Hausas and Yorubas were as unalike as Pequots and Creeks. Nor did the subgroups in each of these cultural blocs act in concert. The French, English, and Spanish fought wars with each other, contending for power and advantage in the seventeenth and eighteenth centuries, just as Hurons and Iroquois or Creeks and Cherokees sought the upper hand. Our task is to discover what happened when peoples from different continents, diverse among themselves, came into contact with each other at a particular point in history. It is social and cultural *process* and *change* that we are primarily concerned with—how cultures were affected and their destinies changed by the experience of contact with other cultures. Anthropologists call this process "acculturation" and historians call it "social change" but in either event the important thing to remember is that we are studying a dynamic process of interaction that shaped the history of native Americans, Europeans, and Africans in North America in the seventeenth and eighteenth centuries.

It is well to remember that when we speak of "cultural groups" or "societies" we are referring to abstractions. A *society* is a group of people organized together so that its needs—the sustaining of life at the most basic level—can be met. *Culture* is a broad term which embraces all the specific characteristics of a society—technology; modes of dress and diet; economic, social and political organization; styles of shelter; religion; language; art; values; methods of child-rearing; and so forth—as they are functionally related to each other. Put most simply, "culture" means a way of life, the framework within which any group of people—a society—comprehends the world around it and acts in it. But "culture" and "society" are also terms which imply standards or norms of behavior, the mean of individual characteristics. This is what is meant when we refer to "cultural traits" or "group behavior." To employ such terms is to run the danger of losing sight of the individual human beings, none of them exactly alike, who make up the culture. Culture is a mental construct which we employ for the sake of convenience so that highly varied and complex individual behavior can be broadly classified and compared.

Because we are Americans, belonging to the same nation, speaking the same language, living under the same law, participating in the same economic and political system—all of which make up the American "culture" —does not mean that we are all alike. Otherwise there would be no generation gap, no racial tension, no political conflict. The same can be said of Germans, Koreans, and Nigerians. Furthermore, certain Americans may have more in common with individual Nigerians or Koreans than with some of their fellow Americans. Nonetheless, taken collectively, Americans organize their lives differently and behave differently from people in other parts of the world. While we must be alive to the problems of a cultural approach to history, it at least provides us with a way of understanding the interaction of the great mass of individuals of widely varying backgrounds who found themselves cohabiting one part of the "New World" several centuries ago.

One other cautionary note is necessary. Though we will often speak of racial groups and racial interaction, these terms do not refer to genetically different groups of people. For half a century anthropologists poured their intellect and energy into attempts to classify all the peoples of the world, from the pygmies of Borneo to the Aleuts in Alaska, according to genetic differences. Noses were measured, cranial cavities examined, body hair noted, lips described, and hair and eye color classified in an attempt to define scientifically the various physiological types of man and then to demonstrate that these characteristics coincided with degrees of "cultural development." It should come as no surprise that this massive effort of Western white anthropologists resulted in the conclusion that the superiority of the Caucasian peoples of the world could be "scientifically" proven.

Genetic sciences today have wiped away this half-century effort and we are now far less convinced that significant genetic differences separate "racial groups" as previously classified by anthropologists. In retrospect it is apparent that different groups of Europeans in the New World fashioned variant codes of race relations based on their own needs and attitudes concerning how people should be classified and separated. Thus "Negro" in Brazil and in the United States came to have different meanings that reflected conditions and values, not genetic differences. As Sidney Mintz wisely reminds us, "The 'reality' of race is thus as much a social as a biological reality, the inheritance of physical traits serving as the raw material for social sorting devices, by which both stigmata and privileges may be systematically allocated."[4]

---

[4]Sidney Mintz, "Toward an Afro-American History," *Journal of World History*, 13 (1971): 318.

Thus there is little basis for distinguishing cultural groups at the biological or physiological level. We are dealing not with genetically different groups but with human populations from different parts of the world, with groups of people with cultural differences. Most of all, we will be looking at the way in which these peoples, brought into contact with each other, changed over the course of several centuries—and changed in a manner that would shape the course of American history for generations to come.

chapter 1

Before Columbus

The history of the American peoples begins not in 1492, the date which most of our history books take as their point of departure, but more than 30,000 years before the birth of Christ. For it was then that humans first discovered what much later would be called America. Thus American history can begin with some fairly simple questions: Who were these first inhabitants of the "New World"? Where had they come from? What were they like?

Almost all of the evidence suggesting answers to these questions comes from archaeologists who have excavated ancient sites of early life in North America, unearthing objects of early material culture—pots, tools, ornaments, and so forth—and pieced together the skeletal remains of the "first Americans." Aided by carbon-14 dating techniques, they have dated the arrival of man in America to about 30,000 B.C. and there is some evidence to suggest that even this date will have to be moved back as much as five or ten thousand years.

Agreement is general among anthropologists that these first inhabitants of the continent were men and women out of Asia—nomadic peoples from the inhospitable environment of Siberia who migrated across the land-bridge of the Bering Straits that connected Siberia with Alaska in search of more reliable sources of food. Thousands of years later, about 10,000 B.C., this land bridge disappeared under water as the great glaciers of the Ice Age began to melt, raising the water level in the Bering Straits region by as much as two or three hundred feet. But for several thousand years Asian peoples in search of a more life-sustaining environment than was provided by the forbidding Siberian tundra drifted in bands across this temporary freeway to the New World.

Although most anthropologists agree today that the migration was of Asian peoples, particularly from northeast Asia, the skeletal remains of these migrants also reveal non-Asian characteristics. It is probably that they represented a potpourri of different populations in Asia, Africa, and Europe, which had been mixing for thousands of years. But whatever the infusion of genes from peoples of other areas, these first Americans were Asiatic in geographical origin.

Proliferation of Cultures

Once in the North American continent, these early wanderers began a long trek southward and then eastward, following vegetation and game. It is important to remember that people in Europe at this time were also still living as seed-gatherers and hunters. Generations probably passed before these nomads reached the Pacific Northwest, and the entire movement, which ultimately reached the tip of South America and the east coast of North America, took thousands of years. When we speak of the migratory movements of the peoples of America, it is the southward and eastward movement that must be noted first. The distances, of course, were immense—15,000 miles from the Asian homeland to Tierra del Fuego, the southernmost limit of South America, and 6,000 miles from Siberia to the eastern edge of North America.

During the centuries which these long migrations spanned, the first Americans became widely dispersed over an immense land mass. One band would split off from another, and this process, repeated many times in many areas, marked the beginning of the emergence of separate cultures numbering in the hundreds on the continent. Cultural differences over a period of thousands of years became more distinct as people in different ecological regions organized their lives and related to the land in ways that their natural habitats required. Europeans would later indiscriminately lump together a wide variety of native cultures under a single rubric "Indian." But in reality myriad ways of life had developed by the time Europeans found their way to the very old "New World." For example, if Europeans had been able to drop down on native villages from the Atlantic to the Pacific coasts and from Alaska to the Gulf of Mexico in 1492 they would have found "Indians" living in Kwakiutl rectangular plank houses on the Northwest Coast; in rectangular gabled houses in Choctaw country in the lower South; in Gothic domed thatched houses in Wichita territory; in earth lodges in Pawnee prairie country; and in barrel-roofed rectangular houses arranged in Algonquian villages in most of the Northeast woodlands. Separate societies had developed a great variety of techniques for providing basic shelter because they lived in areas where building materials and weather conditions varied widely. The same diversity marked the ornaments and clothes they fashioned and the natural foods they gathered.

This diversity of native cultures is similarly evident in the languages they spoke. According to linguistic scholars, Indian languages, at the point when Europeans first came into contact with North American cultures, can be divided into twelve linguistic stocks, each as distinct from each other as Semitic languages are from Indo-European languages. Within each of these twelve linguistic stocks, a great many separate languages and dialects were spoken, each as separate as English from Russian. In all, about two thousand languages were spoken by the native Americans—a greater diversity than in any other part of the world.

How can we account for this striking diversity of Indian cultures? To a large extent the explanation lies in an understanding of environmental conditions and the way in which bands of people adapted to their natural surroundings, molding their culture in ways that would allow for survival in their region. As elsewhere in the prehistoric world, human beings were basically seed gatherers and game hunters. They were dependent for life on a food supply over which they had very little control. Struggling to control their environment, they were frequently at its mercy. To take a single example, as great geologic changes occurred in North America about 8000 B.C., vast areas from Utah to the highlands of Middle America were turned from grasslands to desert waste. Big game and plants requiring plentiful water could not survive these changes and Indian cultures in these areas had either to move on, finding new sources of food, or modify their cultures to the new conditions. Only small game and desert-adapted plants could survive these climatic changes and it is probable that during this process some societies moved on, some became extinct, and some adapted to new conditions.

Another way of understanding the process of cultural change and the proliferation of culture groups is to focus on agriculture—the domestication of plant life. Like all living organisms, human beings depend ultimately on plants to survive. For both men and animals plants are the source of fuel or energy. The ultimate source of this energy is the sun. But to tap this solar energy humans and animals must rely on plants because plants are the only organisms capable of producing significant amounts of organic material through the photosynthetic process. Plant food was—and still is—the strategic element in the chain of life, for it sustained man and it sustained the animals that provided him with a second source of food.

The Agricultural Revolution

When man learned to control the life of plants—*agriculture* is the term we give to the process—he took the first revolutionary step toward controlling the environment. It was the domestication of plants that began to emancipate human beings from their status as near-slaves to the physical world, facing extinction if the food supply decreased or vanished through forces beyond human control. To learn how to harvest a seed, plant it, and nurture it, was to assume some of nature's functions and, in so doing, to gain partial control over what heretofore had been uncontrollable. With this acquisition of partial control came vast cultural changes.

When the process of agriculture began in the New World is difficult to date with precision but it is estimated at about 8000 to 5000 B.C. In Europe, Asia, and Africa agriculture was also developing. Whether it occurred earlier in one part of the world or another is not as important as the fact that the "agricultural revolution" began independently in several widely separated parts of the world.

When the production of food replaced the collection of food, dramatic changes occurred in the life of societies. First, plant domestication allowed for a more sedentary as opposed to nomadic or seminomadic existence. Secondly, it permitted great increases in population, for even with as little as 1 percent of the land under cultivation enormous increases in the food supply could be obtained. Thirdly, it reduced the amount of time and energy needed to obtain a food supply and thus created more secure conditions for social, political, and religious development; artistic expression; and technological innovation. And lastly, it led in most areas toward a sexual division of labor, with men engaging in the hunt for game and women organizing the cultivation of crops.

Thus the agricultural revolution began to reshape the cultural outlines of native societies. Population growth and the beginnings of sedentary village life were accompanied by increasing social and political complexity. In some areas, the tribe began to evolve into larger social entities with certain individuals or groups, arranged hierarchically, organizing and controlling the production and the distribution of food surpluses. Tasks became more specialized and a more complex social structure became elaborated. In many of these changing cultures the religious specialist became the dominant figure, just as had happened in other parts of the world where the agricultural revolution had occurred. The religious figure organized the common followers, directed their work, and exacted tribute as well as worship from them; in return he pledged to protect the community from hostile forces.

When Europeans first reached the "New World," native Americans were in widely different phases of this agricultural revolution and thus their cultures were marked by striking differences. A glimpse at several of the societies with which Europeans first came into contact in the early sixteenth century will illustrate the point. In the Southwest region of North America, Hopi and Zuñi cultures had been engaged in agricultural production and a sedentary village life for some 3,000 years before the Spanish first arrived. By about 700 to 900 A.D. these tribes had begun to abandon the ancient pit houses dug in cliffs and to construct rectangular rooms arranged in apartment-like structures. By about 1200 A.D. "pueblo" culture, as it was termed by the Spanish, had developed planned villages composed of large terraced buildings, each with many rooms. These apartment-house villages were constructed on defensive sites—within rock shelters on sheer rock faces, on flat summits, or on steep-sided mesas—locations that would afford the Hopis and Zuñis protection from their northern enemies, the Apaches. The largest of them, at Pueblo Bonita, contained about eight hundred rooms and may have housed as many as a thousand persons. No larger apartment-house type construction would be seen on the continent for several hundred years, until the late nineteenth century in New York City.

By the time of Spanish arrival the Hopis and Zuñis were also using irrigation canals, check-dams, and hillside terracing as techniques for bringing water to what had been for centuries an arid, agriculturally marginal area. At the same time, the ceramic industry became more elaborate, cotton replaced yucca fiber as the main clothing material, and basket weaving became more artistic. In its technological solution to the water problem, in its artistic efforts, in its agricultural practices, and in its village life, Pueblo society on the eve of Spanish arrival was not radically different from peasant communities in most of the Euro-Asian world.

The Aztecs

Farther south, where Spaniards concentrated their first colonizing efforts, a far different culture was flourishing. This was the fabled Aztec empire in the Valley of Mexico. In this region highly favorable environmental conditions had brought the agricultural revolution to its most advanced stage on the continent. Consequently, it was here that cultural change had proceeded the fastest. By about 900 B.C. pre-Aztec society had developed extensively in population, in ability to grow crops, and in the complexity of its social structure. Tension had already begun to grow between certain holy centers of power that had developed and hinterland areas—that is to say between the cities and the countryside. These urban centers became the focus of artistic development, dictatorial political power, and trade. During the late medieval period, while Europe was involved in a prolonged period of wars, in which competing aristocracies struggled for advantage and derived the benefits from the labor of masses of peasants, a similar phenomenon was occurring thousands of miles to the west. More than a thousand overlords contended for domination of the mass of people and it was during this time that the Aztecs emerged as the most militaristic and powerful of the elite groups in the area. During a series of wars, they established control over a vast population of perhaps four to five million, equal at that time to the combined population of France and England. Staggering blood sacrifices; vast pomp, ceremony, and sumptuary displays; and government by terror characterized the century before Spanish arrival. Aztec power was also translated into huge architectural projects—colossal temples, monuments, tombs, and plazzas—and into elaborate artistic work in ceramics, metal, and stone.

Coming in anticipation of finding only "primitive" people, many of the Spanish soldiers believed they were having visions when they reached Tenochtitlan, the capital city of the Aztec empire. "Some of the soldiers among us who had been in many parts of the world, in Constantinople, and all over Italy, and in Rome," wrote Bernal Diaz del Castillo, one of Cortez's soldiers, "said that so large a market place and so full of people, and so well regulated and arranged, they had never beheld before."[1] The Spanish soldiers gaped at works of engineering, painting, sculpturing, and urban design that staggered their imaginations. Well they might, for Tenochtitlan's population, estimated at 60,000 on the eve of Spanish conquest; the brilliant artistry of its skilled artisans; and the elaborate integrated agricultural economy in the surrounding region, which employed extensive irrigation systems, elaborate hillside terracing, and artificial islands in the lakes, placed the Aztec center of power beyond the imagination of Europeans whose own capital cities provided no parallel.

Other Early Indian Cultures

Several thousands miles northeast of the Aztec empire native American cultures strikingly different from that of the Zuñis, Hopis, or Aztecs

[1] Bernal Diaz del Castillo, *The Discovery and Conquest of Mexico, 1517–1521* (New York: Farrar, Straus and Cudahy, 1956), pp. 218–19.

were evolving. From the midlands of North America to the Atlantic coastal plain a variety of tribes belonging to three main language groups —Algonquian, Iroquoian, and Siouan—were growing in strength. Their existence in eastern North America, which has been traced as far back as 10,000 B.C. was based on a mixture of agriculture, food gathering, game hunting, and fishing. Like other tribal groups that had been touched by the agricultural revolution, they gradually adopted semi-fixed settlements and developed a trading network linking together a vast region. Unlike the hierarchy-conscious Aztecs, whose masses of agriculturalists worked to support a splendiferous, theocratic state apparatus, these woodlands people were egalitarian villagers leading a far simpler life.

MOUNDBUILDERS

Among the most impressive of these societies were the so-called Mound-builders of the Ohio River Valley, who constructed gigantic sculptured earthworks in geometric designs, sometimes in the shapes of gigantic humans, birds, or writhing serpents. When colonial settlers first crossed the Appalachians, after almost a century and a half on the continent, they were astounded at these monumental constructions, some reaching as high as seventy feet. Their stereotype of eastern Indians as forest primitives would not allow them to believe that these were built by native peoples, so myths were invented to explain how survivors of the sunken islands of Atlantis or descendants of the Egyptians and Phoenicians had wandered far from their homelands, built these impressive monuments, and then disappeared. Archaeologists and anthropologists now inform us that the Moundbuilders were the ancestors of the Creeks, Choctaws, and Natchez. Their culture evolved slowly over the centuries and by the advent of Christianity had developed considerable complexity. In southern Ohio alone about ten thousand mounds, used as burial sites, have been pinpointed, and another one thousand earth-walled enclosures have been excavated, including one enormous fortification with a circumference of about three and one half miles and enclosing about one hundred acres—the equivalent of fifty modern city blocks. Archaeologists know that the Moundbuilders participated in a vast trading network covering the eastern half of the continent because a great variety of items that have been found in the mound tombs can be traced to other parts of the continent—large ceremonial blades chipped from obsidian from rock formations in Yellowstone National Park; embossed breastplates, ornaments, and weapons fashioned from copper nuggets from the Great Lakes region; decorative objects cut from sheets of mica from the southern Appalachians; and ornaments made from shark and alligator teeth and shells from the Gulf of Mexico.

INDIAN TRIBES OF EASTERN NORTH AMERICA
ON THE EVE OF EUROPEAN CONTACT

100   0   100   300
Scale of miles

MISSISSIPPI CULTURE

By about 500 A.D. the Moundbuilder culture was declining, perhaps because of attacks from other tribes or perhaps because of severe climatic changes that undermined agriculture. To the west another culture, based on intensive agriculture, was beginning to flourish. Its center was beneath present-day St. Louis, and it radiated out to encompass most of the Mississippi watershed, from Wisconsin to Louisiana and from Oklahoma to Tennessee. Thousands of villages were included in its orbit. By about 700 A.D. this Mississippian culture, as it is known to archaeologists, began to send its influence eastward to transform the life of most of the less technologically advanced woodland tribes. Like the Moundbuilders of the Ohio region, these tribes, probably influenced by Meso-American cultures through trade and warfare, built gigantic mounds as burial and ceremonial places. The largest of them, rising in four terraces to a height of one hundred feet, has a rectangular base covering nearly fifteen acres, larger than that of the Great Pyramid of Egypt. Built between 900 and 1100 A.D., this huge earthwork faces the site of a palisaded Indian city which contained more than one hundred small artificial mounds marking burial sites. Spread among them was a vast settlement, "America's first metropolis," as an archaeologist has recently called it, containing some 30,000 people by current estimations.

The finely crafted ornaments and tools recovered by archaeologists at Cahokia, as this center of Mississippi culture is called, include elaborate ceramics, finely sculptured stonework, carefully embossed and engraved copper and mica sheets, and one funeral blanket fashioned from 12,000 shell beads. They indicate that Cahokia was a true urban center, with clustered housing, markets, and specialists in toolmaking, hide dressing, potting, jewelry-making, weaving, and salt-making.

Several centuries before Europeans arrived on the Atlantic seaboard the Moundbuilder and Mississippian cultures had passed their prime and, for reasons that are not yet clear, were becoming extinct. But their influence had already passed eastward to transform the woodlands cultures in the eastern part of the continent. Although the widely scattered and relatively fragmented tribes that were settled from Nova Scotia to Florida never matched the earlier societies of mid-continent in architectural design, earthwork sculpturing, or artistic expression, they were far from the forest primitives that Europeans pictured. Touched by the Hopewellian and Mississippian cultural explosions about 900 A.D. they added limited agriculture to the skills they had already acquired in exploiting a wide variety of natural plants for food, medicine, dyes, flavoring, and smoking. In the mixed economies that resulted, all the resources around them were utilized—open land, forests, streams, and shore.

For the most part, these people of the Northeast Woodlands, on whose lands European fishermen began camping and drying their codfish in the late fifteenth century, lived in villages, especially after they had been influenced by the agricultural traditions of the Ohio and Mississippi Valley societies. Locating their cornfields near fishing grounds and learning to fertilize the young plants with the heads of fish, they settled into a more sedentary pattern of life. Domed wigwams of birch and elm, copied in the early years by Europeans, were clustered together in villages which were often palisaded. The birch-bark canoes, light enough to be carried by a single man from stream to stream, gave them a means of trading and communicating over a vast territory. The extent of development among these Eastern Woodlands societies on the eve of European contact is indicated by the archaeological evidence of a Huron town in the Great Lakes region which contained more than one hundred large structures housing a total population of between four and six thousand. Settlements of this size were larger than the average European village of the sixteenth century and larger than all but a handful of European colonial towns in America after a century and a half of colonization.

Along the Atlantic seaboard, from the St. Lawrence Bay to Florida, Europeans encountered scores of local tribes of the Eastern Woodlands groups. Each maintained cultural elements peculiar to its people, although they shared in common many things such as agricultural techniques, pottery design, social organization, and toolmaking. But the most important common denominator among them was that each had mastered the local habitat in a way that sustained life and insured the perpetuation of their people. In the far northern regions were Abnakis, Penobscots, Passamaquoddys, and others who lived by the products of the sea and supplemented their diet with maple sugar and a few foodstuffs. Farther south, in what was to become New England, were Massachusetts, Wampanoags, Pequots, Narrangansetts, Niantics, Mahicans, and others—small tribes occupying fairly local areas and joined together only by occasional trade. South of them, in what we call the Mid-Atlantic area, were Lenni Lenapes, Susquehannocks, Nanticokes, Pamunkeys, Shawnees, Tuscaroras, Catawbas, and others who subsisted on a mixture of agriculture, shellfish, game, and wild foods. They too were settled in villages and lived a semi-sedentary life.

One of the most heavily populated regions of the Atlantic coast was the southeast where rich and complex cultures, some of them joined in loose confederacies, were located. Belonging to several language groups, these peoples could trace their ancestry back at least 8,000 years. Some of the most sophisticated pottery-making in the eastern half of the continent occurred in the Southeast beginning about 2000 b.c. Hopewellian burial mound techniques were also integrated into these cultures, and by a few hundred years before De Soto marched through the area in the 1540s grandiose ceremonial centers, whose construction involved earth-moving on a vast scale, had become a distinct feature of this culture area. In touch with Mississippian culture, the tribes of the Southeast had evolved elaborate ceramic and basket-weaving techniques, long-distance trade, and in some cases, as with the Natchez, hierarchical and authoritarian social and political organizations. These people included the powerful Creeks and Yamasees in the Georgia and Alabama regions to the Apalachees in Florida and along the Gulf of Mexico, to the Choctaws, Chickasaws, and Natchez of the lower Mississippi Valley, to the Cherokees of the southern Appalachians, as well as several dozen smaller tribes scattered along the southeast coast.

Reliable populations figures that would give us an understanding of the total number of all these different peoples on the eve of European contact are difficult to obtain. Anthropologists have argued for decades about "pre-conquest" population levels and have searched for methods that might provide reliable estimates. The latest work on the subject has raised previous estimates greatly, and many scholars now believe that the pre-contact population of the Americas may have been as high as 100 million. There can be no doubt that the eastern half of North America was not nearly so densely populated as areas of Central and South America and that even by the most liberal estimates the whole of North America contained not more than 10 million people of whom perhaps 500,000 or so occupied the regions along the coast within reach of the Europeans during the first century of contact. The point to emphasize, however, is that even if we scale down by half the estimates of the most recent demographers and anthropologists, we are left with the startling realization that Europeans were not crossing the Atlantic ocean to occupy a barren wilderness, but were invading the land which in many areas was as densely populated as Europe itself.

The Iroquois

Among the eastern woodlands cultures we may focus briefly on the Iroquois peoples in order to gain a more vivid impression of how life and society were organized in at least one Indian culture. The Iroquois were to become not only one of the most populous but the most powerful of the northeastern tribes. Their territory stretched from the Adirondack Mountains to the Great Lakes and from what is now northern New York to Pennsylvania. Five tribes—the Mohawks ("People of the Flint"), Oneidas ("People of the Stone"), Onondagas ("People of the Mountain"), Cayugas ("People at the Landing"), and Senecas ("Great Hill People")— composed what was later called by Europeans the League of the Iroquois or in Iroquoian language *Ganonsyoni*, "The Lodge Extended Lengthwise" or that which spread far. The Iroquois confederation was a vast extension of the kinship group that characterized the northeastern woodlands pattern of family settlement and the *Ganonsyoni* embraced perhaps 10,000 people at the beginning of the seventeenth century.

The origin of the League of the Iroquois has fascinated historians for more than a century. Some argue that the Iroquois were weak and disorganized when English and French settlement began in the early 1600s and infer that the League was forged as a means of responding to the European presence. But earlier studies, which have regained wide acceptance, tend to show that the League was formed in the late fifteenth century and derived from the Iroquois' own attempts to solve a difficulty that had plagued them for generations in their "loosely organized ethnic confederacy"—the problem of blood feuds and chronic small-scale violence with neighboring Algonkian tribes. Increases in population in the northeast, triggered by more extensive development of agriculture, had heightened the need for hunting during this period. This brought tribes which had previously made little contact with each other into even more frequent conflict situations. Iroquois villages were palisaded in the fifteenth century, a sign of intensifying conflict, and the males of the villages apparently became more and more preoccupied with war and killing. When Jacques Cartier sailed up the St. Lawrence River in 1534 he heard from members of Algonkian tribes that their enemies, the Iroquois, had been driven from the Laurentian region several generations earlier.

Legend has it that the unification of Iroquoia was led by Hiawatha, a Mohawk sachem. About 1450 Hiawatha lost several of his relatives and in his bereavement wandered off into the wilderness. In what was probably a hallucinatory state he had a vision in which a supernatural creature named Dekanawidah appeared before Hiawatha and appointed him as his agent. Dekanawidah, writes Anthony Wallace, "dictated a code for the revitalization of Iroquois society" and Hiawatha carried it from village to village, recruiting disciples who regarded him as a prophet.[2] Hiawatha's visions gradually took the form of a plan for a new and strong confederacy of the loosely affiliated Iroquois villages. The key to the plan was a prohibition of blood revenge by any Iroquois against any member of the five tribes. In the event of a killing, a ritualized condolence ceremony was to perform the function of relieving bereavement depression, which before could only be satisfied by blood revenge. A council of forty-nine chiefs, delegated by the five nations and meeting at Onondaga, was granted power to make decisions for all the villages. Thus a political structure was erected to maintain intra-Iroquois peace and gradually to draw surrounding tribes into the confederacy.

As Hiawatha's preaching of the visions of Dekanawidah was gradually accepted, a loose ethnic confederacy was transformed into a more cohesive political confederacy. The prohibition of intra-Iroquois blood feuds al-

[2]Anthony F. C. Wallace, "The Dekanawidah Myth Analyzed as the Record of a Revitalization Movement," *Ethnohistory*, 5 (1958): 126.

lowed villages to grow and gain stability, population to increase, and the Iroquois to develop the political mechanisms not only to solve their internal problems but to gain and maintain a more unified front in negotiating with their Algonquian neighbors for the use of hunting territories to the north or in admitting dependent tribes to settle on their territory. That all of this was occurring during the century before European arrival was fortuitous because it facilitated the development of a fairly well-coordinated Iroquois policy for dealing with the European newcomers. In most respects this "revitalization movement" was similar to those that have sprung internally from societies in stress in other parts of the world at widely separated times. The appearance of a messianic figure who touches off a new wave of morality, codifies a new approach to life, and thus revitalizes the society in its time of troubles is a story that to Europeans, with their own Christian mythology, should have sounded a familiar note. Indeed the message of Dekaniwidah expressed the sense of covenant and communitarianism that would be a hallmark of Puritanism in New England several centuries later. "We bind ourselves together," said Dekaniwidah, "by taking hold of each other's hands so firmly and forming a circle so strong that if a tree should fall upon it, it could not shake nor break it, so that our people and grandchildren shall remain in the circle in security, peace and happiness."[3]

In the period before European arrival, then, the minimum purpose of the League of the Iroquois was to strengthen the villages, bind them together, and make Iroquoia "invulnerable to attack from without and to division from within." Later the philosophers of the League expounded a maximum purpose that again found a parallel in the Puritan sense of mission—"the conversion of all mankind, so that peace and happiness should be the lot of the peoples of the whole earth," and so that all people should blend together in one human confederacy. Dekaniwidah is alleged to have said, "The white roots of the Great Tree of Peace will continue to grow, advancing the Good Mind and Righteousness and Peace, moving into territories of people scattered far through the forest."[4]

If some aspects of Iroquois culture were shared by Europeans, others were different enough to convince the colonists that their society had little in common with that of the indigenous people. For example, work in the villages of Iroquoia was done communally and land was owned not by individuals but by all in common. An individual family might till its own patch of land but it was understood that this usage of land in no way implied private ownership. Likewise, hunting was a communal enter-

[3]Anthony F. C. Wallace, *The Death and Rebirth of the Seneca* (New York: Alfred A. Knopf, Inc., 1970), p. 42.
[4]*Ibid.*, p. 42.

prize. Though individual hunters differed in their ability to stalk and kill deer, the collective bounty of the hunting party was brought back to the village to be divided among all. Similarly, several families occupied a long house but the house itself, like all else in the community, was regarded as common property. For the Iroquois the concept of private ownership of property—the idea that each person should own his own land or house—would have struck at the heart of the most important theme in their value system—the cooperative or communal principle. "No hospitals [poorhouses] are needed among them," wrote a French Jesuit in 1657, "because there are neither mendicants nor paupers as long as there are any rich people among them. Their kindness, humanity and courtesy not only makes them liberal with what they have, but causes them to possess hardly anything except in common. A whole village must be without corn, before any individual can be obliged to endure privation." About the same time a Dutch missionary wrote: "The chiefs are generally the poorest among them, for instead of their receiving from the common people as among Christians, they are obliged to give to the mob."[5]

Village settlement was organized by extended kinship groups. Contrary to European practice, the Iroquois family was matrilineal, with family membership determined through the female line. Thus a typical family was composed of an old woman, her daughters with their husbands and children, and her unmarried granddaughters and grandsons. Sons and grandsons remained with their kinship group until they married; then they joined the family of their wife. Divorce was also the woman's prerogative; if she desired it, she merely set her husband's possessions outside the long house door. Thus Iroquois society was organized around the matrilineal "fireside". In turn, several matrilineal kinship groups, related by a blood connection on the mother's side, as between sisters, formed a *ohwachira*, or a group of related families. These *ohwachiras* were grouped together in clans. A village might be made up of a dozen or more clans. Villages or clans combined to create a nation (or "kinship state," as it has been called) of Senecas or Mohawks.[6]

Iroquois society was not only matrilineal in social organization, but invested the women of the community with a share of the political power. Political authority in the villages derived from the *ohwachiras* at whose heads were the senior women of the community. It was these women who

[5]Reuben Gold Thwaites, ed., *The Jesuit Relations and Allied Documents; Travels and Explorations of the Jesuit Missionaries in New France, 1610–1791* (Cleveland: Burrows Brothers, 1899), 43: 271; Johannes Megapolensis, Jr. "A Short Account of the Mohawk Indians," (1644), in J. Franklin Jameson, *Narratives of New Netherland, 1609–1664* (New York: Charles Scribner's Sons, 1909), p. 179.

[6]William N. Fenton, "The Iroquois in History," in *North American Indians in Historical Perspective*, eds. Eleanor Burke Leacock and Nancy Oestreich Lurie (New York: Random House, Inc., 1971), p. 139.

named the men representing the clans at village and tribal councils and who named the forty-nine sachems or chiefs who met periodically at Onondaga as the ruling council for the confederated Five Nations. These civil chiefs, the *rotiyanehr*, were generally middle-age or elderly men who had earlier gained fame as warriors but now "forsook the warpath for the council fire."[7] The political power of the women was not limited to the appointment of male representatives to the various ruling councils. When individual clans met, in a manner resembling the later New England town meeting, the senior women were fully in attendance, caucusing behind the circle of men who did the public speaking, lobbying with them, and giving them instructions. To an outsider it might appear that the men ruled, because it was they who did the public speaking and formally reached decisions. But their power was shared with the women. If the men of the village or tribal council moved too far from the will of the women who had appointed them, they could be removed, or "dehorned." Only so long as they satisfied the will of the women who had placed them in office were they secure in their positions.

The division of power between male and female within Iroquois society was further extended by the role of the women in the tribal economy. While men were responsible for hunting and fishing, the women were the primary agriculturists of the village. In tending the crops they became equally important in sustaining the community. Moreover, when the men were away on hunting expeditions, which frequently required long treks away from the village over a period of weeks, women were left entirely in command of the daily life of the community. Even in military affairs women played an important role for it was the women who supplied the moccasins and food for warring expeditions, and a decision to withhold these supplies was tantamount to vetoing a military foray. Thus power was shared between the sexes and the European idea of male dominancy and female subordination in all things was conspicuously absent in Iroquois society.

In attempting to understand the nature of the Iroquois-European interaction it is useful to inquire into the development of the Iroquois "personality" and patterns of individual behavior. Psychologists tell us that most of our personality traits, our way of responding to people and events that surround us, are firmly rooted in our early upbringing. The modes of child-rearing adoped by a society, then, are important in understanding the collective behavior of any group of people. The Iroquois and other woodlands people, no less than Europeans, designed child-rearing practices to transmit to their children knowledge and skills necessary for the survival of the society. They also passed down an understanding of

[7]*Ibid.*, p. 138.

their cultural and historical heritage in order to inculcate group identity and a strong feeling of loyalty and responsibility to the group. Thus Iroquois parents taught their children how to hunt, to make tools, to grow crops, and to identify plants and animals, just as Englishmen taught their children the rudiments of everyday survival. Similarly both societies worked to fill the child with a sense of his or her heritage and instilled group loyalty through rituals and ceremonies.

One aspect of child-rearing on which European and Iroquoian cultures differed was in the attitude toward authority. In Iroquois society the autonomous individual, loyal to the group but independent and aloof rather than submissive, was the ideal. "Liberty in its fullest extent becomes their ruling passion," a Quaker observed in the early nineteenth century, and his description echoed the earliest Jesuit accounts of two centuries before.[8] Boys were expected to become good hunters and loyal and selfless members of the clan. They were not respected if they were dependent, submissive, or unduly cowed by authority. They were trained early in life, as Wallace has put it, "to think for themselves but to act for others."[9] They were being prepared to enter an adult society which was not hierarchical, as in the European case, but where individuals lived on a more equalitarian basis, with power more evenly distributed among men and women or old and young than in European society. Because material possessions were not prized and private ownership of property was of no importance the competitive principle operated only insofar as his prestige as a hunter or warrior was concerned. The pursuit of wordly goods at the expense of a fellow clansman would have gained him only scorn in his village, and deference to fellow villagers would have been incongruous. In European society, where material possessions were greatly coveted and where the social structure made elaborate distinctions between rich and poor, godly and ungodly, literate and nonliterate, male and female, and politically enfranchised and unenfranchised, far more attention was given to maintaining proper respect for authority. Submission to authority and the maintenance of hierachical lines became principles around which child-rearing was organzed.

To perpetuate their cultural values Iroquoian parents had no need to concern themselves obsessively with authority and thus a far greater degree of permissiveness characterized their child-rearing techniques. Parents did not believe in harsh physical punishment; they encouraged their young to imitate adult behavior and were tolerant of fumbling, early attempts. In the first months of a baby's life the mother nursed and protected the child and at the same time hardened it by baths in cold

8Quoted in Wallace, *Death and Rebirth of the Seneca*, p. 38.
9*Ibid.*, p. 34.

water. Weaning was not ordinarily begun until the age of three or four. Rather than beginning strict regimens of toilet training at an early age the child was allowed to proceed at its own pace in achieving control over its natural functions. Early interest in the anatomy of the body and in sexual experimentation was accepted as natural. All this was in sharp contrast to European child-rearing techniques, which stressed the importance of accustoming the child to authority from an early age and backed this up by taking the child from the breast at about two years, by toilet training at an early age, by making frequent use of physical punishment, by condemning early sexual curiosity, and by emphasizing obedience and respect for authority as central virtues. Iroquois parents would have regarded as misguided the advice of John Robinson, the Pilgrim's pastor, to the parents of his congregation: "And surely there is in all children . . . a stubbornness, and stoutness of mind arising from natural pride, which must, in the first place, be broken and beaten down; that so the foundation of their education being laid in humility and tractableness, other virtues may, in their time, be built thereon. . . . For the beating, and keeping down of this stubbornness parents must provide carefully . . . that the children's wills and willfulness be restrained and repressed. . . . Children should not know, if it could be kept from them, that they have a will of their own, but in their parents' keeping."[10]

The approach to authority also differed for adult members of the society. Iroquois culture, like most Indian cultures of North America, had none of the complicated machinery of European society which operated to direct and control the lives of its members. No laws and ordinances, sheriffs and constables, judges and juries, or courts or jails—the apparatus of authority in European societies—were to be found in the northeast woodlands prior to European arrival. Yet boundaries of acceptable behavior were firmly set. Though priding themselves on the autonomous individual, the Iroquois maintained a strict sense of right and wrong. Rather than relying on formal instruments of authority, however, they governed behavior by inculcating a strong sense of tradition and attachment to the group through communally performed rituals. It was this sense of duty, bolstered by a fear of gossip and a strongly held belief in the power of evil spirits to punish wrongdoers, that curbed antisocial instincts among the Iroquois. In European society a criminal or unethical act might be dealt with by investigation, arrest, prosecution, sentencing, and imprisonment and involved at various steps along the way the power and authority of a number of people and institutional devices. But in Indian society a less complex system operated to transform the aberrant

[10]Quoted in John Demos, *A Little Commonwealth: Family Life in Plymouth Colony* (New York: Oxford University Press, Inc., 1970), pp. 134–35.

individual. He who stole another's food or acted invalorously in war was "shamed" by his people and ostracized from their company until he had atoned for his actions and demonstrated to their satisfaction that he had morally purified himself.

Although Europeans who came to North America were unprepared to find anything but "primitive" people, they were fascinated to observe the parts of Iroquois religious tradition which urged individuals to look to their dreams for clues to unresolved problems and to engage in a kind of group psychotherapy in order to receive help from their fellow tribesmen. More than two centuries before Sigmund Freud's development of psychoanalytic theory, the Iroquois and other northern Indian cultures had achieved an understanding of many of the basic tenets of modern psychology. They recognized that the mind had both conscious and unconscious levels; that unconscious desires were often expressed symbolically in dreams; that these desires, if unfulfilled or unresolved, could cause psychic and psychosomatic illness; and that those suffering from nightmares or haunting dreams could often find relief by recounting his or her dreams to a group, whose members attempted to help the individual find the meaning of and the cure for the subconscious problem.

An incredulous Jesuit priest, Father Ragueneau, described this theory of dreams as he witnessed it in Huron villages in 1649. The Indians, he reported, believed that

> in addition to the desires which we generally have that are free, or at least voluntary in us, . . . our souls have other desires, which are, as it were, inborn and concealed. These, they say, come from the depths of the soul, not through any knowledge, but by means of a certain blind transporting of the soul to certain objects; these transports might in the language of philosophy be called *Desideria innata*, to distinguish them from the former, which are called *Desideria Elicita*. Now they believe that our soul makes these natural desires known by means of dreams, which are its language. Accordingly, when these desires are accomplished, it is satisfied; but, on the contrary, if it be not granted what it desires, it becomes angry, and not only does not give its body the good and the happiness that it wished to procure for it, but often it also revolts against the body, causing various diseases, and even death . . . In consequence of these erroneous ideas, most of the Hurons are very careful to note their dreams, and to provide the soul with what it has pictured to them during their sleep. If, for instance, they have seen a javelin in a dream, they try to get it; if they have dreamed that they gave a feast, they will give one on awakening, if they have the wherewithal; and so on with other things. And they call this *Ondinnonk*—a secret desire of the soul manifested by a dream.[11]

[11] Quoted in Anthony F. C. Wallace, "Dreams and the Wishes of the Soul: A Type of Psychoanalytic Theory among the Seventeenth-Century Iroquois," *American Anthropologist*, 60 (1958): 236.

It would be mistaken to romanticize Iroquois culture or to judge it superior to the culture of the European invader. To do so would only be to invoke the same categories of "superior" and "inferior" that Europeans used to justify the violence they unleashed when they arrived in the New World and to forget that exercises in ranking cultures depend almost entirely on the criteria employed. Instead of grading cultures, almost always an exercise in ethnocentrism, we must understand that Iroquois society, like English or French society, was a total social system undergoing change—change which in the eyes of its members would help to effectuate what they regarded as important. Iroquois culture, like English or French culture, was very old and had undergone major transformations before Europeans arrived. In dynamic relationship with their environment and with neighboring peoples they had become more populous, more sedentary in their mode of settlement, more skilled in agricultural techniques, more elaborate in their art forms. They were also emerging as one of the strongest, most politically unified, and militaristic native societies in the Northeast woodlands. Even after the formation of the League of the Iroquois, which had as one of its objectives the abatement of intertribal warfare, an impressive amount of fighting seems to have occurred between the Five Nations and surrounding Algonkian peoples. Many of these conflicts involved a quest for glory and some of them may have been initiated to test the newly forged alliance of the five tribes against lesser tribes which could be brought under Iroquoian subjugation. Whatever the reasons, the Iroquois on the eve of European arrival were feared and sometimes hated by their neighbors for their skill and cruelty in warfare. Their belief in the superiority of their culture was as pronounced as that of the arriving Europeans.

Of course the Iroquois were not the only Indian tribes that Europeans encountered in the early seventeeth century. Along the Atlantic seaboard, from the St. Lawrence Bay to Florida, the English, Spanish, Dutch, and French met a vast number of tribal groups. They ranged in population and power but even in areas of low population density, dynamic cultures had evolved. In several regions intertribal conflict had resulted in political unifications or confederacies with which Europeans would have to reckon. As was to become evident, even small numbers of Indians could present a considerable problem for those intent on occupying their land.

chapter 2

Europe Reaches the Americas

From the fifteenth to the twentieth centuries one of the dominant movements in human history has been the attempted Europeanization of the
world—or what might be best understood as the militant expansion of
European peoples and European culture into other continents. Only in
the last half-century has this process been reversed, as ancient cultures
have struggled to regain their autonomy through wars of national and
cultural liberation. For Western historians this global expansion has been
closely equated with the spread of "civilization," that is, the carrying of
an allegedly superior European culture to so-called "primitive" areas of
the world. Thus, as various cultures were engulfed by colonizing Europeans, the notion grew stronger and stronger that "progress," in the form
of the growing outreach of European civilization, was being served.

Yet the cultural superiority of Europeans at the time when the western
hemisphere was disclosed to (not discovered by) them is far from clear in
retrospect. Indeed, the very notion of "superior" and "inferior" cultures

has been called into question and it is now time to abandon these concepts in our study of history. What is more important is the fact that it was "New Worlds," placed at the service of colonizing Europeans, that catapulted Europe out of a prolonged period of stagnation and regression. For more than a century before the Atlantic Ocean was turned into a known body of water Europe had suffered depopulation through epidemic disease and prolonged wars; economic recession as reflected by withering production and trade; and a general inertia of Christian culture in a period characterized by an absence of progress in the natural sciences, a decay of the universities, and the crumbling of the Holy Roman Empire. The most dynamic force in Europe in the fourteenth and fifteenth centuries was Islamic culture, which was rapidly expanding into Africa and edging in upon Europe from the East. Western Europe, before the "age of discovery," was characterized by pessimism, cynicism, and despair. It was an age of morbid introspection and melancholy. More than anything else it was the resources of Africa, Asia, and the Americas —gold, silver, land, and people—that brought about a commercial revival and triggered four centuries of European expansion and development. In attempting to find a water route to the oldest parts of the Old World, Columbus stumbled upon what was a new world only in the European imagination. But this fortuitous error sparked the imagination of Europeans—perhaps their most valuable quality—and touched off a revival of enterprise and overseas expansion that lasted for more than four hundred years.

Spanish Expansion into the New World

Columbus thought he had reached India when he made a landfall on the island of Hispaniola in 1492. This was precisely his quest—to find an all-water route to the Orient so that European traders, who trafficked in the indispensable spices that made European food palatable, could avoid paying tribute to the hordes of Middle-Eastern middlemen who skimmed the profits off any overland trading venture. It is customary to focus on the navigational and geographical importance of Columbus's voyages, but the truth is that his sea wanderings would have been written off as an expensive failure once it was realized that he had not found the illusive water route to India, if it had not been for the discovery of gold on Hispaniola in 1493. Without gold and other precious minerals, the new-found lands were only obstacles on the water road to the East.

But while his discovery was accidental, Columbus was still an archetypical figure of European expansion. He was still thoroughly medieval in his patterns of thought, but he was also ambitious, adventuresome, ready to translate an idea, however ridiculed, into action, and audacious enough to maintain his course even when his sailors were ready to mutiny in despair of ever seeing dry land again. Capitalizing on great advances in marine technology and on the Portuguese explorations of the previous century, Columbus, like the Vikings five hundred years before him, discovered that the ocean west of Europe was not illimitable. He had the European quality of arrogance that in the centuries ahead was to prove so valuable in colonization—and so destructive of human life.

Once gold was found, a wholesale rush of enterprising young men from the lesser nobility in Spain began the transatlantic adventure. By the 1550s they had explored, conquered, and claimed for their Queen the Isthmus of Panama, Mexico, most of South America except Brazil and the far southern plains, and the southerly reaches of North America from California on the Pacific Coast to the Floridas on the Atlantic Coast. Led by military figures such as Cortez, Pizzaro, and Coronado, they established the authority of Spain and the Catholic Church over an area which dwarfed their homeland in size and population. By the end of the sixteenth century the major centers of native population had been conquered, some sixty ships were annually crossing the Atlantic between Seville and the Spanish colonies, slaves by the thousands were being imported from Africa and silver in fabulous quantities was being extracted from mines in New Spain.

For the first century of European expansion, from about the 1490s to the 1590s, the colonization of the Americas was dominated by Spain. Her only rival was Portugal, whose energies went primarily into colonizing the Atlantic Azore islands lying some 800 miles off the coast of Portugal, and establishing centers of trade on the east and west African coasts. Not until the 1550s did Portugal stake out a claim in Brazil that was to become the center of her New World activities. But by the end of the century sugar production was claiming the labor of most of some 25,000 Portuguese colonists and perhaps an equal number of African slaves in Brazil.

English Entry into the Colonial Race

By the time England awoke to the promise of the New World, the two Iberian powers were firmly entrenched in it. England was the most backward of the European nations facing the Atlantic in exploring and colonizing the Americas. Only the voyages of John Cabot, who was in reality the Genoa-born Johann Caboti, gave England any title to a place in the New World sweepstakes. And such voyages as Cabot made in the 1590s were never followed up. Even the famous expeditions of John Hawkins in the 1560s must be discounted as unimportant in the expansion of Europe into America because Hawkins was primarily involved in high-class piracy—raiding Spanish trade in the Caribbean with the backing of Catholic-hating English merchants, who hoped to induce their government to sponsor and underwrite their isolated and unorganized attempts to drive a wedge into the Spanish and Portuguese New World monopoly.

English entry into the colonial race had its origins not only in the desire to share in the exploitation of New World resources but in the ideological war that raged in Europe throughout the last half of the sixteenth century. All of the western European powers facing the Atlantic with the exception of the Scandinavian countries were involved in this ideological struggle between those who professed Catholicism and those who adhered to Protestantism. This national and ideological struggle must be viewed as a continuation of issues and interests first raised in the Reformation and Counter-Reformation; and it is important to understand that so far as the colonization of the New World was concerned it would be carried out "in an extraordinarily violent and ideologically polarized period of western history."[1]

For students in the twentieth century the national rivalry is easier to understand than the ideological struggle. Colonies in newly discovered parts of the globe would be sources of additional strength to the mother country, for colonies provided new markets, new sources of raw materials, and, if they contained gold and silver, could add to the total supply of specie by which the strength of nations was then measured. Thus England, at the end of the sixteenth century, was eager to establish a foothold on the North American coast, for Spain and Portugal already dominated the South American continent parts of the Caribbean and had laid claim to the southern portions of the North American landmass as well. If the English did not move soon, it would be too late. By the same token, Spain was intent upon resisting any English incursions into what they regarded as a Spanish sphere of influence. As Englishmen took the first tentative steps toward empire, the Spanish planned seaborne attacks on any English settlement that might dare to exist on the Atlantic coast of North America. The first known map of the tiny English settlement at Jamestown, Virginia, drawn by an Irish Catholic crew member on an English ship that delivered colonists to the Chesapeake settlement, was smuggled back to Spain. It was regarded as a prized document since it provided the information necessary to conduct a surprise attack on this first English foothold on the North American coast.

[1] John Shy, "The American Military Experience: History and Learning," *The Journal of Interdisciplinary History*, 1 (1970–71): 211.

Religious Goals of Colonization

Closely tied to these nationalistic conceptions of overseas possessions were the religious goals of colonization. Both Catholics and Protestants looked upon the occupation of the New World, at least in part, as a religious crusade. Spain had been involved for centuries in conflict with the "infidel" Moors and it was only in the same year that Columbus reached the New World that the expulsion of the Moors from Christian Spain had been completed. Conquest of the New World was not only a national quest but a religious quest for a continent filled with "heathen" people awaiting Christianization.

The religious motive was complicated by the Catholic-Protestant division within Christianity. For Europeans heathens were heathens; but it remained an open question as to whether their conversion would be to Catholicism or to Protestantism. That Christians could be so bitterly divided, that they could engage in religious wars for several centuries, inflicting mass destruction in the name of God, may seem puzzling to those raised in a secular society. But the intensity of this conflict and competition within Christian Europe becomes more understandable when we remember that to men and women of this age—as in centuries before —religion was the organizing principle of life. Man's control over his environment was slight since his power to control natural forces was severely limited by the extent of his scientific and technological knowledge. Thus he was far more wont to attribute to supernatural forces what he could not himself understand or control. And these forces of nature seemed awesome indeed—awesome enough to be worshipped, awesome enough to organize one's life around. Faith, not reason, governed life, and thus men of different faiths found themselves passionately committed to defending their ideology and attacking those with variant views.

These "isms"—Protestantism and Catholicism—are best understood, then, as prescribed codes of living, as ways of making sense out of the uncontrollable forces and events that surrounded human existence, and a way of giving order and meaning to one's world and one's place in it. In this sense these ideological commitments were not markedly different from the "isms" of today—communism, socialism, democracy. These too are systems of thought and belief, ways of organizing the life of society and channeling its energies and values. They, too, give meaning to all we do and provide us with a sense of identity. Most people believe in one of these "isms" no less passionately than their predecessors believed in Protestantism, Catholicism, or Islam. Our own wars, fought today with even greater ferocity and technological ruthlessness in the name of ideological systems provide a way of understanding why Christians and Moslems or Catholics and Protestants would fight so relentlessly to defend or spread their particular faith in the early modern period.

During much of the sixteenth century England had swayed back and forth between religious ideologies, living first under the Protestant regimes of Henry VIII and his sickly son, Edward VI, and then under the Catholic reign of his daughter Mary Tudor, who had married Philip II of Spain—the chief pillar of Catholic power in Europe. When Mary Tudor died and Henry's second daughter, Elizabeth, took the throne in 1558, England was returned to Protestantism. Like her father, Elizabeth favored Protestantism primarily as an expression of national independence. First and foremost, she meant to create the conditions for national growth and prosperity. Although in economic matters she enjoyed some success, the religious question always hung above her head. Philip II of Spain, her brother-in-law, regarded her as a Protestant heretic and plotted against her incessantly.

THE SPANISH ARMADA

In 1587 the smoldering conflict between Catholic Spain and Protestant England broke into open conflict and England braced itself for the seaborne attack that was expected from the Spanish armada—regarded as the most powerful navy in the world. The battle that ensued is known simply as the Spanish Armada. In the spring of 1588 the Spanish fleet set sail for England, reaching its destination late in July. For two weeks a battle raged at sea. To Europe's amazement the English, aided by the Dutch, prevailed. The Spanish defeat did not establish English superiority at sea or bring England any overseas territory in recognition of her victory. It did not even propel England into the overseas colonial race. But it did prevent a crushing Catholic victory in Europe and temporarily ended Spanish dreams of European hegemony. The Armada brought a temporary stalemate in the wars of religion and made clear for a generation—until 1618, when the beginning of the Thirty Years War again threw Europe into open religious conflict—that religious uniformity was not to be imposed by force. England was free to pursue her own destiny, free from domination of other European powers, national and ideological.

The Beginnings of
English Colonization

With the way clear for overseas expansion, the "westward fever" began to catch hold in England at the end of the sixteenth century. One unsuccessful and inconsequential effort had already been made—the planting of a small settlement on Roanoke Island, off the coast of North Carolina, in the 1580s. But after the Armada the English gentry and merchants began to sense the profits which beckoned from the New World. In North America one might find a source of raw materials as rich as the Spanish and Portuguese had found in their South American colonies. Gold and silver might await the bold of heart. The evasive northwest passage to the Orient, through what was still regarded as a continent of narrow proportions, might be found.

Urging their countrymen on were two men, uncle and nephew, both named Richard Hakluyt. In the last quarter of the sixteenth century the Hakluyts devoted themselves to explaining the advantages of settling the remote regions on the other side of the Atlantic. In pamphlet after pamphlet they set forth a battery of arguments in favor of colonization. Glory and adventure awaited everybody: for the nobility at court colonization promised an empire in the New World, a source of new baronies, fiefdoms, and feudal estates; for the merchant there were new markets and a landmass filled with exotic produce that could be marketed at home; for the clergymen there awaited a continent filled with "savages" to be converted for the greater glory of Christ; for the commoner there beckoned a field of adventure and limitless economic opportunity; for the impoverished day laborer there was the prospect of starting life anew in a land where boundless land and opportunity could be found. In pamphlets such as *A Discourse on Western Planning* the Hakluyts publicized and propagandized the idea that the time was ripe for planting English stock across the Atlantic. Shakespeare contributed his bit to the national excitement by writing a play, *The Tempest*, about those who crossed the ocean to further the greatness of their country.

English participation in the age of exploration and colonization began with a generation of adventurous seadogs and gentlemen such as Walter Raleigh, Francis Drake, Humphrey Gilbert, and Richard Grenville. With little capital and minimal support from the Crown, they attempted much and ended mostly in failure. We give their exploits much room in our history books because they were the first to try. But England could not become a serious colonial power in the New World until the government, as in Spain and Portugal, gave active support to colonizing schemes, and, more important, until the merchant community and the rising middle class in England began plowing investment capital into overseas colonizing experiments. Thus all the early efforts came to little or nothing: the voyages of Hawkins in the 1560s on the Spanish Main; the Roanoke voyages of 1585 to 1588, which ended in failure; the Sagadahoc settlement on the coast of Maine in 1607, which lasted only a year; and even the settlement of Jamestown, Virginia, in 1607, which limped along for a generation before securing a real foothold.

In all these feeble first efforts the English lacked the principal ingredients that had marked the successful Spanish and Portuguese colonial efforts. They had little support in the form of subsidies, ships, and naval protection from the national government. They had minimal support from the Church, in contrast to the extensive participation of the Catholic Church in the Spanish and Portuguese colonies. They had virtually no aid from the army or from men like the conquistadors who were of military background. And they had little support from citizen investors—a broad mass of middle- and upper-class people who would risk money in colonizing experiments. Thus as long as English colonization rested in the hands of the English nobility—restless sons of aristocrats and favored courtiers of the Crown—nothing much could be expected. It took far more than outfitting a few ships and gathering up a few hundred adventurous or desperate individuals to surmount the obstacles inherent in overseas colonization. It was one thing to reach the New World in small wooden ships and to land several hundred men with supplies for several months; but it was quite another to organize these people into a social and economic organization that could survive in a frightening, new environment, much less successfully exploit the resources locked in the earth.

If the government, the church, and the military elements of English life could not be drawn into colonizing schemes, then what was needed was the wealth and support of the rising middle class of English society. Such men, who at the beginning of the Tudor period had been relatively insignificant, had been making enormous strides forward in the second half of the sixteenth century. It was this redistribution of economic and political power, which historians call the "rise of the gentry," that was indispensably important to the successful settlement of North America. The colonization movement would probably never have succeeded in the hands of the English nobility, unsupported by this much broader segment of English society. This support came grudgingly in the first half of the seventeenth century and even then English investors were far more drawn to the quick profits of sugar cultivation in the West Indies than to the uncertainties of mixed farming, lumbering, and fishing on the North American mainland.

To the difficulties of generating adequate financial and military support was added the reality that whether they focused on the North American continent or the Caribbean islands, Englishmen squarely confronted the rival claims of other European nations—claims that in many cases were backed up by actual occupation of territory. Spain already had about 90,000 colonists in her overseas possessions and although most of them were in Peru and Mexico, where major populations centers had been established at Potosi, Mexico City, and Cartagena, they had also planted frontier outposts in southwestern North America and at various points along the Atlantic Coast from Florida to the Chesapeake Bay. Spanish claims extended as far north as Newfoundland. The English approaching the North American mainland were well aware of the Spanish threat, and nothing testified so poignantly to this as the fact that after initial settlements were planted the English built their forts facing the sea —to fend off Spanish attacks—rather than facing inland where Indian danger lay. Englishmen habored no doubts that they were engaged in semi-piratical intrusions on the established colonies of Spain.

Englishmen were also approaching a continent occupied by Frenchmen. Since 1524, when Giovanni da Verrazzano had explored the eastern edge of North America in the employ of the king of France, the French had also been seized by visions of finding the Northwest Passage to China and cities of gold. Frenchmen could settle, however, only where the Spanish had no use for the land. Thus after abortive attempts to plant colonies in Florida and Brazil, which were wiped from the map by the Spanish and Portuguese, the French contented themselves with developing the frozen expanses of Canada. French fishermen had been working the coasts of Newfoundland and Nova Scotia since the early sixteenth century and the development of a considerable fur trade with the Indians of the area began about 1535. These efforts had convinced the French that the St. Lawrence River area could be profitable, even if the climate was inhospitable. Only the St. Lawrence and Hudson Rivers provided access by water into the interior of the northern parts of the continent and in 1603 the French wisely chose to plant their first settlements near the mouth of the St. Lawrence. They thus began their quest for another form of New World gold—the skins of fur-bearing animals.

Englishmen approaching the North America coast, therefore, had to reckon with Spain and France, whose territorial claims dictated that the English look to the middle part of the Atlantic seaboard for a toehold on the continent. But it was another people, the indigenous inhabitants of the land, that claimed English attention most forcefully of all. What did men like Gilbert and Raleigh know about the native occupiers of the land as they approached the forbidding coast of North America in the 1580s? How would they be received by these people whom Columbus, thinking he had reached Cathay, mistakenly called Indians? How would Englishmen obtain the use or possession of land they occupied? And how were ideas about the nature of Indian peoples influenced by this thorny question of sovereignty over the land?

English Images of the North American Natives

We can be sure that these Englishmen experienced the apprehensions that regardless of time or place fill the minds of those who are attempting to penetrate the unknown. But it is also apparent that they also had well-formed ideas about the Indian people of the New World. Beginning with

Columbus's report on the New World, published in several European capitals in 1493 and 1494, a mass of reports, stories, and propagandistic accounts had been circulating among sailors, merchants, geographers, and churchmen who were participating in or promoting the early voyages of discovery, trade, and settlement. These became the basis for an understanding of the New World by any adventurer approaching the eastern edge of land in the West Atlantic Ocean.

From this considerable literature, the early colonists were likely to have derived a split image of the natives of North America. On the one hand they had reason to believe that the Indians were a gentle people who would be receptive to those who came not to harm them but to live and trade with them. Columbus had written of the "great amity towards us" which he encountered in San Salvador in 1492 and described the Arawak Indians there as "a loving people without covetousness," who "were greatly pleased and became so entirely our friends that it was a wonder to see." The Indians "brought us parrots and cotton thread in balls, and spears and many other things, and we exchanged for them other things, such as small glass beads and hawks' bells, which we gave to them."[2] Verrazzano, the first European to navigate the eastern edge of the continent, wrote with similar optimism from the Bay of New York in 1524:

> After a hundred leagues we found a very agreeable place between two small but prominent hills; between them a very wide river, deep at its mouth, flowed out into the sea. . . . We took the small boat up this river to land which we found densely populated. The people were almost the same as the others, dressed in birds' feathers of various colors, and they came toward us joyfully, uttering loud cries of wonderment, and showing us the safest place to beach the boat.[3]

From this time on, accounts of natives of the New World included many such enthusiastic descriptions of native people and their eagerness to receive European explorers and settlers. This positive side of the image of the Indians not only reflected the friendly reception which Europeans apparently received in Newfoundland, parts of Florida, and elsewhere in the Caribbean and South America, but also represented a part of the vision of the New World as an earthly paradise—a Garden of Eden where war-torn, impoverished Europeans could find a new life amidst nature's bounty, which had allowed native people to live for centuries in sensual leisure. That Columbus thought he had found the Gihon—one of the Biblical rivers flowing from Eden—when he reached the Orinoco River in 1498 is vivid testimony to this strain in the European mentality.

[2]Quoted in Wilcomb E. Washburn, ed., *The Indian and the White Man* (Garden City, N.Y.: Doubleday & Co., Inc., 1964), p. 4.
[3]Lawrence C. Wroth, *The Voyages of Giovanni da Verrazzano, 1524–1528* (New Haven: Yale University Press, 1970), p. 137.

Theodor DeBry, a Flemish engraver, appealed to European fantasies of the New World in his depiction of the first encounter in North America between native Americans and colonizing Englishmen—at Roanoke Island in 1585. (The New York Public Library, Rare Book Division.)

Dutch New Amsterdam, depicted here in 1626, became English in 1664 but maintained its Dutch architecture and atmosphere throughout the colonial period. (The New York Public Library.)

t' Fort nieuw Amsterdam op de Manhatans

Intensity and purposefulness suffused the personality of John Winthrop, leader of the Puritan migration to New England. (Courtesy American Antiquarian Society.)

Another reason existed for drawing a favorable image of the North American natives. The English, like other European colonizers, hoped that trade with native peoples would become a major source of profit on the other side of the Atlantic and in other ways needed the aid of indigenous people. The early English voyages were not primarily intended for the purpose of large-scale settlement and agricultural production. Trade with the Indians, the search for gold and silver, and discovery of the Northwest Passage were the keys to overseas development. Not only would the natives provide a new outlet for English woolens, but all the commodities of the New World could be expected to flow back to England after trade was established. Land had been a key element for the Spanish and Portuguese colonizers in the New World. But land conquest did not figure importantly in the English mind in the early stages of colonizing activity. The intention, rather, was to establish well-fortified trading posts at the heads of rivers where the natives would come to trade. In this mercantile approach to overseas adventuring the English promoters of the late sixteenth and early seventeenth centuries were influenced by earlier English participation in the Levantine and Muscovy trade where English merchants had operated profitably for half a century, not invading the land of foreign peoples and driving them from it, but "trafficking" among them without challenging their possession of the land or attempting to subjugate them. So a special incentive existed for seeing the Indian as something more than a "savage." It was only a friendly Indian who could be a trading Indian. If trade was the key to overseas development, then it is not surprising that English promoters would suggest that the Indian might be receptive and generous—a man who could be wooed and won to the advantages of trade.

However, a counterimage of the Indian was also firmly lodged in the minds of Englishmen approaching the coast of North America. This negative picture of the native, which cast him as a savage, hostile, beast-like animal whose proximity in appearance and behavior was closer to the animal kingdom than the kingdom of men, also derived from the extensive literature of colonization that had emanated from Spanish and French depictions of the New World. As early as the first decade of the sixteenth century Sebastian Cabot had paraded in England three Eskimos taken captive on his voyage to the Arctic in 1502. A contemporary described the natives as flesh eating, primitive specimens, who "spake such speech that no man coulde understand them, and in their demeanour like to bruite beasts."[4] A flood of pamphlets in the second half of the six-

---

[4]Richard Hakluyt, *Divers Voyages touching the discoverie of America, and the Ilands adjacent unto the Same* (1582), Hakluyt Society *Publications*, 1st Ser., 7 (London: The Hakluyt Society, 1850): 23.

teenth century described the natives in terms that could have been little cause for optimism concerning the reception Europeans would receive. These accounts were filled with portraits of the Indians as crafty, brutal, loathsome half-men whose cannibalistic instincts were revealed, as one pamphleteer wrote in 1578, by the fact that "there is no flesh or fishe, which they finde dead, (smell it never so filthily) but they will eate it, as they finde it, without any other dressing [cooking]."[5] Other accounts limned the natives as bestial, living in sexual abandon, and, in general, moved entirely by passion rather than reason.

Apart from tales of travel and adventure in the New World, the English had a far more striking reason for imagining that all would not be friendship and amiable trading when they encountered the native occupants of the North American coast. For years they had been reading accounts of the Spanish experience with Indian peoples in Mexico and Peru —and the story was not a pretty one. Chief among these Spanish accounts was the work of the Dominican friar Bartholomé de Las Casas, whose *Brevissima Relacion de la Destruccion de las Indias* was translated into English and published in 1583 as *The Spanish Colonie, or Brief Chronicle of the Actes and Gestes of the Spaniards in the West Indies*. On the one hand, Englishmen could delight in Las Casas's descriptions of Spanish cruelty and genocide, for such stories confirmed all the worst things which the Protestant English believed about the Catholic Spaniards with whom they were about to go to war. Thus the "Black Legend" concerning the Spanish was amply fed by passages in Las Casas such as the following:

> The Spaniards with their horses, their spears, and their lances, began to commit murders and strange cruelties. They entered into Towns, Boroughs, and Villages, sparing neither women with child, neither them that layed in, but that they ripped their bellies, and cut them in pieces, as if they had been opening of lambs shut up in their fold. They layed wagers with such as with one thrust of a sword could paunch or bowel a man in the middest, or with one blow of the sword most readily and deliverly cut off his head, or that would best pierce his entrails at one stroke. They took little souls by the heels, ramping them from their mother's dugs, and crushing their heads against the cliffs. Others they cast into the river laughing and mocking, and when they tumbled in the water they said, now shift for thyself, such a one's corpse. They put others together with their mothers and all they met to the edge of the sword. They made certain Gibbets long and low, in such sort, that the foot of the hanged touched in a manner the ground, every one enough for thirteen in honor and worship of our Savior and his twelve Apostles (as they used to speak) and setting to fire burned them all quick that were fastened.[6]

[5]Vilhjalmur Stefansson, ed., *The Three Voyages of Martin Frobisher* (London: The Argonaut Press, 1938), 2: 23.

[6]Quoted in William S. Maltby, *The Black Legend in England: The Development of Anti-Spanish Sentiment, 1558–1660* (Durham, N.C.: Duke University Press, 1971), p. 16.

These accounts were ideal for feeding anti-Spanish prejudices and were eagerly quoted by promoters such as the Hakluyts, who were quick to label the Spanish colonizers "hell-hounds and wolves." But such accounts also suggested that when Europeans met "primitive" people, slaughter of this sort was inevitable. Moreover, Las Casas was rebutted by a host of Spanish writers who justified Spanish behavior by insisting that the Indians had precipitated bloodletting and, because of their unalterably bestial nature, could be dealt with in no other way. However useful accounts of Spanish cruelty might be for Protestant pamphleteers, Englishmen embarking for the New World must have wondered whether the same experience awaited them. Few doubted that they enjoyed the same technological superiority as the Spanish. If they desired, they could presumably lay waste to the country they were entering. In addition, the English experience with the Irish, in whose country military officers like Gilbert and Raleigh had gained experience in the subjugation of "lesser breeds" for several decades, suggested that the English were fully capable of every cruelty contrived by the Spanish. However tractable and amenable to trade the Indian might appear in some of the English literature, the image of a hostile savage who awaited Christian adventurers could never be blotted from the English mind. The English knew well, not only from the Spanish and Portuguese experience in the New World, but from their own invasions of Ireland and the Netherlands in the late sixteenth century, that indigenous peoples do not ordinarily accept graciously those who come to dominate them. To imagine the Indian as a savage beast was therefore a way of predicting the future, preparing for it, and justifying what one would do, even before one caused it to happen.

Still a third factor nourishing negative images of the Indians related directly to the natives' possession of land coveted by Europeans. For Englishmen, as for other Europeans, the Indians' occupation of the land presented problems of law, morality, and practicality. As early as the 1580s, George Peckham, an early promoter of colonization, had admitted that some Englishmen doubted their right to take possession of the land of others. In 1609 the thought was raised again by another promoter of colonization, Robert Gray, who asked rhetorically, "By what right or warrant can we enter into the land of these Savages, take away their rightfull inheritance from them, and plant ourselves in their places, being unwronged or unprovoked by them?"[7] It was an appropriate question to ask, for Englishmen, like other Europeans, had organized their society around the concept of private ownership of land and regarded this as

---

[7] *A Good Speed to Virginia* (1609), quoted in Wesley Frank Craven, "Indian Policy in Early Virginia," *William and Mary Quarterly*, 3rd Ser., 1 (1944): 65.

an important characteristic of their superior culture. They were not blind to the fact that they were entering the land of another people, who by prior possession, could lay sole claim to the entire continent.

To some extent the problem could be resolved by arguing that Englishmen did not intend to take the Indians' land but wanted only to share with them what seemed a superabundance of territory. In return, they would extend to the Indians the advantages of a richer culture, a more advanced civilization, and, most importantly, the Christian religion. It was this argument that the governing council in Virginia used in 1610 when it advertised in England that the settlers "by way of marchandizing and trade, doe buy of them [the Indians] the pearles of earth, and sell to them the pearles of heaven."[8] That the Chesapeake tribes had indicated no desire to exchange their land for such Christian instruction as a ragged band of Englishmen could provide—"the pearles of heaven"—was not indicated.

A second and more portentous way of answering the question of English rights to the land was to deny the humanity of the Indians. Thus, Robert Gray, who had asked if Englishmen were entitled to "plant ourselves in their places," answered by arguing that the Indians' inhumanity disqualified them from the right to possess land. "Although the Lord hath given the earth to children of men," he wrote, "the greater part of it [is] possessed and wrongfully usurped by wild beasts, and unreasonable creatures, or by brutish savages, which by reason of their godles ignorance, and blasphemous Idolatrie, are worse than those beasts which are of most wilde and savage nature."[9] This line of reasoning was filled with danger for the Indian, for while many leaders of colonization would avow, as one of them put it, that "every foote of Land which we shall take unto our use, we will bargayne and buy of them," others would find it more convenient to suggest that Indians, merely by being "Godless" and "savage," as defined by Englishmen, had disqualified themselves from rightful ownership of the land.[10] In this sense there was much to be gained by developing deeply negative images of native peoples. The darker the image—the more it defined aboriginal peoples in nonhuman

---

[8] *A True Declaration of the Estate of the Colonie in Virginia* . . . (1610), in *Tracts and Other Papers, Relating Principally to the Origin, Settlement, and Progress of the Colonies in North America* . . . , Peter Force, comp. (Washington D.C., 1884), 3: No. 1, p. 6.

[9] *A Good Speed to Virginia* (1609), quoted in Gary B. Nash, "The Image of the Indian in the Southern Colonial Mind," *William and Mary Quarterly*, 3rd Ser., 29 (1972): 210.

[10] William Strachey, *The Historie of Travell into Virginia Britania* (1612), eds. Louis B. Wright and Virginia Freund, Hakluyt Society *Publications*, 2d Ser., 103 (London: The Hakluyt Society, 1953): 26.

terms—the stronger was the European claim to the land of the New World. Defining the Indian as a "savage" or "brutish beast" or "tawny serpent" did not give Europeans the power to dispossess Indians of their land. But it gave them the moral force to do so if and when physical force should become available. The Spanish, Portuguese, Dutch, French, and English did not differ much in this regard.

A pamphlet published in England, as the first English colonizing expedition was preparing to embark for Roanoke Island, off the North Carolina coast, illustrates how both the positive and the negative images of the Indian were operating in the English mind. It was written by Sir George Peckham, who had accompanied Humphrey Gilbert on a voyage of exploration to Newfoundland in 1583. Published in London as *A True Report, of the late discoveries, . . . of the Newfound Landes,* Peckham's account was a clear expression of the emerging formula for English colonization: exterior expressions of goodwill, explanations of mutual benefits to be derived from the contact of English and Indian cultures, and yet, lurking beneath the surface, dark images and the anticipation of violence. Peckham's pamphlet began with elaborate defenses of the rights of maritime nations to "trade and trafficke" with "savage" nations and assured Englishmen that such enterprises would be "profitable to the adventurers in perticular, beneficial to the Savages, and a matter to be attained without any great daunger or difficultie." Some of the natives, he allowed, would be "fearefull by nature" and disquieted by the "straunge apparrell, Armour, and weapon" of the English, but "courtesie and myldnes," along with a generous bounty of "prittie merchaundizes and trifles as looking Glasses, Bells, Beades, Braceletts, Chaines, or collers of Bewgle, Christall, Amber, Jett, or Glasse" would soon win them over and "induce their Barbarous natures to a likeing and mutuall society with us."[11]

With this explanation of how he hoped the English might act, and how the Indians might respond, Peckham proceeded to reveal what he must have considered the more likely course of events:

> But if after these good and fayre meanes used, the Savages nevertheless will not be heerewithall satisfied, but barbarously wyll goe about to practise violence either in repelling the Christians from theyr Portes and safe Landinges or in withstanding them afterwardes to enjoye the rights for which both painfully and lawfully they have adventured themselves thether; Then in such a case I holde it no breache of equitye for the Christians to defende themselves, to pursue revenge with force, and to doo whatsoever is necessary for attayning of theyr safety; For it is allowable by all Lawes in such distresses, to resist violence with violence.[12]

[11]David Beers Quinn, ed., *The Voyages and Colonizing Enterprises of Sir Humphrey Gilbert,* Hakluyt Society *Publications,* 2nd Ser., 84 (London: The Hakluyt Society, 1940): 450–52.

[12]*Ibid.,* 453.

With earlier statements of the gentle and receptive qualities of the Indians almost beyond recall, Peckham reminded his countrymen of their responsibility to employ all necessary means to bring the Indians from "falsehood to truth, from darkness to light, from the highway of death, to the path of life, from superstitious idolatry, to sincere christianity, from the devill to Christ, from hell to Heaven."

Thus two conflicting images of the Indian wrestled for ascendance in the English mind as the first attempts to colonize in the New World began. At times the English tended to see the native as a backward but receptive person with whom amicable and profitable relations might be established. But the negative image, filled with visions of violence and bloodshed, probably reverberated even more strongly in the minds of those who were sailing toward land already occupied by people of a different culture.

First English-Indian Encounter

The experience at Roanoke Island is of no importance in the overall history of European colonization of the New World. The two handfuls of men who were set ashore did no more than struggle for survival for three years, and when their annual provisioning ship was delayed in 1588 by the approaching Spanish Armada off the coast of England, they promptly perished, either by starvation or by Indian attack. But their story is important in a way that is left unexamined in the history books. This was the first extended encounter between Indians and the English-speaking, Protestant variety of European. For Indians of the Chesapeake area what transpired would help to fix impressions of who and what these Englishmen were. Likewise, the three accounts of the Roanoke expedition, published in London by those who had been there but had returned to England after the first year, helped to plant in the minds of all other Englishmen coming to America in the early seventeenth century ideas of what kind of people they were likely to encounter.

Though differing in detail, all the accounts agree that the Indians of the Carolina coast were receptive to the English. Arthur Barlow, a member of the first expedition, wrote that "we were entertained with all love, and kindness, and with as much bountie, after their manner, as they could possibly devise. We found the people most gentle, loving and faithful, void of all guile, and treason." Barlow remarked that the Indians were "much grieved" when their hospitality was shunned by the suspicious English.[13] Other accounts, while less complimentary to the Indians,

[13]David Beers Quinn, ed., *The Roanoke Voyages, 1584–1590*, Hakluyt Society *Publications*, 104 (London: The Hakluyt Society, 1955): 108.

also averred that the indigenous people were eager to learn about the artifacts of English culture and, though wary, extended their hospitality. Since the English came in small numbers, the Indians probably did not regard them as much of a threat. Curiosity about the "others" seemed to be strong on each side. So far as can be determined from the surviving evidence, no conflict occurred until the English discovered a silver cup missing and dispatched a punitive expedition to a nearby Indian village. When the Indians denied taking the cup, the English, deciding to make a show of force, burned the village to the ground, and destroyed the Indians' supply of corn. After that, relations deteriorated. Aware of their numerical disadvantage and the precariousness of their position, the English employed force in large doses to convince the local Indians of their invulnerability. As one member of the expedition admitted, "Some of our companie towardes the ende of the yeare, shewed themselves too fierce, in slaying some of the people, in some towns, upon causes that on our part, might easily enough have been borne withall."[14] Given this course of events, the coastal tribes must have concluded that the English were untrustworthy, quick to resort to arms, and dangerously unpredictable. "What was lost in this famous lost colony," we have recently been reminded, "was more than the band of colonists who have never been traced. What was also lost and never quite recovered in subsequent ventures was the dream of Englishman and Indian living side by side in peace and liberty."[15]

In spite of their difficulties, the principal members of the Roanoke colony who returned to England entertained considerable respect for Indian culture. Thomas Hariot wrote that "although they have no such tooles, nor any such craftes, sciences and artes as wee; yet in those things they doe, they shewe excellencie of wit."[16] John White, a painter of some skill who had accompanied the expedition, brought back scores of sketches and watercolors which showed the Indians at various aspects of work and play. White's drawings reveal a genuine appreciation of the Indians' ability to control their environment through their methods of hunting and agriculture, their family and communal life, and other aspects of their culture.

For two decades after the Roanoke experiment, Englishmen launched no new colonial adventures. A few English sea captains, representing merchants who dabbled in the West Indies trade, looked in on the coast of North America and attempted to barter with the Indians. They re-

[14]*Ibid.*, 381–82.
[15]Edmund S. Morgan, "Slavery and Freedom: The American Paradox," *Journal of American History*, 59 (1972–73): 16.
[16]Quinn, ed., *Roanoke Voyages*, 104: 371.

ported that their relations were generally friendly. But no further English attempts at colonization would come until after the death of Queen Elizabeth in 1603 in whose reign so much had been done to propagandize American colonizing and to obtain for it the backing of the Crown and the mercantile wealth of the nation. North America, so far as it was an arena of European colonization, still belonged to the Spanish and French.

chapter 3

Cultures Meet on the Chesapeake

The first permanent English settlement in the New World was founded at Jamestown, Virginia, in 1607. But properly speaking, it was not a colony at all, at least in the sense of being a political unit governed by the mother country. Rather it was a business enterprise, the property of the Virginia Company of London, made up of stockholders and a governing board of directors which answered directly to James I. Its primary purpose in the eyes of its founders was to return a profit to its shareholders—merchants, political figures at the royal court, and others who had invested their capital in the hopes that the remarkable success of the Spanish and Portuguese in Mexico, Peru, and Brazil could be duplicated.

The King's charter to the Virginia Company of London begins with the suggestion that the company was to concern itself with bringing the Christian religion to such people "as yet live in darkness and miserable ignorance of the true knowledge and worship of God." This reference to Christianizing the Indians of the Chesapeake area no doubt concerned many Englishmen in an era when the rivalry with Spain for the uncommitted peoples of the earth was analogous to the ideological struggle for the uncommitted people of the "Third World" by communist and capitalist countries after World War II. But far more important in the minds of those who were subscribing to shares in the Virginia Company was to receive a return on their investment. As Captain John Smith, who was to become a central figure in the drama unfolding in Virginia, later wrote: "We did admire how it was possible such wise men could so torment themselves and us with such strange absurdities and impossibilities: making Religion their colour, when all their aime was nothing but present profit. . . . For I am not so simple to think that any other motive than wealth will ever erect in Virginia a Commonweale."[1]

How would the Virginia Company enrich its stockholders? Nobody was quite sure, but it was assumed that profits in the New World would come in a variety of ways: through the discovery of gold and other minerals; by trade with the Indians; by production of pitch, tar, potash, and other products of the forest needed by the English navy; through the development of a fishing industry; and, best of all, by discovering the illusive passage through the American continent to Cathay. Some of these objectives had been realized in other English joint-stock ventures: by the Muscovy Company in Russia, the Levantine Company in the Middle East, and the East India Company in the Far East. Why not in North America?

Once sufficient capital was obtained, the principal problems were to recruit laborers who would go to the colony as employees of the Virginia Company and to establish the kind of administration and authority which would channel their energies toward the desired goals. Both of these problems proved thorny in the early years.

The tiny fleet that set sail for Virginia in December 1606 was the final fruit of a year's planning in London by investors and the board of governors of the Virginia Company. Three ships carrying about 120 colonists embarked under the command of Captain Christopher Newport. Sixteen weeks later, after stopping in the West Indies for water and provisions, a landfall was made on the Chesapeake Bay. Men and provisions were put ashore and after a few days the ships disappeared over the horizon, leaving the small band of Englishmen alone in an unknown land.

Early Misfortune

What followed in the next nine months, before Captain Newport returned with supplies and additional settlers, was a dismal tale of human

---

[1]Edward Arber and A. G. Bradley, eds., *Travels and Works of Captain John Smith* (Edinburgh: J. Grant, 1910), 2: 928.

weakness and misfortune. Attempts were made to explore the area, to build a fort and shelters within it, to plant crops, and to organize a bit of fishing. But the colonists seemed to have spent much of their time dividing into factions and organizing plots against each other. The supplies quickly dwindled and men were soon on starvation rations. Some deserted to the Indian villages where food was plentiful. Dysentery plagued the settlement. One of the members of the resident council of governors was expelled by his exasperated colleagues. A second was sentenced to execution as a spy of the Spanish, who were thought to be planning the elimination of the colony. A third was saved from hanging only by the arrival of the reprovisioning ships from England. When Newport returned in January 1608 only 38 of the original settlers were still alive. Three days later fire destroyed most of the crude buildings in Jamestown and most of the freshly unloaded supplies.

Twice in 1608 and once in 1609 the Virginia Company of London sent out ships with new settlers and supplies. But the "starving time" continued and, as one of the leaders later wrote: "dissentions and jarrs were daily sowne amongst them [the settlers], so that they choaked the seed and blasted the fruits of all men's labors."[2] Although more than 900 settlers were sent to Virginia in the first three years, by the winter of 1609–10 only sixty survivors remained in the colony and some among them had resorted to cannibalism in their distress. "Such was the insufferable sloth and unreasonable Perverseness of far the greater Number," wrote an eighteenth-century Virginian, "that they would sooner have perished, than have been at pains to gather food."[3] In London, while the directors of the Virginia Company circulated promotional pamphlets such as *Good Speed to Virginia* and *Virginia Richly Valued*, the street talk rumored that the colony was a dismal failure and investors glumly counted the money they had wasted on this ill-starred enterprise. Men asked what had gone wrong with the plan to establish English presence in North America.

One of the flaws in the plans of English promoters of colonization was that they had badly miscalculated the reality of the North American coast. Most investors and participants in the colony were hoping to duplicate the Spanish experience in Mexico and Peru. They dreamed of dragging from the earth the precious minerals which would make them wealthy. They hoped to utilize a native labor force or at least to profit

[2]John Rolfe, *A Relation of the State of Virginia* (1616), quoted in Perry Miller, "Religion and Society in the Early Literature: The Religious Impulse in the Founding of Virginia," *William and Mary Quarterly*, 3d Ser., 6 (1949): 29.

[3]William Stith, *The History of the First Discovery and Settlement of Virginia* (New York: Joseph Sabin, 1865), p. 98.

from trade with the Indians. But Virginia was not Mexico or Peru. Its earth contained neither gold nor silver and thus all the frantic digging that was done in the early months and all the loading of ships with mica-speckled dirt, which the colonists thought must be gold, brought only a depletion of energy and shattered dreams. "Our gilded refiners, with their golden promises," wrote John Smith, "made all men their slaves in hope of recompence. There was no talke, no hope, nor worke, but dig gold, wash gold, refine gold, load gold [in order to load] a drunken ship with so much gilded [mica-filled] durt."[4]

Doubling the disappointment was their inability to utilize the labor of the Indians of the region. Most Englishmen who came to Virginia in the initial stage of colonization probably assumed that without undue effort they could exploit the Indians of the New World. Upon their backs could be built a prosperous society. Cortez had conquered the mighty Aztec empire with a few hundred men and then turned the labor of thousands of Indians to Spanish advantage. Pizzaro had done the same in Peru. Why should it not be so in Virginia?

But in the Chesapeake region the English found that the indigenous people were not so densely settled and could not be so easily subjugated. Smith later wrote that the Spaniards were fortunate enough to colonize "in those parts where there were infinite numbers of people who had manured the ground so that food was provided at all times."[5] Moreover, the Spanish got the "spoil and pillage" of the well-developed regions they colonized because they brought with them a military force capable of overpowering the native society. But the English settled in Virginia where there was no wealthy Indian empire to conquer. Nor could some 30,000 Indians of the Chesapeake region be molded into a labor force at the Europeans' command, for the English brought with them neither an army of conquistadors nor an army of priests to convert Indians to the European religion. Unable to exploit or utilize the native population, the Virginia settlers found the New World paradise far from utopian.

A third flaw in the English plan of settlement related to the composition of the original settlers at Jamestown. Of those who arrived in the early years, many were gentlemen-adventurers who were ill-equipped to undertake the rugged work of colony building and proved to be only a drain on the tiny settlement's resources. By the same token there were far too few laborers and farmers—men who could cut trees, build houses, and farm the soil. John Smith complained that a small number of adventure-seeking gentlemen would have been well enough; but "to have more

[4]Arber and Bradley, eds., *Works of Smith*, 1: 104.
[5]Quoted in Sigmund Diamond, "From Organization to Society: Virginia in the Seventeenth Century," *American Journal of Sociology*, 63 (1958): 460.

to wait and play than worke, or more commanders and officers than industrious labourers" was foolishness, "for in Virginia a plaine Souldier
that can use a pickaxe and spade, is better than five Knights."[6] Those
who had been bred to a life of labor were not much better. "A more
damned crew hell never vomited," growled the president of the Company
and his opinion was echoed and embellished by one of Virginia's first
historians, who described the original colonizers as "unruly Sparks,
packed off by their Friends, to escape worse Destinies at home . . . , poor
Gentlemen, broken Tradesmen, Rakes and Libertines, Footmen, and
such Others, as were much fitter to spoil or ruin a Commonwealth, than
to help to raise or maintain one."[7] This inappropriate selection of colonists not only created manpower problems but led to chronic social tension. Men of high social standing were regarded in England as essential
to the strength and stability of society. But in a wilderness settlement on
the edge of a vast, unknown continent they only created resentment, unwilling to work themselves and unable to command the respect of those
under them.

The most enlightening example of the social tension created when
Englishmen moved to a new environment on the opposite side of the
Atlantic Ocean is the case of Captain John Smith. Smith claimed no
aristocratic blood; his father was a simple west country tenant farmer.
Concluding at an early age that the life of a poor farmer held nothing
for him, Smith had set out for more exciting fields of endeavor. Before
he had reached his mid-twenties he had traveled and fought his way
across Europe and back as a professional soldier in the employ of various
local warloads who purchased his services. He fought duels in Transyl-
vania, battled the Turks on the plains of western Hungary, was captured
and enslaved for several years in Istanbul, escaped into Russia, and
worked his way back to England by way of North Africa. Because of his
military experience, his skill as a cartographer, and because he had friends
in London who were interested in the Virginia enterprise being mounted
in 1606, Smith was recruited as a member of the first Jamestown expedition. His experience suggested that he would be a good man to have along
when the going got rough.

Even on the ocean voyage Smith had fallen out with some of the leaders
of the expedition, men with gentry blood flowing in their veins, and had
been clapped in irons on the *Susan Constant*. When the secret orders were
opened upon arrival on the Chesapeake, it was disclosed that Smith had

[6]*Ibid.*, 461.

[7]George Sandys to John Ferrar, 1623, in Susan M. Kingsbury, ed., *The Records of
the Virginia Company of London* (Washington, D.C.: Government Printing Office,
1906–35), 4: 23; William Stith, *History of Virginia*, p. 103.

been named a member of the Virginia governing council. This aroused further resentment. Smith had little patience with men who reckoned that their social origins excused them from manual labor and he did not hesitate to say so. As it happened, he was one of the few among the initial colonists who possessed the courage and ability to explore and map the region around Jamestown, establish contact with the Indians, negotiate with them, and attempt any rational organization of the colony's slender human resources. The net effect of his exertions, however, was to alienate the gentlemen councilors around him. They saw his aggressiveness and disdain for their social superiority as a calculated attempt to gain control of the colony and to depose them in the process. Attempts were made to eliminate Smith as a dangerous influence at Jamestown but by September 1608 Smith had outlasted most of his enemies and for a year ruled the colony as president of the governing council.

Reorganization and Tobacco

After three years of near anarchy and a failure to find ways of exploiting the Chesapeake region to the benefit of the Virginia Company's stockholders, the directors in London perceived that what was needed in the colony were not soldiers of fortune but ordinary farmers who could extract from the land the necessary food supplies to sustain the colony and begin the cultivation of a staple crop. A reorganization of the company was accomplished in 1609 and a large number of settlers were lured to Virginia by promises of free land at the end of seven years labor for the company.

Under this new system of recruitment about 1,200 new emigrants were drawn to Virginia in 1610 and 1611. But even with this new source of manpower the Virginia Company was unable to develop staple crops or find a way of returning a profit to its investors. The colony limped along and the company barely remained afloat. By 1616 death and re-emigration to England had reduced the population to 350. Again the company raised the inducements for going to the Chesapeake. This time 100 acres of land was offered outright to anyone in England who would journey to the colony. Instead of pledging limited servitude for the chance to become sole possessor of land, an Englishman trapped at the lower rungs of society at home could now become an independent landowner in no more time than it took to reach the Chesapeake.

Under this new program, the Virginia Company gave up, once and for all, the hope of making a fortune for its shareholders through the employment of a work force, either native or English. Now the company oper-

ated simply as an organization for the promotion and sale of land. Its
aim was to encourage as many Englishmen as possible to come to Virginia
to pursue their fortunes independently. In time, if the colony proved
itself valuable, its vast land resources could be sold at profit. Other concessions were also made. In 1619 the resident governor was ordered to
allow the election of a representative assembly, which would participate
in governing the colony and thus bind the colonists emotionally to the
land. In the same year the company shipped a boatload of unmarried
women to the colony in order to improve morale and touch off a small
population explosion.

In response to these concessions more than 4,500 colonists arrived between 1619 and 1624. They came no longer as employees of the Virginia
Company of London or as individuals to be governed entirely at the
discretion of the resident council and the governing council in London.
Through its failures, the company had learned that only by promising
immediate ownership of land and by allowing a degree of local government could they hope to keep the colony alive and growing. The colony
had been initiated not by men seeking political or religious freedom but
by profit-hungry investors in England and fortune-hunting adventurers
and common riffraff from the back alleys and prisons of England. But
after almost two decades the original plans had been abandoned as men
adjusted unrealistic expectations to the realities of the New World.

It was not only the reorganization of the Virginia Company and the
new inducements to settlement that lifted the colony out of the depths
of social disorder and unprofitability in the early years. It was also the
discovery that tobacco—"the jovial weed," as it was called—grew excep-
tionally well in the soil of the Chesapeake region. Tobacco, which became
one of the seventeenth century's most widely used narcotics, had been
first brought to Portugal from Florida in the 1560s, but it was Francis
Drake's boatload of the leaf, procured in the West Indies in 1586 and
then popularized among the upper class by Raleigh, that converted it
from medicinal purposes to a social addiction. By the early seventeenth
century England was swept with the smoking craze. Young bloods in English society developed various tricks and affectations as a part of the
smoking cult: the "Ring," the "Whiffle," the "Gulp," and the "Reten-
tion" became a part of the new social habit. Even the violent opposition
of King James could not arrest the popularity of smoking tobacco. Sound-
ing like a modern physician, James anonymously published *Counterblast
to Tobacco* in which he described smoking as "a custom loathsome to the
eye, hateful to the nose, harmful to the brain, dangerous to the lungs,
and in the black stinking fumes thereof, nearest resembling the horrible
stygian smoke of the pit that is bottomless." But it was to no avail as
English society imported more and more tobacco leaf from the New
World. At first the West Indies supplied the bulk of the crop, but experi-

ments with tobacco culture in Virginia proved phenomenally successful. Exports of leaf increased from 2,300 pounds in 1616 to 200,000 pounds in 1624 and had skyrocketed to 3,000,000 pounds by 1638. Tobacco had become to the Chesapeake region what sugar was to the West Indies and silver was to Peru and Mexico.

INDENTURED SERVANTS

Tobacco, of course, would not grow by itself, and so as the demand for tobacco grew, English planters on the Chesapeake sought a source of cheap labor. In the Spanish and Portuguese colonies the settlers had been able to incorporate the native populations into a forced labor system that approximated slavery. But the English discovered that they lacked the power in the early years to enslave the local tribes. So it was to England that the tobacco planters looked for their labor supply—and particularly to the most depressed segment of the population, made up of young men who were willing to sell their labor for four to seven years in exchange for passage across the Atlantic and a chance, after they had served their time, to become independent landowners and tobacco planters in the New World. These men were called indentured servants because they indented themselves to serve a master for a specific period of time. They differed from the earlier employees of the Virginia Company only in that they had contracted their labor to an individual rather than to a company. Put to work in the tobacco fields, an indentured servant could tend about 1,000 to 2,000 tobacco plants, which could be expected to yield tobacco worth about £100 to 150 a year. Few men in England could generate an equivalent income for a year's labor.

After tobacco proved successful in Virginia, a fairly small number of landowners clamored for indentured servants in order to increase the amount of land under cultivation. Brought to the colony by the shipload, they were auctioned off at the dock to the highest bidder. The more servants a landowner could purchase, the greater the crop he could produce; larger crops brought more capital with which to purchase land and additional servants. Thus, as one historian has recently written: "Virginia differed from later American boom towns in that success depended not on acquiring the right piece of land but on acquiring men. Land that would grow tobacco was everywhere, so abundant that people frequently did not bother at first to secure patents for the amounts they were entitled to. Instead men rushed to stake out claims to men, stole them, lured them, fought over them—and bought and sold them, bidding the prices to four, five, and six times the intial cost."[8]

Life for these indentured servants was harsh, for they were the personal

[8]Edmund S. Morgan, "The First American Boom: Virginia 1618 to 1630," *William and Mary Quarterly*, 3d Ser., 28 (1971): 183.

property of a small number of tough, ambitious planters who possessed not only the wealth but the political and social power in the colony. The largest plantation owners controlled local government and brooked no restraints on their behavior. What might happen to a man who challenged a system controlled by the few became apparent to an ordinary immigrant named Richard Barnes in 1624. His tongue loosened by alcohol in a local tavern, Barnes uttered some "base and detracting" words against the resident governor. For this it was ordered that he "be disarmed and have his arms broken and his tongue bored through with an awl and shall pass through a guard of 40 men [with muskets] and shall be butted by every one of them and at the head of the troop kicked down and footed out of the fort; and he shall be banished out of James City and the Island, that he shall not be capable of any privilege of freedom of the country . . . [hereafter]."⁹

Barnes was not an indentured servant but a freeman; for indentured servants who defied the will of the ruling group of tobacco planters life could be even more hazardous, for servitude in early Virginia was different from early chattel slavery only in degree. Unrestrained by the courts which in the mother country protected the rights of servants against unduly oppressive masters, servant owners treated their bondsmen as pieces of property. John Rolfe, one of the leading figures of the colony, reported in 1619 that the "buying of men and boys" and even the gambling at cards for servants in Virginia "was held in England a thing most intolerable." Six years later, an English merchant refused to take a boatload of indentured servants to Virginia because, as he explained, "servants were sold here up and down like horses." What occurred in "boomtime Virginia," Edmund Morgan has written, was "not only the fleeting ugliness of private enterprise operating temporarily without check, not only greed magnified by opportunity, producing fortunes for a few and many," but also the beginning of "a system of labor that treated men as things."¹⁰

English-Indian Relations

While Virginia's promoters and investors were adapting their plans to the realities of the Chesapeake environment, the settlers were not only developing means of exploiting the land and immigrant labor but also encountering the native people of the region. Will it or not, there could be no development of the region's resources without directly confronting the indigenous inhabitants of the land. From the time that the first Jamestown expedition touched land, Indians and Englishmen were in

⁹*Ibid.*, 193.
¹⁰*Ibid.*, 198.

continuous contact in North America. Moreover, permanent settlement required acquisition of land by white settlers—land which was in the possession of the Indian. That single fact was the beginning of a chain of events which governed the entire sociology of red-white relations.

It is not possible to know exactly what Englishmen expected of the Indians as they approached the Chesapeake Bay in the spring of 1607. Nor is it possible to be certain whether the Indian destruction of a Spanish mission in the same area a generation before bespoke a generalized hostility toward Europeans. But it seems likely that given the English belief that the Roanoke colony had been reduced to a pile of bones by the Indians a generation earlier, and given the Indians' sporadic experience with Europeans as a vindictive and militaristic people, neither side was very optimistic about the receptiveness of the other. The pessimistic view of the English must have been greatly intensified when the Jamestown expedition was attacked near Cape Henry, the most seaward point of land in the Chesapeake Bay region, where the first landfall was made. From this point on, the English proceeded with extreme caution, expecting violence and treachery from the Indians, even when they approached in outwardly friendly ways. Thus, when the one-armed Captain Newport led the first exploratory trip up the newly named James River, just weeks after a tiny settlement had been planted at Jamestown, he was confused by what he encountered. The Indians, a member of his group wrote, "are naturally given to trechery, howbeit we could not find it in our travell up the river, but rather a most kind and loving people."[11] This account describes how the English were wined and dined by the Indians, who explained that they were "at oddes" with other tribes, including the Chesapeake tribe that had attacked the English at Cape Henry, and were thus willing to ally with the English against their enemies.

Ethnographic research conducted more than three centuries after the events indicates that the Indians of the region were accurately describing their situation when they said they were "at oddes" with other tribes. Some fifty small tribes lived in the Chesapeake Bay region. Powhatan was the paramount chief of several dozen of these, and for years before the English arrival had been consolidating his hold on the lesser tribes of the area, while warding off the inland tribes of the Piedmont. In this kind of situation it is possible that Powhatan saw an alliance with the English as a means of extending his power in the tidewater area while simultaneously neutralizing the power of his western enemies. At the same time, his unpleasant experience with Europeans, including a clash just

---

[11]Philip L. Barbour, ed., *The Jamestown Voyages Under the First Charter, 1606–1609* Hakluyt Society *Publications*, 2d Ser., 136 (London: The Hakluyt Society, 1969;) 103–4.

three years before with a passing English ship whose crew had been hospitably entertained but then had killed a local chief and kidnapped several Indians, probably made Powhatan extremely wary of these newcomers.

John Smith and others were quick to comprehend the intertribal tensions as well as the linguistic differences among the Indians. But apparently they could not convince themselves that some tribal leaders could find their arrival potentially to their advantage. Perhaps because they viewed their position as so precarious, with dysentery, hunger, and internal strife debilitating their tiny settlement, they could only afford to regard all Indians as threatening. Thus hostile and friendly Indians were seen as different only in their outward behavior. Inwardly they were identical—"savage," treacherous men who only waited for a chance to drive the English back into the sea from which they had emerged.

During the first months of contact, the confusion in the English mind was revealed again and again. In the autumn of 1607, for example, when food supplies were running perilously low and all but a handful of the Jamestown settlers had fallen too ill to work, the colony was saved by Powhatan, whose men brought sufficient food to keep the struggling settlement alive until the sick recovered and the relief ship arrived. Many saw this only as an example of Powhatan's covert hostility rather than as an attempt of the chief to serve his own interests through an alliance with the English. "It pleased God (in our extremity)," wrote John Smith, "To move the Indians to bring us Corne, ere it was halfe ripe, to refresh us, when we rather expected . . . they would destroy us."[12] As a man of military experience among "barbarian" people in all parts of the world, Smith was not willing to believe that the Indians, in aiding the colony, might have found the survival of the English in their own interest. Another leader of the colony could only attribute the Indians' generous behavior to the intervention of the white man's God. "If it had not pleased God to have put a terrour in the Savages heart," he wrote, "we had all perished by those wild and cruell Pagans, being in that weake estate as we were."[13]

In December 1607 Smith was captured during one of his exploratory incursions into Powhatan's country and marched to Werowocomoco, the seat of Powhatan's confederacy. Powhatan seems to have wanted to employ this opportunity to impress the English with his power and arranged a mock execution ceremony for Smith. At the critical moment, as the executioners prepared to deliver the death blows, the chief's favorite daughter, Pocahontas, threw herself on Smith to save him. About twelve years old, Pocahontas had been a frequent visitor to Jamestown, undoubt-

[12]Arber and Bradley, eds., *Works of Smith*, 1: 8–9.
[13]Barbour, ed., *Jamestown Voyages*, 136: 144–45.

edly as an emissary of her father, and was well known to Smith. But rather than understanding the rescue in symbolic terms, as Powhatan's way of indicating his strength but also his desire to forge a bond with the newcomers, Smith and other Virginians took Pocahontas's gesture as a spontaneous outburst of love for the English—an un-Indian-like act attributable to English superiority or perhaps to God's intervening hand. Hostility was on the English mind, sporadic hostility had already been experienced, and thus Powhatan's deliverance of the English leader, at a time when the colony was almost defenseless, was perceived as further evidence of the natives' irreversible hostility.

In the aftermath of the incident, Pocahontas became a kind of ambassador from Powhatan to the struggling Jamestown colony, an agent who became fluent in the English language and kept Powhatan informed on the state of the internally divided Englishmen. By late 1608, more colonists had arrived in Jamestown, and Smith, as the new president of council, adopted an aggressive stance, burning Indian canoes, fields, and villages in order to extort food supplies and to cow Powhatan and his lesser chiefs into submissiveness. Fully aware that Virginia could not be effectively resupplied from England every few months and that the colonists were unable to sustain themselves in their new environment, Smith sought a forced trade with Powhatan. By the end of 1608 the chief had determined to let the Englishmen starve, a policy made manifestly clear not only by his refusal to trade but by his withdrawal of the Pocahontas emissary. On penalty of death the young Indian daughter of the chief was forbidden to enter the English settlement. "Captain Smith," intoned Powhatan at a confrontation of the two leaders in January 1609, "some doubt I have of your coming hither, that makes me not so kindly seek to relieve you as I would [like]. For many do inform me your coming is not for trade, but to invade my people and possess my country."[14]

Smith's response, as the leader of a colony where some men were deserting to the Indians while others starved, was to raid Indian villages for provisions. Powhatan's response was to attack the English wherever he could. Even the arrival of fresh supplies and several hundred new colonists in July and August did not help, for the provisions were quickly exhausted and the men quickly proved that they consumed more than they produced. When the relief ships departed in October 1609, with John Smith aboard one of them, Virginia embarked upon a winter of despair. Under the surveillance of Powhatan, who ambushed foraging colonists when he could, the death toll mounted. George Percy, Smith's successor, wrote that after the horses had been eaten, the dysentery-

---

[14]Quoted in Philip L. Barbour, *Pocahontas and Her World* (Boston: Houghton Mifflin Company, 1970), p. 46.

wracked Virginians "were glad to make shift with [such] vermin as dogs, cats, rats, and mice." When these were exhausted men resorted to "things which seem incredible, as to dig up corpses out of graves and to eat them —and some have licked up the blood which hath fallen from their weak fellows. And amongst the rest, this was most lamentable, that one of our colony murdered his wife, ripped the child out of her womb and threw it into the river, and after chopped the mother in pieces and salted her for his food, the same not being discovered before he had eaten part thereof."[15]

Powhatan's policy of withdrawing from trade with the encroachers had succeeded. By the spring of 1610 the Spanish ambassador to England, Alonso de Velasco, reported accurately that "the Indians hold the English surrounded in the strong place which they had erected there, having killed the larger part of them, and the others were left, so entirely without provisions, that, they thought it impossible to escape." Virginia could be easily erased from the map, Velasco counseled his government, "by sending out a few ships to finish what might be left in that place."[16] What the Spanish ambassador did not know was that two relief ships had reached Jamestown in May 1610 but found the situation so dismal that Sir Thomas Gates, arriving to assume the governorship of the colony, decided to embark the remaining sixty survivors, set sail for England, and admit that Englishmen could not permanently inhabit the shores of the Chesapeake. On June 7, 1610, Gates ordered the forlorn settlement stripped of its meagre possessions, loaded the handful of survivors aboard, and set sail down the James River for the open sea. The ships weighed anchor for the night after reaching the Chesapeake Capes and planned to start the return ocean voyage on the following day.

On the next morning three ships hove into sight. They carried 150 new recruits sent out by the Virginia Company and a new governor, Sir Thomas West, Lord De la Warre. Jamestown, at its moment of extinction, was reborn.

Newly armed and provisioned, the revitalized Jamestown colonists revived and extended their militaristic Indian policy. The new attitude toward the Powhatan Confederacy was apparent in the orders issued in 1609 for governing the colony. Three years before, the Virginia Company had instructed, "In all your passages you must have great care not to offend the naturals, if you can eschew it."[17] Now the governor was or-

[15]Quoted in *ibid.*, pp. 64–65.
[16]Quoted in Grace Steele Woodward, *Pocahontas* (Norman, Okla.: University of Oklahoma Press, 1969), p. 120.
[17]E.G.R. Taylor, ed., *The Original Writings of Correspondence of the Two Richard Hakluyts*, Hakluyt Society *Publications*, 2d Ser., 77 (London, 1935): 494.

dered to effect a military occupation of the region between the James and York rivers, to make all tribes tributary to him rather than to Powhatan, to extract corn, furs, dyes, and labor from each tribe, and, if possible, to mold the natives into an agricultural labor force as the Spanish had done in their colonies. As the English settlement gained in strength, Smith's successors continued his policy of military foraging and intimidation. From 1610 to 1612 Powhatan attacked the colonists whenever opportunities presented themselves and the English mounted attacks that decimated three small tribes and destroyed two Indian villages. Most of the corn that sustained the colony in these years seems to have been extracted by force from Powhatan's villages.

In 1613 the English kidnapped Pocahontas in a move designed to obtain a return of English prisoners and a quantity of weapons that the Indians had obtained over the years and to force payment of "a great quantitie of Corne," as Pocahontas's abductor, Captain Samuel Argall put it.[18] Understanding that his daughter was not in harm's way, Powhatan made limited concessions to the English but refused to satisfy all of the ransom conditions. But in the following year, when the widower John Rolfe, who had been experimenting in the cultivation of tobacco since 1610, vowed to marry Pocahontas, Powhatan was reluctantly persuaded of the political advantages of allowing the first Anglo-Indian marriage in Virginia's early history. Pocahontas became the instrument not only of an uneasy truce between the two societies, but returned to England with Rolfe and other members of Powhatan's Confederacy in 1616 in order to promote further colonization on the Chesapeake. She died on the eve of her departure for Virginia in 1617 after helping to raise the money that pumped new lifeblood into the Virginia Company and consequently sent hundreds of new fortune-seekers to the Chesapeake— a part of the population buildup that would lead to a renewal of hostilities five years after her death.

CULTURAL INTERCHANGE

Notwithstanding misconceptions, suspicion, and violence on both sides, the English and the Powhatans lived in close contact during the first decade of English settlement and cultural interchange occurred on a broad scale. Although it has been a commonplace in the popular mind since the moment when Europeans and native Americans first met that the Europeans were "advanced" and the Indians were "primitive," the technological differences between the two cultures, as anthropologist

[18]Quoted in Woodward, *Pocahontas*, p. 156.

Nancy Lurie has recently reminded us, were equaled or outweighed by the similarities between these two agricultural societies.[19] The main technological advantages of the English were their ability to traverse large bodies of water in wooden ships and their superiority in the use of iron to fashion implements and weapons. But the Indians quickly incorporated such iron-age items as kettles, fishhooks, traps, needles, knives, and guns into their material culture. In return they provided Englishmen with an understanding of how to use nets and weirs to catch the abundant fish and shellfish of the Chesapeake waters and introduced the Europeans to a wide range of agricultural products that were unknown in Europe before the New World was reached. Thus Englishmen in Virginia learned from the natives of the region how to cultivate tobacco, corn, beans, squash, pumpkins, wild rice, and other food products. The English introduction to a wide range of medicinal herbs, to dyes, and to such important devices as the canoe was also a part of the process of cultural interchange.

Such interaction proceeded even while hostility and sporadic violence occurred in the early years. And it was facilitated by the fact that some Indians lived among the English as day laborers while a number of settlers fled to Indian villages rather than endure the rigors of life among the autocratic English rulers and oppressive tobacco planters. This kind of interchange brought a knowledge and understanding of the other culture. Thus even while the English pursued a policy of intimidation in the early years, they were not blind to the resilience and strength of the Indians' culture. Smith himself marveled at the strength and agility of the Chesapeake tribes, at their talent for hunting and fishing, and admired their music and entertainment. He noted that they practiced civil government, that they adhered to religious traditions, and that many of their customs and institutions were not unlike those of the Europeans. Smith's statement that "although the countrie people be very barbarous; yet have they amongst them such government, as that their Magistrats for good commanding, and their people for due subjection, and obeying, excell many places that would be counted very civill" illustrates the tendency of the English mind to embrace contradictory images of the Indian as both savage and civilized. Other Englishmen, such as the Anglican minister, Alexander Whitaker, who proselytized among the Indians, wrote that it was a mistake to suppose that the Indians were merely savage people "for they are of body lustie, strong, and very nimble: they are a very understanding generation, quicke of apprehension, suddaine

[19]Nancy Lurie, "Indian Cultural Adjustment to European Civilization," in *Seventeenth-Century America: Essays in Colonial History*, ed. James M. Smith (Chapel Hill: University of North Carolina Press, 1959), pp. 38–45.

in their dispatches, subtile in their dealings, exquisite in their inventions, and industrious in their labour."[20] So while both sides adjusted uneasily to the presence of the other, they were both involved in cultural borrowing. It was a process between two peoples separated by a cultural gap that was not nearly so large as the Europeans found it convenient to imply by labeling one culture "savage" and the other "civilized."

RENEWED HOSTILITY AND AGGRESSION

After the increase of population that accompanied the rapid growth of tobacco production, relations between the two peoples underwent a fundamental alteration. While giving Virginia a money crop of great potential, the cultivation of tobacco created an enormous new demand for land. As more and more men pushed up the rivers that flowed into the Chesapeake Bay to carve out tobacco plantations, the Indians of the region perceived that what had previously been an abrasive and sometimes violent relationship might now become a disastrous one. Powhatan had died in 1618, just as the tobacco culture was beginning to expand rapidly. His cousin Opechancanough watched the English expansion uneasily for four years. Then in 1622 he set about to coordinate a unified attack on all the English settlements. It was the murder of a greatly respected Indian of the Powhatan Confederacy that ignited the assault on the Virginia settlements in 1622, but the highly combustible atmosphere generated by a half-dozen years of white expansion and pressure on Indian hunting lands was the more fundamental cause.

Although it did not achieve its goal of ending English presence in the Chesapeake area, the Indian attack of 1622 wiped out almost one-third of the white population. Included among the victims was Opechancanough's nephew by marriage, John Rolfe. It was the final straw for the Virginia Company of London. Shortly thereafter it declared bankruptcy, leaving the colony to the governance of the Crown. The more important result was that those who survived the attack were left free to pursue a ruthless new Indian policy. Even though several leaders in the colony confided to men in England that the real cause of the Indian attack was "our owne perfidious dealing with them," it was generally agreed that henceforward the colonists would be free to hunt down the Indian wherever he could be found. No longer would it be necessary to acknowledge an obligation to "civilize" and Christianize the native. A no-holds-barred approach to

---

[20]Arber and Bradley, eds., *Works of Smith*, 1: 43–84; Whitaker, *Good News from Virginia* (1613), quoted in Roy H. Pearce, *The Savages of America: A Study of the Indian and the Idea of Civilization* (Baltimore: The Johns Hopkins University Press, 1953), p. 13.

"the Indian problem" could now be taken. One leader in the colony wrote revealingly after the attack:

> Our hands which before were tied with gentlenesse and faire usage, are now set at liberty by the treacherous violence of the Sauvages. . . . So that we, who hitherto have had possession of no more ground than their waste and our purchase at a valuable consideration to theire owne contentment gained; may now by right of Warre, and law of Nations, invade the Country, and destroy them who sought to destroy us; whereby wee shall enjoy their cultivated places, turning the laborious Mattacke into the victorious Sword . . . and possessing the fruits of others labours. Now their cleared grounds in all their villages (which are situate in the fruitfullest places of the land) shall be inhabited by us, whereas heretofore the grubbing of woods was the greatest labour.[21]

A note of grim satisfaction that the Indians had succeeded in wiping out one-third of the English population can be detected. Now the colonizers were entitled to devastate Indian villages and to take rather than buy the best land. John Smith, writing from England two years after the attack, noted that some men held that the attack "will be good for the Plantation, because now we have just cause to destroy them by all meanes possible." Another writer expressed the genocidal urge that was prevalent when he reasoned that the Indians had done the colonists a favor by sweeping away the previous English reluctance to annihilate the Indians. He enumerated with relish the ways that the "savages" could be exterminated. "Victorie," he wrote, "may bee gained many waies: by force, by surprize, by famine in burning their Corne, by destroying and burning their Boats, Canoes, and Houses, by breaking their fishing Weares, by assailing them in their huntings, whereby they get the greatest part of their sustenance in Winter, by pursuing and chasing them with our horses, and blood-Hounds to draw after them, and Mastives to teare them."[22]

Once the thirst for revenge was slaked, the only debatable point was whether the extermination of the Indians would work to the benefit or disadvantage of the colony. One prominent planter offered "reasons why it is not fittinge utterlye to make an exterpation of the Savages yett" and then assured his neighbors that it was not genocide he was against but the destruction of a people who, if properly subjugated, could enrich all Virginians through their labor. But both subjugation and assimilation required more time and trouble than the Virginians were willing to spend.

21Edward Waterhouse, "A Declaration of the State of the Colony and Affaires in Virginia . . . " (1662), in Kingsbury, ed., *Records of Virginia Company*, 3: 556–57.
22*Travels and Works of Smith*, 2: 578–79; Waterhouse, "State of the Colony," in Kingsbury, ed., *Records of Virginia Company*, 3: 557.

The simpler course, consistent with instructions from London to "root out [the Indians] from being any longer a people," was to follow a scorched earth policy, destroying villages and crops each summer with military expeditions.[23] In 1629 a peace treaty was negotiated but then rejected because it was decided by the council that a state of "perpetual enmity" would serve the colony better. It was a policy predicated on the belief that acculturation of the two peoples, even if possible, was not desirable.

In the aftermath of the Indian attack of 1622 an unambiguously negative image of the Indian pervaded the Virginian mentality. Words such as "perfidious," "cunning," "barbarous," and "improvident" had been used earlier to describe the natives, but their culture still commanded considerable respect in English eyes. After 1622 the Indians' culture was seldom deemed worthy of consideration. More and more abusive words crept into English descriptions of the Indian and negative qualities were projected onto him with increasing frequency. Whereas John Smith and others of the first decade had described the Indians as "ingenious," "industrious," and "quick of apprehension," the author of a history of the massacre, writing just after the event, asserted that the Chesapeake Indians "are by nature sloathfull and idle, vitious, melancholy, slovenly, of bad conditions, lyers, of small memory, of no constancy or trust . . . by nature of all people the most lying and most inconstant in the world, sottish and sodaine: never looking what dangers may happen afterwards, lesse capable than children of six or seaven yeares old, and lesse apt and ingenious."[24] This vocabulary of abuse reflects not only the rage of the decimated colony but an inner need to provide a justification for colonial policy for generations to come. Hereafter, the elimination of the Indians could be rationalized far more easily, for they were seen as cultureless, unreconstructible savages rather than merely as hostile people whose culture, though different in some respects from the English, fitted them admirably for survival in the Chesapeake area.

CONTINUED ENMITY

In the two decades that followed the Indian attack of 1622 Virginia grew to about 6,000 settlers. By 1645 the colony was shipping several million pounds of tobacco annually to England. Although the Crown appointed a royal governor to rule in conjunction with an appointed coun-

[23] John Martin, "The Manner Howe to Bringe the Indians into Subjection," in Kingsbury, ed., *Records of Virginia Company*, 3: 705–7.
[24] Waterhouse, "State of the Colony," in Kingsbury, ed., *Records of Virginia Company*, 3: 562–63.

cil and an elected House of Burgesses, the real power in the colony lay at the local level where each tobacco planter operated autonomously, with little regard for centralized authority. Men like Governor John Harvey, appointed in 1626, could complain that these planters acted "rather for their owne endes than either seekinge the generall good or doinge right to particuler men."[25] But there was little he could do to foster a spirit of community or to curb the appetites of the land-hungry, profit-conscious tobacco planters. When he attempted to formulate a conservative Indian policy in the 1620s, for example, proposing that a lasting peace be negotiated with the Indians and the Chesapeake tribes left unmolested on the land they were occupying, the planters refused to cooperate. These were men who had clawed their way to the top of the rough-hewn frontier society and they had no intention of allowing the governor to interfere with their engrossing of large tracts of land or their continuation of an aggressive Indian policy. When Harvey tried again in 1635 to impose his will, a coterie of Virginia's leaders plotted against him, provoked violence, and evicted him from the colony while sending petitions back to the mother country complaining of his arbitrary and unreasonable policies.

It was such tough, self-made, ambitious men as these, unhindered by religious or humanitarian concern for the Indians and unrestrained by government, that the Chesapeake tribes had to confront after 1630. They also had to face the rapidly shifting demographic balance—the drastic decline of their population by disease and war during the first quarter-century of English presence and the rapid increase of English after 1624. These were factors beyond the control of the Chesapeake tribes. But even though they did not auger well for the future the natives continued to follow their traditional way of life. The years of contact with European culture did little to convince them that they should remodel their religion, social and political organization, or values and beliefs on English patterns. Only the technological innovations and material objects of the newcomers were incorporated into Indian culture; the other aspects of European culture were resisted or rejected.

The Indian uprising of 1644 is additional proof, as Lurie has recently written, "that the Indians' method of adjusting to changes wrought by the Europeans continued to be an attempt to prevail over or remove the source of anxiety—the settlers—rather than to adapt themselves to the foreign culture." Though fewer in number than in 1622, the tribes attacked under the leadership of the aged Opechancanough, who was carried to the battle on a litter. The English suffered as many casualties as

25Quoted in Bernard Bailyn, "Politics and Social Structure in Virginia," in Smith, ed., *Seventeenth-Century America*, p. 97.

a generation before. That the young warriors, who could have known about the earlier war only through accounts passed down in the oral tradition, were willing to risk an all-out attack, knowing the grim reprisals that would rain down on them if they were defeated, is an indication of "the stubborn resistance of the Indians to cultural annihilation."[26] Though the Powhatan tribes were again the losers in the war of 1644, partially because the aid they expected from white Marylanders, whose relations with Virginia had always been abrasive, did not materialize, their determination apparently convinced the Virginians that Indians could rarely be cowed into submissiveness. Rather than risk future wars, the colonists reversed the policy of the 1620s and in 1646 signed a formal treaty with the survivors of the Powhatan Confederacy which drew a line between red and white territory and promised the Indians safety in their areas. It was the beginning of the modern reservation system, for it recognized that assimilation of the two peoples was unlikely and guaranteed to the indigenous people a sanctuary from white land hunger and aggression. In return the Powhatan tribes were to render military assistance in the event of an attack by tribes outside the Chesapeake area and were to pay a yearly tribute to the Virginia colony in beaver skins.

DECAY OF INDIAN STRENGTH

When a census was taken in Virginia in 1669, only 11 of the 28 tribes described by John Smith in 1608 and only about 2,000 of the 30,000 Indians present when the English arrived were still left in the colony. That the English prevailed in the clash of cultures was partly due to the continued immigration of new settlers to the colony at a time when the Indians were suffering population decline. The waning strength of the Indians may also have been related to the technological inferiority of their weapons, although this is uncertain since the bow and arrow could be at least as effective as the musket in forest fighting. More important in the Indians' decline was their inability to unify against the incoming European peoples. They outnumbered the English during the first two decades of settlement and might have expected to be further aided by the fierce internal divisions that gripped the Virginia colony for years. But in times of military crisis the colonists were better able to unify, if only momentarily, than the tribes of the Chesapeake region.

Another factor played an equal if not more important role in the slow decay of Indian strength: the functionlessness of the Chesapeake tribes within the English economic and social system. This can be best under-

[26]"Indian Cultural Adjustment," in Smith, ed., *Seventeenth-Century America*, pp. 51–52.

stood by looking comparatively at the English and Spanish systems of colonization. In the Spanish colonies, the densely settled Indians had been utilized effectively as a subjugated labor force, both in the silver mines and in agriculture. The Spanish had unerringly located the native population centers in Mexico and Peru and made them the focal points of their colonizing efforts. Because the Indians supplied the bulk of the labor for colonial extractive and productive enterprises in the early decades, it was not only desirable but necessary to assimilate them into the European culture. Moreover, the Spanish church had a vested interest in the Indians. They sent hundreds of missionaries to the colonies with the express purpose of obtaining as many conversions as possible for the greater glory of the church. Thirdly, because the Spanish emigrants were overwhelmingly male, Indian women came to serve the indispensable function of mistress, concubine, and wife. Though they were regarded as inferior to Spanish women, thousands of them became the sexual partners, inside and outside of marriage, of Spanish men and in this way were of the utmost importance to the colonizers. Of course none of these services could be obtained until the native societies had been subordinated to Spanish authority. And the most merciless forms of mass killing and terrorization were employed by the Spanish to insure their ascendancy in the first period of contact. Thereafter, however, the Indians were seen not primarily as a threat to Spanish colonization, though the possibility of native uprisings was always present, but as a population that could answer the economic, religious, and biological needs of the European newcomers. Important incentives existed for drawing the natives into Spanish culture, for mixing with them, and protecting them. In spite of catastrophic spread of European diseases, which may have reduced the Indian population by as much as 75 percent in the first century of contact, an impressive degree of acculturation and assimilation took place in the colonial period.

In Virginia none of these factors pertained except in the most limited way. The English brought no military force comparable to the conquistadors to subjugate the sparsely settled Chesapeake tribes and drive them into agricultural labor. The Anglican church sent only a handful of clergymen to the colony and they made only token efforts to mount a missionary campaign. Their power over local settlers so far as relations with the Indians was concerned was minimal. Nor was there a prolonged need for Indian women that might have brought about greater assimilation. The imbalance of males and females, though it existed in the early decades of settlement, was redressed by about mid-seventeenth century because English women were imported and emigration after mid-century tended to be by family far more often than in the Spanish case. Interracial marriages were almost unknown in Virginia and the few contacts between white men and Indian women that did take place were limited to the frontier areas where trappers and traders occasionally consorted with native women.

The only way in which the Indian served the needs of the white colonist was in the fur trade where the Indian served as trapper and hunter. But the fur trade was always of negligible importance in the early Virginia settlements, and by the 1620s tobacco dominated the Virginia economy. What the colonist primarily wanted from the Indian was his cleared land, as was made manifest in the aftermath of the 1622 attack. Within the first generation of European settlement, it was demonstrated that neither side possessed the military capacity to subjugate the other. But for the English subjugation was unnecessary. The Indian, it was understood, had little to contribute to the goals of English colonization and was therefore regarded merely as an obstacle. Once defined in these terms, the Chesapeake tribes became the subject not of assimilative policies but apartheid plans which called for separation or removal. In almost a perfect reversal of Spanish Indian policy the English in Virginia after 1622 worked to keep the two cultures apart, to minimize assimilation and acculturation. Like the Spanish policy it was a plan based on the calculation of self-interest. Differences in the exploitable resources of the Spanish and English colonies, in the density of Indian population, in the demographic composition of the colonizing and colonized societies, and in the social backgrounds of the colonists, rather than differences in national character, attitudes toward the indigenous people, or in national policy, were chiefly responsible for the pursuit of assimilation in Spanish American and the pursuit of racial separation in Virginia.

chapter 4

Cultures Meet in the Northeast

While Indians of the Powhatan confederacy were planning their attack on the white settlements of the Chesapeake in 1622, Englishmen were mounting an "invasion" of Indian territory five hundred miles to the north. The word "invasion" is used not so much because Puritans, like other Europeans, were entering land occupied by indigenous people but because for Puritans life itself was a militant campaign against the Devil. The initial arrival of the Pilgrims on the western edge of the Atlantic in 1620 marked the beginning of a movement of English Protestants whose ideas, values, and institutions did more to shape the contours of colonial society than any other group. Yet in their relationships with people of other cultures Puritans were not significantly different from their country-men of other religious persuasions.

Puritanism

Puritanism was, among other things, a religious reform movement. Since the reign of Henry VIII, where England had turned toward Protestantism, Catholic-Protestant tensions had racked the country. When Elizabeth ascended the throne in 1558 she attempted to effect a religious compromise. But to avowed anti-Catholics the Church of England that flourished under her reign was at best a halfway house between a corrupt and a pure church; at worst it was barely distinguishable from the Church of Rome with its liturgy, vestments, rituals, and oppressive bureaucracy. Some Englishmen wanted greater purity in the church, a more radical cleansing of Catholic elements. They called themselves Puritans.

Puritanism was also a political and social response to long-range changes that had been occurring in English society. Men and women of this era were living at a time when the traditional feudal society was giving way to a more modern social order. From our vantage point, four centuries later, we can see that England was undergoing "modernization," which included overturning the traditional church, the growth of the cities, collectivization of land, an increase in trade, and the rise of a capitalistic society in which the individual had far more autonomy. The most visible manifestations of these long-term trends were uprooted peasants cast off the land, an increase in vagabondage and poverty, and frightening increases in urban crime as people crowded into the cities, particularly into London, which grew from about 75,000 in 1550 to 200,000 in 1600.

Part of the changes overcoming English society concerned values and individual behavior. In the older medieval ethos society was arranged in a fixed system of hierarchies—in church, government, economic organizations, and family. Life in any English rural village reflected this emphasis on rank and order. Every individual was contained within a web of elaborate relationships which conferred duties and responsibilities on each member of the community. There was the manorial hierarchy with lord, steward, and tenants; the parish hierarchy with vicar, churchwardens, and overseers of the poor; the hierarchy of the established church with archbishop, bishops, deans, canons, and visitors; and the hierarchy of economic enterprise with corporations, guilds, masters, journeymen, and apprentices. But in the period of modernization individuals were gradually working themselves free of the authority of corporate groups. Little by little inroads were made on the religious authority which dictated individual belief; on the political authority which strictly governed civil behavior and defined political rights in a limited way; and on the economic authority in which prices, wages, and conditions of work were closely regulated by guilds and monopolies granted by the Crown. Thus "protesters" or Protestants began challenging the authority of the Church of Rome; individual entrepreneurs challenged the right of the guilds to regulate work; individual enterprisers challenged monopolies which excluded outsiders from areas of economic activity; and agricultural operators began buying small farmsteads and consolidating them into larger agricultural units, dislocating tenant farmers in the process.

To Puritans, English society seemed beset by dangerous currents of social change. Everywhere individuals were breaking free of institutionalized restraints. In religious matters this was welcome when it involved the attempt to place the individual in a more direct relationship with God by removing the traditional intermediaries—especially the Catholic Church. But individualism in other areas of life was deemed corrosive because it left people to their own devices, where they promptly acted out the worst fantasies of social anarchy. Social order, respect for authority, morality—all seemed to be crumbling amidst the new social and economic order. Everywhere one saw "idle and masterless men," as one social critic summed it up.

The concept of "every man alone," the atomic individual operating freely in time and space, is at the core of our modern system of beliefs and behavior. But to intellectuals, social critics, and religious leaders of the late sixteenth century it conjured up only frightening visions of chaos. Individualism as a mode of behavior threatened the concept of community—of people bound together by obligations and responsibilities. In the older conception of society each person had gained rights not as an individual but as a participating member of one of the corporate parts of society. It was upon these corporate entities, organizations, and groups —religious, political, economic, and social—that rights were conferred. The individual by himself was thought of as frail and unimportant. Now, under a newer ethic, the individual rather than the group became the conceptual unit of thinking. To Puritans this translated into a frightening vision of anticommunity.

As a social and political movement Puritanism intended to address itself to this problem of the individual versus the community. It intended to reverse the march of disorder, wickedness, and "masterlessness" which it saw burgeoning in English society. Through a new discipline the Puritans hoped to create a regenerated social order and thus to restore the lost equilibrium of their society. Their method or plan was to prescribe an ethic which stressed work or industriousness, in whatever one's calling, as a primary way of serving God. One did not have to occupy a high station or follow a profession; one had only to work hard in whatever station one found oneself, be that lawyer, blacksmith, or common laborer. Each "calling" was equally worthy in God's sight and, followed assiduously, would lead the individual toward spiritual grace. Status and money were unimportant; the test was a person's dedication to his work. Thus one of the Puritan leaders wrote: "If thou beest a man that lives without a calling, though thou hast two thousands to spend, yet if thou hast no calling, tending to publique good, thou art an uncleane beast. God sent you unto this world as unto a Workhouse, not a Playhouse."[1]

Secondly, the Puritans sought to organize themselves into religious congregations where men and women could work together, discipline themselves, and work for mutual salvation. Virtuousness would be fostered by a group concern, each member not only working for his or her own perfection but also scrutinizing the behavior of others for signs of waywardness. Thirdly, the Puritans adopted the idea that if they were going to reform their society at large and not just themselves, they would have to assume responsibility—moral stewardship—over all those around them. In a chaotic and criminal world God's "elect" must not save only themselves but must assume the burdens of civil government so as to reform society at large. Others who could not find the Puritan truths in their hearts might have to be coerced and controlled, directed and dominated. Thus, all would be bound together in covenant to do God's work. In this sense Puritanism was meant to be an instrument of radical politics designed to capture the machinery of civil government so as to effect a conversion of the whole society. A mass-based movement with an ideological vision was to rule the land—a radical departure from traditional thought, which held that kings ruled by their divine right and delegated their authority to those below them.

The rise of Puritanism during Elizabeth's reign, and the subsequent persecution of Puritans by her successor, James I, is a story well told in other historical works. For our purposes it is enough to understand that despite their initial successes, Puritans were increasingly harassed under James and by the 1620s many were convinced that if the work of reforming English society was ever to be completed, the crusade for a new design in living would have to be first carried out in another part of the world. That economic opportunity also beckoned, at a time when many of them were feeling the effects of depression in England, was not an unimportant part of their decision. But their ideological commitment marked them off from the colonizers in Virginia. These were men and women fired by

---

[1]Quoted in Perry Miller and Thomas H. Johnson, *The Puritans* (New York: American Book Company, 1938), pp. 325–26.

a vision of building a Christian utopia, dedicated to organizing themselves around the concept of community, and possessed of the belief that industriousness, frugality, and self-discipline were indispensable parts of worshipping their God. In Virginia, by contrast, the spirit of communalism was conspicuously absent, an ideological vision was lacking, and economic ambitions, rather than being contained and limited within a set of moral prescriptions, were pursued in and of themselves.

The Puritans were by no means the first Europeans to reach the shores of what was to be called New England and what was the homeland of a number of Algonquian-speaking, sparsely settled tribes. Fishermen of various European nationalities had been working the Newfoundland Banks and drying their catches on Cape Cod and the coast of Maine since the late sixteenth century. Hundreds of fishing ships had visited the New England coast and made contact with local Indians before 1607 when the first English attempt at colonization was made in the region. The attempt at colony-building in that year was short-lived, for the small number of settlers who disembarked on the coast of Maine were beset with food shortages, fire, and inhospitable winds. Not until 1620 was another attempt at colonization made, this time by several hundred English Pilgrims who had earlier fled to Holland and now decided to establish themselves in the New World. Slowly in the 1620s other fur-trading and fish-drying settlements took root along the coast. But none of these could compare with the great Puritan migration which began in 1630 with eleven ships and some seven hundred passengers and which by 1640 had brought about 12,000 people to New England.

The Quest for Utopia

Led by a member of the English gentry, John Winthrop, the Puritans set about the work of building their "Citty on the Hill" as they called their experiment in utopia building. The hope was to establish communities of pure Christians who collectively swore a covenant with God that they would work for his ends, knowing that he in return would watch over them. The individualistic impulses that had flowered in England were to be brought under control as all worked for the common good. To accomplish this the Puritans agreed to employ what we might call totalitarian means. There could be no diversity of opinion concerning religious orthodoxy in the new communities. Government would be limited to those who were visibly filled with God's grace as determined by those already in the church. Offenders, both civil and religious, would be rooted out and punished severely. Every aspect of life would be integrated into the quest for utopia—economic activity, political activity, intellectual activity, and religious activity. In other words, the Puritans were attempting to integrate all the elements of their culture into one unified quest at a time when contemporary European society was characterized by greater diversity and individualism. Participants in the experiment, at least initially, were agreeing to give up some of their freedoms in order to accomplish greater goals. Homogeneity, not diversity, was sought, and protecting the rights of the community rather than the rights of its individual members was the main concern. This was to be a society consensual in origin but authoritarian in operation. What the Puritans in England had formulated as an ideology of rebellion was now to be employed as an ideology of control.

As in Virginia, the early months were difficult. More than two hundred of the first seven hundred immigrants perished and a hundred more, chronically depressed by their first winter in the forbidding New England climate, returned to England the next spring. But Puritans kept coming. Villages began "hiving out" along the shores of Boston's Back Bay, along the rivers that emptied into it, south into what became Connecticut, and north along the Massachusetts coast. Crops were planted, fishing begun, and Massachusetts quickly achieved the viable economic base which had been so sorely lacking in Virginia in the early years. No doubt this success can be explained not only by the militant work ethic and discipline shared by most of the settlers, but also by the quality of leadership exercised by men such as Winthrop, John Cotton, John Eliot, and Thomas Shepard, who were experienced in local government, in law, and in the power of exhortation. The typical early leader in Virginia was a soldier of fortune or a roughneck adventurer whose instincts were almost entirely predatory. Massachusetts was led in the early years by university-trained ministers, experienced members of the English lesser gentry, and men almost compulsive in their determination to fulfill what they regarded as God's prophecy for New England.

Early Dissension

Nevertheless, Massachusetts experienced dissension and conflict in the early decades, both within its communities and in contact with the natives of the region. Even on the voyage across the Atlantic some inklings that the sun would not always shine on the Puritan experiment began to appear. In the middle of the voyage Winthrop was compelled to remind some of the less submissive members of the expedition that respect for authority was to be a fundamental part of this new venture. Factional and individualistic tendencies had already raised their heads. Once on firm ground, and surrounded by boundless land, it was not easy to squelch acquisitive instincts or to keep people closely bound in covenanted communities. Restless men began moving away from the center of authority. Others, remaining at the center, agitated for a broader-based political system and a decentralization of authority that would give the individual towns the right to manage their own affairs. After only two years Winthrop wondered if the Puritans had not gone "from "from the snare to the pit." Thirteen years later he was still struggling to convince those around him that "if you stand for your natural corrupt liberties, and will do what is good in your own eyes, you will not endure the least weight of authority, but will murmur and oppose, and be always striving to shake off that yoke."[2]

Winthrop's troubles multiplied. In 1633 Roger Williams arrived in New England and now the established leaders were faced with a contentious and visionary man who defined religious orthodoxy in terms different from theirs and had no intention of changing his views to conform with those already accepted as orthodox. Williams preached that the Puritans were not truly pure because they would not proclaim their complete separation from the Church of England. He argued that their interpretation of the Bible was incorrect. And perhaps most discomfiting, he charged that the colonists were intruding on Indian soil and illegally depriving the natives of their rights. By 1635 Williams had resisted all those who struggled to make him retreat from his views and defied the civil magistrates to try or punish him for his teachings. Convinced that Williams would split the colony into competing religious groups; destroy all stability, cohesion, and authority; and bring about the disintegration of the colony through his religious perfectionism, the Massachusetts magistrates banished Williams from the colony and attempted to ship him back to England. But Williams escaped the authorities and trekked southward where in time he started a small settlement of his followers—the seed of the colony of Rhode Island.

Even as Williams was being banished to his distant Eden, the authorities were confronted with another preacher of unorthodoxy—Anne Hutchinson. Brilliant and charismatic, she had proven her value to the community as a midwife and spiritual counselor in the months after her arrival in early 1634. But in the next two years she emerged as more than a counselor. She gathered many in the community around her for religious discussions and then took to dissecting the previous Sunday's sermons and raising points of criticism concerning the theological interpretations of John Wilson, Boston's minister. Before long she was the center of a movement called Antinomianism—a variant interpretation of Puri-

[2]Quoted in Richard S. Dunn, *Puritans and Yankees: The Winthrop Dynasty of New England, 1630–1717* (Princeton: Princeton University Press, 1962), p. 24.

tan doctrine which stressed the mystical elements of God's grace and the futility of applying rules and regulations to govern the process by which each individual came to terms with his or her God. By 1636 Boston was dividing into two camps and Anne Hutchinson was drawing to her circle not only those who believed in her theological discourses but most of the discontented in the community—merchants who chafed under the government's price controls, young people who disliked the rigid rule of their elders in church and government, and artisans who resented wage controls imposed to arrest the inflationary trend that had made its appearance.

Determined to rid itself of this second threat to uniformity of opinion, the magistrates indicted Anne Hutchinson in 1636 and after a long and symbolic trial, in which the outcome was predetermined, she was banished from the colony for preaching eighty-two erroneous theological opinions. The sentence read to her at the trial's end conveys the fear that had been aroused in Boston and the determination of the magistrates to squelch further division within the community. "Forasmuch as you, Mrs. Hutchinson, have highly transgressed . . . and offended and troubled the Church with your Errors," intoned the judge, "and have drawn away many a poor soule, and have upheld your Revelations; and forasmuch as you have made a lye . . . Therefor in the name of our Lord Jesus Christ . . . I doe cast you out . . . and deliver you up to Satan . . . and account you from this time forth to be a Hethen and a Publican . . . and I command you in the name of Jesus Christ and of this Church as a Leper to withdraw your selfe out of the Congregation."[3] With a number of her followers, Anne followed the route of Roger Williams to Rhode Island. The colony's leaders, the guardians of the dream of a Christian utopia, had demonstrated the lengths to which they were prepared to go to perpetuate homogeneity.

But New England could not really remain homogeneous, no matter how many nonconformists were banished from its midst. Nor could the acquisitive instincts which ate at the concept of community and fed individualistically inclined settlers, leaders included, be forever dampened. The work ethic inevitably brought material gains and with worldly success men developed the ambition to reach still higher—precisely what the Puritan leaders feared would destroy the stable harmonious system they were trying to build. Population increases, geographical expansion, and trade contacts with the outside world all worked against the idea of a closed corporate community suffused with religiosity. In spite of the lead-

[3]Quoted in Emery Battis, *Saints and Secretaries: Anne Hutchinson and the Antinominan Controversy in the Massachusetts Bay Colony* (Chapel Hill: University of North Carolina Press, 1962), p. 246.

ers' protestations that "The care of the public must oversway all private respects," Massachusetts, even in the early years, demonstrated the difficulty, if not the impossibility, of setting down land-hungry Englishmen in the New World and expecting them to restrain their appetites and their individualistic urges. The centrifugal forces of the environment were more than a match for the centripetal forces of religious ideology.

Puritans and Indians

Given the Puritan ideal of community and the centrality of the idea of reforming the world in their image, it might have been thought that the conflict and limited acculturation that characterized Anglo-Indian contacts on the Chesapeake might have been replaced in New England with less hostility and greater interaction. But this was not to be the case.

The Algonquian-speaking tribes of the New England area probably never totaled more than 25,000. Most of them were settled in small villages along the coast and river valleys, but like the Chesapeake area, the northeast coast was only sparsely populated when Europeans arrived. By the time the first permanent settlements were planted in the 1620s, Abenakis, Massachusetts, Narragansetts, and Wampanoags, the largest tribes of the area, had already been in contact with European culture for several generations. Fishermen who dried their catches and engaged in minor trade had provided insights into European culture since the last quarter of the sixteenth century, and short-lived French and English attempts at settlement in the first decade of the seventeenth century gave the Indians further information about European behavior. When George Popham, leader of the English colony on the coast of Maine, landed in 1607, he was surprised to find the Indians generally friendly though wary, as well they might have been since an exploratory expedition two years earlier had kidnapped several Indians and taken them back to England. But relations remained nonviolent until the English, for unknown reasons, attacked the Indians and, according to the account of a later observer, "maltreated and misused them outrageously."[4] Further incidents of kidnapping in 1608 and again in 1614, when twenty-four Indians were captured and sold into slavery in Malaga, must have increased native distrust of white men, although not sufficiently to dampen the interest in English trade goods. Thus when John Smith visited the New England coast on a trading venture in the latter year, he found the natives eager to barter their fish and furs.

---

[4]Quoted in Alden T. Vaughan, *New England Frontier: Puritans and Indians, 1620–1675* (Boston: Little, Brown and Company, 1965), p. 14.

Only two years later, English fishermen stopped on the coast and left behind the deadliest of all the Europeans' weapons—an epidemic virus. It struck with lightning speed, leaving thousands of Indians dead in a short time. Five years later an Englishman moving through the area wrote that "the bones and skulls . . . made such a spectacle . . . that as I travailed in that Forrest, nere the Massachussetts [tribe], it seemed to mee a new found Golgotha."[5] Probably one-half of all the native inhabitants of the New England area succumbed to the disease. It was a powerful example of the role that microorganisms brought by Europeans to the New World played in decimating indigenous cultures. In Europe these bacteriological infections—smallpox, diphtheria, scarlet fever, yellow fever, and others— had wrought demographic disaster in the fifteenth and sixteenth centuries. But infected populations gradually built up immunities against them. The Indians, however, had no such immunities when Europeans arrived as human carriers of these microorganisms, and the effects could therefore be swift and deadly. Whole tribes were often wiped out in the space of a few years, leaving vast areas depopulated. The greater the density of Indian population, the swifter the spread of the disease. In Mexico and other parts of the densely populated Spanish empire, the Indian population losses were far more severe than in sparsely settled coastal North America. But in selected local areas, such as New England, this unplanned but highly effective bacteriological warfare could have important effects.

When the Pilgrims arrived in 1620, they came on the heels of this recent depopulation of the northeastern coastal region. It was their further good fortune to encounter Squanto, a Wampanoag Indian who had been kidnapped by an English ship captain in 1614. Squanto had been sold by his abductor in Spain but somehow made his way to England where he joined an English captain on several trips to the New England coast. On the second of these trips Squanto found that most of his tribe had been killed by the plague but he remained in the Cape Cod area and was there when the Pilgrims landed. Through Squanto's friendship the Pilgrims were rendered important assistance in the early years.

William Bradford, the leader of the Pilgrim colony, wrote a decade after the initial settlement that the English had come anticipating the "continual danger of the savage people, who are cruel, barbarous, and most treacherous"—characteristics that made "the very bowels of men to grate within them and make the weak to quake and tremble."[6] But

[5]Thomas Morton, "New English Canaan," in *Tracts and Other Papers Relating Principally to the Origin, Settlement and Progress of the Colonies in North America,* Peter Force, comp. (Washington, D.C., 1836), 2, No. 5: 19.

[6]William Bradford, *Of Plymouth Plantation, 1620–1647*, ed. Samuel Eliot Morison (New York: Alfred A. Knopf, Inc., 1966), p. 26.

given the record of kidnapping and broken trust which the English had established in their periodic visits to the coast before 1620, the characterization better fit the English than the local tribes. In all probability the local Indians were deeply suspicious of the Pilgrims but no incident of violence at Plymouth occurred until after the newcomers discovered the natives' underground cold-storage cellars and stole as much of the corn, placed there for winter's use, as they could carry off. Even then the Indians chose to minimize contact with the settlers, though after death had reduced the Plymouth colony to about fifty persons by the spring of 1621 the vulnerability of the English might have invited Indian attack.

The Wampanoags' need for a military ally to aid them in their struggle with the neighboring Narragansetts probably explains why they tolerated English abuses and even signed a treaty in 1621 which formed the basis for trade and mutual assistance with the precariously situated English. The logic of the Wampanoag diplomacy was revealed when Miles Standish and other Pilgrims aided them in a dispute with their enemies in 1621.

This amity lasted only a year however. In 1622 the arrival of about sixty non-Pilgrim newcomers to the colony brought serious friction. The new colonists settled themselves at Wessagusset, some distance from the Pilgrim colony, stole corn from the neighboring Massachusetts, and planned attacks on them. Under cover of a story that the Indians were conspiring against both white communities, Standish, who had long harboured grudges against several insulting Massachusetts, led an offensive against the friendly Indians, killing eight of them and impaling the head of the sachem Wituwamet on top of the fort at Plymouth as a symbol of white power. Hearing of the deterioration of relations, John Robinson, formerly the Pilgrims' minister in Holland, wrote Governor Bradford in dismay, asking why the English indulged in needless violence. What was happening to "civilized" men in the wilderness? asked Robinson. Were they beginning to act like "savages," forgetting that they were supposed to represent order and piety? Robinson singled out Miles Standish, the militia captain of Plymouth, for feeding his ego through killing Indians. "It is . . . a thing more glorious, in men's eyes, than pleasing in God's, or convenient for Christians, to be a terrour to poor barbarous people. And indeed I am afraid lest, by these occasions, others should be drawn to affect [this kind of behavior] in the world."[7] As for the Indians, they "could not imagine, from whence these men should come," wrote Thomas Morton, a friend of the Indians, "or to what end, seeing them performe such unexpected actions." From that time on the English colo-

_____
[7] *Ibid.*, p. 375.

nists were called "Wotowquenange, which in their language signifieth stabbers or Cutthroates."[8]

When the Puritan migration began in 1630, Indians of the New England coast had more than a generation of experience with English culture. Little that they had encountered could have rendered them optimistic about future relations, although their own intertribal hostilities continued to make the settlers potentially valuable allies, and their desire for trade goods persisted. As for the Puritans, they were publicly committed to interracial harmony but privately preparing for the worst. The charter of the Massachusetts Bay Company, for example, spoke of the commitment to convert the Indians to Christianity. The "principall ende of this plantacion," it pronounced, was to "wynn and incite the natives of [the] country, to the knowledg and obedience of the onlie true God and Savior of mankinde, and the Christian fayth."[9] But the instructions of the Company to John Winthrop revealed more accurately what was anticipated. According to these orders, all men were to be trained in the use of firearms; Indians were prohibited from entering the Puritan towns; and any colonists so reckless as to sell arms to the Indians or instruct them in their use were to be deported to England where they would be severely punished. While ordering that the Indians must be fairly treated, the Company was reflecting the garrison mentality that settlers, once landed and settled, would manifest even more strongly. No missionary activity was to be initiated for thirteen years.

In the first few years of settlement the Indians did little to arouse Puritan wrath. Their sagamores, or chiefs, made overtures of friendship; the eastern Massachusetts tribes supplied the colonists with corn during the difficult first winter; and a minor trade was started. It was with surprise that one Puritan leader recounted that during the first winter, when the Puritans "had scarce houses to shelter themselves, and no doores to hinder the Indians access to all they had in them, . . . where their whole substance, weake Wives and little ones lay open to their plunder; . . . yet had they none food or stuffe diminished, neither Children nor Wives hurt in the least measure, although the Indians came commonly to them at those times, much hungry belly (as they used to say) and were then in number and strength beyond the English by far."[10]

This state of coexistence lasted only a few years. Smallpox struck the

---

[8]Thomas Morton, "New England Canaan," p. 76, quoted in Neal H. Salisbury, "Conquest of the 'Savage': Puritans, Puritan Missionaries, and Indians, 1620–1680" (Ph.D. diss., University of California, Los Angeles, 1972), p. 86.

[9].Nathaniel B. Shurtleff, *Records of the Governor and Company of the Massachusetts Bay in New England*, 5 vols. (Boston: W. White, 1853–54), 1: 17.

[10]Edward Johnson, "Wonder-Working Providence," quoted in Salisbury, "Conquest of the 'Savage'," pp. 63–64.

eastern Massachusetts tribes in 1633 and 1634, killing several thousands as far north as Maine and as far south as the Connecticut Valley. For the colonists it was proof that God had intervened in the Puritans' behalf at a time when the expansionist impulses of the settlers were beginning to cause friction over rights to land. The town records of Charlestown for example, observed that "without this remarkable and terrible stroke of God upon the natives, [we] would with much more difficulty have found room, and at far greater charge have obtained and purchased land."[11] As in Virginia, it was the need for land that provided the incentive for steering away from rather than toward equitable relations between the societies. That the population buildup came so quickly in Puritan New England only hastened the impulse of Europeans to regard Indians as objects to be removed rather than subjects to be assimilated.

Land Acquisition

Puritan theories of land possession help to clarify this willful move to classify Indians in such a way that only violence rather than assimilation or coexistence could occur. Like other Europeans, Puritans claimed the land they were invading by right of discovery. This theory derived from the ancient claim that Christians were everywhere entitled to dispossess non-Christians of their land. A second European legal theory bolstering Puritan claims was that land not "occupied" or "settled" went by forfeit to those who attached themselves to it in a "civilized" manner. Before he set foot in the New World John Winthrop wrote:

> As for the Natives in New England, they inclose noe Land, neither have any setled habytation, nor any tame Cattle to improve the Land by, and soe have noe other but a Naturall Right to those Countries, soe as if we leave them sufficient for their use, we may lawfully take the rest, there being more than enough for them and us.[12]

Thus in Puritan eyes entitlement to the land of New England required nothing more than the assertion that because their way of life did not conform to European norms, the Indians had forfeited all the land which they "roamed" rather than "settled." By European definition the land was *vacuum domicilium*—unoccupied. Indeed occupation or settlement was not possible by a people who were "uncivilized."

That the Puritans boldly occupied the land, acknowledging no need

---

[11]Quoted in Vaughan, *New England Frontier*, p. 104.

[12]"Generall Considerations for the Plantation in New England . . . " (1629), in *Winthrop Papers*, 5 vols., ed. Allyn B. Forbes (Boston: Massachusetts Historical Society, 1929–47), 2: 118.

to obtain Indian consent through negotiation or purchase, gives some idea of the position of strength they occupied among the disease-ravaged local tribes. Legal theories were proclaimed to justify this early seizure of land but such rationalizations would have counted for little if the coastal tribes had been in a position to resist this unilaterally contrived policy. In Virginia similar arguments for the rights of the invaders to native land were enunciated, but the small number of Virginians in the first several decades were in no position to antagonize the Chesapeake tribes through outright seizures of territory.

That land policy was formulated primarily in response to the presence or absence of countervailing power was made manifest in 1633 when the English in New England broke the precedent established in the first three years and purchased a tract of land from a local sachem. This was not, however, an accommodation to Indian rights or demands but a response to Dutch pretensions in the New England region. Since 1624 the Dutch, under the auspices of the Dutch West India Company, had controlled the Middle Atlantic region, focusing their efforts in New Amsterdam (later New York City) and Fort Orange (later Albany). Their trading contacts with the Indians stretched northward up the Hudson River and southward to Delaware Bay. But their territorial claims reached farther— all the way to New England—although they did not have sufficient manpower or resources to attempt settlement in this area. But in 1633 the Dutch purchased a tract of land from the Pequot Indians, who controlled the Connecticut River Valley. Since Englishmen were obliged to recognize the land titles of other Europeans, who were "civilized" and not "savage," the Dutch purchase forced the hand of the Plymouth settlers whose trading rights and sphere of influence were not jeopardized. The only way of contesting the Dutch purchase was to make a counterpurchase of their own. The Plymouth traders did just this, buying the same tract of land that the Dutch had purchased, but from a tribesman who had earlier been driven from his land by the Pequots. Francis Jennings has written, "Although strong advocates of rights of conquest when it suited their purpose, Plymouth men now contended that their client Indian had not lost his true rights through the Pequot conquest, and the Plymouth deed was solemnly set up against the Dutch deed."[13]

Such an isolated land purchase from the Indians, though it proved that the presence or absence of opposing power was the controlling factor in land policy, had little effect on general policy. In 1633 and 1634 Roger Williams argued strenuously that the royal patent to the Massachusetts Bay Company did not legally convey title to the soil of New England, which could be gained only by purchase from its original owners, as the

[13]"Virgin Land and Savage People," *American Quarterly*, 23 (1971): 531.

Dutch had recognized. But Williams's position was summarily dismissed by the Massachusetts government and the firebrand Williams was soon banished from the colony, at least in part because of this disturbing argument. In Rhode Island, Williams was offered land by a Narragansett chief and thus found "among the savages," as he wrote, a place where he and his followers could peaceably worship God according to their consciences. Winthrop's response to Williams's argument was that "if we had no right to this lande, yet our God hathe right to it, and if he be pleased to give it us (takinge it from a people who had so long usurped upon him and abused his creatures) who shall controll him or his terms?"[14] By claiming that God directed all Puritan policy, Winthrop thus charged anyone who murmured dissent with opposing not only Puritan policy but God himself.

The practice of purchasing Indian land progressed slowly as settlement continued. But the purchases were almost always made in order to obtain a favorable settlement in a situation where the same tract of land was coveted by both English and Dutch settlers or by rival English groups. In such cases a deed to the land in dispute from an Indian seller was the best way to convince a court of one's claim. Even in those cases where intra-European rivalry necessitated the purchase of Indian land, the sale could be accomplished through a variety of stratagems designed to reduce the cost to the white settler. Turning livestock into cultivated Indian fields over a period of time was an effective way of convincing an Indian that his land was losing its value. Alcohol was frequently used to reduce the negotiating skill of the Indian seller. Another method was to buy the land at a rock-bottom price from an Indian sachem who falsely claimed title to it and then to take to court any disputing sachem who claimed ownership. Before an English court, with its white lawyers, judges, and juries, the Indian claimant rarely won his case. Perhaps most effective of all was fining Indians for minor offenses of English law—walking on the Sabbath or illegally entering a town, for example—and then "rescuing" him from the debt he was unable to pay by discharging the fine in return for a tract of his land. As would be amply demonstrated later, none of these tactics worked in areas where Indian tribes were strong and unified. But among the sparsely settled, decimated, and divided tribes of southern New England they were highly effective.

The Puritan Sense of Mission

All of the factors that operated in Virginia to produce friction between the two societies—English land hunger, a deprecatory view of native culture, and inter-tribal Indian tension—were to be found in New England.

14Quoted in *ibid.*, 534n.

They were vastly augmented by another factor not present on the Chesapeake—the Puritan sense of mission. For men of such high moral purpose, who lived daily with the anxiety that they might fail in what they saw as the last chance to save corrupt Western Protestantism, the Indian stood by his differentness as a direct challenge to the "errand into the wilderness." The Puritans' mission was to tame and civilize their new environment and to build in it a pious commonwealth that would "shine like a beacon" back to decadent England. But how could order and discipline be brought to the new environment unless its inhabitants were tamed and "civilized"? Governor William Bradford of Plymouth tellingly described the land he was entering as "a hideous and desolate wilderness full of wild beasts and wild men."[15] Both land, beast, and man must be brought under control, for to do less was to allow chaos to continue when God's will was to impose Christian order. As Roy H. Pearce has explained, the Indian stood as a vivid reminder of what the English knew they must not become. He was the counterimage of civilized man, thought to be lacking in what was most valued by the Puritans—civility, Christian piety, purposefulness, and the work ethic. If such men could not be made part of the Puritan system, then the Puritans would have demonstrated their inability to control this corner of the earth to which God had directed them. Such a failure would surely be answered by God's wrath. So Puritans achieved control of themselves—internal control—through controlling the external world containing forests, fields, and Indians.[16]

The greater one's doubts about the success of this utopian experiment, doubts magnified by internal dissension, the greater the inner need to stifle self-doubt through repression and extension of control. Thus in New England, Indians became obstacles in two senses: as in Virginia and elsewhere they were a physical obstacle since they possessed the land and could not be subjugated so as to serve English ends; and they were a psychological obstacle since while they remained "savages" they threatened the identity of individual Puritans and the collective success of the Puritan Way.

To eliminate "savagism" one did not necessarily have to eliminate the "savages." From their writings one would believe that the Puritans would have much preferred to convert the "heathen" to Christianity. But this could only be accomplished through great expenditures of time and effort. The Spanish and Portuguese had sent hundreds of missionaries along with the conquistadors and settlers. But the Puritans came only with their own ministers and these men had more than enough to do to maintain piety and moral standards within the white community. Thus proselytizing the natives of New England never received a high priority.

15Bradford, *Plymouth Plantation*, p. 62.
16Roy H. Pearce, *The Savages of America: A Study of the Indian and the Idea of Civilization* (Baltimore: The Johns Hopkins Press, 1953), pp. 3–24.

Rather than convert the "savages" of New England, the Puritans attempted to bring them under civil government; that is, to make them strictly accountable to the ordinances that governed white behavior in Massachusetts. Insofar as Indians were willing to subject themselves to the new white code of behavior, usually out of fear, the Puritans could prevail, keeping a close eye on all Indians within the areas of white settlement and bringing them to court for any offenses against white law. In this way many of the smaller tribes of eastern Massachusetts, disastrously weakened by European disease or living in fear of strong and hostile neighbors, did what was necessary to satisfy the newcomers. But inevitably the question of control became a military problem when the Puritans encountered a tribe that was sufficiently strong to resist the loss of its cultural identity and its political sovereignty.

Such were the Pequots—a strong and aggressive tribe that had migrated into southern New England in the century before English arrival. By the 1630s they had subjugated the lesser tribes of the region and viewed the Narragansetts as their only rival in southern New England. The Pequots worked hard to convince the neighboring Narragansetts that only by uniting against the English could either tribe survive. But their arguments went unheard. Following the advice of Roger Williams, the Narragansetts agreed to ally themselves with Massachusetts Bay, leaving the Pequots virtually alone in their determination to resist the English.

Hostilities between the Pequots and English were triggered by the murder in Pequot country of two white ship captains and their crew of seven, who, according to the Pequots, had abducted two braves. One of the captains, John Stone, was cordially hated among the English, for he had attempted to murder Governor Prence of Plymouth and had later been banished from Massachusetts for other misdeeds. Two years later Captain John Oldham was found murdered on his pinnace. Using these incidents as justification for a punitive expedition against the unsubmissive Pequots, a joint Connecticut-Massachusetts force marched into Pequot country and demanded the murderers, who, as it turned out, were not Pequots, as well as "one thousand fathoms of wampom for damages" and some Pequot children as hostages. The Pequots correctly perceived that the issue was more general than the death of the two Englishmen. The broader question was whether or not they would submit to Puritan rule and permit incursions into the Connecticut River Valley region which they possessed. They chose to resist.

In the war that ensued, the English and their Narragansett allies found the Pequots more than a match until they were able to surround the main Pequot fort on the Mystic River in Connecticut in May 1637. The English and Narragansetts attacked before dawn, infiltrated the fort, and set fire to the Pequot wigwams inside before beating a fast retreat. In the melee inside the fort about forty Narragansetts suffered wounds at the hands of the English, who found it difficult to distinguish between Indian enemies and allies. Retreating from the fiery fort, the English regrouped and waited for fleeing survivors from the inferno. Before the day was over a large part of the Pequot tribe had been slaughtered, many by fire and others by guns. Those who escaped or who were not at the fort were hunted down. Males were executed and women and children were enslaved and sold to other tribes or shipped to the West Indies in chains. One of New England's first historians, William Hubbard, wrote that dozens of captured Pequots were put on board the ship of Captain John Gallup, "which proved [to be] Charon's ferry-boat unto them, for it was found the quickest was to feed the fishes with 'em."[17] One of the militia captains wrote that at Mystic Fort "God . . . laughed [at] his Enemies and the Enemies of his People to Scorn, making them as a fiery Oven . . . [and] filling the Place with Dead Bodies." But William Bradford wrote that "it was a fearful sight to see them thus frying in the fire and the streams of blood quenching the same, and horrible was the stink and scent thereof; but the victory seemed a sweet sacrifice, and they gave the praise thereof to God, who had wrought so wonderfully for them, thus to enclose their enemies in their hands and given them so speedy a victory over so proud and insulting an enemy."[18] Two generations later Cotton Mather, a pillar of the Puritan ministry, reiterated: "in a little more than *one* hour, five or six hundred of these barbarians were dismissed from a world that was *burdened* with them."[19]

Such savagery as the "civilized" Puritans demonstrated at Mystic Fort was shocking to the Narragansett "savages" who fought with the Puritans. According to one English officer, they came after the victory and "much rejoiced at our victories, and greatly admired the manner of Englishmen's fight, but cried Mach it, Mach it; that is, It is naught, it is naught, because it is too furious and slays too many men," a poignant comment on the different styles and functions of warfare in the two societies.[20]

For the Puritans the extermination of the Pequots was proof of their

[17]William Hubbard, *A Narrative of the Troubles with the Indians in New England* (1677), quoted in Carolyn T. Foreman, *Indians Abroad 1493–1938* (Norman: University of Oklahoma Press, 1943), p. 29.

[18]John Mason, "A Brief History of the Pequot War," Massachusetts Historical Society *Collections*, 2d Ser., 8 (Boston: 1826): 140–41. Bradford, *Plymouth Plantation*, p. 296.

[19]Cotton Mather, *Magnolia Christi Americana; or, The Ecclesiastic History of New-England* (New York: Russell & Russell, 1967), 2: 558.

[20]John Underhill, "News from America," quoted in Salisbury, "Conquest of the 'Savage'," p. 81.

political and military ascendancy. Its additional function was to provide a response to anxiety and threats that had become widely diffused throughout the colony. These fears were associated not only with the threat of the Pequots but also with the dissensions within Puritan society. It is well to remember that the war came on the heels of three years of intense internal discord centered around the challenges to the power of the magistrates by Roger Williams and Anne Hutchinson. These challenges, in turn, involved not only theological questions but economic restrictions, the distribution of political power, and competing land claims among English settlers in Massachusetts, Connecticut, and Rhode Island. Their colonies beset with controversy, the Puritan leaders talked morbidly about God's anger at seeing his chosen people subvert the City on the Hill. In this sense, the Puritan determination to destroy the Pequots and the level of violence manifested at Mystic Fort can be partially understood in terms of the self-doubt and guilt that Puritans could expiate only by exterminating so many of "Satan's agents." Dead Pequots were offered to God as atonement for Puritan failings.

Victory over the Pequots decisively established English sovereignty over all the Indians of southeastern New England except the Narragansetts and removed the one remaining obstacle to expansion into the Connecticut River Valley. Relations with the Narragansetts remained turbulent, and at one point, in 1643, when the Narragansett sachem Miantonomo sold a large tract of valuable land on Narragansett Bay to the arch heretic Samuel Gorton, who was cordially hated throughout Puritan New England for his outspoken criticism of Massachusetts policy, the English countenanced the murder of Miantonomo by his Mohegan enemies, clients to the Connecticut government.

Sporadic friction of this sort aside, the tribes of southern New England, reduced to about one half of their former population by a generation of contact with English colonists, adjusted as best they could to the realities of Puritan power. A fur trade of some importance kept the two societies in touch with each other and provided the means by which English iron goods became incorporated into the material culture of the Indians. The trade flourished in the late 1630s and early 1640s, but by mid-century the beaver supply in the eastern woodlands had been seriously depleted and the Indians were trading the pelts they could obtain to the Dutch, who unlike the Puritans, were willing to barter firearms for furs. But in spite of these trade contacts, most of the tribes that had survived the coming of the English chose to maintain their native way of life. Only a few of the weaker and more depopulated groups followed the handful of missionaries, finally spurred to action in 1643 by English critics who rightly charged that conversion had been studiously ignored for more than a decade. After ten years of effort less than a thousand Indians of the region were settled in four villages of "praying Indians" and fewer than one hundred of these declared their conversion to the Puritan form of Christianity. Even among these, defections would be numerous in the 1670s when war broke out in Massachusetts. As in the case of Virginia, the natives incorporated certain implements and articles of clothing obtained in the European trade into their culture, but overwhelmingly, even after major military defeats, they preferred to resist acculturation when it meant adopting English religion, forms of government, styles of life, or patterns of social and economic organization.

For Puritans and non-Puritans who had migrated into New England in increasing numbers after mid-century, the Indian served no useful purpose. As in the Virginia case, the rough balance of English males and females eliminated the need for Indian women as sexual partners. The church took only a minor interest in the Indian, who in any event could rarely satisfy the qualifications that Puritans placed upon their own people for church membership. The Indian trade withered to relative unimportance in the economy of the settlers as fishing, lumbering, shipbuilding, and agriculture became the mainstays of the economy. This lack of function within the organization of European culture, combined with the special tendency of Puritans to regard the Indian as unreconstructible savages, made acculturation and assimilation all but impossible.

chapter 5

Patterns of Indian-European Interaction

Because the history of colonial America has been written primarily as the record of the English in North America it is easy to overlook the fact that for most of the seventeenth century the eastern edge of the continent was the scene of bitter intra-European rivalry. The English were periodically pitted against the Dutch, Swedes, French, and Spanish. And conflict did not stop there, for the English themselves were locked in a series of disputes and insurrections which plagued colonization in the first two-thirds of the seventeenth century and led to armed conflict up and down the seaboard in the last quarter of the century. In many instances native groups were able to capitalize on this intra-European and intra-English tension in their attempts to fashion strategies of adaptation and survival. But they were also being subjected to the invasion of a bewildering variety of Europeans who, despite linguistic and cultural diversity and competitive strivings, kept growing in number and were able to bury their differences when the threat of Indian resistance scented the breeze. By looking comparatively at Anglo-Indian, Dutch-Indian, and French-Indian relations we can learn much about the New World confrontation of cultures.

The Mighty Dutch

For both the English and the Indians who inhabited the Middle Atlantic region—the area for which the Delaware and Hudson River Valleys served as focal points—it was the Dutch who posed the biggest problem from the 1620s until the 1670s. Hollanders had achieved independence from their own colonial masters, the Spanish, only in 1609, but even by then they had become the principal carriers of seaborne commerce in Western Europe and had begun interloping in the Spanish and Portuguese trade to the New World, trading illegally with settlers who were glad to violate the commercial policies of their own countries in order to get more favorable prices from the Dutch in the cloth and slave trade. Then, in a generation of spectacular achievement, the Dutch forged into the forefront of the race for wealth in the New World. In 1621 the Dutch West India Company, impressively capitalized and fully supported by the government, was launched. Its goals were commerce and conquest— to gain control of as much of the European-African-New World trade as possible and to plant colonies wherever the opportunity arose. Success came almost at once and in a few decades resulted in such a staggering acquisition of power that perhaps even American megacorporations in the mid-twentieth century could not be said to exert the influence that the Dutch West India Company did in the second quarter of the seventeenth century. In 1628 its fleet intercepted and captured the entire annual Spanish flotilla, homeward bound from the Caribbean. Enough gold was scooped up in this single exploit, about fifteen million guilders, to pay a 50 percent dividend to the Company's shareholders with enough left over to finance a military campaign against the Portuguese settlements in northeastern Brazil. For the next half century the Dutch controlled shipping to the New World and in the process reduced the Spanish and Portuguese trade to insignificance.

At the same time the Dutch began incursions on the African slave trade of their competitors. They had built bases of their own on the African coast as early as 1611 but in the 1620s and 1630s they began assaulting Portuguese forts and trading posts. By 1637, when they captured the center of Portuguese slaving activities, Elmina Castle on the Gold Coast, they had all but driven the Portuguese from the Atlantic slave trade. Bases on the African coast were linked to bases in the Caribbean which had been seized from the Spanish—Curacao, Saba, St. Martin, and St. Eustatius. This was accompanied by assaults on Portuguese Brazil, beginning in 1624 and culminating in 1630, when the Dutch overwhelmed the Portuguese and took control of their highly profitable sugar plantations on the northeast coast, the most important source of sugar for the kitchens of Europe. Other arms of the vast Dutch trading empire reached the East Indies, India, Ceylon, and Formosa.

On the North American mainland the mighty Dutch were also active. They had initiated a trade in furs with the Indians in 1609 on the first voyage of Henry Hudson, who sailed as an employee of the Dutch East India Company. Five years later they established a tiny trading post high on the Hudson River near Albany. Shortly after the chartering of the West India Company in 1621 a permanent settlement was planted on the present site of New York City. Called New Amsterdam, it became the center of Dutch colonization in North America for the next half century. Furs rather than sugar or gold were the source of profit for the colony of New Netherland and as early as 1628 the small Dutch settlement was sending home almost 8,000 furs a year. The Dutch radiated out in small numbers from this center in the Hudson River Valley for the next four decades. They planned settlements to the north in the Connecticut River Valley, to the south in the Delaware River Valley, across the Hudson River in what was to become New Jersey, and to the east on Long Island. Their numbers were not large and in time they would be overwhelmed by the more numerous English. But their power at sea was never to be underestimated, as the Virginians found out as late as 1667, when Dutch raiders captured twenty tobacco ships in the James River, and in 1673 when they repeated this success. Thus, while the Dutch never settled more than 10,000 people in their Middle Atlantic colonies, they were able to exert a strong influence on English affairs. In time the English became far more populous, and when three Anglo-Dutch wars were fought in Europe between 1650 and 1675, the colony at New Netherland became a target of English attack. It was captured by the English in 1664, recaptured by the Dutch in 1673, and then was almost immediately retaken by the English. This marked the end of Dutch political authority in North America.

The French

The French, like the Dutch, were a force in the New World before the English. And like the Dutch, their activities in the late sixteenth and early seventeenth centuries were confined to harrying Spanish and Portuguese shipping, trading surreptitiously with Iberian settlers in the Caribbean and South America, and planting tiny fishing and trading settlements on the North American mainland. The French had begun early, in the 1530s, when Jacques Cartier made several voyages of discovery to

Newfoundland and the Gulf of St. Lawrence. Cartier's explorations made the St. Lawrence waterway knowable to Europeans, although at the time it was not evident to them that this was one of the two accesses by water into the heartland of the continent. Some unsuccessful attempts at planting tiny settlements followed in the 1540s but the French soon discovered that the real wealth of the northern regions lay not in gold or diamonds but in fish and furs, particularly the latter. By the end of the sixteenth century about five hundred European fishing ships came annually to Canadian waters and the French were predominant among them. When tiny French settlements at the mouth of the Rio de Janeiro and on the southeastern coast of North America were wiped out by the Portuguese and Spanish respectively in 1560 and 1565, the French decided to concentrate to the north where their commercial activities would be free from Spanish and Portuguese molestation.

As valuable as fishing was, the fur trade turned out to be vastly more profitable. Nothing more was required than to bring trade goods desired by Indians across the Atlantic, anchor a few ships in a sheltered bay of the St. Lawrence, and wait for Indian traders to arrive with pelts. Military conquest was unnecessary and in fact would only adversely affect the trade nexus with the Indians. Even large settlements were not required, for the fur trade involved a simple barter relationship between the French and the Indians.

In time the French decided to plant permanent settlements in North America because they realized that without a colonial population base French trading posts would be subject to the predatory raids of the Dutch, English, or any other colonizing nation. Thus a colony was settled in 1604 at Port Royal, Nova Scotia, and by 1608 a second settlement was planted at Quebec. This evidence of an intention not only to trade and fish but to solidify claims to the northern part of the continent was enough to induce the English, a thousand miles to the south, to mount a campaign of extermination against the French. Although England and France were not at war, the governor of Virginia, Sir Thomas Dale, commissioned a seasoned explorer and Atlantic seadog, Samuel Argall, to attack the French settlements in 1613. Just a few months after he had abducted Pocahontas in Virginia, Argall wiped out the French settlement at Port Royal. For the next few decades the French struggled to plant tiny settlements and maintain them in the face of growing English opposition centered in New England. But France was preoccupied with the Thirty Years War in Europe and could spare neither men nor money for overseas development. By 1643, after almost half a century of colonization, there were still fewer than four hundred Frenchmen in New France. Most of them were Indian traders or Jesuit priests, who had come in considerable numbers to convert the Indians. As one royal governor of Canada later remarked, only two kinds of business existed in New France—the conversion of souls and the conversion of beaver.

It was under the leadership of Samuel Champlain, backed by the Company of New France, another joint-stock operation, that New France was established on a more permanent footing. By offering land for the taking the company lured settlers from France to establish an agricultural society, permanently settled and dedicated to replicating French institutions in the wilderness. By 1660, though still less than two thousand Frenchmen lived in the colony as compared with ten times that number in New England, scattered towns were appearing along the St. Lawrence River.

Dutch-Indian Relations

How did the Dutch and French inhabitants of these small but strategically located settlements relate to the Indian societies they encountered? Were differences in national character or ideology important in Dutch-Indian and French-Indian interaction? Or was the Anglo-Indian experience in Virginia and New England duplicated? By adopting a comparative approach to European-Indian relations we can better understand the uniqueness or typicality of the English experience and test certain classic generalizations such as that of the famous historian Francis Parkman, who wrote a century ago that in North America "Spanish civilization crushed the Indians; English civilization scorned and neglected him; French civilization embraced and cherished him."[1]

For the Dutch, so long as the fur trade was thriving and represented the primary source of profit in New Netherland, relations with the Mahicans of the Albany area and the local tribes in the vicinity of New Amsterdam remained amicable. The Dutch did all in their power to preserve the Indians' goodwill, for it was obvious that since they were vastly outnumbered and dependent upon trade for profit they needed the Indians far more than the Indians needed them. Unlike the Virginians on the Chesapeake or the Puritans in New England, their principal goal was not farming and large-scale settlement but simply the profitable bartering of European trade goods for the skins of the beaver, otter, and deer. From the Indian point of view there was little to be feared from the European presence, for the Dutch came in small numbers, had no apparent design on Indian land, and were eager to trade commodities that Indians wanted and could obtain by trapping animals which existed abundantly in their territory.

[1]Quoted in Mason Wade, "The French and the Indians," in *Attitudes of Colonial Powers toward the American Indian*, ed. Howard Peckham and Charles Gibson (Salt Lake City: University of Utah Press, 1969), p. 61.

Struggles to Control Fur Resources

As desirable as exchanging furs and skins for European trade goods seemed to the Indian tribes, it contained a hidden danger of utmost significance. Prior to the arrival of Europeans, Indians had hunted for subsistence; because their needs were not great this perpetuated the conservation of game. But once the skins of fur-bearing animals had been incorporated into the international Atlantic market, the Indian began hunting relentlessly in what became a process of game extermination. Under such conditions the beaver supply was exhausted with frightening speed in particular areas. When this occurred, as it did to the Mahican suppliers of the Dutch during the first quarter of the seventeenth century, the fur merchants of the Dutch West India Company began to cultivate their enemies, the Mohawks, who were the easternmost of the Iroquois tribes whose territories stretched westward to the Great Lakes. The Iroquois became the major suppliers of pelts to the Dutch and this role transformed them into a formidable power in the Northeast.

To the north of the Dutch settlements the French were also engaged in fur trading with the powerful Huron tribes, which commanded the territories north of the Great Lakes. In time, the advantages to be reaped from an even larger fur trade with the Dutch and the depletion of furs in the tribal territories under their control enticed the Iroquois into attacking the Hurons. If successful, the Iroquois could divert the vast fur resources of the Canadian north from Montreal, the center of French trading activities, to Albany, the main Dutch trading post. In effect, this was an effort to make Amsterdam rather than Paris the major recipient of North American beaver skins. By 1633 the Iroquois were bringing as many as 30,000 pelts a year to the Dutch trading posts. But the need to obtain control of more distant hunting grounds or to assume the role of middlemen, receiving pelts from more westerly hunters and transporting them eastward to the Dutch at Albany, became intense. Thus in a period of a few decades in the early seventeenth century an ancient smoldering Iroquois-Huron hostility was greatly intensified and transformed into an open competition for control of western furs. The Iroquois-Huron enmity was further transformed by the introduction of European firearms. Supplied to the Iroquois by the Dutch, they were used in the 1640s in what amounted to a war of extermination against the Hurons. As one Canadian historian has written: "Before the coming of the Europeans, the Indians' wars had been limited; their motivation and their primitive weapons had precluded too heavy casualties. Afterward their wars became wars of extermination—total war fought for economic ends, and increasingly for ends sought by Europeans."[2] Fighting for individual prestige or blood revenge was replaced by fighting for control of trade.

What is all the more remarkable about the transforming nature of the European presence on the largest and most powerful Indian cultures of the Northeast was that so few Europeans were involved. In the second quarter of the century the great Huron nation, comprising 30,000 people or more, was nearly destroyed by European disease and the attacks of Iroquois enemies inspired by the desire for European trade goods. At the same time the victorious Iroquois used the European trade connection vastly to increase their power. All this was triggered by tiny Dutch and French settlements and trading posts scattered along the waterways of the St. Lawrence and Hudson River Valleys whose total population, even after almost a half-century of settlement, totalled no more than three thousand.

What could happen to smaller Indian tribes, which had neither the strength nor the geographical advantage to play a role in the all-important fur trade, was amply illustrated by the fate of the dozen or so Indian bands that lived in the vicinity of New Amsterdam in the 1640s. A few years before, the Dutch West India Company had begun recruiting more settlers in order to build up the agricultural base of the society. Between 1638 and 1643 the population doubled from about one to two thousand. This required land purchases from local Indian tribes such as the Rockaways, Canarsees, Massapequas, and Merrics. Having sold their land, however, the Indians saw no reason to leave it until Dutch farmers took it up. Thus agriculturalists from both societies were living side by side in areas such as Long Island, Rockaway, and Staten Island. When Dutch cattle trampled Indian fields or the half-wild dogs of the Indians attacked Dutch cattle, tempers flared. The resident governor of the Dutch West India Company, Willem Kieft, added to the tension by attempting to repair the sagging finances of the colony through taxing all local Indians. This attempt to extract tribute from the Indians was resisted and the local tribes were not reluctant to venture the opinion that Kieft "must be a very mean fellow to come to live in this country without being invited . . . and now wish to compel them to give him their corn for nothing."[3]

Violence between the Dutch and the Indians

Dutch expansionism and sharp trading with Indian bands in the region inevitably brought sporadic violence. When this involved loss of life

[2]William J. Eccles, *The Canadian Frontier, 1534–1760* (New York: Holt, Rinehart and Winston, Inc., 1969), p. 59.

[3]Quoted in Allen W. Trelease, *Indian Affairs in Colonial New York: The Seventeenth Century* (Ithaca, New York: Cornell University Press, 1960), p. 66.

among the Dutch, the usual response was to demand the surrender of the responsible Indians to Dutch justice. In effect the Dutch, like the English in New England, were demanding a recognition of their sovereignty. In 1642 a band of Hackensacks, across Newark Bay from New Amsterdam, murdered two Dutch farmers whose cattle had been trampling Indian corn and who allegedly had swindled the Indians in trade. The Hackensack sachems offered to pay the victim's widow a wampum atonement to "wipe away her tears"—the normal procedure in Indian tradition. But they refused to yield up the murderers, which would have been admission that they regarded themselves as living under Dutch law. Instead they asked Governor Kieft to halt the dangerous trade in alcohol and to prevent incursions on Indian land.

For the Dutch, as for the Puritans, the question became one of authority. And just as the Puritans sought a military solution to this kind of political problem, the Dutch responded at the first opportunity to establish by force what they could not secure through exhortation or negotiation. In 1643, a band of Wecquaesgeeks in Westchester, who two years before had murdered a Dutchman, were attacked by a party of warriors, possibly Mahicans, from the Albany region. Seventeen Wecquaesgeeks were killed and others taken prisoner. In terror, the remainder of the band fled to the Dutch settlements at New Amsterdam and begged for protection. The Dutch received them and allowed them to resettle in two locations near the town. But Kieft and other leaders in the colony could not resist the temptation to exterminate the encamped Wecquaesgeeks as a means of making unmistakably clear to all tribes within New Amsterdam's orbit that they must accept Dutch trading terms, pay tribute when required, and place themselves under Dutch authority.

On the night of February 25, 1643, eighty Dutch soldiers, under orders to take women and children prisoner but to kill only the men, attacked the Wecquaesgeek encampment. One of the Dutch leaders reported that:

> Young children, some of them snatched from their mothers, were cut in pieces before the eyes of their parents, and the pieces were thrown into the fire or into the water; other babes were bound on planks and then cut through, stabbed and miserably masacred, so that it would break a heart of stone; some were thrown into the river and when the fathers and mothers sought to save them, the soldiers would not suffer them to come ashore but caused both old and young to be drowned . . . A few escaped to our settlers, some with the loss of a hand, others of a leg, others again holding in their bowels with their hands, and all so cut, hacked and maimed, that worse could not be imagined; they were indeed in such a state that our people supposed they had been surprised by their enemies, the tribe of Maquaes [Mohawks].[4]

Another attack at the second Wecquaesgeek encampment produced

[4]Quoted in *ibid.*, pp. 72–73.

similar results. But the attempt to exterminate the tribe and thus de-moralize all Indian bands in the region backfired. Throughout the area of Dutch settlement Indians began a campaign of revenge. When Roger Williams arrived in New Amsterdam to embark for Europe on a Dutch ship, he witnessed "their Bowries . . . in Flames, Dutch & Eng[lish] were slaine, mine Eyes saw . . . flames at their Townes . . . & ye Flights & Hur-ries of Men, Women & Children, the present Remoovall of all that Could for Holland."[5] For the next two years at least a dozen Indian bands at-tacked isolated farms and settlements on the periphery of New Amster-dam, taking the lives of several hundred Dutch and English, including Anne Hutchinson and her family, who had migrated to Long Island by way of Rhode Island after having been expelled from Massachusetts seven years before.

Though the Indians sorely harassed the Dutch settlements and crum-bled both the morale and the finances of the colony, they were ultimately the losers. It is estimated that more than a thousand Indians lost their lives before hostilities ceased in 1645. By far the most serious losses oc-curred near what is now Pound Ridge in Westchester County. A company of men, led by Captain John Underhill, the hero of the Mystic Fort mas-sacre of the Pequots six years before, surprised an Indian settlement in the dead of the night and shot and burned to death more than five hun-dred Tankitekes, Wiwanoys, and Wappingers.

Thus Dutch-Indian relations in the New Amsterdam region were not significantly different from English contacts with native cultures in New England and on the Chesapeake. After the first few years, little was to be gained from trade since the beaver in the area had been exhausted and the Dutch depended upon their Albany traders to tap the rich fur resources of the interior. Nor could the local Indians serve any useful purpose as potential converts to the Dutch form of Christianity, for the Dutch West India Company had little interest in sending over mission-aries to convert the local Indians, who were looked upon as ignorant, brutish people separated from the Dutch by an unbridgeable gulf. Neither did the Dutch require Indian wives, for they were plentifully supplied with European women almost from the outset.

In this situation, with land settlement replacing trading as the dom-inant economic activity, the local tribes became only obstacles to Dutch expansion and Dutch authority. That they were internally divided, sepa-rated into bands of Wappingers, Hackensacks, Wecquaesgeeks, Tappans, Nyacks, Canarsees, and others, made it all the easier for the Dutch to fix upon a military solution to the "Indian problem." Unlike the invaluable Mohawks of the upper Hudson region, upon whom the Dutch depended for the all-important fur trade, the Indian bands and tribes of the lower

[5]*Ibid.*, p. 74.

Hudson served no function in the Dutch hierarchy of needs. Only so long as they possessed greater strength than the Dutch were friendly relations with them preferable to unfriendly relations. Kieft's War of 1643–1646 did not defeat them entirely. A number of bands concerted themselves in 1655 and attacked New Amsterdam, killing at least fifty Dutch, taking a hundred or more prisoners, and setting fire to houses and stored food. These hostilities continued throughout the 1650s and into the next decade. But their strength was ebbing after decades of attritional warfare, and while the Dutch were resupplied in men and arms from Europe, the Indians had only their own dwindling resources to call upon. When the English overpowered the Dutch in New Netherland in 1664, they encountered only demoralized remnants of an earlier Indian population.

By contrast Dutch-Indian relations at Albany were peaceful and profitable. Probably not more than one hundred Dutch resided there in the 1640s but they neither attacked nor were attacked by the powerful Mohawks, for both peoples admirably served each other's needs. Even though they were greatly outnumbered, the Albany settlers did not hesitate to sell arms and ammunition to their Indian trade partners. By contrast, in New Amsterdam, where the colonists were far more numerous than the Indians and the Indians far more divided, strict regulations against the sale of firearms were enforced. This policy is not difficult to understand when the competition for land in the New Amsterdam region is compared with the cooperative activities of Dutch and Mohawks in the Albany region. Firearms were provided to the Mohawks in the knowledge that they would be used by the Indians to gain control over Huron tribesmen aligned with the French. In this sense, every gun in Indian hands contributed to the profitable flow of beaver skins to Amsterdam by way of the Hudson River rather than to Paris by way of the St. Lawrence River. Such a profitable trade did not necessarily bring mutual respect and admiration between Dutch and Mohawks. Thefts, attacks on animals, and trampled fields were also common in the mixing of the two cultures. But as the most careful historian of Indian relations in seventeenth-century New Netherland has written, "Peace was maintained because both sides had everything to lose and nothing to gain by hostilities. . . . The two races regarded each other less often as corn thieves, trespassers, or Indian givers than as sources of economic prosperity; what they thought of each other personally was beside the point."[6]

New Netherland Becomes New York

When England, after a generation of civil conflict culminating in the restoration of Charles II in 1660, decided to make a second great effort in

[6]*Ibid.*, p. 115.

the colonization of the West Indies and the North American mainland, the Dutch colony of New Netherland was one of the first objectives. Anglo-Dutch commercial rivalry had been intensifying since mid-century and the Dutch colony, situated between the English colonies on the Chesapeake and those in New England, was an inviting target. To take it would remove the Hollanders entirely from the eastern seaboard and consolidate the English empire in North America. To this end a military expedition led by Richard Nicholls seized New Netherland in 1664 almost without resistance from the Dutch, who had only a tiny garrison to stand in the way. New Netherland became New York and its Dutch inhabitants were obliged to incorporate themselves into the English colonial system. Though several generations would pass before the English made up even half the population of New York, political authority, trade, and military affairs would now be securely contained within the British imperial system.

For the Indian tribes of New York, the change of political authority had little significance. Insofar as their relations with Europeans were concerned, Dutch and English were hardly distinguishable. Nothing in the arrival of the English could change the fact that disease and war had already decimated the Algonkian tribes on the lower Hudson. Nor were the English inclined to alter the pattern of relationships since they had now taken over a European administration upon which the local Indians had become pathetically dependent. The English undoubtedly counted it as their good fortune that they were colonizing in an area where the work of subjugating the indigenous population had already been accomplished. Nor were they more inclined than the Dutch to proselytize among the local tribes when more important commercial matters laid claim to their energies.

The last third of the seventeenth century in New York witnessed the further decline of the small tribes in the area of Manhattan, Long Island, and the lower Hudson River Valley. The Indian population dwindled as the natives struggled for existence through a mixture of hunting, fishing, farming, and day labor in white settlements. Their relationship to the Europeans became almost entirely servile. A Long Islander summed it up in 1670: "There is now but few upon the Island, and those few no ways hurtful but rather serviceable to the English, and it is to be admired, how strangely they have decreast by the Hand of God, since the English first setling of those parts."[7]

Hostile Indians had become friendly Indians, but the friendliness was only the outward expression of internal social and political disorganization and the cultural dependency that accompanied it. In this state of

[7]Daniel Denton, *A Brief Description of New York* (1670), quoted in *ibid.*, p. 179.

demoralization alcohol became ever more important to the local tribes. It too contributed to their demise while serving as a painkiller for the eroded quality of life. The New Yorkers knew that the bargaining power of the Indian waned after sufficient rum had been proferred him. Although selling alcohol to Indians was prohibited, "yet every one does it," remarked one observer in 1679.[8] Two years later a Minisink sachem bitterly remonstrated that alcohol had caused the death of sixty of his people in three years. That the provincial council was obliged to affirm in 1679 and several times again in the 1680s that Indians in the colony "are free & not slaves," and should not be made lifetime servants against their will was poignant proof that the dwindling Indian population was losing not only its cultural autonomy but its physical freedom as well.

At Albany the advent of the English brought no significant change in Indian relations. The Iroquois continued to deal with merchants who were primarily Dutch, to negotiate with interpreters who were Dutch, and to receive European trade goods, in return for their furs. The furs, of course, after passing through New York, were destined for English rather than Dutch markets and the goods they received originated in a different part of the European world; but this was of little consequence to Iroquois trappers. Far more important than the substitution of English for Dutch political administration was the fact that the fur trade itself had been in a state of long-term decline since about 1660 and nothing in the English conquest of the colony could reverse this trend. The decline was caused by the exhaustion of beaver in the eastern areas of the Great Lakes and the difficulties of outwitting the French for control of the western beaver sources.

French-Indian Relations

While the Dutch and English struggled to control the western fur trade, the French in the north had been forging relations with Indian societies of the St. Lawrence and upper Great Lakes regions. For the French the Indians were absolutely vital, and this dependency upon the indigenous people, along with a pronounced difference in the attitude of the Catholic church, led to Indian relationships in the seventeenth century that set most French colonies apart from other Europeans in North America. The differences began with numbers. The French were so few in number that they could not have entertained the slightest hope of survival without the friendship of the native peoples surrounding them. In 1640, after

---

[8]*Journal of Jaspar Danckaerts, 1679–1680*, ed. Bartlett B. James and J. Franklin Jameson (New York: Charles Scribner's Sons, 1913), p. 79.

Finely-crafted combs and decorative objects such as these, recovered from Hopewell moundbuilder sites, were fashioned centuries before European arrival. (Courtesy The Ohio Historical Society.)

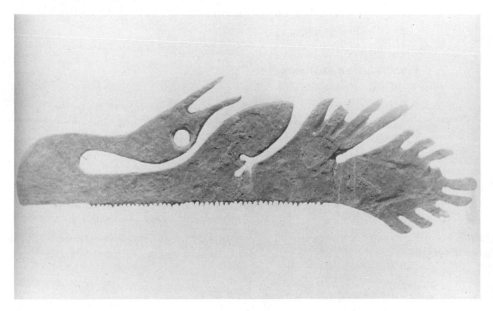

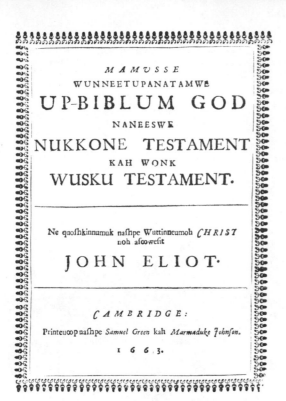

MAMUSSE
WUNNEETUPANATAMWE
UP-BIBLUM GOD
NANEESWE
NUKKONE TESTAMENT
KAH WONK
WUSKU TESTAMENT.

Ne quoſhkinnumuk naſhpe Wuttinneumoh *CHRIST*
noh aſooweſit

JOHN ELIOT·

CAMBRIDGE:
Printeuoopnaſhpe *Samuel Green* kah *Marmaduke Johnſon.*
1 6 6 3.

The Algonquian translation of the Bible, a part of John Eliot's attempts to
Christianize the Indians of Southern New England, was not only a religious
instrument but also a part of establishing Puritan political control. (Reproduced by permission of The Huntington Library, San Marino, California.)

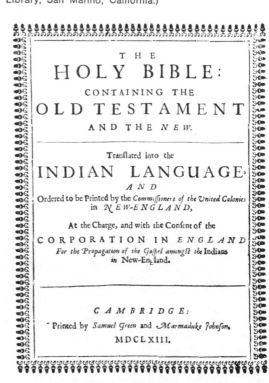

THE
HOLY BIBLE:
CONTAINING THE
OLD TESTAMENT
AND THE *NEW*.

Tranſlated into the
INDIAN LANGUAGE,
AND
Ordered to be Printed by the *Commiſſioners of the United Colonies*
in *NEW-ENGLAND*,

At the Charge, and with the Conſent of the
CORPORATION IN *ENGLAND*
For the *Propagation of the Goſpel amongſt the* Indians
in New-England.

CAMBRIDGE:
Printed by *Samuel Green* and *Marmaduke Johnſon.*
MDCLXIII.

Lapowinsa, a Delaware chief, sat for his portrait in 1735. Two years later he gave up a vast tract of land to William Penn's sons in the disreputable "Walking Purchase." (Courtesy The Historical Society of Pennsylvania.)

Tomochichi, who was born before the first Englishman set foot in the Carolinas, sat for his portrait with his nephew in 1734. (Courtesy Smithsonian Institution, National Anthropological Archives, Bureau of American Ethnology Collection.)

These Cherokee chiefs, accompanied by a British officer, visited London after the Cherokee War of 1760–1761. Colonial Williamsburg Foundation, Department of Collections.

Indian cannibalism existed primarily in the minds of Europeans, but depictions such as this, by Theodor DeBry, played a role in the characterization of Indians as "savages." (The New York Public Library.)

This Mohawk chief journeyed to England in 1710 to treat with the English government. His grandson, Joseph Brant, made the same trip 65 years later and joined the British in the American Revolution. (Courtesy Library of Congress.)

four decades of colonizing activity, the entire French population in North America was about 240, not the equal of any one of a number of New England towns. Even a generation later, in 1663, the French population had increased only to 2,500, less than the town of Boston or of several Huron towns in the upper Great Lakes region.

That a high proportion of these Frenchmen were male added to the dependency on the Indian neighbors. In contrast to the English and Dutch settlements, where the sex ratio among Europeans was far more balanced, Frenchmen took Indian mistresses, concubines, and wives with equanimity. They exhibited no embarrassment at this mixing of blood and were hard put to understand English qualms about interracial relations. In Nova Scotia, where French women were uncommonly scarce, intermarriage was so common that one authority believes that by 1676 virtually all the French families had Indian blood in their veins. In the more settled areas of the St. Lawrence River Valley, where the Algonkian tribes were less sedentary and Jesuit priests raised some objections to racial mixing, interracial fornication rather than interracial marriage was more customary. The Jesuits frowned on church marriages between the two cultures but they could do nothing about the sexual urges of their parishioners. "In the Night time," wrote Baron de Lahontan, "all of them, barring the Jesuits, roll from House to House to debauch the Women Savages." Farther west at the trading posts, "miscegenation between the *coureurs de bois* and the Indian women was the rule rather than the exception."[9]

The practice of racial intermixture became official government policy by the 1660s when Colbert, Louis XIV's architect of imperial reorganization, called for a full-fledged integration of the races. Colbert ordered the French settlers "to civilize the Algonquins . . . and the other savages who have embraced Christianity, and dispose them to come and settle them in community with the French, live with them, and bring up their children in their manners and customs." In spite of the opposition of the Catholic church, Colbert also encouraged intermarriage and urged the governor of New France to bring about a mingling of the cultures "in order that, having but one law and one master, they may form only one people and one blood."[10] It was a policy contrived to bring the Indians under stricter French control, but at the same time designed not to destroy or weaken, but to assimilate, the indigenous population. A half century later, two lettered Virginians, William Byrd and Robert Bever-

[9]Alfred G. Bailey, *The Conflict of European and Eastern Algonkian Cultures, 1504–1700; A Study in Canadian Civilization* (Sackville, N.B.: The Tribune Press, 1937), p. 112.

[10]Quoted in *ibid.*, p. 107.

ley, pondered this "Modern Policy" adopted by France in Canada (and in Louisiana) and lamented that English "false delicacy" in the early years on the Chesapeake had kept them from making a "prudent Alliance" through intermarriage such as the French had done.[11]

It has been pointed out by one Canadian scholar that when miscegenation occurred, it was almost always between French men and Indian women and that the offspring of these liaisons followed the mother. This meant that Indian blood was rarely added to the French gene pool. Though this is true, it is equally important to note the social effects of widespread miscegenation. Frequent intermixing brought contacts of the most intimate nature between the two peoples, and this intimacy could not help but bring about greater mutual understanding. That New France was both undermanned and "underwomaned" provided two important reasons for forging amicable and intimate relations with the native peoples of the St. Lawrence region.

Of equal importance in the establishment of nonviolent relations was the fact that virtually every man in New France during the first half century was there either to trade furs or to evangelize among the Indians. Both tasks required Indian cooperation and only rarely could either be accomplished through coercion. Thus French traders traveled hundreds of miles into the remote Great Lakes regions of the Hurons, establishing trading posts, learning the language and customs of the tribes, and engaging in a process of mutual acculturation. In the English and Dutch settlements the Indian trader was the exception rather than the rule, since the vast majority of the settlers, especially after the first few years, were agriculturalists engaging in an activity to which the Indian had nothing to offer once his techniques of cultivating crops indigenous to the region were made known to the Europeans.

Those who were not traders in New France were generally Jesuit priests. They established missions, martyred themselves in hostile Indian country, and worked for the greater glory of their God through conversion of Indians to Catholicism. Fur trading and missionary work often went hand in hand, with missions established at important river junctions where the fur trade took place. Though some Jesuits trekked northward to the farthest shores of the Gulf of St. Lawrence and westward as far as Georgian Bay, their main efforts were concentrated among the 30,000 Hurons who were settled in the Great Lakes region in towns of several thousand. The Jesuits were far more willing than the Puritans to believe

[11]William K. Boyd, ed., *William Byrd's Histories of the Dividing Line betwixt Virginia and North Carolina* (Raleigh: North Carolina Historical Commission, 1929), pp. 3–4; Robert Beverley, *The History and Present State of Virginia . . .*, ed. Louis B. Wright (Chapel Hill: University of North Carolina Press, 1947), pp. 38–39.

that Indian beliefs in a supreme being, in the immortality of the soul, and in supernatural forces could be revised sufficiently to find acceptance from their Christian God. Whereas the Puritans insisted that Indians of the New England area erase their values, renounce their way of life, and abandon their religious beliefs as a starting point in accepting Christianity, the Jesuits studied the Indian structure of belief and attempted to build on it rather than wholly to replace it. The statement of Father Ragueneau in 1647, while it would have struck the Puritan clergy as the work of the Devil, is revealing of the positive Algonkian response to Catholicism:

> One must be very careful before condemning a thousand things among their customs, which greatly offend minds brought up and nourished in another world. It is easy to call irreligion what is merely stupidity, and to take for diabolical working something that is nothing more than human; and then, one thinks he is obliged to forbid as impious certain things that are done in all innocence, or, at most, are silly but not criminal customs . . . I have no hesitation in saying that we have been too severe in this point.[12]

This greater flexibility and willingness to accept native culture on its own terms, even while demeaning it, led to a far greater degree of interaction between the cultures in New France than in New England. Where Puritans settled, the meager missionary activity that was undertaken was focused on the weakest tribes—those that had lost or were losing their political autonomy and their cultural self-sufficiency. Weakened by disease and warfare and demoralized by the steady growth of European society, they abandoned major parts of their culture and attempted to refashion themselves in the white man's image. Living in "praying villages," they imitated English clothing styles, work habits, and forms of worship. In contrast, the greatest successes of the Jesuits in New France were among the most powerful Indian societies. The Jesuits built on the existing Indian culture, asking not that the natives strip away their cultural heritage but that they add to it.

The special nature of the French relations with the Algonkians is also revealed in the French attitude toward Indian sovereignty. In all European-Indian contacts the concept of sovereignty, as it was used to connote political authority, can be regarded as a kind of litmus test of the balance of power between the two cultures. In relations with Indians, whom all European peoples regarded as an inferior people, sovereignty was the ultimate goal to be obtained, for it meant recognition by native peoples that they were no longer strong enough to maintain their political autonomy. Whenever sovereignty was surrendered, subjugation was not far

[12]Quoted in Eccles, *Canadian Frontier*, p. 48.

behind if it had not already preceded it. Thus when the New Englanders fought the Pequots in 1637 the goal was to exterminate or bring under English jurisdiction the one powerful tribe that refused to accept Puritan sway in this region. Similarly, as soon as the Chesapeake colonists were sufficiently strong, they forced the Indians to recognize their sovereignty, a process that began with the policies of John Smith to exact tribute from the tribes of the Powhatan Confederacy. But in New France, the governing council was debating as late as 1664 whether an Algonkian Indian who had raped the wife of a French settler should be prosecuted in the French court of justice. As one of Canada's foremost historians has said,

> The whole question of French relations with the Indians was here shown in clear relief; for if the Indians who committed what were crimes under French law could be held accountable to the officers of that law, it could be said that the French were truly sovereign. If they could not, if the Indians considered themselves as subject only to their own rudimentary laws for crimes committed against French subjects, then clearly they were free, independent, and sovereign in their own right within the confines of the French colony; and this could only mean that New France, in effect, had divided sovereignty, French and Indian.[13]

Of course declaring sovereignty and implementing it were two different matters and all European colonizers, having judged their strength sufficient to pronounce their sovereignty, were still faced with the job of imposing it. In New France in 1664 the decision was made to consult with the chiefs of nearby tribes on the matter. When a conference was arranged, the Indian spokesman pointed out that friendly relations had been maintained for decades in spite of individual acts of crime and violence on both sides; and that each side must do its best to control its members. The French in this case agreed with the Indians that the offender should not be prosecuted. A half century later, in 1714, when Indians declared that the French had no right to jail or punish them for drunkenness, since they were not subject to the laws of the colony, and believed that the liquor, not the drinker of it, was responsible for breaches of conduct, the official reply was acquiescence along with the admission from the French that "the matter is extremely delicate." The French, assenting to the Indians' assertion that they were individually autonomous and collectively sovereign, passed laws prohibiting the sale of alcohol to the Indians. When crimes were committed by Indians under the influence of alcohol, the French courts attempted to discover the illegal supplier, prosecute him for violating French law, and charge him with damages committed by the drunken Indian.

The French policy did not necessarily reflect greater humanitarianism,

[13]*Ibid.*, p. 77.

understanding of the Indian, or acceptance of his culture. First and foremost it was a policy born of weakness. As Eccles has written: "The French
were unable to impose their law on the Indians, and for one good reason;
to have attempted to do so with any degree of vigor would have alienated
the Indians, and this the French could not afford to do."[14] But out of
this policy founded on weakness, ironically, came the most lastingly amicable relations between Europeans and native Americans on the continent. By regulating their own subjects in the sale of alcohol and by continuing to recognize the sovereignty of the Algonkians, the French were
able to coexist peacefully with native societies to a degree unprecedented
elsewhere in North America. That their settlements were so small and
competed so little for cleared land doubtless helped in this regard.

In spite of the relatively pacific character of French-Algonkian relations, the Indians were not altogether spared the ravages that beset other
native cultures after European arrival. Epidemic diseases were not a
matter of policy or national character and they struck the Hurons as
mortally in 1649 as they had the eastern Massachusetts Indians three
decades earlier. Nor could the French, however good their intentions,
have averted the attacks on their Huron allies by the Iroquois after the
European rivalry for the fur trade began. Once the beaver supply in the
traditional Iroquois hunting grounds was exhausted, the Five Nations
were obliged to assume the role of middlemen between the Huron and
Ottawa tribes north of Lake Erie and Ontario and the Albany traders.
When this could not be accomplished through diplomacy, as in the late
1640s, war was employed. Within a few years they had virtually destroyed
the Hurons, Petuns, and Eries living around Lake Erie. Thereafter war
raged intermittently, as the Iroquois exploited the remaining beaver in
their newly conquered territories and perfected the art of hijacking fleets
of fur-laden canoes from the Ottawa country to the north as they headed
for French markets at Montreal.

FRENCH-NATCHEZ RELATIONS

That the French national character counted for much less than economic and demographic factors involved in the relationship with Indian
societies was amply demonstrated by the French experience with the
Natchez of the lower Mississippi region in the early eighteenth century.
The Natchez were a highly structured and ritualistic people, the southernmost descendants of the ancient Moundbuilders. In their social stratification, theocratic authority, hereditary class system, and celebration of
war they more closely approximated European culture than any other
group in eastern North America. After De Soto had passed through their
country in 1542, they experienced virtually no contact with Europeans

[14]*Ibid.*, pp. 78–79.

until the arrival of Robert La Salle, the French explorer who laid claim to the lower Mississippi Valley for France in 1682. For another three decades, until the French established a small trading post on the Mississippi in 1713, they had only casual contact with French missionaries and French and English traders.

When the French began building a permanent settlement in Natchez country in the second decade of the eighteenth century as part of their plans to control the interior of the continent and encircle the English, they brought soldiers, women, and black slaves with them. Trade with the Natchez was only incidental to the French purposes. When minor skirmishing flared in 1715 and the Indians murdered four Frenchmen in retaliation for the ill treatment they had received, the French turned their superior weaponry on them without reservations. When a second war broke out in 1722, Bienville, the French governor, burned three Natchez villages to the ground and demanded that the Natchez emperor, Tattooed Serpent, send him the head of one of the minor chiefs in violation of tribal custom which made all chiefs immune from the death penalty.

This kind of draconic policy led only to further hostilities. In 1729, when the French demanded land cessions without compensation, including the site of an important Natchez village, the Natchez responded by mounting an offensive designed to eliminate their oppressors. Nothing could have been clearer by this time than that the French had found the Natchez useless for their purposes in the lower Mississippi and felt no qualms about attempting to eliminate them. Though the Natchez were successful in overpowering the French at Fort Rosalie in 1729, killing several hundred Frenchmen and taking prisoner at least as many women, children, and black and Indian slaves, the French were only temporarily beaten back. Reinforcements arrived in 1730 and with the aid of Choctaw allies they stormed the Natchez strongholds with cannon. More than 1,000 Natchez were killed, many captives were burned at the stake, and some 400 were sold into slavery in Santo Domingo. The surviving Natchez, scattering in small bands, sought refuge with other southeastern tribes. By the end of the year the Natchez nation, once nearly 5,000 strong, had ceased to exist as a sovereign people. Finding no way of utilizing the Indians to their own advantage, the French had worked toward the elimination of these ancient sun-worshipping people with a thoroughness that might have aroused the envy of the English in New England, the Dutch in New Amsterdam, or the Spanish in Mexico.

Colonization Efforts in South Carolina

While Iroquois, English, Hurons, and French struggled for control of the northern fur trade, other Englishmen were mounting a colonizing effort a thousand miles to the south—in what was to be called South Carolina. Later this vast fertile region was to become the center of the plantation slave system in North America, but in the 1660s, when English settlement began, it was no more than another wilderness frontier in English eyes. But it was also a frontier in which another European people, the Spanish, had been interacting with native societies for more than a century and a half. Spanish explorers and adventurers, among whom Ponce de Leon's name is the most familiar, had been charting the south Atlantic and Gulf Coasts since the late fifteenth century and making occasional contacts with the natives of the region. By 1520 the tribes of the coastal plain must have been fully aware of the dangers inherent in contact with Europeans, for in that year Lucas Vasquez de Ayllon, a Spanish imperial officer and member of the Royal Council of Hispaniola, lured some fifty Indians aboard his ships and whisked them away into slavery in the West Indies. "By such means," wrote a contemporary writer, Peter Martyr, "they sowed hatred and warfare throughout that peaceful and friendly region, separating children from their parents and wives from their husbands."[15]

For the next half-century Spaniards planted small settlements on the southeastern coast of the continent, engaging in minor trade with the Indians of the area, establishing missions manned by Franciscan fathers, and evicting the French in 1565 after they dared to plant a settlement in the vicinity of the later Port Royal. Several attempts were made to bring the entire Gulf region under Spanish control. From 1539 to 1542 Hernandez De Soto led an expedition deep into the country of the Creek tribes, several hundred miles from the coast, and in 1559 Spaniards drove northward from Mexico in a concerted attempt to establish their authority in the lower Gulf region. Everywhere they went the Spanish enslaved Indians and used them as provision carriers. On occasion, as in 1597, the various coastal tribes concerted themselves in an attempt to wipe out the Spanish missions and trading posts on the Atlantic Coast and drive the Spaniards back to Florida. But the Franciscans kept returning as if God had meant for them to settle all the Indians of the region within the sound of the mission bell. When the first English settlers arrived at the mouth of the Ashley River in April 1670 they found themselves only fifty miles from the northernmost Spanish mission, just south of the Savannah River.

For the scattered and politically disunited tribes of the Carolina country—Guales, Yamasees, Apalachees, Tuskegees, Hitchitis, Westos, Creeks,

---

[15]Quoted in John R. Swanton, *Early History of the Creek Indians and their Neighbors*, Smithsonian Institution, Bureau of American Ethnology, Bulletin 73 (Washington, D.C.: Government Printing Office, 1922), p. 33.

Cusabos, and many others—the arrival of the English provided both opportunities and dangers, depending on their previous position. For the
missionized Indians of northern Florida the English probably appeared
as a threat for they would now be subject to English attacks and the on-
slaught of other tribes drawn into the English orbit. For the coastal
Indians of the region around the mouth of the Ashley River, which was
the site of the English colonizing center of Charleston, the English may
have appeared as saviors, for these tribes had been under heavy attack
from their western neighbors for a number of years. "We have them in a
pound," exclaimed one of the first English colonists in a letter to London,
"for to the Southward they will not goe, fearing the Yamases, Spanish
Comeraro as the Indians terms it. The Westoes are behind them a mortall
enemie of theires, whom they say are ye man eaters. Of them they are
more afraid then the little children are of the Bull beggers in England.
To ye Northward they will not goe for their they cry that is Hiddeskeh,
that is to say sickly, soe that they reckon themselves safe when they have
us amongst them."[16] For the Creeks, to the west of the Westos, the English may also have seemed to provide an answer to their problems with
hostile neighbors, for if they could secure an alliance with the English,
they might gain indisputable control of the Carolina interior.

Thus the English arrived in Carolina at a time when internecine tribal
conflict enabled the settlers to forge an immediate alliance with the
coastal tribes in what amounted to a mutual security pact. Prior to English arrival the Westos had gained an edge in the intra-Indian hostility
largely because they had been able to build a trade connection with Indian traders in Virginia, who provided them with guns. But now the
Westos found that they would have to use their English weapons against
incoming Englishmen who had allied with their enemies. Within months
of their arrival the English had secured the firm friendship of the local
tribes in the coastal area. Not long thereafter the Creeks, several hundred
miles to the west, were sending emissaries to the coast, professing their
friendship and suggesting a military alliance.

For the English colonists, the intricacies of intertribal rivalry, once
unravelled, offered unsuspected opportunities. Most of the original settlers came from the English sugar island of Barbados. They had anticipated using African slave labor to carve out sugar plantations, just as
they had done in the Caribbean. But soon after their arrival it became
apparent that a far faster way to wealth was beckoning. The southeastern
part of the continent, it was apparent, was more densely populated than
the northeast. If the major tribes—Cherokees, Creeks, and Choctaws—

---

[16]Quoted in *ibid.*, p. 67.

could be drawn into trade, vast wealth might be reaped from contact with the native peoples. The Spanish had done little to exploit this potential, for their main goal had been to stake out a claim to the territory and protect it by establishing missions that would gather local Indians to the sedentary agricultural mission life.

One of the first Englishmen in Carolina, Henry Woodward, quickly perceived the trade potential of the area. He had come to Carolina on a scouting expedition in 1666, remained for two years with the Cusabos, a coastal tribe, when the rest of the expedition left, and became the first Englishman to penetrate the interior of the Carolina country—"a Country soe delitious, pleasant and fruitful," he reported, "that were it cultivated doubtless it would prove a second Paradize."[17] Woodward and the other leaders were also aware that the Virginians had already opened a profitable trade with the Catawbas and Westos to the west and northwest of the Carolina settlement at Port Royal.

It was not beaver that beckoned in the Carolina Indian trade, for this valuable animal that had enriched so many traders to the north was available only in small numbers in the warmer climate of Carolina. Instead it was deerskin, also highly marketable in continental Europe and available in the Carolina country in great profusion. "There is such infinite Herds," wrote one of the Carolina leaders in 1682, "that the whole Country seems but one continued Park."[18] From 1699 to 1715 Carolina exported an average of 54,000 deerskins a year and thereafter the trade increased, reaching more than 150,000 skins in some years.

INDIAN SLAVE TRADE

In the first two decades, however, what began as a trade for deerskins was transformed almost immediately into a trade for Indian slaves. There is little evidence that this was anticipated by the early Carolina settlers and in fact the rapid growth of the Indian slave trade caused shock and consternation in London. African slavery was already a familiar part of New World colonization and Indians had been enslaved in other colonies following their defeat in war. But nowhere in the North American colonies of England had an Indian slave trade based on predatory raids been known. Yet from the early years of settlement and for the next three decades it was the cornerstone of commerce for the Charleston merchants. That the early Carolinians were so inured to the use of slave labor from

[17]Verner W. Crane, *The Southern Frontier, 1670–1732* (Ann Arbor; University of Michigan Press, 1956), p. 13.
[18]Quoted in *ibid.*, p. 111.

their experience in Barbados, where slavery was institutionalized much earlier than in the mainland colonies, helps to explain their unquestioning acceptance of Indian slavery.

In most respects the Indian slave trade resembled the African slave trade. The Carolinians did not themselves penetrate the interior but formed alliances with coastal native groups, which they armed, rewarded richly with European trade goods, and encouraged to make war on weaker Indian groups, some of them ancient enemies. By the early 1670s slave coffles were marching through the Carolina backcountry to the coast much as they were filing through the African interior to the trading forts on the West African coast. Once in Charleston, they were transferred to ships for the "middle passage" to other colonies, much as Africans crossed the Atlantic during the process of forced relocation. Most of the Carolina Indian slaves were destined for the West Indies, although a sizable number remained in Carolina and hundreds were shipped northward to New York and the New England colonies, as is evident from reading the colonial newspapers in the northern cities, which frequently printed advertisements for runaway Indian slaves. In 1708 the population of the white settlements in Carolina included about 5,300 whites, 2,900 African slaves, and 1,400 Indian slaves.[19] Of the latter about 500 were men, 600 women, and 300 children. By this time, however, most male Indian slaves were being shipped out of the colony, for it was difficult to keep Indian men from escaping and they posed the problem of insurrection, as in 1700 when an Indian slave rebellion in South Carolina was aborted. Nonetheless, a sizable number of Indian slaves, particularly women and children, were subdued and inured to slave life in the white settlements.

Indian slave artisans and house servants would be a familiar sight in Charleston, as well as in northern colonial towns, for many years. For example, the small settlement of Kingston, Rhode Island, with a white population of 935 in 1730, contained 223 Indian slaves, as well as 333 black slaves.[20] By 1715 the truculence of these Indian men, held captive in their own country, had become so great that three New England colonies were obliged to pass laws forbidding further importations from South Carolina. The preambles of all three laws spoke of the "malicious, surly and revengeful" behavior of these southern Indians and justified the abolition of the trade not on humanitarian grounds but because of "divers conspiracies, insurrections, rapes, thefts, and other execrable crimes [which] have been lately perpetrated in this and the adjoining col-

[19]*Ibid.*, p. 113.
[20]Almon W. Lauber, *Indian Slavery in Colonial Times within the Present Limits of the United States* (New York: Columbia University Press, 1913), p. 110.

onies by Indian slaves."[21] Nonetheless, Indian slavery continued to be a familiar part of colonial life, as revealed in the wills of upper and middle-class whites, down to the Revolution.

POLITICS

The development of the Indian trade in skins and slaves was intimately tied to the peculiar character of Carolina's early politics. South Carolina was founded in the era of Restoration colony building—the planting of settlements in the aftermath of a long period of English civil war and the reinstallation of the English monarchy. Strategic considerations dictated that England cement her claims on the North American coast by removing the Dutch in the Middle Atlantic area and strengthening her pretensions against the Spanish by settling colonies south of the Chesapeake. With this in mind, Charles II, restored to the throne in 1660, issued charters for a cluster of colonies in the Mid-Atlantic region—New York, New Jersey, Pennsylvania, and Delaware—and for the colony of Carolina on the lower Atlantic coast. In each case, the charters, specifying title to vast tracts of land and conferring rights of government, were granted to favorites and creditors of the king. Thus colony building in the Restoration period served not only to strengthen English claims against the Spanish and Dutch in North America but to reward the faithful who had stood by Charles II when he was in exile during the republican regime of Oliver Cromwell in the 1650s. In the case of Carolina, the recipients of the King's favor were some of his staunchest supporters during the Cromwellian period—the Duke of Albemarle, who had been a leading officer in the royalist army; the Earl of Clarendon, the King's chief minister; the Earl of Craven, a prominent royalist during the years of English civil war; Sir William Berkeley, the governor of Virginia; and Sir John Colleton, a prominent Barbados planter and supporter of the monarchy during its years of eclipse. All these men had claims on the King; all had political power which the King was anxious to keep on his side after his Restoration; and all saw the opportunity to extend their wealth and power by colonizing in America.

When Charles II granted a proprietary charter to these men in 1663, they immediately set about devising a framework of government which they thought would avoid the kind of instability that had beset earlier English attempts at colonizing and, at the same time, lure a large number of settlers to Carolina. As proprietors, they had rights nearly equivalent to those of feudal landlords. All land within the limits of their patent must be purchased from them and they were free to charge a yearly

21*Ibid.*, p. 292.

tribute, called a quit-rent, on each acre of land they sold. They also possessed wide administrative, judicial, and executive powers; in fact, their authority was somewhat greater than the king himself possessed in England.

The main work of devising a blueprint for the Carolinas fell to Anthony Ashley Cooper, an expert in colonial affairs who had served on Cromwell's Council of State for Plantations while at the same time maintaining friendly connections with the exiled King. In 1669 Ashley drafted a constitution for Carolina with the assistance of his friend and protege John Locke, who was the tutor of Ashley's children and secretary to the Council for Trade and Plantations. Ashley and Locke were uninterested in the utopian schemes for the New World that had possessed the minds of the Puritans.

What Ashley and Locke devised was a bizarre combination of the modern and feudal. In order to attract colonists land was offered not at a bargain price; it was offered for nothing. At first eighty acres were offered to each adult male who would emigrate; later the ante was increased to 150 acres per immigrant. But this liberal land system was grafted onto a semi-medieval system of government. The Fundamental Constitutions of Carolina provided the eight Carolina proprietors, their deputies, and a limited number of quasinoblemen with a monopoly of legislative, administrative, and judicial power in the colony. They would hold undisputed reign through an elaborate system of courts, committees, and councils— all tied to the wisdom and authority of eight proprietors in London.

The reality of settlement in Carolina bore little correspondence to what its founders had planned. Nobody who came to the colony took the distant London proprietors very seriously, least of all the tough, unsentimental, nonideological planters who streamed in from the Barbados and Virginia where depressed economic conditions had made a new start in the Carolina wilderness seem attractive. They came to take up 150 acres of free land and they quickly laid claim to the best land they could find without respect for the elaborate plans projected by the proprietors for settling in compact, rectangular patterns. The land they occupied first lay along the rivers, the arteries of transportation by which they could transport their crops to market.

In government, as in land affairs, they did what they pleased. The London proprietors appointed a governor to take command, but he quickly found out that without the cooperation of the local planters he could do nothing. Men tough and independent enough to undertake the hardships of carving out plantations in the swampy lowlands of eastern Carolina were not going to be fitted into a rigid system of land occupation or into a hierarchical system of government that placed the power to make decisions 3,000 miles away. Viewing the London proprietors as self-interested aristocrats who knew nothing about the rigors and problems of frontier life, they set about shaping their own institutions of government.

Carolinian-Indian Relations

The establishment of an Indian trade in pelts and slaves became the issue around which the designs of the proprietors and the desires of the individual planters met head-on in the first decades of settlement. The proprietors sent strict instructions that settlers were not to engage in the Indian trade and appointed agents, led by Henry Woodward, to supervise the trade monopoly and make pacts with the natives. They also condemned the Indian slave trade as a field of enterprise, reasoning that it might plunge the colony into a unending series of Indian wars that would ruin Carolina's reputation as a safe place for prospective settlers.

To the most ambitious and ruthless early settlers this conservative Indian policy was unacceptable. They understood that agriculture was a poor second to the Indian trade as a means of accumulating a quick fortune in Carolina and they saw no reason to allow the London proprietors to monopolize the trade, especially since they had no means of enforcing their policy. Therefore steps were taken to thwart proprietary Indian policy. At the outset of settlement the proprietors had formed a trade partnership with the Westo tribe, located about fifty miles from the coast. The Westos were known for their aggressiveness and had been attacking the coastal tribes for years, aided by the technological superiority they had gained through a gun trade with Virginia. By employing Henry Woodward the proprietors were able to draw the Westos into a trade agreement and make them the cornerstone of proprietary Indian policy in the early years. The Westos would not only supply deerskins but would act as a buffer between the Carolina settlements and the Spanish mission system to the south.

In attempting to thwart the proprietary trade monopoly, the independent planters realized that their choices were either to wean the Westos away from the proprietors or to destroy them. In the beginning, private traders, ignoring the proprietary monopoly and orders against enslaving Indians, incited a number of incidents with the local tribes, particularly the Kussos, and then sent out punitive expeditions designed to bring home Indian captives to be sold into slavery. Although they objected strenuously that the settlers were provoking war with local tribes in order to enslave them, the proprietors could do little to stop this kind of entrepreneurial activity. In 1677, recognizing what had already happened, the proprietors gave permission for the Charleston traders to deal with local

Indian tribes but reasserted their monopoly of the more profitable inland trade with the Westos and Creeks. The local response was to contrive a war against the Westos themselves. The Carolina planters had no desire to risk their own lives against the Westos and in fact lacked sufficient strength to defeat the powerful tribe. But they solved their problem by arming a migrating group of Shawnees, who had filtered across the Appalachian Mountains, and offering them lavish gifts to defeat and enslave the proprietary-linked Westos. In early 1680 the subcontracted war against the Westos began. Three years later the Carolina proprietors in London learned that not more than fifty of their former allies and trading partners were still alive in Carolina. The rest had been killed or sold into slavery. Destroyed with the Westos was the proprietary Indian trade monopoly. As an historian of early proprietary policy has written: "Their complete failure to put down the traffic in Indian slaves, to which the Westo War gave a notable impetus, was significant of their failing authority."[22]

For the next few decades the private traders, who had now grasped control of the provincial government, armed the Shawnees, or Savannahs as they became known, and engaged in "an orgy of slavedealing."[23] The governor and members of his council, the nominal instruments of proprietary policy, were themselves involved in the profitable purchase of slaves, which their Savannah allies took in a series of raids on interior tribes. The search for more and more slaves took the Savannahs farther and farther afield until by the end of the seventeenth century they were conducting slave operations deep into the interior and far down the coast into Spanish Florida. The culmination of this form of economic enterprise came in the first decade of the eighteenth century. In 1704, a Carolina Indian trader, Thomas Moore, led about 1,000 Creek warriors and fifty of his countrymen into Apalachee territory. Other raids in the next six years left the Spanish mission system, initiated in 1573, in a shambles. Some 10,000 to 12,000 Timucas, Guales, and Apalachees were caught in the net of English slavery. Marched to Charleston, they were sold to the slave dealers and shipped out to all points in the growing colonial empire of England.

The London proprietors were helpless to stop these perversions of their Indian policy. When they denounced the Indian slave trade as immoral and reckless, the colonists replied that the public safety required the elimination of some of the lesser tribes and maintained that transporting them out of the colonies or using them as slaves kept them "from being

---

[22]Crane, *Southern Frontier*, p. 20.
[23]*Ibid.*, p. 139.

put to Cruell deaths" by the Savannahs. The proprietors were not fooled
by this twisted logic. They understood perfectly, as they informed the
local government, that the colonists were playing on the Savannahs'

> covetousness of your gunns Powder and Shott and other European
> Comodities . . . to ravish the wife from the Husband, Kill the father to
> get the Child and to burne and Destroy the habitations of these poore
> people into whose Country wee were Ch[e]arefully received by them, cher-
> ished and supplyed when wee are weake, or at least never have done us
> hurt; and after wee have set them on, worke to doe all these horrid wicked
> things to get slaves to sell the dealers in Indians [and] call it humanity to
> buy them and thereby keep them from being murdered.[24]

For several decades after the Westo War the Carolina traders conducted
a slave trade with their Savannah allies and at the same time developed
a profitable trade in deerskins with the interior Creeks. Complaints were
frequently leveled that the Indian trade was filled with abuses and that
the cheating of the Indians would eventually disaffect the trading tribes
and incite them to war. But regulation of the trade, though it was debated for years, was "hopelessly entangled in the bitter factionalism of
Carolina politics" with the proprietary and antiproprietary groups vying
for control of the trade.[25] As had been predicted, abuses of the trade
and encroachments on Indian land finally led the Savannahs to conclude
that their alliance with the Carolinians was suicidal in its implications.
Understanding that attempts to obtain fair treatment stood little chance
of success and that war against those who exploited them might be too
costly, most of the Savannahs decided in 1707 to migrate northward into
the backcountry of Maryland and Pennsylvania. But rather than let the
Savannahs extricate themselves from the trade dependency, the Carolinians offered huge bounties to a tribe of about 450 Catawba Indians to
attack and extirpate the Savannahs. Twice in 1707 and 1708 small numbers of Carolinians, led by the son of a former governor, joined the Catawbas in attacks on the Savannahs. Governor John Archdale justified
the policy by writing that "thining the barbarous Indian natives" had
seemed necessary and admitted that by the end of the first decade of the
eighteenth century the two principal tribes of the coastal area, the
Westos and the Savannahs, were virtually extinct.[26]

For the Indian tribes of the Carolina region the arrival of the English
had disastrous effects. Previously the coastal tribes had been incorporated

---

[24]Quoted in *ibid.*, pp. 139–40.

[25]*Ibid.*, p. 145.

[26]John Archdale, "A New Description of . . . Carolina" (1707), in Alexander A.
Salley, *Narratives of Early Carolina, 1650–1708* (New York: Charles Scribner's Sons,
1911), p. 285.

in the Spanish mission system. Though this had rendered them dependent and altered their way of life, it had not destroyed them. The settlement of South Carolina, on the other hand, had catastrophic effects, for it introduced a trade in European cloth, guns, and other goods that greatly intensified Indian warfare, pitted one tribe against another, and greatly reduced the population. Even the stronger tribes of the area, with whom the English forged trade alliances, found that after they had used English guns to enslave smaller and weaker tribes, they were themselves scheduled for elimination.

Yet in spite of the attritional effects of trading with the English, the Indian desire for trade goods was so strong that nothing could deter new tribes from forging alliances while others were being destroyed. The Creeks, the strongest and most populous of the interior tribes, were abandoning their old villages on the Chattahoochee River in the late seventeenth century and migrating eastward to the Altamaha in order to be closer to the English. Even a terrible smallpox epidemic that spread through the interior Indian villages in 1697 did not convince the Creeks that the European connection might better be spurned. Vast quantities of deerskins, carried on the backs of native burdeners, moved eastward along the Indian trail that led from more than five hundred miles in the interior to the coastal trading center of Savannah. Supplied with English weapons, the Creeks also served the English by making war on the Spanish and their Indian allies and on the Choctaws of the Alabama and Mississippi region. "Through the media of intensified warfare, hunting and trading," a historian of the Creeks has written, "the Creeks became, comparatively speaking, a fiercely acquisitive and affluent Indian society," and yet "abjectly dependent upon the English trading system."[27]

Whether the zone of interaction was in the St. Lawrence River Valley, the Hudson River Valley, the southeastern coastal sea islands and marshlands, or the lower Mississippi River Valley; whether the Europeans involved were French, Dutch, or English; whether the Indians involved were Hurons, Mohawks, Narragansetts, Westos, Creeks, or Natchez; European-Indian relations revolved around one basic axis. For the Europeans the essential components of colonization were land, trade, and physical security. For Indians land, trade, and physical security also were primary goals, but to these must be added the preservation of political and cultural sovereignty. In the zones of interaction where Europeans came in small numbers to pursue trade and did not threaten the Indian land base, relations could be generally amicable. In Dutch Albany and French Canada, Europeans and Indians followed mutually profitable pur-

[27]David H. Corkran, *The Creek Frontier, 1540–1783* (Norman: University of Oklahoma Press, 1967), p. 53.

suits. The Europeans did not threaten the political sovereignty, the land base, or the cultural integrity of native societies; Indians, in turn, had no desire to attack those who provided greatly coveted trade goods.

But in areas where Indian land or political autonomy was at stake or where an Indian slave trade was desired, widespread conflict occurred irrespective of the national origins of the Europeans involved. Europeans were usually the vanquishers in these encounters, but native groups fought with a determination that far exceeded their numbers. Internal divisions among the coastal tribes—the inability to unite politically to insure their own survival—is the commonly cited explanation for their eventual defeat. But to imply that Indians were incapable of political unifications because of their "backward" cultures is to forget that Europeans were also badly divided. In more than two centuries of colonization in North America the different groups of European settlers never composed their national antagonisms sufficiently to unite against Indian enemies. Indeed the English colonists were so badly divided among themselves in Metacom's War of 1675 that they were only barely able to defeat an enemy whom they greatly outmatched in men and supplies. The picture of Metacom's difficulties in obtaining the aid of neighboring tribes is real; but it must be considered alongside the picture of Governor Andros of New York invading Connecticut as the war was in progress and Bostonians expelling from their town English refugees from burned-out frontier villages.

In the end, we are best equipped to understand the pattern of interaction and conflict between the various Indian and European societies by appreciating that each group pursued its own interests as steadfastly as it could, limited primarily by the resources available to it and restricted partially by conditions and attitudes that predated European arrival. Europeans of all nationalities took what they could get in North America and adapted their methods to the circumstances that pertained to any particular area. Indians made similar calculations of self-interest and employed a similarly wide range of strategies in pursuing it. For both, survival and the enhancement of their own culture were the paramount objectives.

chapter 6

The Coastal Cultures: Resistance and Accommodation

That the Indian was rarely a passive agent in the first century of contact with European culture was dramatically apparent in the last third of the seventeenth century in Massachusetts and in the first quarter of the eighteenth century in South Carolina. During this period Indian tribes in both New England and the South rose up in determined attempts to prevent becoming a colonized people. In other areas, such as Virginia and Pennsylvania, small tribes resisted encroachment by foreigners but, bereft of Indian allies and weakened by population decline, moved out of the path of European expansion or succumbed to confinement on reserved parcels of land. In many cases, however, Indian tribes chose to initiate war against the cultural and territorial invaders or to withdraw from contact rather than accept the role of a dominated people. Rather than conceiving of these coastal native societies as brittle and static, and thus unable to adapt to the arrival of dynamic European culture, we might better perceive them as malleable societies with which the colonists had little desire to acculturate. In the face of this European ethnocentrism Indian societies improvised a variety of responses to these colonists, ranging from cooperation to resistance to withdrawal. Each of these can be seen as an attempt to preserve their corporate unity and cultural integrity. This was a period of great crisis and stress for the coastal tribes, but those who have argued that it involved wholesale cultural disintegration have offered little proof to substantiate this claim. What seems most remarkable is that most of the coastal cultures which were experiencing the brunt of European population buildup retained their basic values intact and "continued to view the changing world from the frame of logic of their own cultures."[1]

Following the Pequot War of 1637 in New England, the Narragansetts, who had joined the English against the Pequots, attempted to maintain their autonomy by keeping their distance from the English colonists. But the Narragansetts occupied precisely the territory toward which Puritan expansion into the Connecticut River Valley was destined to go. In 1643 the colonies of Massachusetts, Connecticut, and Plymouth, eager to forge an offensive league against the powerful Narragansetts, and also against the pestiferous deviant colony of Rhode Island, formed the New England Confederation. Military preparedness was the goal of the Confederation, governed by a commission made up of two representatives from each of the Puritan colonies. Strength was added to the Puritan front by alliances with the Mohegans, enemies of the Narragansetts. In 1643, when the Narragansetts became involved in a battle with some Mohegans, the New England Confederation mounted a military expedition to chasten them. Calculating the odds against them, the Narragansetts submitted and signed a treaty which saddled them with the cost of the expedition. The costs were apparently paid in land and by such tactics the Puritans were gradually able to clear away the chief obstacle to territorial expansion.

While Puritans were pushing southward and westward, their population growing to some 25,000 by 1650 and 50,000 by 1675, a few men were attempting experiments in Christianization among the remaining fragments of the eastern New England tribes. Led by John Eliot, Thomas Mayhew, and Daniel Gookin, these efforts were concentrated among the Indians whose numbers and cultural integrity had been deeply eroded by epidemics, war, and dependency upon European trade goods. Several thousand "praying Indians" were established in fourteen villages where they attempted to become white men in red skins—adopting English

[1] T. J. C. Brasser, "The Coastal Algonkians; People of the First Frontiers," in *North American Indians in Historical Perspective*, eds. Eleanor Burke Leacock and Nancy Lurie (New York: Random House, Inc., 1971), p. 76.

methods of agriculture, praying to the English God, adopting English hair styles, dress, and customs. The repudiation of their culture was the price of admission to "civilization." And yet, as a recent student of these praying villages has pointed out, "While the towns perhaps appeared to represent a transition phase preceding full assimilation into white society, no such assimilation was ever mentioned as even a remote possibility. The reservation Indians of seventeenth-century New England, as many of those in the United States to this day, were relegated to a state of suspended animation between two cultures, not being a real part of either."[2]

Other New England tribes, where stronger leaders and greater numbers prevailed, resisted the missionary work of men like Eliot and Gookin. As Neal Salisbury has written, "Christianization was successful only with Indians whose identities had previously been shattered by the English conquest" or where conquest was not attempted, as in the case of the successful missions on Martha's Vineyard.[3] Even the more cohesive tribes, which had maintained a degree of independence from the expanding Puritan society, were aware by the early 1670s that their position was precarious and steadily worsening. Their options were limited. They could submit to the English colonies, selling their land, putting themselves under Puritan government, and performing day labor within the white man's settlements. They could sell their land for whatever they could get and migrate westward, attempting to place themselves under the protection of the stronger Iroquois tribes at their backs. Or they could attempt what had never been successfully undertaken before anywhere in the continent—a pan-Indian offensive against a people who greatly outnumbered them and had at their disposal a far greater arsenal of weapons.

Metacom's War

It was the third alternative that the Wampanoags chose. In part this can be explained by the leadership of Metacom, or King Philip as the English called him. Metacom was a son of Massasoit, the Wampanoag leader who had allied himself to the Plymouth settlers when they first arrived in 1620 and fought with them against other tribes throughout his life. Massasoit had died in 1661 and Metacom had watched his older brother, Wamsutta, preside over the deteriorating position of the Wampanoags. In 1662 Wamsutta died mysteriously after the Plymouth officials had interrogated him about rumors concerning an Indian conspiracy. For the next decade, Metacom, as sachem of the Wampanoags, brooded over the position of his people and was forced to accept one

[2]Neal H. Salisbury, "Conquest of the 'Savage': Puritans, Puritan Missionaries, and Indians, 1620–1680" (Ph.D. diss. University of California, Los Angeles, 1972), p. 212.
[3]*Ibid.*, p. 242.

humiliating blow after another. The worst came in 1671 when he was compelled to surrender a large stock of guns and accept a treaty of submission in which he agreed to follow the advice of the New England Confederation in matters relating to the sale of land to white colonists. From that time on he began building a league of Indian resistance, convinced that the steady loss of Wampanoag land and arms, combined with the corrosive effects of the Puritans' alcohol and the discriminatory character of the white man's government, would be reversed only by Indian initiative.

Adding to the Indian mentality that was developing was the decline of the fur trade. By 1670 the beaver supply of the eastern areas was all but extinct. Coastal tribes such as the Narragansetts and Wampanoags had little chance to trade for furs from the interior since this market was firmly in the hands of the Iroquois. Dependent on trade goods, but no longer able to provide the white trader with commodities he wanted, the Indians' plight was becoming hopeless. Alcohol became a way of deadening the pain, but in the long run it too only contributed to the sense of desperation.

That Metacom was able to recruit support for his resistance movement is an indication that the Wampanoags, despite the setbacks of the previous decades, were far from a demoralized people. They lacked neither resources nor spirit to rebel. Still valuing their ancient cultural traditions, they sought new alliances with surrounding tribes and embarked upon a war which in itself was a symbol of hope and a commitment to the advent of a revitalized life.

The triggering incident of Metacom's War was the trial of three Wampanoags haled before the Puritan courts for an act of tribal vengeance involving the murder of a Christianized, Harvard-educated Indian, John Sassamon, who had served for a time as Metacom's secretary and advisor. Sassamon was a man caught between two cultures. Though he had fled white civilization some time after his Harvard experience, he was moved to inform the government at Plymouth in the spring of 1675 that the Wampanoags were preparing for a general attack on the English settlements. When he was found murdered shortly afterwards, the Plymouth officials were able to produce an Indian who claimed he had witnessed the murder and could identify the felons. Three Wampanoags swung at the end of English ropes in June 1675 and their conviction carried with it the implication that the conspiracy allegedly being organized by Metacom was a reality.

War did not break out immediately. In fact the haphazard and sporadic burning and looting that occurred during the next few weeks conveys the impression that Metacom was attempting to restrain the more fiery young men of his tribe who were pushing hard for a war that would renew their sense of integrity and bring back to their culture the honor that had been compromised by their fathers over the years. But the war came in full force by the end of the summer. The execution of the three Wampanoags had been the catalyst but the underlying cause was the rising anger of the young Wampanoag males, who refused to accept the inheritance of their fathers. Unwilling to face a lifetime of submission to an alien culture and rankling with the thought that so much had been sacrificed in order to accommodate the white invader, they girded themselves for battle. Revitalization of their culture through war was probably as important a goal as the defeat of the white encroacher, who so often in the past had humiliated the New England tribes while occupying more and more of their land.

In the first few months of the war, Metacom's followers conducted daring, hit-and-run attacks on villages in the Plymouth colony. These were accomplished without the assistance of the other major tribes in New England—the Narragansetts, Nipmucs, and Mohegans. But the failure of the English colonists to unify militarily for an immediate assault on the Wampanoags brought new allies to Metacom's side. When they found that Metacom and his warriors were easily evading their pursuers, attacking his flanks and conducting guerrilla-type operations, many Indians decided that this was the opportunity that they had long awaited. Tribe after tribe joined Metacom and by late summer Indian attacks were occurring all along the New England frontier. Although the English retained the allegiance of the Niantics and Mohegans, the Pocomtucks, and Pocassets, the latter inspired by the female leader Weetamoo, joined the Indian cause. Most important, the Narragansetts, who had attempted to stay officially neutral while apparently offering clandestine aid to the Wampanoags, were driven into the war by Puritan attacks on them. Even the Nipmucs, a tribe of local Indians near Springfield, who had silently nursed grievances for years but were thought by the colonists to be a faithful ally, joined the offensive by late summer. A few months later the River Indians of the upper Hudson were mobilizing for an attack on the New Englanders. Their plans were aborted only when the governor of New York incited the Mohawks to attack them.

By the time of the first November snowfall the entire upper Connecticut Valley had been laid in waste by Indian forays and the New England frontier was reeling under the attacks of the highly mobile Indian warriors. By March 1676, Metacom's forces were attacking Medfield and Weymouth, less than twenty miles from Boston, and Providence, Rhode Island. "At various points," writes the most recent historian of the war, "the line of English settlement had been pushed back toward the coast, and people in all but the largest and best-defended seaports were in a state of almost constant apprehension."[4] Thoughts of English superiority began to fade as ambush after ambush punished the colonial forces. "The English soldiers, with their heavy, cumbersome equipment," we learn, "began to doubt their own ability to stand up to the Indians, man for man."[5] Draft resistance became epidemic by the spring of 1676 and eastern communities grumbled at the influx of refugees from the frontier towns. Food scarcities in the towns produced opportunities for profiteering among those who controlled supplies. Even in times of military crisis, it seemed, the centrifugal forces which had been compromising the Puritan concept of community for a generation were difficult to overcome.

In the spring of 1676 the Indian offensive began to wane, not as the result of colonial military victories but because of food shortages and disease among the Indians. In what had become a war of attrition, they were finding it more and more difficult to obtain food supplies and weapons to replenish their depleted stores. Attempts to obtain guns and ammunition from the Mohawks near Albany met with some success but when the New York authorities succeeded in cutting off this vital source of supply, Metacom's forces were left in a precarious position. Slowly in the summer of 1676 groups of Indians began to surrender, while others headed westward seeking shelter among tribes there. Most of the leaders who surrendered or were captured were executed. But to pay for the costs of the war many others, including Metacom's wife and son, were sold into slavery and shipped to West Indian and Mediterranean slave markets. Metacom himself was killed in a battle near the Wampanoag village where the war had begun. Regarded by the Puritans as an agent of Satan —"a hellhound, fiend, serpent, coitiff and dog," as one leader put it—his head was carried triumphantly back to the English settlements.[6] By the end of the summer the war was over, although "hunting redskins became for the time being a popular sport in New England, especially since prisoners were worth good money, and the personal danger to the hunters was now very slight."[7]

At the end of the war several thousand English and perhaps twice as many Indians lay dead. Of some ninety Puritan towns, fifty-two had been attacked and twelve destroyed by the "tawney serpents," as Cotton Mather revealingly called them. The Indian villages were devastated even more completely. Not for forty years would the white frontier advance again

---

[4]Douglas E. Leach, *Flintlock and Tomahawk: New England in King Philip's War* (New York: W. W. Norton & Company, Inc., 1966), p. 170.

[5]*Ibid.*, p. 183.

[6]Quoted in Alvin M. Josephy, Jr., *The Patriot Chiefs: A Chronicle of American Indian Resistance* (New York: The Viking Press, Inc., 1958), p. 35.

[7]Leach, *Flintlock and Tomahawk*, p. 237.

to the point where it had been on the eve of the war. For the Indians of coastal New England it was the last gasp. Had they been able to secure the aid of the Abnakis, a powerful tribe on the northern frontier that had strong connections with the French, or with the Mohawks, the easternmost Iroquois nation, the outcome might have been different. But ancient intertribal hostilities were not yet forgotten; perhaps even more important, the stronger interior tribes valued their trading partnership with the English far more than the survival of the coastal Indians. For the survivors there remained only the bitter fact that the English had prevailed and must now be recognized as their "protectors." In the aftermath of the war even the tribes that had remained neutral or rendered military assistance to the colonies were subjected to far more rigorous regulation. By a law passed in 1677 most remaining Indians, regardless of their religious preferences, were confined in one of the four surviving praying villages. A few hundred others became "poor tenant farmers and hired servants" in the English communities. Even the missionary movement among the Indians was dealt a crushing blow, for after the war their were few Indians to Christianize and those who remained were securely penned within a few Indian towns where they became wards of a Puritan colony that cared little for their religious status so long as their control on the land was broken.

In spite of the finality of the English victory, which was accomplished by the exhaustion of the Indian effort rather than through English military superiority, Metacom's War demonstrated that some of the coastal tribes were prepared to risk extinction rather than become a colonized and culturally imperialized people. A truly assimilationist policy was never attempted by the Puritans because they were not prepared to accept the Indians except as unresisting subjects controlled by but not included within English society. The weakest of the coastal tribes succumbed to this policy but the stronger chose to resist, even at the risk of annihilation, against a society that outnumbered them in men and material resources. But at the war's end the Indians of New England, except on the northern frontier, had been catastrophically reduced in population, land resources, political autonomy, and economic independence.

Bacon's Rebellion

While New Englanders fought for their lives during 1675 and 1676, the Chesapeake colonists were also locked in a struggle for survival that involved not only war between the red and white communities but war within the white community. By the time Metacom's War was over in New England, several hundred whites and a larger number of Indians lay dead in Virginia and Maryland, the capital city of Jamestown lay smoldering in ashes, and a thousand English troops were on their way across the Atlantic to suppress what the king took to be an outright rejection of his authority in Virginia. This deeply tangled conflict, called Bacon's Rebellion, took its name from the twenty-nine-year old planter Nathaniel Bacon, who had come to the Chesapeake only two years before.

Bacon's Rebellion seemed to come almost without warning. Virginia had grown rapidly since mid-century, achieving a population of about 40,000 by 1670 and annually exporting some 15,000,000 pounds of tobacco to England. Sir William Berkeley presided over the colony's fortunes as royal governor, an office he had held intermittently for more than twenty years. Pitted against both the Indians and the royal governor was Bacon, who had been educated at Cambridge in England, enjoyed status as a second cousin of the governor and a member of his council, and arrived in Virginia with sufficient wealth to purchase an already established tobacco plantation, complete with a number of slaves.

But Bacon and many others who were seeking economic gain in Virginia were deeply troubled by declining social opportunity and by the Indian policy fashioned over the years by Governor Berkeley. In 1646, at the end of the second Indian uprising against the Virginians, a treaty was signed that guaranteed the Chesapeake tribes the territory north of the York River, which ran northwest from the Chesapeake Bay into the interior of Virginia. Red and white leaders had agreed that the price of peace was granting each culture exclusive land rights in specified regions. For almost three decades after 1646 conflict had been avoided. In fact, a profitable trade for furs with several tribes had developed, although some in Virginia grumbled that it was monopolized by the governor and his circle of favorites. This stabilization of Indian relations, however, became increasingly odious to the wave of new settlers who arrived in Virginia in the 1650s and 1660s, and especially to a mass of white indentured servants who had served their time only to find that in an era of depressed tobacco prices they could not compete with established planters. As their numbers grew, they put more and more pressure on the Virginia government to open up the lands north of the York River for settlement. Why should this area be reserved forever for a handful of Indians, they argued, when the Virginia charter ran all the way to the "South Sea," leaving plenty of room to the west for the local tribes? Governor Berkeley wrote home on several occasions that one of every three or four men were landless or impoverished and that all of them "we may reasonably expect, upon any Small advantage the Enemy may gaine upon us, would revolt . . . in hopes of bettering their Condicion by Shareing the Plunder of the Country with them."[8]

[8]Edmund S. Morgan, "Slavery and Freedom: The American Paradox," *Journal of American History*, 59 (1972–73): pp. 21–22.

This land hunger and constriction of opportunity turned to violence in July 1675 when a group of Doeg Indians, affronted by the failure of a planter to pay them for goods they had traded, attempted to steal his hogs. Their plans were thwarted and several Indians were killed by English gunfire. When the Doegs took revenge by killing several of the offending whites, thirty of the neighboring planters launched a retaliatory assault. Ten Doegs and fourteen Susquehannocks who had been allied to the Virginians for many years lay dead at the end of the foray. When the Virginia government did nothing to make reparations for the deaths of the friendly Susquehannocks, the Indians sought revenge through attacks on outlying settlements along the Maryland and Virginia frontier.

The incident, as white Virginians would later admit, came as the inevitable result of the land fever and hatred of Indians that led to "takeing up the very Townes or Lands they [the Indians] are seated upon, turning their Cattell and hoggs on them, and if by vermin or otherwise any be lost, then they exclaime against the Indians, beate & abuse them (notwithstanding the Governors endeavour to the contrary). . . . "[9] Even more at the root of the indiscriminate attacks of the English was the fact that the Virginia Indians had been reduced in number and power so drastically in the previous decades as to offer only weak resistance to the "land lopers," as they were later labeled. Such men saw the opportunity to open up all land still remaining in Indian hands through the out-and-out annihilation of the remnants of the Chesapeake tribes. Less than one thousand Indian males remained in the Virginia region by this time and these, as Governor Berkeley had written in 1671, "are absolutely subjected, so that there is no fear of them."[10] Such weakness was an invitation to white violence. The Marylanders and Virginians could easily put a thousand well-armed men in the field and it was just this that occurred in September 1675. About one thousand Chesapeake planters and militiamen marched against an abandoned stockade on the Potomac River, which had been assigned to the Susquehannocks by the colony of Maryland. Surrounding a village containing about one hundred braves with their families, they demanded that the chiefs come out to parley. When the Susquehannocks denied any responsibility for the frontier attacks, their chiefs were led away from the village and murdered.

Though the Virginia militia officers involved were tried for this crime, they were given only small fines or cleared of the charges by local courts. Appalled by this English "savagery," Governor Berkeley denounced the

[9]"Virginia's Deploured Condition" (1676), Massachusetts Historical Society *Collections*, 4th Ser., 9 (Boston, 1869): 164.
[10]Quoted in Wilcomb E. Washburn, *The Governor and the Rebel: A History of Bacon's Rebellion in Virginia* (Chapel Hill: University of North Carolina Press, 1957), p. 20.

attack and the legal proceedings. But he found scanty support in the colony and could do little more than express his concern. So long as the Indians were heavily outmatched and served only as an obstacle to further expansion, few Virginians would speak in their behalf or act against those who precipitated hostilities with them. With the Susquehannocks now fully committed to war, despite the overwhelming odds against them, Virginia prepared for their version of what they had already heard was happening to the north under the leadership of Metacom. Like a brushfire, rumors swept the colony that the Susquehannocks were offering vast sums to western Indian nations to join them in attacking the Europeans and even that a confederacy linking Metacom's followers and the southern Indians was being cemented.

Bent on revenge, the Susquehannocks attacked during the winter of 1675–76. The assault took the lives of thirty-six colonists. Angered and apprehensive, the frontiersmen turned on the Indians closest at hand, the settled Appomattoxs and Pamunkeys who lived within the white area of settlement on reservations which a post-war writer admitted "had long been coveted by neighboring Virginians."[11] In what has been labeled a "blood sacrifice" by a recent historian of the war, Nathaniel Bacon assumed the leadership of a frontier movement and began annihilating friendly Indians in the region.[12] Arguing that the subject Indians "have been soe cunningly mixt among the severall Nations or familyes of Indians that it hath been very difficult for us, to distinguish how, or from which of those said Nations, the said wrongs did proceed," Bacon asked Governor Berkeley for a commission to lead his volunteers against any Indians that could be found.[13] When Berkeley refused to legitimize indiscriminate attacks, the fiery Bacon announced his intention to proceed with or without the governor's approval. Berkeley declared Bacon a rebel, stripped him of his councilor's seat, and led an expedition of about three hundred Virginia planters to capture Bacon. The frontier leader in turn gathered his forces around him and headed for the wilderness and "a more agreeable destiny then you are pleased to designe mee," as he defiantly informed the governor.[14]

Governor Berkeley's solution to the deteriorating situation was to dispatch punitive expeditions to chastise any Indians who had attacked the white settlers but then to attempt peace negotiations. Meanwhile he intended to build a string of forts along the frontier to be manned by 500 men who would range among the forts and keep peace between the two

11"Virginia's Deploured Condition," p. 166.
12Washburn, *The Governor and the Rebel*, p. 35.
13Quoted in *ibid.*, p. 37.
14*Ibid.*, p. 41.

peoples. It was a defensive—and an expensive—policy. The money to build and garrison the forts could come from only one place—the pocketbooks of the planters who would have to pay increased taxes over the next few years.

Berkeley misjudged both the white settlers and the Indians. The Susquehannock sachems could not control their own warriors, who again launched attacks even as their chiefs were negotiating with the governor. As for the white Virginians, they wanted nothing of the expensive policy of containment which the governor had concocted. The tobacco market had slipped badly in recent years, an epidemic had carried off half the colony's cattle in the previous summer, a drought had cut deeply into the 1675 harvest, and now, they argued, the governor was suggesting a weak and expensive solution to the biggest Indian crisis in three decades. In their minds the problem was more easily and less expensively solved.

By May 1676 Bacon had declared himself the leader of the rebellious frontiersmen, who were determined to pursue their own Indian policy. Their first target was a fortified settlement of Occaneechee Indians, who had been regarded as friendly and who had recently destroyed a band of Susquehannocks encamped near them as evidence of their fidelity to the Virginians. Attacking the unsuspecting Occaneechees at midnight, Bacon's men annihilated the tribe. Later critics claimed that £1000 in beaver skins inside the Occaneechee fort had whetted the appetites of Bacon's men. With his following increasing at every new attack on the Indians, Bacon then marched to Jamestown to confront the governor, who had charged him with treason against the government. Bacon demanded a commission to legitimize his attacks on the Indians and under great pressure the governor finally acceded. But when Bacon left with his Indian fighters, Berkeley again declared him in rebellion, gathered as many supporters as he could, and attempted to pursue Bacon's force. For the rest of the summer Bacon and Berkeley, each with several hundred supporters, maneuvered around each other, seeking support, sniping at each other's heels in quasimilitary forays, and puzzling over how to stop the chain of events that had started with a disagreement over Indian policy. Time was on the side of Berkeley because once the Indians had been crushed, the Virginia rebels were anxious to return to their homes. Moreover, Berkeley's reports of the rebellion in England had brought the dispatch of a thousand royal troops, who would arrive in Virginia with a royal investigating commission in January 1677. But by that time Nathaniel Bacon was dead of swamp fever and his followers had melted back into the frontier region.

Although the Virginians who followed Bacon were disaffected by high taxes, favoritism in government, and the tight grip on power and profit exercised by Berkeley and his friends, it was the governor's protective Indian policy before the first bloodshed and his unaggressive policy thereafter that provided the strongest insurrectionary impetus. A war of extermination was demanded by men who in the 1670s no longer feared an Indian population shrunken by disease and sporadic fighting in the previous decades. Peace had been useful for three decades because Virginia had little more than 8,000 settlers and the agreement by which all Indians were excluded from land south of the York River allowed plenty of room for expansion. But Virginia's population had quadrupled in the intervening thirty years while the Indians had only grown weaker. It was not peace that frontier Virginians now wanted but war.

The investigators of the Royal Commission perceived this genocidal mentality shortly after arriving in Virginia. In a message to the House of Burgesses, which was debating a peace treaty with the remaining Indians, the commissioners denounced the "inconsiderate sort of men who soe rashly and causelessly cry up a warr, and seem to wish and aime at an utter extirpation of the Indians." The commissioners called it "a base ingratitude, a nameless Prodigie of infatuation, and mere madness" that Bacon and his followers "would make a breach with, or strive to destroy and extirpate those amicable Indians, who are soe farr from hurting them or us, that we must confess they are our best guards to secure us on the Frontieres from the incursions and suddaine assaults of those other Barbarous Indians of the Continent . . . "[15] When a peace treaty was signed in May 1677, one of its articles gave further evidence that the frontier Virginians had seen the Indians only as functionless obstacles that stood in their way. In the fourth article, the treaty referred specifically to the "violent intrusions of divers English into their [the Indians'] lands, forceing the Indians by way of Revenge, to kill the Cattle and hoggs of the English."[16] Thus the purposeful goading of Indians into retaliatory attacks, which could then be used as a reason for a war of extermination, was explicitly recognized by the Virginians themselves as a major cause of the rebellion.

But to argue that Bacon and his followers "causelessly cry up a warr" was to misunderstand a fundamental reality of white attitudes toward the coastal tribes in the last quarter of the seventeenth century. The Baconians had correctly assessed the value of an Indian war and did not disguise their conviction that they had everything to gain from precipitating a conflict with both friendly and unfriendly tribes. Some frontiersmen were to die attacking the Indians, others were to be killed in fights with Berkeley's troops, and twenty-three were captured and executed for

[15]Quoted in *ibid.*, p. 117.
[16]*Ibid.*, p. 161.

treason. But the advantages reaped from the war were considerable for those who survived. As one historian has written, "the effects of the Rebellion had been devastating, and after their long history of war and defeat, the Indians of the tidelands and piedmont regions found it increasingly difficult to preserve their accustomed habits of existence."[17] In effect, the few thousand surviving Virginia Indians had been reduced to a miserable existence on small tracts of assigned land where they were guaranteed protection from land-hungry white settlers, who were forbidden to settle closer than three miles. But a viable way of life had all but been denied to the remnants of the Powhatan Confederacy. As in New England white expansion could now proceed, virtually unchecked, until it reached the territorial limits of stronger interior tribes.

The real significance of Bacon's Rebellion, so far as interracial relationships were concerned, is that it proved that even the highest authorities in an English colony, dedicated though they might be to preserving peace between the two societies, could not prevent genocidal attacks by white settlers. Though he represented the authority of the king in Virginia, Berkeley could do little to control those who saw the Indians as an impediment to the aggrandizement of land on the Virginia frontier. After 1675 the House of Burgesses, reflecting the interests of local planters, had withdrawn the governor's power to disallow individual land grants, an authority which the governor had exercised since 1666 to prevent settlers from taking up land too close to Indian settlements. Thereafter it was a simple matter to intimidate Indians into selling their land in the area of white settlement. As the Secretary of Virginia wrote in 1678, "the english would ordinaryly either frighten or delude them into a bargaine and for a trifle get away the grownd . . . , then he comes and settles himselfe there and with his cattle and hoggs destroyes all the corne of the other Indians of the towne. . . . This was a great cause of this last warr, and most of those who had thus intruded and were consequently the principall cause of it were notwithstanding amongst the forwardest in the rebellion and complained most of grievances."[18] Against this kind of tactic even a royal governor was helpless. Power in the colonies tended to devolve to the local level and this made it impossible for even the most fair-minded colonial governor to stabilize intercultural relations. Probably nobody vested with authority tried more consistently than William Berkeley to hold back the aggressive genocidal tendencies that suffused the land-hungry Englishmen on the seventeenth-century Chesapeake fron-

---

[17]Nancy Lurie, "Indian Cultural Adjustment to European Civilization in *Seventeenth-Century America: Essays in Colonial History*, ed. James M. Smith (Chapel Hill: University of North Carolina Press, 1959), p. 55.
[18]Quoted in Washburn, *The Governor and the Rebel*, p. 161.

tier. But for his troubles, Berkeley saw his colony plunged into civil war, the capital city burn to the ground, and a personal estate valued at £8000 evaporate under the attacks of those who were prepared to fight against both their fellow Englishmen and the Indians.

For the Susquehannocks and other tribes of the coastal region the lesson must have been unmistakably clear. Even when they recognized the authority of the Europeans, declared themselves subject to English law, and abided by that law, and even when they fought against the Indian enemies of the white government, they could not expect to live in peace. The same authority that bound them to treaties of amity and mutual defense with the colony of Virginia was the authority that was unable to control its own white subjects. Their attempts to cooperate with English society were met with English renunciation of accommodations except as a temporary policy. Moreover, they learned that even when European society was divided against itself, as in Virginia in 1676, they could be overmatched by the more populous and better armed fragment of white society that conducted military operations on two fronts. Scattered in small towns, each representing a fragment of a tribe that had once been larger and more powerful, the coastal Indians were doomed whether they chose war or peace. The price of survival in Virginia, as in New England, was the sacrifice of an independent tribal identity and submission to white civilization as tenant farmers, day laborers, and domestic servants.

The Arrival of the Quakers

It was in the area between New England and the Chesapeake in the decades following Metacom's War and Bacon's Rebellion that Indians of the coastal cultures retained their land and their way of life the longest. In part this was because only a small number of Europeans settled in the region during the half-century when the populations of Massachusetts, Connecticut, Maryland, and Virginia were growing rapidly. An equally important factor was that when Europeans did arrive in large numbers, they came as devotees of a religious philosophy called Quakerism that was dedicated to the principle of nonviolence and just relations among men of all religions and races. As long as this philosophy of the Society of Friends held sway, interracial relations in the Delaware River Valley stood in stark contrast to other parts of North America. But when the Quaker commitment to pacifism waned and Quakers lost political control of the area, the last chance for an autonomous Indian existence along the coastal plain of North America quietly disappeared.

Quakers began emigrating to the middle Atlantic region in the mid-

1670s, first to East and West Jersey, which had formerly been part of New Netherland, and then in the 1680s to Pennsylvania, which was to become the center of the Quakers' hopes for a utopia in the New World. Like their Puritan cousins, Quakers burned with the bright heat of religious conviction. In their religious ideology they shared much with the Puritans, for they too regarded the English Protestant Church as corrupt and renounced its formalistic elements. But they carried the Puritan revolt against English Anglicanism to its extreme, decrying all intermediary institutions standing between the individual believer and his God. In this sense, the Quaker was essentially a mystic, persuaded that every believer might find God's grace within one's self through one's own power, unaided by priests, ministers, liturgy, or other devices.

Quakers had been severely persecuted in England after the rise of their movement in the 1650s and therefore began to formulate plans for founding colonies of their own in the New World. They sent their advance agents to Massachusetts, where they were reviled, mutilated, deported, and even hung for practicing their faith; to the West Indies; to Rhode Island; to the Chesapeake; and then in the 1670s and 1680s to New Jersey and Pennsylvania. In the period of Restoration colony building, the latter colony had been granted to one of the most important English Quakers, William Penn. Penn was determined to make it the center of the New World Quaker movement. In Pennsylvania, according to his vision, people of all races, religions, and national backgrounds would be able to live together in peace. However unwelcome the Quakers might be elsewhere in the New World, where war and violence were thought to be unavoidable aspects of carving out English settlements in the presence of Indians, French, Spanish, and Dutch, peace and interracial harmony were to reign in Pennsylvania.

Thus when Quakers arrived in the Delaware River Valley they threatened no violence to the Indians. However, the natives of the area—a loose collection of small tribes of which the Delawares were the largest—had little reason to believe that these Europeans would be different from any others whom they had known for three quarters of a century. Over the decades they had witnessed the arrival of the Dutch, Swedes, the Dutch again, and finally the English. From this exposure to three variants of European culture, each speaking a different language and professing a different form of Protestant religion, the Indians had learned of European technology, material culture, and values. By the time the Quakers arrived, the Delawares had extensive experience with European firearms and alcohol, two key commodities in the trade they conducted in beaver, otter, and deerskins. Like almost every other tribe that came in contact with the Europeans, they had suffered a major population decline. On the eve of the Quaker arrival the Delaware warrior strength was estimated at 1,000, probably less than half what it had been before three smallpox epidemics struck the tribe between 1620 and 1670.

According to the most recent history of the Delawares, the English take-over of the Delaware River Valley in the 1660s was far more threatening to the Delawares than the earlier presence of the Dutch or Swedes.[19] This may have been because the English arrival brought to the area new landless settlers, who began to exert unwelcome pressure for land. But wholesale violence and large-scale dispossession of land such as had occurred both north and south of the Delaware River Valley had not been a feature of the Delawares' contact with Europeans. Now the Delawares were on the verge of experiencing a wholly new kind of European presence, for with the arrival of William Penn and the Society of Friends in 1681, a new era, almost unparalleled in the seventeenth-century history of European-Indian relations in North America, was about to begin.

The Quakers who emigrated to Penn's new colony were primarily agriculturalists, which meant that like other colonists, they gave primary importance to the acquisition of adequate amounts of land. Nor did they differ from their fellow countrymen in seeking material success. Quakers, like Puritans, had been recruited in England from the rising middle groups of society and, as their spectacular success in Pennsylvania over the next few generations was to demonstrate, the economic urge pulsated in them as vigorously as in others on the continent. But Quakers also had an ideological vision. They believed that despite an historical record which seemed to prove otherwise, people of different cultures and beliefs could live together in friendship and peace. Their optimism was not the product of ignorance, for they were fully aware of what had happened when Europeans and Indians met in other parts of North America, including the bloody conflicts that had almost eliminated the Indians in the two most populous areas of British North America only five years before Penn received his grant for Pennsylvania. Yet they were ideologically committed to pacifism, eager to avoid the conflict which had beset other colonies, and convinced that what others had not achieved could be accomplished in the Quaker "Holy Experiment."

Even before he set foot in Pennsylvania, Penn laid the groundwork for peaceful relations. In a letter to be transmitted by his commissioners who preceded him to Pennsylvania he wrote to the Delawares: "The king of the Countrey where I live, hath given unto me a great Province therein, but I desire to enjoy it with your Love and Consent, that we may always live together as Neighbours and friends. . . ."[20] In this single statement

[19]C. A. Weslager, *The Deleware Indians: A History* (New Brunswick, N.J.: Rutgers University Press, 1972), p. 140.
[20]Quoted in *ibid.*, p. 156.

Penn recognized the Indians as the rightful owners of the territory and gave notice that only with their consent would he allow settlers to establish their farms and towns. As proprietor, Penn had been granted title to all the lands within the bounds of his charter. Colonists must purchase land from him. But he in turn sent advance notice that he would sell no land until he had first purchased it himself from the local chiefs. Penn strengthened his commitment by pledging his word that the injustices suffered previously by the Indians would no longer be tolerated. Strict regulation of the Indian trade and a ban on the sale of alcohol were promised. Voltaire was later moved to write, though not with strict accuracy, that this was "the only league between those nations [Indians] and the Christians that was never sworn to, and never broken."[21]

When the first Quaker settlers arrived, led by Penn's cousin, they immediately began land negotiations with the Delawares, or Lenni Lenapes, as the called themselves. The Indians may have been suspicious of Penn's promises, which must have sounded like other European expressions of goodwill that had not lasted much beyond their initial enunciation. But the Delawares were no doubt impressed with the lavish supply of trade goods that were offered for the land along the Delaware River north of the site of what was to become the capital city of Philadelphia. Included were quantities of wampum, blankets, duffels, kettles, hoes, axes, knives, mirrors, saws, scissors, awls, and items of clothing. Also included were rum, powder, shot, and twenty guns, indicating that even those who professed nonviolence and wished to ban the sale of alcohol as a way of stabilizing relations could not afford to deny to Indians the trade goods they most desired.

Penn's arrival in his colony in 1682 brought him face to face with the Delawares. It was pacifism, not violence, that was on his mind and the Indians may have detected this in his eagerness to learn about their culture and language. Penn traveled extensively in eastern Pennsylvania, visiting the Delaware settlements and learning their language, as only a handful of Englishmen did in a century and a half of colonization. "I have made it my business to understand it," he wrote, "that I might not want an Interpreter on any occasion. And I must say, that I know not a language spoken in Europe that hath words of more sweetness in Accent and Emphasis, than theirs."[22]

Still another factor conducive to peaceful relations was the absence of any extensive Indian trade. The fur trade was centered north of Pennsylvania and though Penn made efforts to divert the interior trade so that

[21]Quoted in Thomas E. Drake, "William Penn's Experiment in Race Relations," *Pennsylvania Magazine of History and Biography*, 68 (1944): 372.
[22]Weslager, *Delaware Indians*, p. 166.

it would pass through Philadelphia rather than Albany and New York, he was singularly unsuccessful in this. This was disappointing to Penn and the Quaker merchants but in the long run it limited contacts between Pennsylvanians and Indians and thus minimized the chances for misunderstanding and hostility. As for trade with more westerly Indians, the timing of the Quaker arrival made this impossible until well after the first generation of settlement. A thriving Delaware Valley fur trade had existed between the Susquehannocks, who hunted in the regions inland from Delaware Bay, and the Dutch and Swedish traders, who had been established in the area since the 1620s. But the Susquehannocks had been weakened by competition and battle with the Iroquois to the north and then on the eve of the Quakers' arrival by hostilities with Marylanders and Virginians during Bacon's Rebellion. Thereafter the remnants of the tribe had migrated northward where they placed themselves under the protection of their former enemies, the Iroquois. This had left eastern Pennsylvania inhabited only by small local tribes; even as late as 1702 a prominent officeholder remarked that Penn's colony seemed "quite destitute of Indians."[23]

So long as Penn's influence was strong in his colony, Indian relations remained generally harmonious, aided in part by the absence of competition for land and the presence of only a meager fur trade. Penn resided in his colony from 1682 to 1683 and 1699 to 1700, but never returned after his second visit. A dozen years later he suffered several disabling strokes and played almost no role in the affairs of his colony during the last six years of his life. Coinciding with his decline were two developments that sent Indian relations in Pennsylvania reeling in the direction they had taken in other colonies: the rise of an Indian trade and the arrival of waves of land-hungry European settlers.

Ironically, the Quaker policy of toleration for all religious and ethnic groups attracted to Pennsylvania in the early eighteenth century the very European groups whose land hunger and disdain for the Indians undermined the Quaker attitude of trust and love for the natives. In 1710 and 1711 came the first of these, a group of Swiss Mennonites who settled on a tributary of the Susquehannah River sixty miles inland from Philadelphia. In 1717 arrived a much larger group of German Protestants, the first of an influx of Palatinate immigrants who by the mid-eighteenth century were to constitute about 40 percent of the colony's population. In the following year the first of another wave of immigrants poured in—this time Scotch-Irish, who began to locate near the present-day Pittsburgh. None of these groups shared Quaker idealism about interracial harmony. They had been driven from their homelands by chronic eco-

---

[23]Francis Jennings, "The Indian Trade of the Susquehanna Valley," *Proceedings of the American Philosophical Society*, 110 (1966): 410.

nomic depression and were concerned only about building a new life, centered around tilling the soil, in the remote regions of Penn's colony. To obtain land reasonably and live in a colony where they were free to practice their religion was all they asked. But they were not prepared in return to accommodate themselves to the local tribes, particularly if land speculators and government officials in Philadelphia were willing to co-operate with them in dispossessing the Indians of their land.

A second irony was that many of the Indians whom these refugees from European oppression were to confront were also recent refugees from oppression. In the late seventeenth and first half of the eighteenth century the valleys of Pennsylvania drained by the Susquehannah River became a sanctuary for a number of tribes that migrated from the south and west after hearing of the benevolent Quaker Indian policy, which they believed might offer a way out of the desperate situations in which they found themselves as a result of contact with European society. From Maryland came the Nanticokes and Conoys to escape war and enslave-ment that had decimated their tribes for several decades. "The People of Maryland," the Pennsylvania government was told by one Indian spokes-man, "do not treat the Indians as you & others do, for they make slaves of them & sell their Children for Money."[24] From Virginia and North Carolina came the Tuscaroras and Tutelos for similar reasons. From the southwest came the Miamis and Shawnees, who had formerly lived in the Ohio Valley and traded with the French. Thus a sizable number of In-dians were drawn into central Pennsylvania in the last third of the seven-teenth century. For the Europeans who were to arrive in the early eight-eenth century it was an unanticipated stroke of good fortune because the Indians facilitated later white settlement by clearing the land for crops, settling village sites near water transportation, and establishing trails for hunting. When the new Pennsylvanians arrived, they would reap the advantages of this preparatory work, using the Indian routes to advance west, occupying Indian town sites, and taking over the cleared fields.

Deterioration of Harmony
in Pennsylvania

The Delaware people and other refugee Indians watched their situation deteriorate even as William Penn lay dying in England. They brought bitter complaints to the government in Philadelphia that new settlers were building mill dams downstream from them and thus blocking the fish from coming upstream to spawn. Settlers were pouring in, squatting

[24]Quoted in Weslager, *Delaware Indians*, p. 182.

on land that had not been sold to the proprietary government. Fraud, alcohol liberally bestowed upon Indian bargainers, and outright intimidation were becoming the instruments of white land policy where Quaker fairmindedness had once reigned. But rather than fight, the tribes preferred to vacate their land, knowing what had happened when the resort to violence was employed in Virginia and New England. By 1724 the main branch of the Delawares had migrated westward, part of them to an area not far beyond the limits of white settlement but others all the way to the Ohio River. But they left heavy with resentment. A generation later, when they allied with the French and attacked their former English allies, the Pennsylvanians would reap the wind they had earlier sown. A leading Pennsylvanian wrote of their displacement: "These poor People were much disturbed . . . yet finding they could no longer raise Corn there for their Bread they quietly removed up the River Sasquehannah, though not without repining at their hard usage. . . . Tis certain they have the same reason to resent this as all those other Indians on this Continent have had for the foundation of their Wars that in some places they have carried on so terribly to the destruction of the European Inhabitants."[25]

The development of a fur trade in Pennsylvania brought the second change that ruined Penn's Indian policy. Penn had hoped for a fur trade from the beginning and even savored the thought of a proprietary monopoly over it. But the northern fur trade, controlled by the Iroquois, was firmly in the hands of the merchants of New York. In the opening years of the eighteenth century, however, the Iroquois became disillusioned with their Dutch and English trading partners in Albany and New York. Complaining of the rising price of trade goods and the malpractices of the traders, they made overtures to the Pennsylvania government and suggested that their western furs could be diverted down the Susquehannah River, which had its sources in the heart of Iroquois country, and from there floated along the Schuylkill River to Philadelphia. Other trade connections were made with the Shawnees who had migrated eastward from far in the interior but maintained trading connections with Indian trappers in the Ohio Valley. At last Pennsylvania's merchants had obtained a way of tying European and native markets together.

James Logan

In Pennsylvania, as in other colonies, the fur trade and competition for land were intricately bound together. This is best understood by look-

25Quoted in Francis Jennings, "The Delaware Interregnum," *Pennsylvania Magazine of History and Biography*, 89 (1965): 178.

ing at the individual who was most intimately involved in both land affairs and the Indian trade in the Quaker colony—James Logan. Scotch-Irish by birth and a weakly committed Quaker, Logan had been brought to Pennsylvania in 1699 by Penn, who saw in the young man a spark of intellect and a passion for work that seemed to make him an ideal candidate for his personal secretary. Penn was not wrong in viewing Logan as a man of great potential. Throughout his life Logan was an avid student of the classics, European languages, philosophy, history, and science. In time he would become known in the colonies as one of the giants of culture and intellect—a shining example of versatile western European man leading the advance of civilization on new frontiers. Logan's personal library was unmatched in America in the pre-Revolutionary period and his contributions to colonial culture before 1750 equalled those of any other European on the continent. But Logan also had a passion for power and wealth. He achieved both. Arriving as Penn's secretary, Logan accumulated a staggering succession of offices including Commissioner of Property, member of Council, Chief Justice of the Supreme Court, Provincial Secretary, Receiver of Proprietary Rents, and trustee of Penn's estate after his death. Operating from all these offices, Logan became a formidable figure in Pennsylvania politics in the first three decades of the eighteenth century. Simultaneously, as a merchant and land speculator, he was becoming one of the colony's wealthiest men.

It was Logan more than anyone else who obtained an inside track on the blossoming Pennsylvania Indian trade. He engaged the services of several French *coureurs de bois* whose lifelong experience as Indian traders made them indispensably important, imported quantities of trade goods from England, and then exercised his many political and administrative powers to oil the wheels of his new profit-making machine. As one historian of the Pennsylvania Indian trade has written:

> In the Indian trade, Logan the merchant was helped enormously to control his markets and his marketing organization by Logan the Commissioner of Property, Logan the Secretary of the province, and Logan the agent of the Penn family. When Logan the merchant did not wish to risk his own money for his own business, Logan the Proprietary agent might lend the Proprietary's money to the trader. . . . After the trader had proved his usefulness, Logan the Commissioner of Property and political boss could arrange quietly with his trusty ally, the Surveyor General, to lay out a tract of land for the trader to use as a base for operations.[26]

In addition, as the colony's secretary, he directed diplomatic negotiations with the Indians and was able to employ his traders as messengers and interpreters—a policy which enhanced the prestige of the traders with the

[26]Jennings, "Indian Trade of the Susquehanna Valley," p. 416.

Indians and gave them further reason to respect the power of Logan the merchant. Still further advantages accrued from the fact that Logan was able to draw upon his trading network for knowledge of the most fertile and best situated areas of the backcountry. The Indians were skilled agriculturalists and familiar with the hinterland; thus they chose wisely in planting their villages. As a Commissioner of Property, Logan allotted proprietary lands to the traders as close as possible to these Indian sites, made large purchases himself, and then began to direct the incoming Swiss, Germans, and Scotch-Irish to these areas. As the number of white settlers increased, Logan's land holdings rose in value. Meanwhile the trampling of unfenced Indian crops by the Europeans' cattle and hogs made Indian agriculture more and more difficult. "The effect of [these] activities on the Indians was first to draw them to the Susquehanna region in pursuit of trade, then to push them ever farther to the west, destroying the sedentary agricultural aspects of their economy and magnifying the importance of hunting and nomadism."[27]

In the second quarter of the eighteenth century eastern Pennsylvania was emptied of its Indian population. The lands of the Delawares which could not be gained through the fur trade or the assignment of settler rights in the immediate proximity of Delaware villages was gained in connivance with other Indians. In this case it was the Iroquois to whom the Pennsylvanians turned for help in expelling the last of the local tribes. With James Logan leading the way, the provincial government proposed an alliance with the Iroquois under which the powerful northern confederacy would assume suzerainty over all smaller Indian tribes residing in Pennsylvania. The object of the alliance, according to the white accounts, was interracial peace—obtainable only when stronger Indian nations assumed the responsibility for managing the affairs of lesser Indian groups. But the real purpose of the alliance was to drive the Delawares from their homelands without having to resort to force. Thus in 1732 one band of the Delawares was obliged by the Iroquois to give up their land at Tulpehocken, about sixty miles from Philadelphia, and migrate higher up the Susquehannah River to Shamokin where they were to live under the supervision of a minor Iroquois chief.

Ten years later the process of dispossessing the Delawares was completed at a conference in Philadelphia. What was at stake was the land between the Lehigh and Delaware Rivers, known as the Forks of the Delaware. In 1735 Logan had produced what he alleged was a copy of an old deed signed in 1686 by which the forebears of the present Delaware leaders had ceded this land to William Penn. But the inability of

27*Ibid.*, p. 420.

Logan to produce an original copy, the lack of any reference to the transaction in the land records at Philadelphia, and the rarely mistaken oral tradition of the Indians, by which land transactions were scrupulously passed from generation to generation, all point to the conclusion that by now the Pennsylvanians were confident enough of their strength to force from the Delawares what they could not get by agreement. The Delaware chiefs Nutimus and Tishecunk protested that if the land had been sold by their ancestors, they would have certain knowledge of it. Logan questioned this, pointing out that they were but "little boys" at the time. Nutimus's reply is worth careful consideration since it provides insight into the two systems of values that were confronting each other and discloses the Indian method of recording history: "He had it from his Father," Nutimus replied.

> Besides from the Indian way of selling Land he could not but know. For the Indians who possess Land had it bounded by Rivers Creeks & Mountains & when they sold, the Chief always with the Leave of the others undertook to sell & when he had agreed he called together the heads of the families who had any Right in the Land, sold & divide among them the goods he got for the Land telling them for what they received those Goods; then the Heads of the families again divided their portion among the Young people of the Family & inform them of the Sale & thus every individual, who have any right must be fully acquainted with the Matter. Besides Whenever a Sale is made, the Chief who sells calls the Chiefs of the Neighboring Tribes who are his friends but have no right, in order to be Witnesses of the Sale & to make them remember it he gives them a share of the Goods. So that no Land can be sold without all the Indians round being made acquainted with the Matter. & this we think a Way to have it better known than You take, for when You have gott a Writing from us you lock it up in ye Chest & no body knows what you have Bought or what you paid for it, and after a while by Selling our Land out in small parcels for a great deal of money you are able to build . . . houses as high as ye Sky while we beg having so little for ourselves & dividing that among our friends must live in Wigwams—yet we never claim any Land we have ever fairly sold, we know we have no Right.[28]

Though the Delaware chiefs challenged the validity of the deed, they were faced with the combined opposition of the Pennsylvanians and the Iroquois. Finally they signed a confirmation of the alleged 1686 document, bowing to veiled threats that to resist would only lead to abrasive contacts followed by violence, as incoming squatters encroached on their lands. Two years later, in 1737, the bounds of the Indian deed were to

---

[28]Quoted in Anthony F. C. Wallace, *King of the Delawares: Teedyuscung, 1700–1763* (Philadelphia: University of Pennsylvania Press, 1949), pp. 21–22.

be "walked off" in accordance with the alleged deed, which granted the Penns all the land from a specified point in Bucks County westward as far as a man could walk in a day and a half. The walk itself provided another opportunity for defrauding the Indians. Two of William Penn's sons, who had recently arrived in Pennsylvania to bolster their sagging estates through the sale of land, personally participated in plans to send secret parties scouting through the woods to blaze a trail which would enable the walkers to cover ground as swiftly as possible. By employing three specially trained walkers to follow the blazed trail the Penns were able to extend their claim almost sixty miles into Delaware territory, far beyond the limits intended by the Delaware chiefs.

Nearly 1,200 square miles were now in the hands of the Penns. Ten square miles were graciously set aside as an Indian reservation. But Nutimus and the other Delaware leaders, bitter at this latest evidence of white dishonesty, refused to move off their land. Hundreds of white settlers began pouring in as small tracts of land were sold by the Penns and by Logan, who had foresightedly made large purchases in the area. The solution to impending conflict was to pay the Iroquois to remove the Delawares. "We now expect from You," signaled Pennsylvania's governor in 1741, "that you will cause these Indians to remove from the Lands in the forks of the Delaware and not give any further Disturbance to the Persons who are now in Possession."[29]

One year later Iroquois representatives gathered in Philadelphia to fulfill their pledge. At a grand council attended by Delaware and Iroquois chiefs and officials of the Pennsylvania government, the Iroquois spokesmen signified a fundamental fact in Indian-white relations: that while English colonists sometimes had the power to swindle, dominate, or subjugate native peoples singlehandedly, they often relied on intertribal hostility and the avidity of Indians for European trade goods to obtain the support of powerful tribes in contests against weaker tribes. "Cousins," expostulated the Iroquois orator,

> Let this Belt of Wampum serve to Chastize You; You ought to be taken by the Hair of the Head and shaked severely till you recover your Senses and become Sober; you don't know what Ground you stand on, nor what you are doing. . . . We have seen with our Eyes a Deed signed by nine of your Ancestors above fifty years ago for this very Land, and a Release Sign'd not many Years since by some of yourselves and Chiefs now living to the Number of 15 or Upwards. But how came you to take upon you to Sell Land at all? We conquer'd You, we made Women of you, you know you are Women, and can no more sell Land than Women. Nor is it fitt you should have the Power of Selling Lands since you would abuse it. This

29Weslager, *Delaware Indians*, p. 190.

land that you Claim is gone through Your Guts. You have been furnished with Cloaths and Meat and Drink by the Goods paid you for it, and now You want it again like Children as you are. . . . For all these reasons we charge You to remove instantly. We don't give you the liberty to think about it. You are Women; take the Advice of a Wise Man and remove immediately. . . . Depart the Council and consider what has been said to you.[30]

With this withering blast from the Iroquois, the Delawares were stripped of their options. For several generations they had recognized themselves as subordinate to the Iroquois. But the tie had been reciprocal, for if the Delawares recognized the authority of the Iroquois in matters of war and diplomacy, the Iroquois also counted on the Delawares as one of the southern "posts" of their league and respected Delaware management of their own land affairs. Now the Delawares left Philadelphia humiliated by their former protectors and bereft of autonomy in their internal affairs. The Iroquois, lavishly entertained for their intercession, left Philadelphia with a train of borrowed horses and wagons burdened down with shoes, stockings, hats, blankets, hatchets, hoes, and other goods. James Logan and the proprietors of Pennsylvania left with title to enough land to provide them with handsome incomes for years. The retreating Delawares would not forget, however, The taunts of the Iroquois that they were women and children would still ring in their ears a dozen years later when they were among the first of the western tribes allied to the French to deliver a series of devastating strikes along the Pennsylvania frontier at the outset of the French and Indian War.

South Carolina-Indian Relations

To the south of the Chesapeake another configuration of forces in the early eighteenth century eliminated all but fragments of the coastal tribes. In the first period of settlement in South Carolina most of the Westos and Savannahs had been destroyed or sold into slavery as the Carolina proprietors and independent merchants in the colony struggled for control of the Indian trade. The proprietors accurately charged in 1695 that the slave dealers had obtained control of the governor's council and "have made warrs and peace with the Indians as it best suited their private advantage in trade."[31] Those upon whom the proprietors had counted most had used their power to subvert proprietary Indian policy

[30]*Minutes of the Provincial Council of Pennsylvania* (16 vols.; Philadelphia and Harrisburg, 1851–53), 4: 578–80.
[31]Quoted in Verner W. Crane, *Southern Frontier, 1670–1732* (Ann Arbor: University of Michigan Press, 1956), p. 120.

for their own advantage. But in the early eighteenth century, in a movement reminiscent of Bacon's defiance of Governor Berkeley's circle, which
had monopolized the Indian trade in Virginia, a group of lesser mer=
chants challenged the control of the Indian trade by the governor and his
councilors. Using the lower house of the legislature as their fulcrum of
power, they attempted to shatter the grip on the lucrative trade held by
those above them. By 1707 the governor was complaining of "the Multitude of Indian traders that now more and more pester the Trade with
their Numbers for their own advantage."[32] But the multitude could not
be staunched. They not only sent more and more of their own Indian
agents into the interior, but they wrested control of Indian policy from
the Council and placed it in the hands of the Assembly.

The new traders, advertising themselves as reformers, unveiled plans
for a careful regulation of the trade. Flagrant abuses such as using alcohol
to numb Indians into unfair contracts and urging them to attack and
enslave tribes friendly to the colony were to end. The governor's son-in-
law and trading partner, James Child, they pointed out, had only recently
sent the Cherokees against some friendly Indians and rewarded them
richly when they brought about 160 slaves to the Charleston slave market.
Instituted in 1707, the reform plan called for "Regulating the Indian
Trade and making it Safe to the Public." All traders were to be licensed
and their activities placed under the supervision of a board of Indian
Commissioners. The traditional techniques of traders—enslaving friendly
Indians, selling rum, and running up enormous Indian debts which could
be used to place the trading Indians in semibondage—were all to be dis-
continued.

To what extent the legislature really intended to reform the Indian
trade, which was yielding enormous profits to those who controlled it, is
not known. Whatever the intentions, the reforms proposed were singularly ineffective. Transferring regulation of the Indian trade from the
provincial councillors to members of the popular assembly party multiplied rather than lessened the abuses. In fact, it was in the years following the reform act of 1707 that arrogance, dishonesty, and abuse in the
trade became so oppressive that they touched off the Tuscarora War of
1711.

The Tuscarora War

The Tuscaroras were a numerous people living in North Carolina in
large villages and "castles" where they gathered hemp, grew crops, and

---

[32]*Ibid.*

tended orchards on tidewater plantations which they had cultivated for generations. For years neighboring tribes, allied with Virginia and South Carolina traders, had raided their villages, stealing their children and selling them to the white slave traders. In 1709 they had watched a swarm of Germans and Swiss, led by a displaced count, Baron de Graffenried, invade their lands with the tacit consent of the provincial government. In local trade they also found that they could expect little from the European's sense of justice. But they recognized the difficulties of forging a pan-Indian alliance and were not unaware of what had happened to those who resorted to force against the colonial settlers. Better than this, they decided, was to migrate northward to Pennsylvania where they might obtain refuge in Penn's Quaker colony. In June 1710 they met at Conestoga with representatives of the Pennsylvania council and the Iroquois League under whose protection they wished to place themselves. Their hopes were shattered, however, for the Pennsylvania government stalled and offered no immediate promises of providing refuge.

Finding withdrawal impossible, the Tuscaroras gathered as many local tribes with similar grievances as possible—Corees, Pamlicos, Matamuskeets, and others—and fell on the European encroachers. About 130 English and Germans were killed in the initial attack. Boiling with internal dissension and as yet thinly populated, North Carolina turned to neighboring colonies for help since she had only a ragtag militia to send against the Indian attackers. Virginia's government promised clothing and money but no men, for the Virginians were not ready to sacrifice their lives to defend the North Carolinians with whom they were bitterly arguing about border land rights. But in South Carolina the embattled North Carolinians found the assistance they needed. Historians have traditionally sung the praises of the South Carolina government for coming to the rescue of her northern neighbors and for assuming "the financial and military burdens" of the war, as one historian has put it.[33] The truth of the matter is that the Indian slave traders of South Carolina gladly entered the fray because they sniffed profit in the breeze. Colonel John Barnwell, an important merchant in the South Carolina Indian trade, led an army of almost 500 men into Tuscarora country. But the army included only thirty whites, for the South Carolinians intended their Indian allies, especially the Yamasees, to do most of the fighting for them. What ultimately lay behind the offer of assistance to the beleaguered North Carolinians was the chance to defeat the Tuscaroras and enslave large numbers of them for sale on the West Indian market. Before Barnwell reached the Tuscarora forts in January 1712 many of the Indians

---

[33]M. Eugene Sirmans, *Colonial South Carolina; A Political History* (Chapel Hill: University of North Carolina Press, 1966), p. 111.

in his army had deserted. But the remainder of the force defeated one group of Tuscaroras and took thirty slaves. To Barnwell's dismay, however, his Yamasee allies deserted with their prizes. "While we were putting the [Tuscarora] men to the Sword," he lamented, "our Indians got all the slaves and plunder, only one girl we got."[34]

Barnwell moved on to destroy hundreds of Tuscarora houses and take several prisoners whom, as he recorded in his journal, were "ordered immediately to be burned alive."[35] Barnwell attempted later to storm another Tuscarora fort, but finding his own forces weakened and badly supplied he arranged a truce. Faced with returning to South Carolina with only a handful of slaves, he broke the truce and scoured the countryside for additional prisoners on his way back to South Carolina. In response to this violation of the truce the Tuscaroras renewed their attacks and the South Carolinians were again invited to enrich themselves by helping their neighbors. A special representative of the North Carolina government, urging a second expedition, advertised the "great advantage [that] may be made of Slaves there being many hundreds of women and children, many we believe 3 or 4 thousand."[36] Undismayed by the wracking dissensions within the North Carolina government, the South Carolinians harked to the advice of their governor, who averred: "What we have already done [in the first expedition] and the return [response] they have made might discourage us from giving them any further assistance, but we act upon nobler principles than to involve the innocent with the Guilty. . . . "[37]

The second expedition was led by another Indian slave merchant, James Moore, a veteran of slaving expeditions in Spanish Florida. Moore recruited an army composed of 33 white colonists and nearly nine hundred Cherokees, Yamasees, Creeks, and Catawbas. Storming the Tuscarora fort at Nooherooka in March 1713, they soundly defeated the North Carolina tribe. Several hundred of the enemy were burned alive in the fort; 166 men regarded as unsuitable for slavery were captured and killed; and 392 Tuscaroras, mostly women and children, were led back to the Charleston slave market. The South Carolina attackers had suffered 57 casualties—22 whites and 35 Indians. In the course of the war the loss of Tuscarora life was estimated at nearly one thousand and as many as 700 may have been enslaved.[38] The scattered remnants of the tribe drifted

---

[34]Quoted in Chapman J. Milling, *Red Carolinians* (Chapel Hill: University of North Carolina Press, 1940), p. 119.
[35]*Ibid.*, p. 120.
[36]*Ibid.*, p. 128.
[37]*Ibid.*
[38]Crane, *Southern Frontier*, p. 161.

northward in the aftermath of the war, seeking shelter under the wing of the Iroquois.

The Yamasee War

Two years after the Yamasees had participated in the defeat and enslavement of the white man's enemies in North Carolina, they were themselves providing the leadership for the largest and most successful anti-European resistance movement in the eighteenth-century history of the southern colonies. Their ability to spearhead a pan-Indian uprising that encompassed not only many of the fragmented remains of the coastal cultures but the powerful and populous interior tribes—Creeks, Choctaws, and Cherokees—brought them as close to wiping out the white colonists as ever native Americans came in the colonial period. Only the last-minute success of the Carolinians in winning the Cherokees to their side saved the colony from an Indian resistance movement that according to the South Carolina assembly included fifteen Indian nations with a total population of more than 30,000.

The Yamasees, like almost every other southern tribe, had eagerly sought trade connections with the English and then lived to regret the dependency fostered by the trade. Even while the Yamasees were attacking weaker tribes in order to supply the Charleston slave traders and were helping the Carolinians subdue the Tuscaroras, they were reaching the desperation point in their relations with the English settlers. Cattle raisers in the coastal area south of Charleston intruded so rapidly in the first decade of the eighteenth century that the Carolina government was obliged to pass an act in 1707 "to Limit the Bounds of the Yamasee Settlement, to prevent Persons from Disturbing them with their Stocks." Despite the argument that the act was designed to help the Yamasees, the real intention, as its title indicated, was to restrict the Indians to reservations in order to open up the rest of the land to white settlers. Three years later the Carolina authorities were struggling with intruders who were taking up land within the territory reserved for the Yamasees.

Even more oppressive were the Indian traders upon whom the Yamasee people had come to depend. The Indian commissioners listened to report after report "of the callous brutality of some of the traders, of petty thieving, of illegal enslavement of free Indians, of the abuse of rum to facilitate sharp dealing, of the use of cheating weights," and, as a Virginia Indian trader informed his London agent in 1715, of the debauching of Indian women when their men were on deer-hunting and slave-raiding expeditions.[39] That the Yamasees were being reduced to a form of peon-

[39]*Ibid.*, pp. 165–66.

age by 1711 was indicated by a report to the Indian Commissioners in that year that they were in debt to the amount of 100,000 skins—the equivalent of four or five years of hunting. When Charleston traders began seizing Yamasee women and children to be sold as slaves in partial payment of these debts, the Yamasees revolted.

The Yamasee attack on Good Friday, April 15, 1715, was carefully co-ordinated with the inland Creeks who had been equally exploited in the trade. One of the three largest interior tribes, the Creeks were spurred on by the French, who had been building forts and trading posts in the lower Mississippi valley since 1701 and trying to woo the Creeks away from the English. It may have been the emerging Creek leader, Brims of Coweta, who planned the attacks in a general strategy to drive the Europeans out of the Southeast. All along the border settlements and wherever traders resided, the Creeks and Yamasees struck, aided by lesser tribes of the coastal plain such as the Saraws, Catawbas, Congarees, Caccamaws, Apalachees, and Santees. Refugees poured into Charleston during the summer of 1715, as the Carolina government tried desperately to patch together a military force from planters, indentured servants, slaves, and volunteers from Virginia and North Carolina. Supplies arrived even from far-off New England as the authorities in Charleston issued gloomy predictions that if the Carolinians succumbed, Indian tribes all over the continent would be inspired to hurl themselves at white coastal settlements. By June, 1715, the *Boston News-Letter* reported that about 90 of the 100 Indian traders in South Carolina had succumbed to the Indians' wrath.

The Carolinians mounted effective counterattacks on the Yamasees in the fall of 1715, but the more numerous Creeks were still carrying the torch to every settlement they could reach. More dangerous, it was learned that they were negotiating with the Cherokees, the largest Indian nation neighboring the southern colonies. Residing in the mountainous southern Appalachia area, the Cherokees, according to an estimate in 1715, could muster nearly 4,000 warriors and boasted a total population four times as large. During the first half-year of the war the Cherokees had remained neutral, but the chances of the hard-pressed Carolinians seemed to rest on obtaining their support or at least preventing a Creek-Cherokee alliance. Thus in an evenly matched struggle, the Cherokees occupied a pivotal position, as was apparent by the frantic attempts of both sides to secure their pledge of allegiance.

The Cherokees themselves recognized the momentous importance of their decision and wavered back and forth, first agreeing to an alliance with the English in August 1715, but then failing to appear for a scheduled November offensive against the Creeks. Realizing that dramatic action was necessary, the Carolina government sent a military expedition of 300 men, including one company of black slaves, deep into the mountainous Cherokee country in order to galvanize the vacillating Indian nation. While the expedition leaders pressed the Cherokees for a commitment, a dozen Creek headmen were also haranguing the Cherokee chiefs and arguing for a joint attack on the white army camped in the woods. The Cherokees were split between a war party and a peace party and when the war party prevailed, they fell on the Creek emissaries and killed them. It was the Cherokees' dependency on English trade goods that finally swung them against the Creeks. As they told the Carolinians, unless they were at war with the Creeks "they should have no way in geting of Slaves to buy amunition and Clothing" from the white traders.[40]

With the Cherokees arrayed against them, the Creeks decided to abandon the towns they had settled in eastern Carolina in order to be nearer the source of English trade goods and to migrate back to their old townsites on the Chattahoochee River. To replace their trading and military connections with the English they sought new links to the French on the Alabama River and the Spanish in Florida. Similarly, the remaining Yamasees fled south to join the Spanish in Florida.

For white Carolinians, the flight of the Creeks and Yamasees left new lands open for the taking. But their thirst for revenge, in a war that cost them more than 400 lives and £400,000, was nearly unquenchable. "Many of the Yammonses and Creek Indians," wrote an Anglican clergyman in the colony, "were against the war all along; But our Military Men are so bent upon Revenge, and so desirous to enrich themselves, by making all the Indians Slaves that fall into their hands, but such as they kill (without making the least distinction between the guilty and the innocent, and without considering the Barbarous usage these poor Savages met with from our vilainous Traders) that it is in vain to represent to them the Cruelty and injustice of Such a procedure."[41]

The Yamasee War defined both the limits of white economic exploitation and the limitations of Indian resistance. Nowhere in colonial America was naked exploitation of the indigenous people less restrained by church, government, or the attitudes of the people than in South Carolina. By 1717 an insignificant population of only about 1,500 males had succeeded in employing the larger tribes to enslave and shatter nearly a dozen small coastal tribes and then had driven a wedge between the Creeks and Cherokees at the moment when an alliance between them might have ended English presence in the region. Throughout this process, covering almost a half-century, the primary weapon of the English had been trade goods. For despite the extraordinary abuses in the Indian trade and the devastating toll that slave raiding took on tribes as far west

40*Ibid.*, p. 182.
41*Ibid.*, p. 179n.

as the Mississippi, it was only with great reluctance, usually accompanied by internal division, that tribes of the Carolina region turned on those who supplied them with European goods.

As in other parts of the continent the key to English success, in an area where they were greatly outnumbered, was the promotion of intertribal hostility. This was not only instrumental in the procurement of slaves, who could be profitably sold in New England and the West Indies, but was a major factor in depopulating tribes whose land then became more accessible to the settlers. This doubly disastrous effect of the English connection became the basis of French attempts to win the Creeks to their side. Since the closing years of the seventeenth century the French had been building forts and establishing contacts with the interior tribes. As early as 1702, Pierre le Moyne Iberville, the architect of the French empire in Louisiana, parleyed with chiefs from the warring Choctaw and Chickasaw nations and attempted to expose the destructive nature of the English connection. For almost a decade, he pointed out, the Chickasaws had allied themselves with the Charleston traders, using English guns to raid the Choctaws and selling the captives they took in order to procure still more guns and ammunition. In the course of taking about five hundred slaves, the Chickasaws had killed more than 1,800 Choctaws and lost some 800 of their own warriors. Englishmen delighted in this arrangement, he explained, for they built their fortunes on the trade in slaves and guns while watching the Choctaws and Chickasaws decimate each other. When the two tribes had sufficiently weakened each other they would no longer be able to protect their land from the English settlers, whose strength grew with the death of every Indian, whether friend or enemy. Iberville offered peaceful trade with both nations, not for slaves but for deerskins.

For the land-hungry English cattle raisers and rice growers of eastern Carolina, who were importing slaves from Africa in ever-growing numbers by the early eighteenth century, the Indian slave trade had no direct benefits since the profits accumulated in the hands of the Charleston merchants. But the secondary benefits were invaluable, for the Indian population of the lower South followed a downward trajectory as a result of the slave trade and thus facilitated southward and westward expansion from the initial settlements in the vicinity of Charleston. The extent of the Indian slave trade is masked in obscurity. But it is certain that while it decreased in the eighteenth century, when the importation of Africans increased from a trickle to a flood, the number enslaved reached into the tens of thousands in the half-century after Carolina was settled by Europeans. The only South Carolina slave census in the colonial period was in 1708 and it estimated about 1,400 Indian slaves among about one thousand white families. But the colonial records, without providing exact figures, indicate that a far greater number were shipped to other colonies, especially to the West Indies. Though exactitude in these matters is unobtainable, a conservative estimate might place the loss in Indian population due to death and enslavement during the first half-century of English settlement at about 50 percent.

When the Creeks, Yamasees, and others revolted against the Charleston traders and their agents in the interior, they came as close as Indian tribes were ever to come in the colonial period to overwhelming the Europeans who had entrapped through cultivating a dependency upon European weapons and other trade goods. Using English guns purchased with Indian slaves, they turned on those who had supplied them. Out of a white population of about six thousand the Indians were able to inflict casualties of about 7 percent in the Yamasee War, almost twice as high proportionately as in New England during Metacom's War. But neither Creeks nor Yamasees nor any other tribe was willing to storm the Europeans at Charleston once the outlying settlements and isolated Indian traders had been destroyed. This called for siege or a massive assault—European forms of warfare which the Indians never adopted. When the Cherokees refused to join the Creeks, the English policy of divide and rule, practiced so extensively in the New World, prevailed. When the English promised them a shower of trade goods for their help, the Cherokees accepted the payoff rather than risk a prolonged war with the Europeans. Even with the best opportunity since the arrival of the English at hand, the Cherokees chose to assist rather than to assault the white colonists. But in the aftermath of war, consistent with the calculation of their own interests, they turned their backs on the Carolina trade, opening a trade with Virginia and haughtily telling their former partners, as a Carolina trader wrote, that "they valued us of Carolina no more than dirt."[42]

The process of decimation, dispossession, and decline among the Indian cultures of the coastal areas was thus accomplished in different ways during the first century of English colonization. In New England and on the Chesapeake the demise was almost complete by the time English settlement was beginning in Pennsylvania and South Carolina. It had come in the north after steady resistance from the stronger tribes, who finally succumbed in pitched battle to an enemy that sought no genuine accommodation with them and was able to keep enough tribes out of the fray to prevail in a war of attrition. In Virginia and Maryland another course of events defeated the coastal cultures. Here the Indians genuinely

[42]Quoted in W. Stitt Robinson, "Virginia and the Cherokees: Indian Policy from Spotswood to Dinwiddie," in *The Old Dominion: Essays for Thomas Perkins Abernethy*, ed. Darrett B. Rutman (Charlottesville: University Press of Virginia, 1964), p. 30.

strove for accommodation following the unsuccessful resistance movements of 1622 and 1644. But as in New England their inability to function in any way that served European society finally led to conflict initiated by whites. Even as a friendly colonized people they were obstacles
in the path of Bacon and his followers.

In Pennsylvania still another variation in the process of decline occurred, for here the English employed Indian allies rather than brute
force to displace the Delawares of eastern Pennsylvania. It was power
diplomacy not military power that became the chief weapon in the white
arsenal, but it must be remembered that it was a policy which the Iroquois found as beneficial as the Pennsylvanians. The process occurred a
half-century later than in New England and Virginia because the middle-
Atlantic region was settled late and in the first decades of settlement
Quaker relations with the Delawares were governed by Penn's peaceful
policy. Moreover, the absence of an active fur trade and competition for
land greatly reduced the chances of friction. But when European refugees
from intolerance and oppression flocked to Pennsylvania the Indians once
again became only an obstacle to white colonization. To both the land
speculators of Philadelphia and the German and Scotch-Irish farmers the
Indian became an unwelcome nuisance. In South Carolina it was not
dead Indians but Indians alive and in chains that benefitted the white
settlers. The buildup of the white population was slow enough and the
desire among the Indians for trade goods intense enough that the white
Carolinians could watch the coastal tribes obliterate each other in the
wars for slaves and when they were exhausted attempt to employ the same
strategy with the more powerful interior tribes.

The result was roughly the same in all the colonies along the seaboard.
By the 1680s in the older colonies and by the 1720s in the newer ones, the
coastal tribes were shattered. Decimated by disease and warfare, the surviving members of these tribes either incorporated themselves as subjects
of stronger inland groups or entered the white man's world as detribal-
ized servile dependents. The Indian's failure to survive was not an unwillingness or inability to intermix with the European newcomers—learning their languages, intermingling with them, adapting to their methods
of trade and negotiation—as some historians have argued. His failure,
rather, was to adapt too well to the material culture of the colonizers. It
was the attachment to European trade goods and the persistence of ancient intertribal hostilities that thwarted pan-Indian resistance, which
alone could have insured the survival of the coastal cultures once it became apparent that their value as trading partners was incidental in
comparison with the value of the land which their destruction would
convert to European ownership.

But while they were decimated and defeated, the coastal cultures performed a major service for the tribes farther inland. Their prolonged resistance gave the interior cultures time to adapt to the European presence and to devise strategies of survival as the westward-moving frontier approached them. "People like the Iroquois," writes T.J.C. Brasser, "owed a great deal to the resistance of the coastal Algonkians, and both peoples were well aware of this."[43] The coastal tribes provided a buffer between them and the Europeans and when the coastal tribes lost their political autonomy, their remnants were often incorporated into the larger interior tribes. These were important factors in the far stronger resistance that the interior Indians offered to European encroachment— a resistance so effective that for the first century and a half of European colonization, the white newcomers were confined to the coastal plain, unable to penetrate the Appalachians where the interior tribes, often allied with the French, held sway.

[43]Brasser, "The Coastal Algonkians," p. 73.

chapter 7

Europe, Africa, and the New World

In the judgment of most historians the African slave trade, beginning in the late fifteenth century and continuing for the next four hundred years, is one of the most important phenomena in the history of the modern world. Besides the obvious fact that it involved the largest forced migration in history, the slave trade and slavery were crucially important in building the colonial empires of European nations and in generating the wealth that later produced the Industrial Revolution. But often overlooked in the attention given to the economic importance of the slave trade and slavery is the cultural diffusion that took place when ten million Africans were brought to the western hemisphere. As slaves, Africans were Europeanized; but at the same time they Africanized the culture of Europeans in the Americas. This was an inevitable, if often overlooked, part of the convergence of these two broad groups of people, who met each other an ocean away from their original homelands.

Just as they were late colonizing the New World, the English lagged far behind their Spanish and Portuguese competitors in making contact with the West Coast of Africa, in entering the Atlantic slave trade, and in establishing African slaves as the backbone of the labor force in their overseas plantations. And among the English colonies in the New World, those on the mainland of North America were a half-century or more behind those in the Caribbean in converting their plantation economies to slave labor. By 1670, for example, Portuguese Brazil had at least 200,000 slaves; English Barbados had about 20,000; but Virginia contained only some 2,000. Cultural interaction of Europeans and Africans did not begin in North America on a large scale until more than a century after it had begun in the southerly parts of the hemisphere. Much that occurred as the two cultures met in the Iberian colonies was later repeated in the Anglo-African interaction; and yet the patterns of acculturation were markedly different in North and South America in the seventeenth and eighteenth centuries.

Early Slave Trade

A half-century before Columbus crossed the Atlantic, a Portuguese sea captain, Antam Goncalvez, made the first European landing on the west African coast south of the Sahara. What he might have seen, had he been able to travel the length and breadth of Africa, was a continent of extraordinary variation in geography and culture. Little he might have seen would have caused him to believe that a natural inferiority characterized African cultures or that the peoples of Africa had failed to develop over time as had the peoples of Europe. This notion of "backwardness" and cultural impoverishment was the myth perpetuated after the slave trade had transported millions of Africans to the Western Hemisphere. It was a myth which served to justify the cruelties of the slave trade and to assuage the guilt of European nations involved in the largest forced dislocation of people in history.

The peoples of Africa may have numbered more than 100 million in the late fifteenth century when Europeans began making extensive contact with the continent. They lived in widely varied ecological zones—in vast deserts, in grasslands, and in great forests and woodlands. As in Europe, most people lived as agriculturalists and struggled to subdue the forces of nature so as to sustain life. That the African population increased so rapidly in the two thousand years before European arrival suggests the sophistication of the African agricultural methods. Part of this skill in farming derived from the Africans' skill in iron production, which had begun in present-day Nigeria about 500 B.C. It was this ability to fashion iron implements that triggered the new farming techniques necessary to sustain larger populations. With larger populations came greater specialization of tasks and thus additional technical improvements. Small groups of related families made contact with other such groups and over time evolved into larger and more complicated societies. The pattern was similar to what had occurred in other parts of the world—in North America, Europe, the Middle East, and elsewhere—when the "agricultural revolution" occurred.

From recent studies of "precontact" African history, it is apparent that the "culture gap" between European and African societies was not very large when the two peoples met. By the time Europeans reached the coast of West Africa a number of extraordinary empires had been forged in the area. The first, apparently, was the Kingdom of Ghana, which embraced the immense territory between the Sahara desert and the Gulf of Guinea and from the Niger River to the Atlantic Ocean between the sixth and tenth centuries. Extensive urban settlement, advanced architecture, elaborate art, and a highly complex political organization evolved during this time. From the eighth to the sixteenth century it was the western Sudan that supplied most of the gold for the western world. Invasion from the north by the Moors weakened the Empire of Ghana, which in time gave way to the Empire of Mali. At the center of the Mali Empire was the city of Timbuktu, noted for its extensive wealth and its Islamic university where a faculty as distinguished as any in Europe had gathered.

Lesser kingdoms such as the Kingdoms of Kongo and Benin had also been in the process of growth and cultural change for centuries before Europeans reached Africa. Their inhabitants were skilled in metal working, weaving, ceramics, architecture, and aesthetic expression. Many of their towns rivalled European cities in size. Some communities of West Africa had highly complex religious rites, well-organized regional trade, codes of law, and complex political organization.

Of course, cultural development in Africa, as elsewhere in the world, proceeded at varying rates. Ecological conditions had a large effect on this. Where good soil, adequate rainfall, and abundance of minerals were present, as in coastal West Africa, the population growth and cultural elaboration was relatively rapid. Where desert conditions or nearly impenetrable forest held forth, social systems remained small and changed at a crawl. Contact with other cultures also brought rapid change whereas isolation impeded cultural evolution. The Empire of Ghana bloomed in western Sudan partly because of the trading contacts with Arabs who had conquered the area about the ninth century. Cultural change began to accelerate in Swahili societies facing the Indian Ocean after trading contacts were initiated with the Eastern world in the ninth century. Thus, as a leading African historian has put it, "the cultural history of Africa is . . . one of greatly unequal development among peoples who, for definable reasons such as these, entered recognizably similar stages of institutional change at different times."[1]

The slave trade seems to have begun in 1472 when a Portuguese captain, Ruy do Sequeira, reached the Coast of Benin and was conducted to the King's court, where he received royal permission to trade for gold, ivory, and slaves. So far as the Africans were concerned, the trade represented no strikingly new economic activity since they had been long involved in regional and long-distance trade across their continent. This was simply the opening of contacts with a new and more distant commercial partner. This is important to note because frequently it has been mistakenly understood that European powers raided the African coasts for slaves and kidnapped hundreds of thousands of helpless and hapless victims. In actuality, the early slave trade was a reciprocal relationship between European purchasers and African sellers. Moreover, trading itself was confined to coastal trade centers where slaves, many captured in the interior, were brought by African agents and sold on terms which the African sellers set. In return for gold, ivory, and slaves, Africans received European guns, bars of iron and copper, brass pots and tankards, beads, rum, and textiles.

Slavery was not a new social phenomenon for either Europeans or Africans. For centuries African societies had been involved in an overland slave trade which transported black slaves from West Africa across the Sahara Desert to Roman Europe and the Middle East. But this was an occasional rather than a systematic trade and it was designed to provide the trading nations of the Mediterranean with soldiers, household servants, and artisans rather than mass agricultural labor. Within Africa itself, slavery had also existed from a very early period, but the scale of it was small and it involved personal service, often for a limited period of time, rather than lifelong, degraded, agricultural labor. Slavery of a similar sort had existed for centuries in Europe, mostly as the result of Christians enslaving Moslems and Moslems enslaving Christians during centuries of religious wars. One became a slave by being an "outsider" or an "infidel," by being captured in war, by voluntarily selling oneself into slavery to obtain money for one's family, or by committing certain heinous crimes. The rights of slaves were restricted and their opportunities for upward movement severely circumscribed, but slaves nevertheless were regarded as members of society, enjoying protection under the law and entitled to certain rights, including education, marriage, and parenthood. Most importantly, the status of slave was not irrevocable and was not automatically passed on to his or her children.

[1] Basil Davidson, *The African Genius* (Boston: Little, Brown and Company, 1969), p. 187.

Thus we find that slavery flourished in ancient Greece and Rome, in the Aztec and Inca empires, in African societies, in early modern Russia, in eastern Europe, and in the Middle East. It had gradually died out in Western Europe by the fourteenth century, although the status of serf was not too different in social reality from that of the slave. It is important to note that in all these regions slavery and serfdom had nothing to do with racial characteristics.

When the African slave trade began in the fifteenth century, it served to fill what was only a minor labor shortage in the economies of its European initiators—Spain and Portugal. Only a trickle of slaves could be absorbed into the domestic economies of the southern European countries; it was African gold, ivory, and pepper that commanded European attention. It is possible, therefore, that were it not for the colonization of the New World the early slave trade might have ceased after a century or more, and been remembered simply as a short-lived incident stemming from early European contacts with Africa at a particular point in history.

With the discovery of the New World by Europeans the course of history was abruptly changed. Once Europeans found the gold and silver mines of Mexico and Peru, and later when they discovered a new form of gold in the production of sugar and tobacco, a vast new demand for human labor was created. At first Indians seemed to be the obvious source of manpower and in some areas Spaniards and Portuguese were able to coerce native populations into agricultural and mining labor forces. But European diseases ravaged native populations and in some areas it was found that the Indian, far more at home in his environment than the white colonizer, was a difficult person to subjugate. Indentured white labor from the mother country was another way of meeting the demand for labor but this source, it was discovered, was far too limited. It was to Africa that colonizing Europeans ultimately resorted. Formerly a new source of trade, the continent now became transformed in the European mind into the repository of vast supplies of human labor—"black gold."

From the late fifteenth to the mid-nineteenth centuries—a period of almost four hundred years—Africans were brought out of their ancestral homelands to fill the labor needs in the European colonies of North and South America and the Caribbean. The most recent estimates place the numbers involved at about ten million people, although as many more may have lost their lives while being marched from the African interior to the coastal trading forts or during the "middle passage" across the Atlantic. Even before the English had arrived on the Chesapeake in 1607 several hundred thousand slaves had been transported to the West Indian and South American colonies of Spain and Portugal. Before the slave trade was outlawed in the nineteenth century far more Africans than

Europeans would have crossed the Atlantic Ocean and taken up life in the New World.

The Atlantic slave trade, designed to furnish the New World plantations of the European powers with a massive labor force, completely altered the ancient slave trade as well as the nature of slavery. For about a century after Goncalvez brought back the first African captives to Portugal in 1441, the slave trade was relatively slight. The slaves whom other Africans sold to Europeans were drawn from a small minority of the population and for the most part were individuals captured in war or whose criminal acts had cost them their rights of citizenship. For Europeans the African slave trade could provide for small-scale labor needs, just as the Black Sea slave trade had done before it was shut off by the fall of Constantinople to the Turks in 1453. Even in the New World plantations, slaves were not in great demand for almost a century after "discovery." Not until the Portuguese succeeded in developing large sugar plantations on the northeastern coastal plains in the late sixteenth century did the New World demand for African slaves begin to intensify. From there sugar cultivation spread rapidly to the tiny specks of land dotting the Caribbean. It was between 1630 and 1680 that most of the Caribbean possessions of England, France, Holland, and Spain were transformed into sugar colonies where small numbers of white settlers ruled over masses of African slaves.

The regularization of the slave trade, brought about by the vast new demand for a New World labor supply and by a reciprocally higher demand in Africa for European trade goods, changed the problem of obtaining slaves. In the face of the accelerating seventeenth-century demand, criminals and "outsiders" in sufficient number could not be found. Therefore African kings were obliged to resort to raids and warfare as a way of obtaining "black gold" with which to trade. European guns abetted the process. Thus, the spread of kidnapping and warfare became intricately connected with the establishment of commercial relations with European powers.

For the Europeans the slave trade itself became an immensely profitable enterprise. In the several centuries of intensive slave trading that followed the establishment of New World sugar plantations, European nations warred constantly for trading advantages on the West African coast. The coastal forts, the focal points of the trade, became key strategic targets in the successive wars of empire. The great Portuguese slaving fort at Elmina on the Gold Coast, begun in 1481, was captured more than a century and a half later by the Dutch. The primary fort on the Guinea coast, started by the Swedes, passed through the hands of the Danes, the English, and the Dutch between 1652 and 1664. Obtaining rights to the slave trade on the African coast and obtaining monopolies for supplying European plantations in the New World with their annual quotas of slaves became a major issue of European diplomacy in the seventeenth and eighteenth centuries. It was the Dutch who were the primary victors in the seventeenth century battle for the West African slave coast; for most of the century a majority of slaves who were being fed into the expanding New World markets found themselves crossing the Atlantic in Dutch ships.

Not until the last third of the seventeenth century were the English of any importance in the slave trade or in the demand for slaves in their North American colonies. English attempts to break into the profitable trade began in a serious way only in 1663, when Charles II, recently restored to the English throne, granted a charter to the Royal Adventurers to Africa, a joint-stock company headed by the king's brother, the Duke of York. Superseded by the Royal African Company in 1672, these companies enjoyed the exclusive right to carry slaves to England's overseas plantations. For thirty-four years after 1663 each of the slaves they brought across the Atlantic bore the brand *"DY"* for the Duke of York, who himself became king in 1685. In 1698 the Royal African Company's monopoly was broken due to the pressure on Parliament by individual merchants who demanded their rights as Englishmen to participate in the lucrative trade. Thrown open to individual entrepreneurs, the English slave trade grew enormously. In the 1680s the Royal African Company had been exporting about five to six thousand slaves annually. In the first decade of free trade the annual average rose above twenty thousand. For the remainder of the eighteenth century English involvement in the trade increased until by the 1790s England had become the foremost slave trading nation in Europe.[2]

How did Europeans of different national origins respond to Africans, as slavery and the slave trade became an intimate part of the colonizing experience in the New World? English reactions to Africans were probably stronger and more negative than those of the Spanish and Portuguese. Though all European countries regarded their civilization as vastly superior to African societies, the Spanish and Portuguese were long familiar with darker-skinned people through centuries of trade and war with people from the Mediterranean Middle Eastern, and North African worlds. But the fair-skinned English, brought face to face with the literally black Africans, seem to have reacted in a particularly negative way. Perhaps it was an unfortunate accident of history that even before Africa had been heard of blackness had become a way of expressing some of the

[2]These statistics on the slave trade, and others that follow are taken from Philip D. Curtin, *The Atlantic Slave Trade: A Census* (Madison: University of Wisconsin Press, 1969).

most ingrained values in English society. "Black" and its opposite, "white," were words with heavy emotional content. Black meant foul, wicked, malignant; it represented night, a time of fear, and thus became associated with the most anxiety-producing aspects of human nature. In English usage black became a partisan word. A black sheep in the family, a black mark against one's name, a black day, a black look, a black lie, a blackguard, and a blackball all were expressions built into the cultural consciousness. White, by contrast, represented purity, virginity, beauty, virtue, and peace. Angels were garbed in white; girls married in white to signify their virginity; the dove of peace was white. Thus Englishmen were culturally conditioned to see evil and ugliness in blackness. In this sense their encounter with the people of West Africa was partially pre-determined by the symbols of color built into English language and culture. The symbology of color was equally a part of Iberian culture but its effects on racial consciousness were tempered by the long associations which the Spanish and Portuguese had had with darker-hued people.

Compounding the negative image were the "heathenism" and the "savagery" of the Africans, as Englishmen viewed them. The reaction of Englishmen in this regard very closely paralleled their response to Indians of North America. The Africans' ignorance of Christianity—their worship of "false Gods"—and their different way of life marked them off from the "civilized" Europeans, just as it had distinguished them from the indigenous people of the New World.

Of course even the most negative impressions of Africans would have been of little historical significance, warranting only a short footnote in the annals of cultural history, if Englishmen and Africans had not begun interacting on a much larger scale—and in a relationship where the people of one color were masters and the people of the opposite color were subjects. That did not begin to happen until the second quarter of the seventeenth century, long after the enslavement of both Indians and Africans had become an indispensable part of the Spanish and Portuguese colonial systems.

Early Slavery in the English Colonies

Even though they were long familiar with Spanish, Dutch, and Portuguese use of African slave labor, English colonists did not turn immediately to Africa to solve the problem of cultivating labor-intensive crops. Indeed the first English reaction to the slave trade had been negative, although only momentarily so. When John Hawkins returned to England in 1562 with several hundred slaves captured in a buccaneering raid on the Spanish Main, Queen Elizabeth pronounced the deed "detestable" and predicted that it would "call down vengeance from heaven upon the undertakers of it." But when the profits which such ventures would bring were pointed out, she demurred in further opposition. Nonetheless, the English were of no significance in the Atlantic slave trade until almost a century later. When they did become involved, it could have caused little surprise, for in enslaving Africans Englishmen were merely copying their colonial rivals in attempting to fill the colonial labor gap. No doubt the stereotype of Africans as uncivilized "beastly" creatures made it easier for the English to fasten chains upon them. But the central fact remains that Englishmen were coming to the New World, like Spanish, Portuguese, Dutch, and French before them, to make a fortune as well as to build religious and political havens. Given the long hostility Englishmen had borne toward Indians and their experience in enslaving them, any scruples they might have had about enslaving Africans were quickly dissipated.

Making it all the more natural to employ Africans as a slave labor force in the mainland colonies was the precedent which had been set by English planters in the Caribbean sugar islands. In Barbados, Jamaica, and the Leeward Islands Englishmen in the second and third quarters of the seventeenth century were learning to copy their European rivals in employing Africans in sugar culture and, through extraordinary repression, to mold them into a slave labor force. By 1675, when there were not more than 4,000 slaves in mainland America and the institution of slavery was not yet unalterably fixed, upwards of one hundred thousand Africans had already been enslaved in the English West Indies. Trade and communication were extensive between the Caribbean and mainland colonists and thus settlers in America had intimate knowledge concerning the potentiality of the slave trade and slave labor.

Whatever the depth of racial prejudice against Africans, therefore, its absence would not have eliminated the labor needs of the English colonies or altered the long-established international precedent for enslaving Africans. Africans, it might be said, were simply the most available people in the world for those seeking a bound labor force and possessed of the wherewithal to obtain it. What is surprising is that the American colonists did not turn to slavery more quickly than they did. For more than a half-century in Virginia and Maryland it was primarily the white indentured servant and not the African slave who labored in the tobacco fields. Those blacks who were imported before about 1660 were held in various degrees of servitude, some for limited periods and a few for life.

The transformation of the labor force in the southern colonies, from one in which white and black indentured servants labored together to one in which black slaves served for a lifetime and composed the bulk of unfree labor, came only in the last third of the seventeenth century in

Virginia and Maryland and in the first third of the eighteenth century in North Carolina and South Carolina. The reasons for this shift to a slave-based agricultural economy in Maryland, Virginia, and the Carolinas are not altogether clear. But the most likely explanation is that English entry into the African slave trade gave the Southern planter an opportunity to purchase slaves more readily and more cheaply than before. Cheap labor was what every tobacco or rice planter sought, and when the price of slave labor dipped below that of indentured labor, the demand for black slaves increased. Thus, in the late seventeenth century the number of Africans imported into the colonies began to grow and the flow of white inden-tured servants diminished to a trickle. As late as 1671 slaves made up less than 5 percent of Virginia's population, according to the royal governor there, and were outnumbered by at least three to one by white indentured servants. In Maryland the situation was much the same. But within a generation, by about 1700, they represented one-fifth of the population and probably a majority of the labor force. A Maryland census of 1707, for example, tabulated 3,003 white bound laborers and 4,657 black slaves. Five years later the slave population had almost doubled.[3] Within an-other generation white indentured servitude had been reduced to insig-nificance and in all of the southern colonies African slaves made up the backbone of the agricultural work force.

To the north in the "middle colonies" of Pennsylvania, New Jersey, and Delaware, where English colonists had settled only in the last third of the seventeenth century, slavery existed on a more occasional basis, since labor-intensive crops were not as extensively grown in these areas and the cold winters brought farming to a halt for a considerable part of the year. New York was an exception. During the period before 1664 when the colony was Dutch, slaveholding had been extensively practiced, encouraged in part by the Dutch West India Company, one of the chief international suppliers of slaves. The population of New York remained largely Dutch until the end of the seventeenth century and the English who slowly filtered in saw no reason not to imitate Dutch slave owners. Thus New York became the largest importer of slaves north of Maryland. In the mid-eighteenth century, the areas of original settlement around New York and Albany remained slaveholding societies with about 20 per-cent of the population composed of slaves and 30 to 40 percent of the white householders owning human property.

As the number of slaves increased, legal codes for strictly controlling their activities were fashioned in each of the southern colonies and some-

[3]Evarts B. Greene and Virginia D. Harrington, *American Population Before the Federal Census of 1790* (New York: Columbia University Press, 1932), p. 124.

what later in the northern colonies. To a large extent these "black codes" were borrowed from English colonies in the West Indies. Bit by bit they deprived the African immigrant of rights enjoyed by others in the society, including indentured servants. And gradually they reduced the slave in the eyes of society and the law from a human being to a piece of chattel property. In this process of dehumanization nothing was more important than the practice of hereditary lifetime service. Once servitude became perpetual, relieved only by death, then the stripping away of all other rights followed as a matter of course. When the condition of the slave parent was passed on to the child, that is, when slavery was extended to the womb, then the institution became totally fixed so far as the slave was concerned.

Thus, with the passage of time Afro-Americans had to adapt to a more and more circumscribed world. Earlier in the seventeenth century they had been treated much as indentured servants; they were bound to labor for a specified period of years and thereafter were free to work for themselves, hire out their labor, buy land, move as they pleased, and, if they wished, hold slaves themselves. But by the 1640s in Virginia blacks were being forbidden the use of firearms. In the 1660s marriages between white women and black slaves were being described as "shameful Matches" and "the Disgrace of our Nation;" during the next few decades interracial fornication became subject to unusually severe punishment and interracial marriage was banned.

These discriminatory steps were slight, however, in comparison with the rapid stripping away of rights that began toward the end of the century. In rapid succession Afro-Americans lost their right to testify before a court; to engage in any kind of commercial activity, either as buyer or seller; to hold property; to participate in the political process; to congregate in public places with more than two or three of their fellows; to travel without permission; and to engage in legal marriage or parenthood. In some colonies, even the rights to education and religion were stripped away, for it was thought that these might encourage the germ of freedom in slaves. From human status, slaves descended to property status. More and more steps were taken to contain them tightly in a legal system that made no allowance for their education, welfare, or future advancement. More and more, the restraints on the slave owner's freedom to deal wtih his slaves in any way he saw fit were cast away. Early in the eighteenth century laws were passed in many colonies forbidding the manumission of slaves by individual owners. This was a step designed to prohibit the possibility that slaves, seeing other Afro-Americans free, would strive for their own freedom and to discourage those who had been freed from encouraging and abetting attempts by their black brothers and sisters also to gain their freedom.

The half-century long movement to strip away all the slave's rights had both pragmatic and psychological components. The greater the proportion of slaves in the society, the greater was the danger to white society, for every slave owner knew that when he purchased a man or woman in chains he had bought a potential insurrectionist. The larger the specter of black revolt, the greater was the effort of white society to neutralize it by further restricting the rights and activities of the slave. Thus, following a black revolt in 1712 that took the lives of nine whites and wounded others, the legislature in New York passed a slave code that rivaled those of the Southern colonies. And throughout the Southern colonies the obsessive fear of slave insurrection ushered in the institutionalization of violence as the means of insuring social stability. Allied to this need for greater and greater control was the psychological need to dehumanize slaves by taking from them the rights that would connote their humanity. It was far easier to rationalize the merciless exploitation of that which had been defined by law as something less than human.

Thus occurred one of the great paradoxes in our history—the building of what some thought was to be a utopia in the wilderness upon the backs of black men and women wrenched from their African homeland and forced into a system of abject slavery. America was seen as a liberating and regenerating force, as David B. Davis has pointed out, but it became the scene of a "grotesque inconsistency." In the land heralded for its freedom and individual opportunity the practice of slavery, unknown for centuries in the mother country, was reinstituted. America, like other parts of the New World, became the scene of "a disturbing retrogression from the course of historical progress."[4] African slaves, as one eighteenth-century Englishman put it, became "the strength and the sinews of this western world."[5] To exchange "strength and sinews" for moral consistency was a trade-off that only a handful of colonists, beginning with a few Quakers at the end of the seventeenth century, saw fit to challenge.

The effect of the mass enslavement of Africans in the American colonies on racial prejudice was profound. Once institutionalized, slavery cast the African into such a lowly role that the initial bias against him could only be confirmed and vastly strengthened. Initially unfavorable impressions of Africans had been combined with labor needs to bring about the mass enslavement of Africans. But it required slavery itself to harden negative racial feelings into a deep and almost unshakable prejudice which continued to grow for centuries. A labor system was devised which kept the African in America at the bottom of the social and eco-

[4]David Brion Davis, *The Problem of Slavery in Western Culture* (Ithaca, N.Y.: Cornell University Press, 1966), p. 25.
[5]Eric Williams, *Capitalism and Slavery* (Chapel Hill: University of North Carolina Press, 1966), p. 30.

THE AFRICANS OF THE SLAVE BARK "WILDFIRE."—[From our own Correspondent.]

THE SLAVE DECK OF THE BARK "WILDFIRE," BROUGHT INTO KEY WEST ON APRIL 30, 1860.—[From a Daguerreotype.]

For slaves, the most traumatic part of acculturating to European colonial life was the dreaded "middle passage." (The New York Public Library.)

European naval architects competed in designing ships which would most efficiently and profitably deliver their human cargoes to the New World. (Courtesy The Library Company of Philadelphia.)

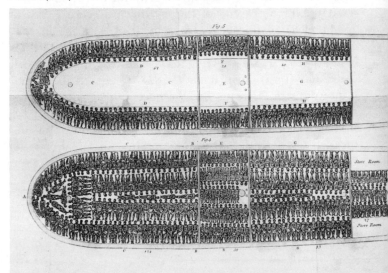

Indigo production, primarily the work of slaves, was of great importance in the creation of wealth in eighteenth-century South Carolina. (By permisssion of the Folger Shakespeare Library, Washington, D.C.)

An eighteenth-century painting from South Carolina reveals the preservation of African cultural forms in North America. The non-secular dance is believed to be of Yoruba origin, as were the stringed instrument and drum. (Colonial Williamsburg Foundation.)

nomic pyramid. Irrevocably caught in the web of perpetual servitude, the slave was allowed no further opportunity to prove the white stereotype wrong. Socially and legally defined as less than a man, kept in a degraded and debased position, virtually without power in his relationships with white society, the Afro-American became a truly servile, ignoble, degraded creature in the eyes of the Europeans. This was used as further reason to keep Africans in slavery, for it was argued that they were worth nothing better and were incapable of occupying any higher role. In the long evolution of racial attitudes in America, then, nothing was of greater importance than the enslavement of Africans.

The Status of Slaves in North
and South America

Because slavery existed in virtually ever part of the New World one can best discover what was unique about the system of bondage that evolved in the American colonies by comparing it with the institution of slavery in other areas of the New World. From recent studies we know that about only 5 percent of the slaves brought to the colonies of the New World came to mainland America. Thus the 350,000 or so Africans who struggled for existence in their new homes in North America between 1600 and 1780 were dwarfed by the two million transported to Portuguese Brazil, the three million taken to British, French, and Dutch plantations in the West Indies, and the seven hundred thousand imported into Spanish America. How did slaves fare in different parts of the New World and how are we to explain the differences in their treatment, their opportunities for emancipation, and their chance, once free, to carve a worthwhile niche for themselves as free persons?

The first comparativists to study slavery in the Americas argued that there were crucial differences between the status of slaves in the Spanish or Portuguese colonies and the English colonies. These differences, they maintained, largely account for the fact that racial mixture is much more extensive today in Latin America than in North America, that formal policies of segregation and discrimination were never embodied in Latin American law, and that the racial tension and conflict which has characterized twentieth-century American life has been largely absent in Latin American countries such as Brazil. Miscegenation can be taken as one poignant example of these differences. Interracial marriage has never been prohibited in Brazil and would be thought a senseless and artificial separation of people. But in the American colonies legal prohibitions against interracial mixing began in the mid-seventeenth century. Virtually every American colony prohibited mixed marriages by the early eighteenth century. These laws, modified from time to time, continued throughout the period of slavery and in many states continued after the abolition of slavery. As late as 1949 mixed marriages were still prohibited by law in twenty-nine states including seventeen outside the South.

Such differences as these, it has been argued, were indicative of the fact that slavery in Spanish and Portuguese America was never as harsh as in Anglo-America nor were the doors to eventual freedom so tightly closed. In Latin America, it is said, the African mixed sexually with the white population from the beginning; he was never completely stripped of his political, economic, social, and religious rights; he was frequently encouraged to work for his freedom; and when the gate for freedom was opened he found it possible to carve a place of dignity for himself in the community. In the North American colonies, on the contrary, the slave lost all of his rights by the early eighteenth century and was thereafter treated as mere chattel property. Emancipation was rare and in fact was prohibited in several colonies in the eighteenth century. Those Afro-Americans who did obtain their freedom, especially after the American Revolution, found themselves permanently consigned to the lowliest positions in society, where social and political rights initially granted him as a citizen were gradually withdrawn. In entitling his book *Slave and Citizen*, Frank Tannenbaum, a pioneer in the comparative study of slavery, signified his view of the differing fates of the African migrant in the two continents of the New World.[6]

By what series of events or historical accidents had the African in the Latin American colonies been placed on the road to freedom while in English North America the road traveled by blacks was always a dead end, even after freedom was granted? Tannenbaum and those who followed him suggested that the answer lay in the different ideological and cultural climates in which the African struggled in the New World. Those who were enslaved in the Spanish and Portuguese colonies entered a culture that was Catholic in religion, semimedieval and authoritarian in its political institutions, conservative and paternalistic in its social relations, and Roman in its system of law. Africans brought to America, by contrast, confronted a culture that was Protestant in religion, libertarian and "modern" in its political institutions, individualistic in its social relations, and Anglo-Saxon in its systems of law. Ironically it was the "premodern" Spanish and Portuguese culture that protected the slave and eventually prepared him for something better than slavery. The Catholic church not only sent its representatives to the New World in far greater number than did the Protestant churches, but it wholeheartedly devoted itself to preserving the human rights of Negroes. Affirming that no individual, no

---

[6]Frank Tannenbaum, *Slave and Citizen: The Negro in the Americas* (New York: Alfred K. Knopf, 1946).

matter how lowly his position or corrupt his beliefs, was unworthy in the sight of God, the Catholic clergy toiled to convert people of every color and condition, wherever and whenever they were found. Indians and Africans in the Latin American colonies were therefore fit subjects for the zeal of the Jesuit, Dominican, and Franciscan priests, and the Church, in viewing masses of enslaved Indians and Africans as future Christians, had a tempering effect on what slave masters might do with their slaves or what legislators, reflecting planter opinion, might legislate into law.

In a similar way the transference of Roman law to the Iberian colonies served to protect the slave from becoming mere chattel property, for Roman law recognized the rights of slaves and the obligations of masters to them. The slave undeniably occupied the lowest rung on the social ladder but he or she remained a member of the community, entitled to legal protection from a rapacious or sadistic master.

Still a third institution mediated between master and slave—the government itself. Highly centralized, the Spanish and Portuguese political systems revolved around the power of the monarch and the aristocracy and this power was expected to radiate out from its metropolitan centers in Europe to the New World colonies. Colonies existed under strict royal governance and since the Crown, closely tied to the Catholic Church, was dedicated to protecting the rights of slaves, slave owners in the colonies were answerable to a social policy formulated at home. In sum, a set of interconnecting institutions, derived from a conservative, paternalistic system of thought, worked to the advantage of the African slave by standing between him and his master. Iberian institutions, transplanted to the New World, prohibited slave owners from exercising unbridled rein over their slaves and insured that the slave, though exploited, was also protected and eventually prepared for full membership in the society.

In the English colonies of North America and the Caribbean, it is argued, these intermediating institutions were notably absent. Slave masters were far more free to follow their impulses in their treatment of slaves and in formulating social and legal policy that undergirded slavery. In North America, government was more localized and democratic, church and state more separate, and individuals less fettered by tradition and authority. Hence slaves were at the mercy of their masters to an unusual degree. The Protestant church had little interest in proselytizing slaves. When it did, its authority was far more locally based than in the Spanish and Portuguese colonies and therefore subject to the influence of the leading slave owners of the area.

Government too was less centralized; England allowed the colonies to formulate much of their own law and exercised only a weak regulatory power over her plantations. Anglo-Saxon law, transferred to the New

World, was silent on the subject of slavery since slavery had not existed in England for centuries. This left colonists free to devise new law, as harsh and exploitive as they wished, to cope with the labor system they were erecting. In America, it is maintained, slave owners molded a highly individualistic, libertarian, and acquisitive culture which would brook few checks on the rights of slave owners to exploit their human property in any way they saw fit. It was property rights which the Anglo-American culture regarded as transcendently important. With relatively few institutional restraints to inhibit slave owners, nothing stood between new African immigrants and a system of total subjugation. Consequently, Tannenbaum and others have argued, a far more closed and dehumanizing system of slavery evolved in the more "enlightened" and "modern" environment of the English colonies than in the more feudalistic and authoritarian milieu of the Spanish and Portuguese colonies.

In the last few decades historians, sociologists, and anthropologists have raised strong objections to this analysis of slavery and race relations in the New World. By looking too intently at Spanish and Portuguese laws, traditions, and institutions in the mother countries, they have said, we may have ignored the gap that often separates legal pronouncements from social reality. Is it possible that in the law books Spanish and Portuguese slaves were carefully protected, but that in actuality the life of slaves was as bad or worse than in the English plantations? Certainly we know that laws do not always reflect actual social conditions. For example, if we had only our post-Civil War legal statutes as a guide to the status of American Negroes in the nineteenth and twentieth centuries, we might conclude that Afro-Americans enjoyed equality with white Americans in the modern era. The laws guarantee nothing less. But what the law specifies and what actually occurs are two different things.

As historians have looked more closely at local conditions in various New World colonies, they have found that the alleged differences between North and South American slavery loom less large. Where the Catholic church and royal authority were well established, such as in urban areas, the treatment of slaves was indeed more humane than in areas of the American colonial South, such as South Carolina, where the Protestant churches took only shallow root. But in rural areas of the Spanish and Portuguese colonies, where slavery was most extensively practiced, the church's sway was not so strong and the authority of the Spanish colonial officials was more tenuous. In these areas individual slave masters were left to deal with their slaves as they saw fit, much as in the English colonies.

Moreover, recent studies have shown that wide variations in the treatment of slaves occurred within the colonies of each European nation. In Puritan New England and Quaker Pennsylvania conditions were never so inhumane as in the Anglo-American South, partly because the Puritan and Quaker churches acted as a restraint on the behavior of slave owners and partly because slaves, always a small percentage of the population, were more frequently employed as artisans and household servants than in the South, where mass agricultural labor was the primary concern of slave masters. Likewise, conditions were far better for slaves in the Brazilian urban center of Recife than on the frontier plantations of the remote southern province of Rio Grande do Sul.

Other factors, quite separate from the ideological or cultural climate of a given area, have claimed the attention of historians more forcefully in recent attempts to delineate differences in slave systems and to isolate the unique facets of English slavery in North America. One such factor is the simple ratio of blacks to whites. Where slaves represented a small fraction of the total population, such as in New England and the mid-Atlantic English colonies, slave codes were devised that left slaves in possession of some rights. Religion and education were commonly believed to be beneficial to slaves and no protests were heard when Quakers and Anglicans set up schools for Negroes in places such as Boston and Philadelphia. Marriage was not infrequent and black parents often baptized their children in the Anglican church, even though death brought burial in a separate "strangers" graveyard. Slaves were freer to congregate in public places and were recognized before courts of law in these areas.

From Maryland to Georgia, however, conditions were markedly different. In the Chesapeake colonies, slaves represented about 40 percent of the population by mid-eighteenth century and in South Carolina they outnumbered whites by the end of the colonial period. In these areas far more repressive slave codes were legislated. The same was true in the English Caribbean islands where whites were outnumbered three to one and often as much as ten to one in the eighteenth century. Surrounded by those whom they had enslaved, control became a crucial factor for white slave owners, who lived in perpetual fear of black insurrections. When they were numerically inferior they took every possible precaution to insure that their slaves would have no opportunity to organize and plot against them. Living in a kind of garrison state amidst constantly circulating rumors of black revolt, white planters heaped punishment on black offenders and retaliated with ferocity against black aggression in the hope that other slaves would be cowed into submissiveness. Castration for sexual offenses against whites and burning at the stake for plotting or participating in insurrection were common punishments in colonies with a high proportion of black slaves. But where slaves represented only a small fraction of the population no such elaborate attempts were made to define their inferior status in precise detail or to leave them so completely at the mercy of their owners.

A second factor affecting the characteristics of particular slave societies was the economic system in which slaves toiled. Where blacks worked in the plantation system, based on the production of cash crops such as cotton, sugar, coffee, or rice, they suffered slavery at its brutal worst. In these areas the expenditure of human life could be appalling. This included the American cotton plantations in the late eighteenth and nineteenth centuries, the Caribbean sugar plantations from the seventeenth to the nineteenth centuries, and the Brazilian coffee plantations of the nineteenth century. The maximization of profit was the overriding goal on such plantations and it was best achieved by literally working slaves to death and then replacing them with newly imported bondsmen.

In fringe areas, by contrast, where slaves were used for occasional labor or as domestic servants and artisans, conditions were much better. Work was not only less depleting, but the opportunity existed for religious and humanitarian ideology to temper the brutality inherent in the master-slave relationship. In Anglo-Dutch New York and Portuguese Recife, slaves were often badly used by their masters but their chances for survival were far greater than on the expanding plantations. When agricultural areas were enjoying boom times and rapid expansion, as in the cases of eighteenth-century South Carolina and nineteenth-century Cuba, the exploitation of slaves was usually found at its extreme worst because special incentives existed for driving them to the limits of human endurance. Perhaps nowhere was the expenditure of life so callously regarded as in the sugar islands of the West Indies. Slaves were regarded "as so many cattle" who would "continue to perform their dreadful tasks and then expire" after seven or eight years, one Englishman wrote in 1788.[7]

Two other factors affecting the lives of slaves operated independently of institutions and ideological currents. The first was whether or not the slave trade was still open in a particular area. When this was so, new supplies of Africans were continuously available and the treatment of slaves was usually harsh. To work a slave to death created no problem of replacement. Where the slave trade was closed, however, greater precautions were taken to safeguard the capital investment that had been made in human property, for replacement could be obtained only through reproduction—a long and uncertain process. The sugar island of Barbados, for example, was a death trap for Africans in the eighteenth century. With fresh supplies of African slaves readily available and with virtually no intermediary institutions to restrain them in the treatment of their human property, sugar planters were free to build their fortunes through an exploitation of slave labor that was limited only by calculations of cost efficiency. That this resulted in a phenomenally high mortal-

---

[7]Quoted in C. Vann Woodward, *American Counterpoint: Slavery and Racism in the North-South Dialogue* (Boston: Little, Brown and Company, 1971), p. 101.

ity—between 1712 and 1762 deaths outnumbered births by 120,000 among a slave population that averaged about 50,000—meant little to the English planters. They could view this carnage as an inevitable if regrettable part of the process by which wealth was created and sugar produced for household consumption in every village in England. Similar conditions existed in the Portuguese coffee-producing areas of northeastern Brazil in the nineteenth century. Irrespective of different national backgrounds and New World cultural environments, "the primary limiting factor upon the white man in the long history of African slavery," a recent historian has reminded us, "arose not out of humanitarian compunction but out of self-interest: the white man came not to destroy altogether, but to capture and sustain life, to be able to put it under virtually total domination for the sake of his own comfort or profit."[8]

The other factor affecting slave life was the prevalence of tropical diseases. In the temperate zones, including most of North America, slaves were far less subject to the ravaging fevers that swept away both Europeans and Africans in the tropical zone. This may be of the utmost importance in explaining why mortality rates were lower and reproduction rates higher in the English colonies than in the Caribbean and South American colonies of various European powers. The startling fact is that only about 5 percent of the slaves brought to the New World came to British North America and yet by the middle of the twentieth century American Negroes represented over 30 percent of all peoples of African descent in the hemisphere. By contrast, Brazil, which imported about 38 percent of all slaves brought to the Americas, had only 36 percent of the African descendants alive in the hemisphere at mid-twentieth century. The British West Indies imported about 850,000 slaves between 1700 and 1780 but the black population of the islands in the latter year was only about 350,000. In contrast the American colonies imported less than 250,000 in the same period but counted about 575,000 Negroes in the population in 1780. These varying rates of population growth reflect many variables—differences in male-female ratios during the slave period, treatment of slaves, fertility rates among free Negroes, and a host of other factors. But however these factors may ultimately be sorted out, it seems clear that the African brought into the North American colonies had a better chance of survival than his counterpart in the tropical colonies where disease environments were so much less favorable for sustaining human life, whether slave or free, black or white.

Although the relative treatment of slaves on the plantations of the different European colonizers is of great importance, it is overshadowed by

[8]Richard Hofstadter, *America at 1750: A Social Portrait* (New York: Alfred A. Knopf, Inc., 1972), p. 107.

another consideration—the access to freedom which slaves found in one colony as opposed to another. While the question of comparative treatment is still being vigorously argued by historians, it seems indisputable that in the Spanish and Portuguese colonies slaves had far greater opportunities to work themselves free of the shackles of slavery than in the English colonies. Census figures for the eighteenth century are fragmentary, but we know that by 1820 the ratio of free Negroes to slaves was about one to six in the United States, one to three in Brazil, one to four in Mexico, and one to two in Cuba. In Spanish Cuba alone, free blacks outnumbered by 30,000 the number of manumitted slaves in all the Southern states in 1800, although the black population of the American South exceeded that of Cuba by about three to one.

Historians who have stressed the greater humanitarianism and the less virulent racism of the Spanish and Portuguese colonizers have interpreted this greater opportunity for freedom in the Spanish and Portuguese colonies as evidence of the relatively flexible and humane nature of the system there and as a testimony to the commitment to preparing the slave for citizenship. But those who argue that demographic and economic factors were preeminently important are more persuasive. They point out that it was the white *need* for free blacks, not humanitarian concern for black freedom, that motivated so many Spanish and Portuguese slave owners to emancipate their human property. Because Englishmen had emigrated to the American colonies in far larger numbers than Spaniards and Portuguese there were enough of them to fill most of the positions of artisan, overseer, cattle tender and militiaman—the "interstitial work of the economy."[9] But the relatively light European emigration to the Spanish and Portuguese colonies left them desperately short of people who could function above the level of manual labor. Therefore it was necessary to create a class of free blacks, working for whites as wage laborers, in order that the economy could function smoothly for the benefit of white landowners, merchants, and investors. Though plantation owners and northern urban slavemasters trained some slaves as artisans, unskilled mass labor was the fate of most Africans in the English colonies because white men had immigrated in sufficient number to fill most of the occupational niches above the level of stoop labor. Where Afro-Americans were functional as freedmen in a white man's society, they were freed; where they were not, they remained slaves. That masters were rarely limited by law in manumitting their slaves in Spanish and Portuguese colonies, as they were in English colonies, testifies more to the fact that the law followed the social and economic needs of society than to

[9]Carl N. Degler, *Neither Black Nor White: Slavery and Race Relations in Brazil and the United States* (New York: The Macmillan Company, 1971), p. 44.

any ideological concern for the slave derived from ancient precedent. If free blacks had not been needed in Latin American society or if it had been more profitable to close the door to freedom than to keep it ajar, it is unlikely that slaves would have been manumitted in such large numbers. There is some evidence to show, in fact, that Brazilian slave owners often emancipated their infirm or aged slaves in order to be free of the costs of maintaining unproductive laborers, a practice also known in the English colonies.

A second way in which free blacks were vital to the interests of white colonizers in Latin America was as a part of the system of military defense. For example, it is clear that English and Portuguese slave systems were strikingly divergent in their attitude toward arming slaves, for whereas this practice was rarely allowed in the English colonies it was widely employed in Brazil. To explain this contrast one needs only to point to the fact that the Brazilian colonists could not hope to repel French attacks in the late sixteenth century, the Dutch invasion in the second quarter of the seventeenth century, and the French assaults of the early eighteenth century without arming their Negro slaves. Carl Degler, who has written a comprehensive comparison of slavery in Brazil and the United States, has written: "Because the mother country . . . was too weak or unconcerned to offer much assistance, all the resources of the sparsely settled colony had to be mobilized for defense, which included every scrap of manpower, including black slaves."[10] In the American colonies, by contrast, the need to arm slaves was comparatively slight. Though colonial shipping was intermittently endangered by the naval raiders of other European powers, the coastal colonies were rarely subjected to attack by European rivals except in New England where slaves were few in number.

When military necessity required it, American slave owners also armed their slaves, ignoring or temporarily setting aside laws which strictly prohibited this. When Nathaniel Bacon's revolt against the government of Virginia was flagging in 1676, he was quick to declare unilaterally liberty for any servants and slaves who would join his cause. Apparently many slaves responded, for among one group of about four hundred rebels at least eighty were runaway black slaves. In South Carolina, where the Spanish threat made the problem of military defense greater than anywhere else in the English colonies, each militia captain was required by law in 1708 "to enlist, traine up and bring into the field for each white, one able Slave armed with a gun or lance."[11] Seven years later, in the

10Ibid., p. 79.
11Verner W. Crane, The Southern Frontier, 1670–1732 (Ann Arbor: University of Michigan Press, 1956), p. 187n.

Yamasee War, the South Carolinians were only too glad to use slaves in attempting to stave off the attacks of their Indian enemies. When Governor Charles Craven forayed into Yamasee country in July 1715, his force of several hundred was about equally composed of white settlers and black slaves.

A third and crucially important way in which the African was more valuable as a freed person than a slave in the Latin American colonies was as a sexual and marriage partner. This pertains primarily to black women. But the phenomenon that so forcefully attracts one's attention is the large degree of racial mixing that occurred in the Latin American countries between Europeans and Indians, Indians and Africans, and Africans and Europeans. Magnus Mörner, a Latin American historian, has pointed out that "no part of the world has ever witnessed such a gigantic mixing of races as the one that has been taking place in Latin America and the Caribbean since 1492."[12] Again, some historians have contrasted the cultural backgrounds of the two European peoples and argued that through centuries of war and economic relations the Spanish and Portuguese had been interacting with the Moors of North Africa and had thereby developed a great plasticity in race relations. The English, by comparison, had remained relatively isolated in their island fortress prior to the late sixteenth century, intermingling with the other cultures to no considerable extent.

But these prior attitudes, transported to the New World, would probably have faded had it not been for compelling circumstances that encouraged miscegenation there. As it happened, Spanish and Portuguese males emigrated without women to a far greater extent than English men, who came predominantly with their families. In the Spanish and Portuguese cases the colonizers carried with them a racial ideology that, while it favored white skin and European blood, was still malleable enough to justify mixing with Indian and African women. In the Latin American colonies, then, interracial sexual relations were common, as the colonizers took Indian and African women as mistresses, concubines, and wives. Such partnerships were accepted with little embarrassment or social strain, for in the absence of European women it was regarded as natural to have sexual relations with or even to marry a woman of dark skin.

Such was not the case in most of the English colonies. English women had come with English men to Puritan New England so that parity between the sexes was established relatively early. This obviated the need for Indian and African women. In the Southern colonies, where white women were in short supply for the first half century or so, African

[12]Magnus Mörner, *Race Mixture in the History of Latin America* (Boston: Little, Brown and Company, 1967), p. 1.

women were also absent since the importation of slaves had remained insignificant until the last decade of the seventeenth century. By the time black women were available in large numbers the numerical disparity between white man and women had been redressed. It was not so much extreme ethnocentrism as it was the presence of white women that made miscegenation officially disreputable and often illegal, though practiced privately to a considerable extent. Had white men continued to be without English women at a time when African women had begun flooding into the Southern colonies, then the alleged English distaste for dark-skinned partners would doubtlessly have broken down. That womenless men are not easily restrained by ideology in finding release for their sexual urges is convincingly demonstrated by the English experience in the West Indian sugar islands. In Barbados, Jamaica, and the Leeward Islands, English women were not as plentiful as in the mainland colonies. But surrounded by a sea of black women, English men eagerly followed the practice of the Spanish and Portuguese, cohabiting with and occasionally marrying their slaves. To outlaw sexual relations with Negro women, as was being done in the American colonies in the eighteenth century, Winthrop Jordan has suggested, would have been more difficult than abolishing the sugar cane.[13] Where white women were absent, black women were needed; where they were needed, they were enthusiastically accepted and laws prohibiting interracial sex and marriage were never passed.

Slavery in the Americas, then, was characterized by a considerable degree of variation, both in the treatment of slaves, the degree of openness in the system, and the willingness of the dominant society to acculturate with the Africans in its midst. The cultural heritage brought to the New World by the various European settler groups played some role in the formation of attitudes, policies, and laws. But the exigencies of life in the New World, including economic, sexual, and military needs, did far more to shape racial attitudes and the system of slavery. That different patterns of settlement and economic development should have played the most dynamic roles in shaping the slave systems was to be expected, for those with the power to shape opinion and mold institutions were bound to do so in a way that helped them achieve their goals.

[13]Winthrop D. Jordan, *White over Black: American Attitudes Toward the Negro, 1550–1812* (Chapel Hill: University of North Carolina Press, 1968), p. 140.

chapter 8

The African Response to Slavery

It is easy to assume that Africans, once sold into slavery and brought to the New World, were simply fitted into a closed system of forced labor where they lived out their lives, abject and de-Africanized, as best they could. So much attention is lavished on the kind of slave system fashioned by slave owners—the black codes they legislated, their treatment of slaves, the economic development they engineered—that the slaves themselves are often forgotten as active participants in a cultural process. How did they live their daily lives in a vastly different culture? To what degree were they acculturated into white European society? How did they experience and respond to the loss of their freedom and the separation from all that was familiar in their native culture? To what degree did they mold a new Afro-American culture, distinct from the European culture surrounding them? Until we adopt the approach of studying the interior lives of slaves, replacing the question "What was done to the slaves?" as

Eugene Genovese has put it, with the question, "What did slaves do for themselves and how did they do it?", we will continue to view slaves only as the object but not the subject of our historical inquiries.[1]

Capture and Transport of Slaves

No accounts of the initial enslavement of Africans, no matter how vivid, can quite convey the pain and demoralization that must have accompanied the forced march to the west coast of Africa and the subsequent loading aboard European ships of those who fell captive to the African suppliers of the European slave traders. As the demand for African slaves doubled and redoubled in the eighteenth century, the hinterlands of western and central Sudan were invaded again and again by the armies and agents of both coastal and interior kings. Perhaps 75 percent of the slaves transported to English North America came from the part of western Africa that lies between the Senegal and Niger Rivers and the Gulf of Benin and most of the others were enslaved in Angola on the west coast of Central Africa. Slaving activities in these areas were responsible for a considerable depopulation of the region in the eighteenth and nineteenth centuries.

Once captured, slaves were marched to the sea in "coffles," or trains. A Scotsman, Mungo Park, described the coffle he marched with for 550 miles through Gambia at the end of the eighteenth century. It consisted of 73 men, women, and children tied together by the neck with leather thongs. Several captives attempted to commit suicide by eating clay, another was abandoned after being badly stung by bees; still others died of exhaustion and hunger. After two months the coffle reached the coast, many of its members physically depleted by thirst, hunger, and exposure.[2]

The anger, bewilderment, and desolation that accompanied the forced march, the first leg of the 5,000-mile journey to the New World, was only increased by the actual transfer of slaves to European ship captains, who would carry their human cargo in small wooden ships to the Americas. "As the slaves come down to Fida from the inland country," wrote one European trader in the late seventeenth century, "they are put into a booth or prison, built for that purpose, near the beach . . . and when the Europeans are to receive them, they are brought out into a large plain, where the [ships'] surgeons examine every part of every one of them, to

[1]Eugene D. Genovese, *In Red and Black: Marxian Explorations in Southern and Afro-American History* (New York: Random House, Inc., 1971), p. 106.
[2]Daniel P. Mannix and Malcolm Cowley, *Black Cargoes: A History of the Atlantic Slave Trade, 1518–1865* (New York: The Viking Press, Inc., 1962), pp. 101–2.

the smallest member, men and women being all stark naked. Such as are allowed good and sound, are set on one side, and the others by themselves; which slaves so rejected are called Mackrons, being above 35 years of age, or defective in their lips, eyes, or teeth, or grown grey; or that have the venereal disease, or any other imperfection."[3] Such dehumanizing treatment, of course, was a part of the commercial process by which "merchan-

[3]Quoted in Basil Davidson, *The African Slave Trade: Precolonial History, 1450–1850* (Boston: Little, Brown and Company, 1961) . p. 92.

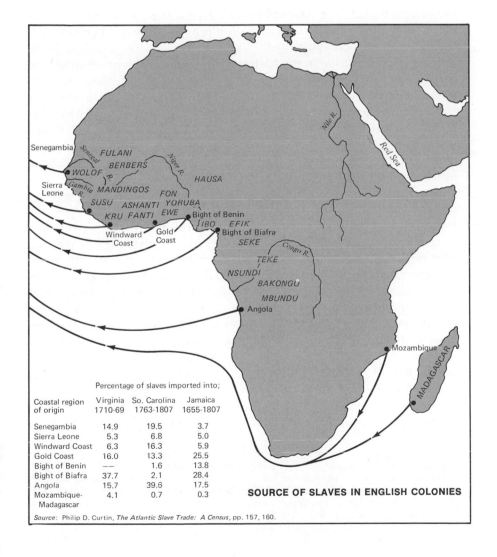

Coastal region of origin	Virginia 1710-69	So. Carolina 1763-1807	Jamaica 1655-1807
Senegambia	14.9	19.5	3.7
Sierra Leone	5.3	6.8	5.0
Windward Coast	6.3	16.3	5.9
Gold Coast	16.0	13.3	25.5
Bight of Benin	——	1.6	13.8
Bight of Biafra	37.7	2.1	28.4
Angola	15.7	39.6	17.5
Mozambique-Madagascar	4.1	0.7	0.3

Percentage of slaves imported into;

SOURCE OF SLAVES IN ENGLISH COLONIES

Source: Philip D. Curtin, *The Atlantic Slave Trade: A Census*, pp. 157, 160.

dise" was selected and bargained for. But it was also part of the psychological process by which an attempt was made to strip away self-respect
and self-identity from the Africans.

Cruelty followed cruelty. After purchase, each slave was branded with
a hot iron signifying the company, whether Spanish, Portuguese, English,
French, or Dutch, that had purchased him or her. Thus slaves purchased
by the English Royal Africa Company in the seventeenth century arrived
in America with *DY*, for the Duke of York, burned into their breasts.
Thus were members of "preliterate" societies first introduced to the al-
phabetic symbols of "advanced" cultures. "The branded slaves," one
account continued, "are returned to their former booths" where they were
imprisoned until a full human cargo could be assembled.[4] The next psychological wrench came with the ferrying of slaves, in large canoes, to the
waiting ships at anchor in the harbor. One English captain described the
desperation of slaves who were about to loose touch with their ancestral
land and embark upon a vast ocean that many had never previously seen.
"The Negroes are so wilful and loth to leave their own country, that they
have often leap'd out of the canoes, boat and ship, into the sea, and kept
under water till they were drowned, to avoid being taken up and saved
by our boats, which pursued them; they having a more dreadful apprehension of Barbadoes than we can have of hell."[5]

The kind of fear that inspired suicide while still on African soil was
prevalent as well on the second leg of the voyage—the "middle passage"
from the West African coast to the New World. Conditions aboard ship
were miserable, although it was obviously to the advantage of the ship
captains to deliver as many slaves as possible on the other side of the
Atlantic. Despite the fact that it was the preservation rather than the
destruction of life that was the main object, brutality was systematic, both
in the form of pitching overboard any slaves who fell sick on the voyage
and in punishing offenders with almost sadistic intensity as a way of creating a climate of fear that would put insurrectionist tendencies out of
mind in other slaves.[6] John Atkins, aboard an English slaver in 1721, described how the captain "whipped and scarified" several plotters of rebellion and sentenced others "to cruel deaths, making them first eat the
Heart and Liver of one of them killed. The Woman he hoisted up by the
thumbs, whipp'd and slashed her with Knives, before the other slaves, till

4*Ibid.*

5Quoted in Mannix and Cowley, *Black Cargoes*, p. 48.

6Equiano, *The Interesting Narrative of the Life of Olaudah Equiano, or Gustavus
Vassa, the African* (London, 1789), rpr. in *Africa Remembered: Narratives by West
Africans from the Era of the Slave Trade*, ed. Philip Curtin (Madison: University of
Wisconsin Press, 1967), p. 92.

she died."[7] Such descriptions could be repeated endlessly, but they all bear on the same points: though the naval architects of Europe competed to produce the most efficient ships for carrying human cargoes to the New World, the mortality on board, for both black slaves below decks and white sailors above, was incredibly high, probably averaging between 10 and 20 percent on each voyage.

That Africans attempted suicide and mutiny so often during the ocean crossings provides us with a strong indication that even the extraordinary degree of force that was used in capturing, branding, selling, and transporting Africans from one continent to another was not enough to make the captives submit tamely to their fate. An eighteenth-century historian of slavery, attempting to justify the terroristic devices employed by slavers, argued that "the many acts of violence they [the slaves] have committed by murdering whole crews and destroying ships when they had it in their power to do so have made these rigors wholly chargeable on their own bloody and malicious disposition which calls for the same confinement as if they were wolves or wild boars."[8] But the modern reader can detect in this characterization of enslaved Africans clear evidence that submissiveness was not a trait of those who were forcibly carried to the New World. So great was this resistance that special techniques of torture had to be devised to cope with the thousands of slaves who were determined to starve themselves to death on the middle passage rather than reach the New World in chains. Brutal whippings and hot coals applied to the lips were frequently used to open the mouth of recalcitrant slaves. When this did not suffice a special instrument, the *speculum oris*, or mouth opener, was employed to wrench apart the jaws of a resistant slave.

Taking into consideration the mortality involved in the capture, the forced march to the coast, and the middle passage, probably not more than one in two captured Africans lived to see the New World. Many of those who did must have been psychologically numbed as well as physically depleted by the experience. But one further step remained in the process of enslavement—the auctioning to a New World master and transportation to his place of residence. All in all, the relocation of any one of some eight million Africans brought westward across the Atlantic from the sixteenth to the eighteenth centuries may have averaged about six months from the time of capture to the time of arrival at the plantation of a European slave master. During this protracted personal crisis, the

---

[7]Davidson, *African Slave Trade*, pp. 94–95.
[8]Edward Long, *The History of Jamaica* (London, 1774), quoted in Mannix and Cowley, *Black Cargoes*, p. 111.

slave was completely cut off from all that was familiar—language, family, wider kinship relationships, tribal religion, and other forms of social and psychological security. Still facing these victims of the European demand for cheap labor was adaptation to a new environment, a new language, and a new work situation.

Adjustment to Slave Life

,The first instinct of the slave who found himself on a Virginia tobacco plantation or a Jamaican sugar plantation was simply to survive. To do this he was obliged, like all of the oppressed, to study carefully the ways of his oppressor. In many cases other slaves were already on the plantation where the slave was taken and it was from them that the techniques of survival were learned. If other slaves were numerous, as on many Southern plantations by the mid-eighteenth century, and if new slaves were frequently arriving from Africa, then it was easier and more relevant to keep elements of the African culture alive and vibrant. But in no case could the African culture simply be erased, for new cultures always effloresce from previous cultures in a gradual process of syncretic change. "While it is certainly true that the African under American slavery changed," writes George Rawick, "he did so in ways that were recognizably African."[9] Music, dance, games, and folktales were among the most persistent cultural survivals, but religion, speech patterns, taboos, and superstitions were also retained in some measure. White slave owners were not unaware of the attempts of their slaves to maintain their cultural heritage and they undoubtedly allowed this insofar as it did not interfere with the "seasoning" of the new immigrants. When it impeded adaptation to the new system of life and work, attempts were made to obliterate such Africanisms. But never in the long history of slavery could memory, habit, and belief be entirely wiped away. The old was altered to suit the demands of a new situation and a new environment. What emerged was a blend of African and European cultural elements.

The shock that was inherent in the capture, sale, and transportation of slaves caused special traumas for the first generation—those who were brought directly from Africa or to the American colonies by way of the West Indies. For their offspring, born into slavery in America, the process of adaptation was far easier. But regardless of whether they were brought to America or born into slavery, Afro-Americans were held in close and intimate contact with English culture. For the "outlandish" or

---

[9]George Rawick, *From Sundown to Sunup: The Making of the Black Community* (Westport, Conn.: Greenwood Publishing Co., 1972), p. 6.

"saltwater" Africans, as planters called their newly-arrived slaves, a break-
ing-in or "seasoning" period was employed to introduce them to life in
the tobacco and rice fields of Maryland, Virginia, and the Carolinas. Since
most slaves had come from agrarian tribes, they were already partially
prepared for agricultural field work. Indeed, the skill of West Africans
in the cultivation of rice may largely explain the fact that, while early
English efforts with this crop in South Carolina were unsuccessful, it became an enormously successful crop after slaves were brought directly
from Africa early in the eighteenth century. This phase of the adjustment
process may have been easier than most others. Planters preferred to import new slaves during the summer months so that they would be able
to work at least one crop before the advent of winter weather, which
afflicted many of them. Usually it took several years for a slave to pick
up the rudiments of the new language, though some were speaking broken English in less than a year. Slaves who had been agriculturalists or
servants in their homeland no doubt found the adjustment to New World
slavery easier than the minority who had occupied higher niches in the
tribal social structure. Planters often complained of the "haughtiness"
and indolence of slaves who had not been raised to a life of labor in their
homeland and at slave auctions buyers were always looking for the type
of slave who was familiar with life in the fields.

In studying the adjustment of Africans to slave life and English culture
historians have arrived at strikingly different conclusions. For many years
it was widely accepted that Africans easily accomplished the geographical
transition from their homelands to America and the social transition from
freemen to slaves. In general, it was believed, they were docile and contented in their new way of life. This view is still incorporated in many
high school and college textbooks, as well as in the general mythology
surrounding the Negro past. Step'n Fetchit of Hollywood movies is the
modern descendant of this happy-go-lucky slave who easily adapted to
the new way of life and found a warm and secure, if task-filled, home on
the Southern plantation. Thus a widely used college history textbook
states:

> Generally when the master and slave were brought into close association,
> a mutual feeling of kindliness and affection sprang up between them,
> which restrained the former from undue harshness toward the latter. We
> find that there were always some brutal masters who treated their black
> servants inhumanely but they were doubtless few in number. Good feel-
> ing between the master and slave was promoted in large measure by the
> happy disposition or docile temperment of the Negro. Seldom was he surly
> and discontented and rarely did he harbor a grudge against his master for
> depriving him of his liberty. On the contrary, he went about his daily
> tasks cheerfully, often singing while at work. . . . The fact that he had

never known the ease and comforts of civilization in his homeland made it less difficult for him to submit to the hardships and inferior position of his condition.[10]

Such an interpretation rests on the assumption that Africans were virtually cultureless before coming to America and possessed innate traits which enabled them to take uncomplainingly to their slave status. Such myths can be exposed for what they are—self-serving justifications for more than two centuries of brutalities inflicted by one people on another. But a more recent formulation of the African response to enslavement must be taken more seriously. It too represents the African as docile and compliant. But the source of this kind of behavior is found not in the kindliness of the master and the generally benevolent character of American slavery but in precisely the opposite—the totally oppressive and closed nature of the plantation system. As postulated by Stanley Elkins in *Slavery: An American Institution*, enslaved African immigrants were so tightly and unremittingly trapped in a web of authority and brutality that they could only survive, physically and psychologically, by developing deeply internalized defense mechanisms. The entire African personality, Elkins argues, underwent a transformation, as the slave adjusted his behavior to conform to the demands of the dominant white figure who stood over him with the power of life and death in his hands. So brutal was the slave system and so weak were the tempering institutions such as church and government that slaves, if they valued their lives, were obliged to become docile and utterly dependent children in order to survive.

This creation of "Sambo," who cringed, fawned, talked, and acted childishly, and ultimately came to identify with the one significant figure in his life—the master—can be best understood, according to Elkins, by drawing the analogy of the Jew in the Nazi concentration camp. Similarly wrenched from familiar surroundings, family, friends, and community values, Jews were brutally enslaved, transported to distant places in slave ships on rails, and then forced into a slave labor situation where the S.S. guard, the modern-day slave overseer, controlled every detail of their lives. To these guards Jews learned to react. Their chances for survival depended upon immediate adaptation to the new system and prisoners became so totally involved in this struggle for physical survival and psychic equilibrium that in time, lacking any other referent of self-esteem except their oppressors, they began to identify with those who had absolute power over them.

[10]Oliver P. Chitwood, *A History of Colonial America*, 3d ed. (New York: Harper & Row, Publishers, 1961), pp. 351–52.

Similarly, Elkins contends, the African slave was trapped in a system where authority was exercised with brutal finality. Brought in shackles to such a system, slaves were infantilized and reverted to childhood silliness and obsequiousness. Born into such a system, slave children had no opportunity to develop normal personalities. In either case, Afro-Americans became compliant slaves, always suppressing anger, never acting conspicuously or independently, rarely asserting the full range of human emotions. The typical plantation slave, writes Elkins, "was docile but irresponsible, loyal but lazy, humble but chronically given to lying and stealing; his behavior was full of infantile silliness and his talk inflated with childish exaggeration. His relationship with his master was one of utter dependence and childish attachment."[11]

Many criticisms of the "Elkins thesis" concerning the adaptation of Africans to slavery have been offered since the book was published in 1959. Some critics have argued that the differences between the concentration camp and the Southern slave plantation are so significant as to render the analogy useless as an analytic tool. "In contrast to the camp inmate," writes a recent critic of Elkins, "the slave had greater freedom from the threat of death and had less need for abject servility in order to avoid it. Besides, unlike the camp inmate, the slave's life was worth considerably more than a bullet."[12] Other critics maintain that "Sambo" is little more than a stereotype created by nineteenth-century Southerners who attempted to defend slavery against the attacks of abolitionists by fabricating a picture of a slave-child who would be hopelessly lost without his or her master. Southern society needed "Sambo" to defend the institution of slavery, so Southerners created him.

Still others have argued that slaves acted like "Sambos" in order to ward off the wrath of those over them but did this as a form of "role-playing," known to slaves as "puttin' on massa." When they feigned childishness or obsequiousness, they did so knowing exactly how their masters wanted them to act and thereby outwitted their oppressors at their own game. Thus one slave reported that he "had been forced to watch the changes of my master's physiognomy, as well as those of the parties he associated with, so as to frame my conduct in accordance with what I had reason to believe was their prevailing mood at any given time."[13] Finally, it is argued that though the Sambo-type personality may have existed, it was simply an extreme form of slave behavior at one end of a spectrum that ran all the way from "Sambo" to his opposite—the

[11] Stanley M. Elkins, *Slavery: A Problem in America Institutional and Intellectual Life* (New York: Grosset & Dunlap, Inc., 1963), p. 82.
[12] John W. Blassingame, *The Slave Community Plantation Life in the Antebellum South* (New York: Oxford University Press, Inc., 1972), p. 93.
[13] *Ibid.*, p. 200.

rebellious, alienated, revolutionary figure such as Gabriel Prosser or Nat Turner.[14]

Historical studies of slavery are now at the point where it is understood that any satisfactory attempt to deal with the African personality under slavery must begin with an analysis of the slave plantation on which most slaves lived and worked. "The behavior of the black slave," John Blassingame reminds us, "was intimately bound up with the nature of the antebellum plantation, the behavior of the master, the white man's perceptions and misperceptions, and a multitude of factors which influenced personal relations."[15] Slavery, then, was a social institution, but it was not so uniform or totalitarian in its operation that it could completely control the lives and the cultural forms of slaves. Despite the enactment of harsh slave codes, the plantation was never so efficiently or rationally managed as to leave the slave without considerable "social space" in which to maneuver. This maneuvering room allowed for a measure of physical and psychic autonomy. Then too, masters and overseers varied greatly in their attitudes and behavior. In fact, the ability of slaves to slow the pace of work, to avenge barbarities inflicted by sadistic masters, and, most of all, to convince masters and overseers that their productivity was linked to obtaining a degree of social room were important parts of the process by which the "slave community" fashioned its own culture. Though slaves might work from sunup to sundown under the overseer's whip and the master's shadow, from sundown to sunup and during the sabbath and holidays, they were largely out of the sight and sound of their owners. Black culture grew in the unintended but inevitable interstices of an institution primarily designed to extract labor from its victims. Only by systematically maiming or killing slaves for moving outside the strict institutional roles assigned them could the perpetuation of black cultural elements have been prohibited. And this would have been to doom the institution of slavery itself.

The African response to slavery must therefore take account of the somewhat flexible and variegated institutional arrangements which structured the life of slaves. It must also distinguish between the response of newly arrived Africans and "country-born" slaves and between slaves who worked as laborers in the fields, as domestic servants in the planters' houses, and as artisans in the shops. The spirit of resistance among "outlandish" Africans, fresh from their homelands, was often immediate and open and was rarely easy to break if we can believe contemporary ac-

[14]See especially Ann J. Lane, ed., *The Debate Over Slavery; Stanley Elkins and His Critics* (Urbana: University of Illinois Press, 1971).
[15]Blassingame, *The Slave Community*, p. 154.

counts in the eighteenth century. "If he must be broke," wrote an English observer, "either from Obstinacy, or, which I am more apt to suppose, from Greatness of Soul, [it] will require . . . hard Discipline. . . . You would really be surpriz'd at their Perseverance . . . they often die before they can be conquer'd."[16] Gerald Mullin's study of fugitive slaves in eighteenth-century Virginia and South Carolina makes clear that newly imported Africans often ran away and did so in ways that reflected the communal folk ethos which they had known on the other side of the ocean. When they took flight, they did so in groups, particularly in the company of slaves from their own country. In 1773, for example, fourteen freshly imported slaves fled as a group from a Virginia slave merchant, plunging into an unknown countryside in search of refuge.[17] Newspaper advertisements in South Carolina in the eighteenth century also reveal this kind of cooperative effort that brought slaves from the same region of Africa together in attempts at escape. The newspapers frequently advertised for groups of runaway "Gambia men" or slaves from the "Fullah Country," and the Carolina backcountry as well as the Spanish-Indian Florida frontier acted as a magnet to those who were bent on escape, especially after 1733 when a Spanish decree invited escaped English slaves to Florida. One North Carolinian was sure that newly imported slaves in his colony, most of them from Guinea, were far less industrious and more active in resisting slavery than "country-born" slaves.[18]

This kind of overt rebelliousness changed as Africans began assimilating into the culture of the English-speaking plantation. Living on plantations with anywhere from several to several hundred other slaves, many of them "country-born," new arrivals learned the routine of planting, transplanting, weeding, worming, harvesting, and transporting crops. But they also learned ways of reducing the tediousness of their tasks and minimizing the exertion which slave masters attempted to maximize. Dragging out the job, feigning illness, breaking tools, and other forms of "gold-bricking" were ways of avoiding physical depletion and also subtle forms of rebellion against slavery itself. Planters like Landon Carter of Virginia complained endlessly that "my people seem to be quite dead hearted and either cannot or will not work."[19] An English observer of

[16]Quoted in Donald D. Wax, "Negro Resistance to the Early American Slave Trade," *Journal of Negro History*, 51 (1966): 11.
[17]Gerald W. Mullin, *Flight and Rebellion; Slave Resistance in Eighteenth-Century Virginia* (New York: Oxford University Press, Inc., 1972), pp. 39–47.
[18]John Brickell, *The Natural History of North-Carolina* (Dublin, 1737; repub. Raleigh, N.C.: [n.p.] 1911), 272–73.
[19]Quoted in Mullin, *Flight and Rebellion*, p. 53.

American slavery noted that the slave "does not appear to perform half as much, as a labourer in England" and added a comment about "the slovenly carelessness with which all business is performed by the slave."[20] More direct forms of resistance were truancy, which usually took the form of hiding out in the woods; outlawry, in which the runaway slave struck by night against slave owners' fields, barns, and houses; crop destruction; barn burning; and organized pilfering in which groups of slaves requisitioned chickens, crops, liquor, tools, and household items by moonlight and sold them in black-market systems that often spread over considerable distances.

When relatively assimilated slaves moved from the field to the house, and changed their role from agricultural workers to household servants, they underwent further transformations which affected behavior. From the slaveholder's point of view the slaves could congratulate themselves for this advance in status, for it brought them closer to "civilized" life, conferred status upon them in the plantation hierarchy, and lightened the burden of their work. And though not many slaves resisted this chance for "advancement," accompanied by opportunities for better food, clothes, and shelter, many were aware that the role of domestic servant carried a heavy price, for it brought them into a far more intimate relationship with their captors and thus inhibited their ability to preserve some of the ancient ways that could be practiced in the relative privacy of the slave quarters. Partially lost to the household slave was membership in the black community and the chance to be out of sight of the white people of the plantation. New demands to acculturate more thoroughly were placed on these slaves, as every aspect of their behavior was now scrutinized by the slave master and slave mistress. Involved in a close, daily relationship with those who dominated their lives, many slaves developed speech problems such as stuttering—an outward sign of an inward difficulty in attempting to act in ways which satisfied the master and mistress but conflicted with real impulses and feelings. Rebelliousness could not take the same forms as in the field and so in the "big house" drunkenness, malingering, and elaborate verbal and emotional contests of will with those whose authority hung over them became the slaves' means of rebelling.

Because the plantation was a small world in itself, relatively self-sufficient and encompassing a wide variety of tasks, it required artisans skilled in carpentry, blacksmithing, milling, bricklaying, weaving, coopering, plastering, leatherworking, and the like. Slaves were trained in these tasks. As skilled workers, they became more fully assimilated into white

[20]Quoted in *ibid.*, p. 54.

culture, moving more freely between house, field, and workshop, and between the plantation and the town, the warehouse and the wharf. Other skilled labor, such as piloting tobacco- and rice-laden rafts and ferries through the maze-like inland waterways of the South, took the slave away from the plantation and out into a larger world. Thus, writes Mullin, "artisans were also bicultural, marginal men who sometimes manifested symptoms of a profound anxiety in interpersonal encounters with their masters."[21] They also became skilled and imaginative in their manner of resistance. They more frequently ran away, sometimes trying to pass for free Negroes in other colonies, hiring themselves out as sailors, trading from carts, and living in towns with other free Negroes and poor whites. They learned to cope with the white world. When they ran away, it was not in groups but individually, and they used their new skills and their new resourcefulness—a measure of how fully they had become ac-culturated—to maneuver their way into situations that would improve their lot. Their status at the top of the slave hierarchy gave them skills and privileges which they were often able to convert into individual or collective attempts to subvert the slave system. A study of slavery in the eighteenth-century capital of Virginia notes the high incidence of run-aways among slave artisans—the most fully acculturated Afro-Americans in the colony.[22]

Viewing the enslavement of Africans in America as an encounter or interaction of two cultures, we can see that the acculturation of slaves involved not only adaptation to the death-dealing daily toil of the plantation but also an education in strategies of survival, resistance, and rebellion. Plantation owners wanted to socialize their slaves as quickly as possible into the small world of the plantation. But ironically, as Mullin points out, "assimilation into colonial society made a few Africans and many of their descendants outwardly rebellious and so, more difficult to control."[23] In striking contrast to the Elkins thesis, which portrays the acculturative process in terms of receding assertiveness and resourceful-ness, the African in eighteenth-century slave society seems to have adapted to his new environment in a creative and persistently resistant fashion. Slave masters extracted labor and obedience from their slaves in an overall sense—if they had not slavery would have collapsed as an eco-nomic and social institution—but they did so only with great difficulty and never with the degree of success they wished for.

[21]*Ibid.*, p. 83.
[22]Thad W. Tate, *The Negro in Eighteenth-Century Williamsburg* (Williamsburg, Va.: Colonial Williamsburg, 1965), pp. 198–99.
[23]Mullin, *Flight and Rebellion*, p. 38.

REBELLION

Rebellion, of course, was the supreme expression of rebelliousness. A number of historians have contrasted the relatively small number of American slave rebellions with the frequent revolts of Brazilian or West Indian slaves and have concluded that Africans in America were far less rebellious than slaves elsewhere in the hemisphere. It is true that there is no American parallel for the massive slave uprisings that occurred in Jamaica in the eighteenth century or the wave of insurrections that kept the city of Bahia in northern Brazil in a state of disruption in the first few decades of the nineteenth century. The largest uprising in colonial America took place in South Carolina in 1739 when about one hundred slaves obtained a cache of arms, killed several whites, and fled toward the Florida frontier where they hoped to take refuge with the Spanish, as handfuls of slaves had done for decades. The plan was squashed by the white militia that intercepted the slave band and, with Indian assistance, defeated them in a pitched battle. And while there were a few other revolts which were nipped in the bud, such as the plot to capture Annapolis, Maryland, in 1740, large-scale rebellions of this kind were rare in the history of American slavery. Nor is there an American parallel to the semi-states created by escaped slaves in Dutch Surinam, French Guiana, Spanish Cuba, and Portuguese Brazil. In these hideaways thousands of runaway slaves fashioned their own communities and held out for decades against periodic assaults of colonial troops. Only Spanish Florida, to which hundreds but not thousands of slaves fled in the eighteenth century, offers an American parallel.

Examples such as these do not really prove the greater rebelliousness of Latin American slaves. What they indicate is that the chances for slaves to mount a successful rebellion increased in inverse proportion to the power of the white community. "The greater number of blacks which a frontier has," warned one observer in 1741, "and the greater the disproportion is between them and her white people, the more danger she is liable to; for these [blacks] are all secret enemies, and ready to join with her open ones on the first occasion."[24] Thus when slaves outnumbered whites six or eight to one, they could be counted on to rebel more frequently than when they were a minority in the population. By the same token, the incidence of flight from slavery was related to the chances for successful escape. In Brazil, where Africans and Indians had mixed

24[Benjamin Martyn], *An Impartial Inquiry into the State and Utility of the Colony of Georgia* (London, 1741), quoted in Peter Hutchins Wood, "Black Majority: Negroes in Colonial South Carolina from 1670 through the Stono Rebellion" (Ph.D. diss., Harvard University, 1972), p. 290.

for generations, there were far more opportunities to hide out or join an Indian community beyond the frontier than in colonial America, where the slave plantations were rarely situated more than one hundred miles from the Atlantic coast and where African-Indian mixing was slight by comparison. Fewer open rebellions in the English mainland colonies do not prove the greater servility of the American slave but serve only to indicate roughly the greater problems which any potential insurrectionist faced in rising against his oppressors in the mainland colonies. In different conditions, rebelliousness became channeled into other forms—more subtle, less dangerous, and more effective.

That almost all the colonies passed special laws against arson and poisoning in the first decades of the eighteenth century and then reorganized these laws a generation later, increasing the severity of punishment, is only one indication of the persistent resistance to enslavement and the enduring hostility manifested by slaves against their masters. In fact, "the sharpest evidence of slave resistance," it has been recently reasoned, "is not the historical record of armed revolts . . . so much as the codes that legalized branding, flogging, burning, the amputation of limbs, hamstringing and murder to keep the slaves 'non-violent.' "[25] A similar kind of evidence that blacks were far from regressing to infantile dependency and abject obedience can be found in the ever-present fear of black rebellion that coursed through the white community. A vivid example of this can be found in the reaction of the Southern colonies to the onset of the Seven Years' War in 1755. William Shirley, commander of the British forces in North America, complained that nothing could be expected of the Southern militias because if they left their local communities the slaves would flee *en masse* to the French, who were promising "liberty & Lands to settle upon." Lewis Evans, a Pennsylvania strategist, also conceded that the Southern militia could not make a move: "The Thing is impossible," he wrote, "they have . . . scarce Whites enough to prevent the Defection of their Slaves; and if any considerable Party should happen to be defeated, when abroad, it could be scarce possible to prevent their total Revolt."[26] The governor of Virginia hoped to spare a few militia units for the intercolonial war effort but greatly feared "the Combinations of the Negro Slaves, who have been very audacious on the Defeat on the Ohio [of Braddock's army]" and prayed that "we shall be able to defeat the Designs of our Enemies and keep these Slaves in proper Subjection."[27]

[25]Sidney Mintz, "Toward an Afro-American History," *Journal of World History*, 13 (1971): 321.
[26]Quoted in Lawrence H. Gipson, *The Great War for Empire: The Years of Defeat, 1754–1757* (New York: Alfred K. Knopf, Inc., 1946), pp. 14–15.
[27]*Ibid.*, p. 15.

Slavery in the North

If slaves were far from submissive in plantation societies, where they often represented half the population, how did they respond to slavery in the Northern colonies where they made up only 3 percent of the population in most of New England and perhaps 10 percent in Rhode Island, New Jersey, New York, and Pennsylvania? To begin with, any answer to this question must recognize that slaves in the North were responding to a different kind of slavery than in the plantation South. Besides representing a small minority in the population, the nature of the slave's work differed in the Northern regions. Infrequently employed in field gangs, Northern slaves typically worked as artisans, farm hands, or personal servants. Whereas a majority of Southern slaves worked on plantations with many other slaves, the typical Northern slave labored alone or with only one or two of his or her countrymen. Moreover, the plantation slave quarters, where blacks could maintain a considerable degree of cultural autonomy and privacy away from the watchful eye of the owner, had no equivalent in Northern slave life. Virtually every Northern slave ate, slept, and lived in the house of the master. All of these factors—their low proportion of the population, wide dispersion, and unrelieved contact with whites—made attempts to retain a link to the African past extremely difficult, while ensuring that acculturation proceeded at a relatively rapid pace.

In the Northern cities slavery was far more deeply rooted than in the countryside. In New York City, where the Dutch had begun a tradition of relying on slave labor during the half-century they controlled the town, almost 20 percent of the population was Afro-American in 1750 and two of every five householders owned at least one slave. In Philadelphia and Boston in the mid-eighteenth century, slaves made up about a tenth of the population and could be found in the homes of nearly every fifth family. In all three cities more than a thousand black slaves labored for their masters in the decade before the Revolution.

Because their labor was typically less arduous and their treatment usually better than on Southern plantations one might expect that slaves in the North would be less resistant to bondage than their fellows in the South. But such was not the case. For example, although black slaves had been assimilating to Anglo-Dutch culture in New York City for almost a century, by the early eighteenth century they had not yet reconciled themselves to slavery. Nor had they yet been shapen into mild-tempered, compliant workers. On the night of April 6, 1712, a group of more than twenty slaves, acting in accordance with a preformulated plan, set fire to a building and then lay in wait for the white men who came to extinguish the flames. Wielding knives, axes, and guns, they killed nine whites and injured others before making their escape. It was later reported that "had it not been for the Garrison [of English soldiers] there, that city would have been reduced to ashes, and the greatest part of the inhabitants murdered."[28] Once suppressed, the plot was investigated and about seventy slaves taken into custody. Forty-three were brought to trial and twenty-five, including several women and Indian slaves, were convicted. The terror of black insurrection which ran like a fever through the white community was evident in the sentences that were imposed: thirteen slaves died on the gallows, one was starved to death in chains, three were burned at the stake, and one was broken on the wheel. Six others killed themselves rather than endure retribution at the hands of the white community. The New York Assembly quickly passed a new slave code, which strictly regulated the slaves' freedom of movement and stripped away most of the rights that until this time distinguished their lot from that of their Southern counterparts. In neighboring colonies, legislators scurried to impose new restrictions on blacks or, as in Pennsylvania, to pass import duties so high as to make further importations of Africans unprofitable.

Even the medieval torture imposed upon the black conspirators of 1712 did not achieve the desired results of cowing Northern Negroes into submissiveness. A generation later, within the living memory of many slaves, a wave of slave unrest swept the Northern seaboard. It began in New Jersey in 1740 with a few incidents of barn burning, which was not uncommon in the North. Two slaves paid with their lives for this act of rebellion. A few months later a rash of thefts and fires struck New York City. Among the buildings ignited was Fort George, which housed the English garrison. Indicted in these incidents were a white tavern keeper, his wife, and an indentured servant girl who served as a prostitute in the tavern. Helped along by some low-grade torture, the servant girl confessed that her master was involved with several slaves in a conspiracy to burn the town to the ground and kill all its white inhabitants. So great was the fear at these rumors that the case was turned over to the Supreme Court of Judicature. The presiding judge's account of the trial remains a valuable source for understanding both slave behavior in New York City and the related fears of the city's white inhabitants.

Two slaves were brought to trial for theft and possible conspiracy. When the conspiracy charge against them could not be substantiated, they were hung for theft, dying "very stubbornly" on the gallows without

[28]Quoted in Kenneth Scott, "The Slave Insurrection in New York in 1712," *New-York Historical Society Quarterly*, 45 (1961): 51.

confessing to anything more. A month later the tavern keeper and his wife were hanged for treason, though they too went to their deaths with closed lips concerning a slave plot. When the servant-prostitute went to the gallows for conspiracy, she died renouncing the statements she had made concerning black insurrectionists. But fear and a desire to cow the city's blacks had overtaken the town by now and the dragnet began pulling in slaves, who were threatened with torture and execution if they did not reveal the identity of the slave conspirators. In the following months 67 confessions were extracted from terrified slaves. Before the trial was over almost a year later 150 slaves and 25 whites had been imprisoned, 18 slaves and 4 whites had been tortured and hanged, 13 slaves had been burned at the stake, and 70 others transported out of the colony to the West Indies.

Many of those arrested, tortured, deported, or killed were probably innocent victims of the fear and anger that overtook New York in 1740 and 1741. Yet the ferocious white response, which might be compared to the Salem witch trials of the 1690s, reflected the pervasive fear in the city that slaves at their core were indeed insurrectionists and could be counted on to repeat their acts of aggression and rebellion against the white community unless the most draconic measures were taken. Had New Yorkers regarded their slaves as docile and childish "Sambos," no such conspiracy would have been believable and no such brutal punishment would have been meted out. New Yorkers were not eager to destroy human property in which they invested. But they lived with a gnawing fear that their slaves would revolt, for they knew from everyday slave behavior that the African captive was a truculent, resistant worker whose desire for freedom seldom flagged. Incidents such as the one in New York show that even in the Northern colonies slaves awaited opportunities to cast off their chains or to inflict upon white society some of the pain that had been apportioned to them.

Even in Boston and in Philadelphia, which was the center of colonial abolitionist activity, there were few misapprehensions about the contentedness or submissiveness of slaves. Magistrates in the colonial period continually faced cases of black resistance to slavery in Boston, and Puritan clergymen such as Cotton Mather often felt compelled to lecture slaves about the glory in God's eyes earned by those who willingly submitting to their masters. But the "fondness for freedom" that led slaves to defy their masters, run away, destroy property, and express their discontent in drunkenness and rowdyism never stopped trying the patience of Bostonians. Puritan clergymen and magistrates attempted to convince slaves that "Your Servitude is Gentle . . . you are treated, with more than meer Humanity, and fed and clothed and lodged, as well as you can wish for." They warned that "If you were Free, many of you would not Live near so well as you do." But still, wrote a Boston judge early in the eighteenth century, slaves engaged in "continual aspiring" after "forbidden Liberty."[29]

In Philadelphia, where the efforts of Quakers to abolish slavery may have produced the most humane type of slavery in North America, slaves also malingered, balked, and struggled for their freedom. Benjamin Franklin, himself a slave owner, wrote in 1770 to a European friend: "Perhaps you may imagine the Negroes to be a mild-tempered, tractable Kind of People. Some of them indeed are so. But the Majority are of a plotting Disposition, dark, sullen, malicious, revengeful and cruel in the highest Degree."[30] The opinion of Joseph Galloway, Franklin's friend and also a slave owner, that the slaves of Philadelphia were intent on obtaining their freedom was borne out in 1777 when the British army entered Philadelphia. A large proportion of the city's slaves, including some belonging to Philadelphians known for their kindly treatment of black servants, made their personal declaration of independence by joining the British troops.

Black Culture in Colonial America

Resistance and rebellion were forms of attacking the system of slavery, of attempting in piecemeal fashion to bring the institution to an end. The balance of power was always massively stacked against the slave in this situation and therefore it is not surprising that the incident of organized group resistance was low. More importantly, we must attempt to understand how slaves, living their lives within the confining limits of the slave system, struggled to maintain as much cultural and personal autonomy as possible in order to resist internalizing the negative stereotypes which slave owners attempted to fasten on them. Viewing the plantation or the city as "a battlefield where slaves fought masters for physical and psychological survival"[31] enables us to turn our gaze to the existential side of black life and culture in colonial America. In this we can focus particularly on three aspects of slave life: religion, work, and the family.

[29]Lawrence W. Towner, "'A Fondness for Freedom': Servant Protest in Puritan Society," *William and Mary Quarterly*, 3d Ser., 19 (1962): 202.

[30]"A Conversation between an Englishman, a Scotchman, and an American," in Verner W. Crane, "Benjamin Franklin on Slavery and American Liberties," *Pennsylvania Magazine of History and Biography*, 62 (1938): 8.

[31]Blassingame, *Slave Community*, p. 184.

RELIGION

Slaves brought with them to the New World a complex religious heritage, and no amount of desolation or physical abuse could wipe out these deeply rooted beliefs. In fact people enduring the kind of daily stress inherent in the master-slave relationship typically turn to their deepest emotive sources for relief. Coming from cultures where the division between sacred and secular activities was much narrower than in European society, where life and afterlife were not regarded as so separate, African slaves made religious activities "areas of considerable potential creativity and social strength."[32]

African religious customs, funeral rites, sacred images, and charms for protection against evil spirits, were no doubt attenuated on New World plantations or melded with elements of Christianity. How fast this happened is not yet known but clearly it varied from place to place. In New England slaves were few in number and the attempts to indoctrinate them in Christian belief were relatively strenuous. Both private religious instruction and public churchgoing was common among slaves and by the mid-eighteenth century many black children were attending schools opened by Anglicans and Quakers. In the Northern towns Anglican ministers frequently married slaves and baptized their children. Also because slaves usually lived within white households in small numbers rather than in slave quarters amidst a black community, Africanisms were probably obliterated much more rapidly than in the South.

On Southern plantations, slave masters were not so eager to see their slaves instructed in Christianity. But the missionary wing of the Anglican church, acting on Morgan Godwyn's broad plan of 1680 to Christianize the Africans and Indians of the English colonies, sent its agents into many areas in the eighteenth century, and other churches also engaged in the instruction of slaves. Moreover, African beliefs and rituals probably persisted far longer than in the North because on the plantation the slave could maintain a far greater sense of a collective experience and was constantly in touch with mother Africa through freshly arriving slaves. Realizing this, slave masters were caught in a dilemma. If the perpetuation of African religion fostered a collective identity and fed the spirit of resistance, then it was imperative to replace it with Christian belief. But at the same time the owner was not eager to have his human property subjected to a new ideology that would make him or her a less willing worker. So when masters permitted their slaves to attend church, it was with the hope that they would learn the Christian ideals of meekness,

[32]Rawick, *From Sundown to Sunup*, p. 32.

humility, and obedience, as the missionaries promised, and not the ideals of the brotherhood of man or the story of the Hebrew flight from oppression.

The problem with Christian instruction was that it was extremely difficult to expose the slave only to the elements of religious thought which would make him submissive while quarantining him from the elements that fed the desire for freedom. Protestant clergymen were careful to impress upon slaves that acceptance of Christ was not to be confused with obtaining freedom, and laws were passed in most colonies to make crystal clear that baptism did not place the master under the slightest obligation to manumit his slaves. But try as they might to suppress it, the idea spread among slaves in the eighteenth-century South that baptism, though not intended to release them from chains, was a first step in this direction. Whether this reflected slave familiarity with the Western tradition that no Christian could enslave another Christian or sprang from another source is uncertain. But the equation of baptism and eventual freedom spread in the early eighteenth century. In 1730, following a period of unusual missionary activity in Virginia, a number of baptized slaves began circulating the word that their acceptance of Christ entitled them to freedom. Several hundred slaves gathered in Norfolk and Princess Anne counties in Virginia to foment a rebellion, but the plan was discovered and four black leaders were hanged. Thereafter the resistance to catechising slaves grew.

Another obstacle to Christianization was the opinion of many slave owners that exposure to the tenets of the carpenter of Nazareth made slaves "proud and saucy," as Thomas Bacon, a Chesapeake clergyman, told slaves. "You must not be eye servants, that is such as will be very busy [only] in your master's presence," warned Bacon.[33] But it was widely believed, as the Swedish traveler in America, Peter Kalm, noted, that if slaves were Christianized, their masters "would not be able to keep their Negroes so subjected afterwards" because of the pride which Africans would develop "on seeing themselves upon a level with their masters in religious matters."[34]

The advent of the Great Awakening in the 1740s ushered in a new era of activity among those eager to Christianize slaves and a new era of receptivity among slaves to the precepts of Christianity. In the Anglican parish of Williamsburg, the capital of Virginia, nearly a thousand slaves were baptized in a single generation from 1746 to 1768. Presbyterians

[33]Bacon, *Sermons Addressed to Masters and Servants. . .* (Williamsburg, Va., 1743), in *Bases of the Plantation Society*, ed. Aubrey C. Land (New York: Harper & Row, Publishers, 1969), p. 232.

[34]*Peter Kalm's Travels in North America*, ed. Adolph B. Benson (New York: Dover Publications, Inc., 1966), 1: 209.

were also active in the Southern colonies beginning about 1740. Samuel Davies, a leading Southern Presbyterian, boasted that he had one hundred slaves in his congregation in Hanover County, Virginia, in 1750 and a few years later claimed that some three hundred blacks received instruction from him. The Anglican Jonathan Boucher recorded that he baptized 315 slaves on a single day in 1767, and by this time a sizable portion of Virginia's slaves, especially those living in the vicinity of small towns such as Williamsburg and Norfolk, had been indoctrinated in Christian religion by Anglicans, Presbyterians, and Methodists.

What gave these efforts special force was the appeal that the Awakeners' style and message had to slaves. For a people whose ancestral religion was grounded primarily in an understanding of nature as indwelling and whose eschatological vision allowed for no sharp differences between the secular and the sacred, religion and daily life being conjoined, Protestantism always had a limited appeal. Highly literate and rational, sanitized of its mystical elements, guarded over by professional clergymen who stressed passivity among worshippers, the Protestant service had little power to render intelligible or tolerable the strange and repressive world in which slaves found themselves. But the revivalism of the Great Awakening, because it preached a personal rebirth, used music and body motion, and asked for the dynamic participation of each individual in an intense emotional experience, seems to have had a tremendous appeal to Africans. Here was a religious outlook which shared enough with ancestral styles and beliefs such as spirit possession, and had meaning for the daily experience of their lives, to allow for the perpetuation of Africanisms at the same time that adaptation to new cultural forms took place.

It was the hope of slave masters that Christian doctrine, whether of the ascetic, rational variety or the emotional, revivalistic variety, would be the opiate of their slaves. Even if their bondsmen shared nothing of what their labor produced, even if they gave up all their rights for a life of perpetual servitude, they could at least comfort themselves with the knowledge that Christianity sanctified the weak, the poor, and the humble. It is with this formulation in mind that those who have studied black religion have traditionally explained that the most important effect of Protestantism on the slave community was to deflect the minds of slaves "from sufferings and privations of this world to a world after death where the weary would find rest and the victims of injustice would be compensated."[35] But slaves did not passively accept what the Anglican or Presbyterian minister chose to inculcate in them. They drew selectively from the white religion and shaped their own religious experience in a

    [35] E. Franklin Frazier, *The Negro Church in America* (New York: Schocken Books, 1964), p. 45.

fashion that not only gave them an area of life which was semi-independent from the control of the master but provided an important psychological mechanism for channeling anger and projecting aggression in ways that would not bring physical retribution from the white community.

Black spirituals reveal a great deal about this two-edged nature of religion. Many of the slave spirituals, which were adaptations of white spirituals or a unique blend of African rhythm patterns, Anglo-American melodies, and adapted words, reflected the pain of the slave experience. Some of the spirituals were called "sorrow songs" and the musical expression of this pain was no doubt cathartic for those who sang them communally. Another theme of the spirituals, however, was that of worth and strength. We cannot know whether such songs as "We Are the People of God," or "I Really Do Believe I'm a Child of God," or "I'm Born of God, I Know I Am" were sung by slaves in the eighteenth century since it is extremely difficult to date their origins. But there is little reason to believe that if slaves found them sustaining in the nineteenth century, they would not have created songs and spirituals with similar themes in the pre-Revolutionary period. What is impressive about these songs is that they portray feelings of worthiness and even a belief that slaves will ultimately prevail because they are superior to the masters. In the midst of a society that worked to convince the slave of his lack of worth, of the poverty of his African culture, of his barbarism, the songs show a strong black self-esteem, an abiding feeling of communal fellowship, and a sense of purpose to life. Black religious music demonstrates how difficult it was for white society to remake the black consciousness and to coerce the black slave into internalizing white values.[36]

The theme of resistance and rebellion was also woven into many of the slave songs. The spiritual celebrating Samson, who sang, "If I had my way, I'd tear this building down," may have had only Biblical meaning for the whites who sang it on Sunday mornings in the parish churches of the South. But for black workers in the field the building was the edifice of slavery and tearing it down meant nothing less than the destruction of the slave system. Similarly, the spiritual "Didn't My Lord Deliver Daniel," which referred to the deliverance of the Hebrews from their enemies, had a more modern meaning for the black slaves who adopted it as one of their own songs.

Almost all the symbolic figures of the black spirituals—Daniel, David, Joshua, Jonah, Moses, and Noah—were children of the Hebrews, figures

---

[36]Lawrence W. Levine, "Slave Songs and Slave Consciousness: An Exploration in Neglected Sources," in *Anonymous Americans: Explorations in Nineteenth-Century Social History*, ed. Tamara K. Hareven (Englewood Cliffs, N.J.: Prentice Hall, Inc., 1971), pp. 99–130.

from the Old Testament who were delivered from their persecutors in this world and not in the afterlife. And they were delivered in ways that had special meaning for slaves. The Red Sea opened to allow the Hebrew slaves to pass through and then closed to engulf Pharaoh's armies; the blind and vulnerable Samson brought the mansion of his conquerors crashing down. In these spirituals slaves were singing about far more than deliverance in the next world. As Lawrence Levine has pointed out, their religious music was not sacred in the narrow sense of being strictly attached to religious ceremony and the Sunday service. It was sacred in a distinctly African way, in the larger context of uniting one's present condition with the ritual and mythical past and linking it also to the possibility of rebirth in the future. Slaves trapped in the grasp of lifelong servitude created their own cultural autonomy "by transcending the narrow confines of the world in which they were forced to live. They extended the boundaries of their restrictive universe backward until it fused with the world of the Old Testament, and upward until it became one with the world beyond. The spirituals are the record of a people who found the status, the harmony, the values, the order they needed to survive by internally creating an expanded universe. . . ."[37] In religious music and in the persistence of plantation conjurers, voodoo men, and witch doctors, we see Afro-Americans struggling to adjust to white culture while still maintaining a separateness from the world of their masters.

WORK

American slaves also succeeded in using daily labor as an instrument for psychological survival and adapted African work habits to New World conditions in a way that made life more bearable. Slaves were only too well aware that the labor they did benefited only the master. But in their daily work they behaved in a number of ways—breaking hoes, uprooting freshly planted seedlings, and harvesting carelessly—that signal their defiance of the exhortations and floggings of the masters and overseers. From these responses masters learned that there were limits beyond which they could not go, for to push too hard was only to prove the law of diminishing returns. To deny the slaves the traditional Sunday holiday or the usual Christmas respite, for example, was only to guarantee that less rather than more work would be done in the future. Similarly, to set work standards too high was only to encourage slaves to accomplish less or to retaliate against their masters. The lesson was clearly stated in 1732 by the South Carolina *Gazette*, which reported that a master who had driven

[37]*Ibid.*, p. 115.

his slaves late into the night, cleaning and barreling a rice crop, found his barn "and all that was in it" burned to ashes by morning.[38]

But slaves also reacted in positive ways to work, expressing preferences "for a rhythm of work and leisure that reflected the pre-industrial culture of both Africa and the slave plantations."[39] They would work harder and longer at tasks that required collective labor but offered resistance to working by themselves. In this preference for collective labor they demonstrated an attitude toward work that was in sharp contrast with the European norm of the individual following his "calling" and laboring independently. Their African background had inured them to collective agricultural labor and they strove to maintain this pattern of work in their lives as slaves.

THE FAMILY

It was at the level of the family—the close intimate connections between man and woman, parent and child, and brother and sister—that slaves developed the most important bastion of defense against the hardships of slavery. Slave law in most colonies did not recognize the legitimacy of slave marriages or families. Historians have pointed to the Spanish and Portuguese colonies, where the Catholic church carefully upheld the sanctity of slave marriage and family life, and taken this as one of the strongest proofs of the unusual harshness of the American system. The charge has often been leveled that American slavery can be seen at its worst in its denial of the right of slaves to even the most basic human right of family association.

Recent scholarship has made it clear that this point of view is historically inaccurate. Not only is it based on the false assumption that white slave owners found it conducive to the efficient and profitable management of the plantation to obliterate family life but it fails to account for the ability of slaves to play an active role in shaping their own social and interpersonal relations within the confines of the "peculiar institution." To be sure, slave masters placed obstacles in the way of slaves as they attempted to recreate African family patterns in the New World. As chattels, they could not make contracts and thus marriage was not legally possible. More important, the sale of either party in a monogamous relationship could precipitously end a union; this is often regarded as the most brutal aspect of slavery.

---

[38] South Carolina *Gazette*, Oct. 14, 1732, cited in Wood, "Black Majority," p. 446.
[39] Eugene D. Genovese, "The History of Slaves," *New York Review of Books* (Sept. 21, 1972), p. 17.

Still another obstacle to stable family life was the general shortage of women, although the excess of males was never so pronounced in the mainland colonies as in the Caribbean islands and many parts of Spanish and Portuguese America. Throughout the seventeenth and eighteenth centuries, so far as can be ascertained from the scanty data available, slaves were imported in a ratio of about three men to two women. This excess of males, especially in the South, meant that permanent or semi-permanent relationships were possible for less than the full number of male slaves. In New York, by far the largest slave holding area in the North, males over sixteen outnumbered females four to three in 1756. One year earlier in Rhode Island parity had been reached among the 2,500 adult slaves; but in Maryland in the same year adult males outnumbered adult females eleven to nine. In St. George's Parish, South Carolina, in 1726 slave men outnumbered slave women five to three.[40] As slave children were born, this disparity between the sexes gradually disappeared, but it was not until a generation or so after the closing of the slave trade in 1808 that parity was reached. In the North, where slaves were sparsely held, this problem was intensified because, although the sex ratio was more even than in the South, most slave owners held only one or two slaves and thus male and female slaves only occasionally lived together under the same roof.

Another barrier to any kind of satisfactory family life was the role which the white male played as sexual aggressor against the black woman. How many black women were assaulted or lured with favors into sexual relations with white masters cannot be known, although judging from the sizable mulatto population by 1800, the number cannot have been small. For a black husband to know of or to witness the assault of a white slaveowner upon his wife was probably the most psychologically destructive and socially disruptive weapon in the white man's arsenal. As Angela Davis has written: "In its political contours, the rape of the black woman was not exclusively an attack upon her. Indirectly, its target was also the slave community as a whole. In launching the sexual war on the woman, the master not only asserted his sovereignty over a critically important figure of the slave community, he would also be aiming a blow against the black man."[41]

The anguish that was thus caused inevitably had traumatic effects on attempts to build a stable relationship because the male head of the fam-

[40]Evarts B. Greene and Virginia D. Harrington, *American Population Before the Federal Census of 1790* (New York: Columbia University Press, 1932), pp. 67, 101, 126; Frank J. Klingberg, *An Appraisal of the Negro in Colonial South Carolina: A Study in Americanization* (Washington, D.C.: The Associated Publishers, 1941), pp. 58–60.

[41]Angela Davis, "Reflections on the Black Woman's Role in the Community of Slaves," *Black Scholar*, 3 (1971–72): 13.

ily was powerless to defend those closest to him from the most intimate and painful form of attack. That so many black novelists and writers in the decades following the end of slavery harked back to this theme, indicates how strongly the pain continued to reverberate in the black consciousness. For example, W. E. B. DuBois, writing three-quarters of a century after emancipation, wrote:

> I shall forgive the white South much in its final judgement day: I shall forgive its slavery, for slavery is a world-old habit; I shall forgive its fighting for a well-lost cause, and for remembering that struggle with tender tears; I shall forgive its so-called "pride of race," the passion of its hot blood, and even its dear, old, laughable strutting and posing; but one thing I shall never forgive, neither in this world nor the world to come: its wanton and continued and persistent insulting of the black womanhood which it sought and seeks to prostitute to its lust.[42]

Even in the face of these formidable obstacles, slaves were able to fashion intimate ties between man and woman, parent and child. Slaves frequently formed monogamous relationships and if these did not last as long as in white society, a large part of the explanation lays in aspects of the system that were beyond the slave's control—the shorter life-span of Afro-Americans, the breakup of marriage because of the sale of one or both partners, and the call of freedom which impelled many slaves to run away. Many planters encouraged their slaves to live together and to take up the role of parent, for they found that slaves were more dutiful and productive when they were tied to a spouse and offspring. It was not so much a concern for the morality of their slaves as an interest in maximizing the output of labor and minimizing insubordination that led owners to promote slave marriage and family life.

Within the black family what were the roles of the man and the woman? This vexed question has assumed new importance because the idea is currently prevalent that the welfare family, headed by a woman, is a replication of a slave matriarchate. In this view the slave mother, as the noted sociologist E. Franklin Frazier has written, "was generally the recognized head of the family group. She was the mistress of the cabin to which the 'husband' or father often made only weekly visits. Under such circumstances a maternal group took form and the tradition of the Negro woman's responsibility for her family took root."[43] Following this formulation, it is assumed that the slave emerged after emancipation with only

[42]W. E. B. DuBois, *Darkwater: Voices From Within the Veil* (New York: AMS Press, 1969), p. 172.

[43]*The Negro Family in America*, quoted in *Black Matriarchy: Myth or Reality?* ed. John H. Bracey, August Meier, and Elliott Rudwick (Belmont, Cal.: Wadsworth Publishing Co., 1971), p. 8.

a faint tradition of normal family life. Buffeted by the problems of trying to adapt as a freeman to an increasingly urban and industrial world, ex-slaves were never able to knit together the same nuclear, two-parent family that served as the norm in the white community. ·

Although the black matriarchal family structure no doubt existed to some extent in the eighteenth-century Southern colonies, doubt remains that this was characteristic of the slave family. Slave men were undoubtedly emasculated in important ways since they could not occupy the dominant role in family and community relationships as they had in the tribal villages of Africa. But the black male did assert his authority by supplementing the food supply through trapping; by organizing the garden plot behind the slave cabin; by disciplining his children; and most of all by being the principal figure in the active resistance to slavery. Slave men did marry slave women and established with remarkable success, given the deterrents inherent in the situation, a relatively stable family life. In some cases slaves were able to preserve these relationships by threatening rebellion. For example, the government of South Carolina, reeling under the blows of the Yamasees in 1715, negotiated a promise of 130 militiamen from Virginia in exchange for an equal number of slave women. But threats of a full-scale slave insurrection if the women were sent northward forced the Carolinians to renege on their part of the bargain.[44].

While slave men struggled to preserve their role in the black family, black women came to occupy a position in the family and in the black community that was strikingly different from that of white eighteenth-century women. More and more in the eighteenth century, especially on the Southern plantation, the ideology of domesticity kept white women confined in the home where they were expected to be the guardians of white virtue and culture. Gradually white women lost the measure of autonomy that had characterized the role of women in European peasant society. Black women, by contrast, remained indispensably important to both the work of the plantation and the stability of the slave community. They worked in the fields and they worked in the slave cabin. It was ironic, Angela Davis has written, that the slave woman "had to be released from the chains of the myth of femininity. . . . In order to function as slave, the black woman had to be annulled as woman, that is, as woman in her historical stance of wardship under the entire male hierarchy. The sheer force of things rendered her equal to her man. . . . Male supremacist structures could not become deeply embedded in the internal workings of the slave system."[45]

[44]David D. Wallace, *South Carolina: A Short History, 1520–1948* (Chapel Hill: University of North Carolina Press, 1951), p. 91.
[45]Davis, "The Black Woman's Role," p. 7.

Female passivity and the retreat to the cult of domesticity, which was beginning to characterize the life of white eighteenth-century women on large plantations and in the upper class of the Northern urban centers, was thus no part of the black woman's life. Caught in the net of slavery, the black woman, paradoxically, maintained a position of strength and autonomy within the black community that made her far more equal to the male than was the case of women in white society. The black family was a partnership of equals in the tasks performed and responsibilities shouldered. In this respect it bore closer resemblance to Algonquian and Siouian family structure than to European family organization, for in Indian cultures women were also vitally important in agricultural work, child-rearing responsibilities were shared, and the woman in general maintained a degree of power and autonomy that was unallowable in white society.

Because slavery was above all else a system for extracting the maximum amount of labor from its victims, it all too often involved cruelties that made family life almost impossible to maintain. But in general, American slaves were better clothed, fed, and treated than those in the West Indies, Brazil, or other parts of the New World where settled white society took only shallow root and plantation owners found it more profitable literally to work their slaves to death and then purchase fresh replacements from Africa. When conditions were at least conducive to sustaining life, slaves were effective in defining a culture of their own. As one black scholar has recently written: "Slaves were able to fashion a life style and a set of values—an ethos—which prevented them from being imprisoned altogether by the definitions which the larger society sought to impose. This ethos was an amalgam of Africanisms and New World elements which helped slaves . . . 'feel their way along the course of American slavery, enabling them to endure.' . . ."[46]

How much of African culture survived under eighteenth-century slavery can never be determined quantitatively. Nor is it especially important to do so. More important is to understand that Africans in the English plantations adapted elements of African culture to the demands of a new life and a new environment. There can be little doubt that slave masters were intent on obliterating all Africanisms that reduced the effectiveness of slaves as laborers and that they had some success in this. It is also true that slavery eliminated many of the cultural differences among slaves, who came from a wide variety of African cultural groups—Fulanis, Ibos, Yorubas, Malagasies, Ashantis, Mandingos, and others. But at the same time, it must be remembered that throughout the eighteenth century, un-

[46]Sterling Stuckey, "Through the Prism of Folklore: The Black Ethos in Slavery," *The Massachusetts Review*, 9 (1968): 418.

like in the nineteenth, large numbers of new Africans were arriving each year. Slave importations grew rapidly in the eighteenth century so that probably never more than half the slaves, and perhaps one-third of the adults, were American-born. This continuous infusion of African culture kept alive many of the elements that would later be transmuted almost beyond recognition. Through fashioning their own distinct culture, within the limits established by the rigors of the slave system, blacks were able to retain semiseparate religious forms, their own music and dance, their own family life, and their own beliefs and values. All of these proved to be indispensable survival techniques in a system of forced labor. Though slaves might feign deference or submissiveness and were severely constrained in many respects, they preserved important elements of traditional culture and learned to carve out important areas of activity, apart from contact with masters and overseers, that gave meaning and importance to life.

chapter 9

The Transformation of
European Culture

In 1650 the European population of the colonies clinging to the eastern edge of the continent was about the same as the daytime population of a major university campus today—roughly 50,000. A half century later this number had multiplied by five to a quarter-million. By 1750 the number had again increased fivefold, including about 200,000 Africans. It was a rate of population increase unknown in other parts of the world. By the middle of the eighteenth century the inhabitants of the English colonies in America were one-third as numerous as the English themselves and the rate at which the gap between the two populations was closing led early demographers such as Benjamin Franklin to estimate that before another four generations passed the colonizers would outnumber those in the land they had left.

The European Immigrants

These rapidly multiplying proto-Americans were not, of course, simply Englishmen. The seventeenth-century immigrants had come primarily from England and mixed with a small number of Dutch, Swedes, and Finns already settled along the seaboard and with a relatively insignificant number of Germans, Scotch-Irish, French, and Africans who arrived late in the seventeenth century. But the eighteenth century belonged to the non-English so far as immigration was concerned. Beginning in the second decade of the century thousands of Germans, Swiss, Ulster Scotch-Irish, and Africans began pouring into the colonies. Some came voluntarily and some involuntarily but whether they arrived as slaves, indentured servants, or free persons, they drastically altered the gene pool of the existing population. By the end of the colonial period, as the Revolution loomed on the horizon, roughly half the inhabitants of the Thirteen Colonies had no English blood in their veins. This proportion of non-English-born was greater than at any time in American history, even after the tremendous influx of Europeans in the late nineteenth and early twentieth centuries.

History has told us primarily about the lives of only an infinitesimally small segment of this population. We know a great deal about the political and military leaders, the men who amassed fortunes, and those whose high positions in the society left their names and their opinions in the official and private records of the time. But the cultural change that was occurring during the century prior to the Revolution bore far more relation to the roughly congruent behavior of the thousands of "historically voiceless" individuals than to the actions of the leaders whose words and deeds form the basis of most of our written history. After the Revolution John Adams would write that "the poor man's conscience is clear; yet he is ashamed . . . he feels himself out of the sight of others groping in the dark. Mankind takes no notice of him. He rambles and wanders unheeded. In the midst of a crowd, at church, in the market . . . he is in as much obscurity as he would be in a garret or a cellar. He is not disapproved, censured, or reproached; he is only not seen."[1] Similarly, historians have "not seen" the largest part of colonial society whose footprints are only now being discerned in the sands of time.

It was the work, the wanderings, the attitudes, and the hopes and fears of the masses of inconspicuous individuals that led to cultural change so distinct in America in the eighteenth century that European aristocrats would never tire of touring the colonies and setting down the characteristics of the people they saw—so different from what they knew in Europe. What they described, though they did it in an entirely untheoretical way, was a set of economic activities, forms of social and political organization, and a constellation of values and beliefs that were fused together in what

[1]Quoted in James A. Henretta, *The Evolution of American Society, 1700–1815* (Lexington, Mass.: D.C. Heath and Company, 1973), pp. 3–4.

we call a culture. During the first three-quarters of the eighteenth century this culture was transformed so extensively that a John Smith or John Winthrop, had they still lived, would have been shocked by what they saw.

SOCIAL CLASSES

The social origins of those who flocked to the colonies in the eighteenth century played a part in the cultural transformation. From the top layers of European society came almost nobody. In the seventeenth century a number of Englishmen at the apex of the social pyramid had taken an active role in colonizing the New World—men such as Walter Raleigh and Richard Grenville in Virginia; the Calverts, who founded Maryland; the proprietors of Carolina and New Jersey, who were insiders at the court of Charles II; and a handful of others. But for the most part they contributed money and organizational ability rather than their lives. Only a few tore free of their moorings in England and emigrated permanently to America. In the eighteenth century such upper-class immigrants were even rarer. Only an occasional Baron de Graffenried or Count von Zinzendorf, usually leading groups of German, Swiss, or Scotch-Irish into the backcountry of Pennsylvania, Virginia, or the Carolinas, represented the upper stratum of European society.

Below the nobility were the country gentry and, grouped with them on the social scale, officeholders, members of the professions, and the wealthier merchants. These were the men who ran the joint-stock companies which had been so important in launching the early seventeenth-century settlements and who continued to provide a major portion of the investment capital necessary for the economic development of overseas territories. In the seventeenth century they contributed substantially to the Atlantic migration, either by coming themselves or by sending their younger sons. The Oxford- and Cambridge-trained Puritan ministers, many of the early merchants of Boston and Philadelphia, and some of the large planters of Virginia, Maryland, and the Carolinas were included in this category. But in the eighteenth century they probably came in smaller numbers.

A rung below the gentry were the yeoman farmers of the countryside and the artisan-shopkeepers of the cities. In the social hierarchy of European communities these were respected men who were entitled to participate in the political life of the community and who bulked large in the membership of the church. Through hard work, good fortune, or a judicious marriage they often propelled themselves upward a rung or two on the social ladder or at least lived to see a son enter one of the professions or embark on a career as a merchant. They may have composed as much as one-third of the immigrants to the colonies. Once there, they pro-

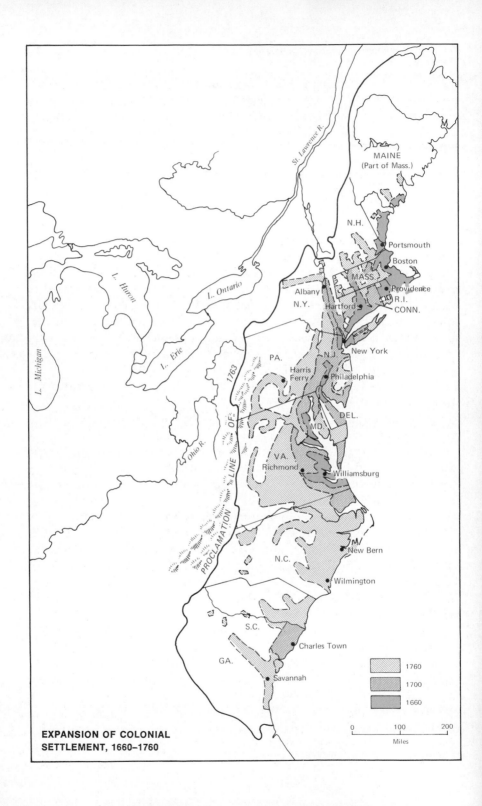

MAINE
(Part of Mass.)

N.H.

Portsmouth
Boston

MASS.

Albany   Providence
N.Y.   R.I.
       Hartford   CONN.

L. Ontario

L. Erie

L. Huron

L. Michigan

St. Lawrence R.

PA.   N.J.
   Harris   New York
   Ferry
        Philadelphia

DEL.
MD.

1763

Ohio R.

VA.
Richmond   Williamsburg

LINE OF

PROCLAMATION

New Bern

N.C.

Wilmington

S.C.

GA.   Charles Town

Savannah

	1760
	1700
	1660

0   100   200
           Miles

**EXPANSION OF COLONIAL
SETTLEMENT, 1660–1760**

vided the backbone of the middle class and often moved rapidly upward in a society that had plenty of room at the top. As a group, they were industrious, ambitious, and skilled enough to advance their fortunes in a way which would have been nearly impossible had they remained at home.

Taken together, these recruits from the nobility, gentry, and middle class of European society accounted for roughly one half of all those Europeans who traveled the water highway to the west side of the Atlantic in the seventeenth century and probably less than a third of the eighteenth-century immigrants. The remaining colonizers consisted of indentured servants—men, women, and children who lacked sufficient sources to pay their way to the New World and who therefore contracted out their labor for a given numbers of years in return for passage. Their backgrounds were mixed. Some were obscure shopkeepers, artisans, schoolteachers, and farmers who were down on their luck or sorely pressed by a downturn in economic conditions. Far more had never risen above the poverty line and anticipated no opportunity to do so. These were the best of them. The worst were petty criminals—people who sometimes left England, Scotland, Ireland, or Germany voluntarily and sometimes at the request of the authorities. Local officials could rid themselves of the community's undesirables and reduce the tax load of property owners, who supported outpensioners and inhabitants of the almshouse, by banishing the disinherited to what they promised would be a new life—or a quick death—in the New World. The Scottish Privy Council, for example, in attempting to organize a colonizing expedition to New York in 1669, sent out warrants to local authorities urging that they recruit "strong and idle beggars, vagabonds, egyptians, common and notorious whoores, theeves, and other dissolute and lousy persons."[2]

INDENTURED SERVANTS

Since the indentured servant came to represent a high proportion of the eighteenth-century immigrants, it is important to understand the mechanics of the profitable business of transporting bound laborers to the colonies. Like African and Indian slaves, white indentured servants were invaluable in a society that was rich in land but poor in labor. Labor in the colonies, Benjamin Franklin wrote in 1759, "is performed chiefly by indentured servants brought from Great Britain, Ireland, and Germany, because the high price it bears cannot be performed in any

[2]Quoted in Peter Gouldesbrough, "An Attempted Scottish Voyage to New York in 1669," *Scottish Historical Review*, 40 (1961): 58.

other way."[3] Franklin was forgetting that black slaves were as numerous as white servants in 1759, even in his hometown of Philadelphia, and that in the Southern colonies they comprised the bulk of the labor force. But his general point is valid: colonial America was being developed by unfree laborers. No matter whether he was a small tobacco planter in Virginia, a shopkeeper in New York, a farmer in Connecticut, or a shipwright in Boston, nearly every established member of colonial society wanted a bound laborer by his side as soon as he had accumulated the £20 to 40 required to purchase one. Additional labor meant the ability to produce additional goods or services, which in turn meant greater profits. In an age before machines, commanding the labor of others became preeminently important and human labor became an European-exported commodity which the colonists most eagerly sought.

The terms of indentured servitude were fairly simple. A servant bound himself or herself by legal contract to a ship captain for a specified length of time, usually four to seven years. In return the captain agreed to transport the servant across three thousand miles of water and place him or her on the auction block in one of the colonial seaports. The ship captain signed the work contract over to the highest bidder at the time of the auction. By the terms of the contract, the servant agreed to serve faithfully in return for food, clothes, shelter, and, at the end of the indenture, a small sum of money, occasionally some tools, and sometimes rights to a few acres of land.

Thus the traffic in bound labor became a regular part of the commerce linking Europe and America. A combination of merchants, ship captains, immigrant brokers, and recruiting agents kept thousands of Europeans on the road to the colonies throughout the pre-Revolutionary period. Like any other cargo, servants were loaded onto boats, carried across the ocean, and sold on the other side. It was a system that provided labor for the established members of colonial society, eventual freedom and the dream of a better life for those caught in the net of European poverty, and gratifying profits to all the middlemen involved. There were, of course, chronic abuses in the system. Just as the trade in Indian and African slaves was ridden with callous disregard for human life, so also the trade in contract labor was often a dirty business. Kidnapping and shanghaiing of drifters and drunks was endemic. Many unfortunate seaport dwellers awakened one morning with a head-splitting hangover to find themselves in the hold of a ship headed westward across the Atlantic. Once on the ship, they found appalling conditions that account for the high mortality rate in the servant trade. The description of Gottlieb Mit-

[3]Quoted in Marcus W. Jernegan, *Laboring and Dependent Classes in Colonial America, 1607–1783* (New York: Frederick Ungar Publishing Co., 1965), p. 55.

telberger, who accompanied a boatload of German servants sailing from Rotterdam to Philadelphia in 1750, conveys some feeling for what those seeking a better life in the American colonies endured for the opportunity to sell themselves into contract labor for some of the prime years of their life:

> During the journey the ship is full of pitiful signs of distress—smells, fumes, horrors, vomiting, various kinds of sea sickness, fever, dysentery, headaches, heat, constipation, boils, scurvy, cancer, mouth-rot, and similar afflictions, all of them caused by the age and the highly-salted state of the food, especially the meat, as well as by the very bad and filthy water, which brings about the miserable destruction and death of many. Add to all that shortage of food, hunger, thirst, frost, heat, dampness, fear, misery, vexation, and lamentation, as well as other troubles. Thus, for example, there are so many lice, especially on the sick people, that they have to be scraped off the bodies. All this misery reaches its climax when in addition to everything else one must suffer through two to three days and nights of storm, with everyone convinced that the ship will go to the bottom with all human beings on board. . . . Children between the ages of one and seven seldom survive the sea voyage; and parents must often watch their offspring suffer miserably, die, and be thrown into the ocean, from want, hunger, thirst, and the like. I myself, alas, saw such a pitiful fate overtake thirty-two children on board our vessel, all of whom were finally thrown into the sea.[4]

Mittelberger described how the limits of endurance were reached on the high seas and then the inmates of the ship turned on each other. But mostly they recalled the villages from which they had come: "Oh! If only I were back at home, even lying in my pig-sty!" Probably one-quarter of those embarking from European ports never lived to see the forests of the New World or, in their weakened condition, died shortly after arrival. For those who did survive the ordeal, the dangers of "seasoning" in North America—the acclimatization to new conditions—lay ahead. In addition there was the physical and psychological adjustment to an environment and a master that were completely unknown. Especially in the Southern colonies, agricultural labor took a deadly toll among those whose masters were determined to get as much labor as possible for the five, six, or seven years of the work contract. Adding to the difficulty of the servant's life was the right of the master to forbid marriage. Because it would invariably lead to pregnancy among female servants, and thus a loss of time, most masters forbid their servants a family life.

Given the harshness of the indentured labor system, it is not surprising to find that colonial newspapers were filled with advertisements for run-

---

[4]Gottlieb Mittelberger, *Journey to Pennsylvania*, ed. and trans. Oscar Handlin and John Clive (Cambridge: Harvard University Press, 1960), pp. 12–15.

away servants, interspersed with notices for runaway slaves. Servants knew the penalties for this: whipping and additional service, usually reckoned at twice the time lost to the master, but sometimes, as in Pennsylvania, calculated at a five-to-one ratio and in Maryland at ten-to-one. Even so, servants fled their masters by the hundreds and occasionally staged minor insurrections. When war came, they flocked to enlist in the British Army. Many masters were willing to take the compensation paid by the army and let a balky servant go.

The great goal of every servant was to obtain a place on the ladder of opportunity—or what, from a vantage point in the villages of Scotland, Ireland, and Germany, *seemed* to be such a ladder. But as one historian has reminded us "it will not do simply to assume that freed servants, especially those from the tobacco fields, were in any mental or physical condition to start vigorous new lives, or that long and ripe years of productivity lay ahead for them."[5] Although it is extremely difficult to follow the lives of freed servants, the most informed study of white servitude indicates that out of every ten indentured servants only one attained a position as a farmer in comfortable circumstances and one more achieved the status of artisan. The other eight died before they obtained their freedom or, after they were released, became propertyless day laborers, vagrants, or denizens of the local almshouse.[6] The life chances of a servant may have been better than this in the seventeenth century but probably worsened in the eighteenth century as some of the early fluidity of society disappeared. Though our attention has been claimed by the handful of servants who prospered or achieved fame—revolutionary leaders such as Daniel Dulany, Charles Thomson, and John Lamb—the statistical probability for rising to even middle-class position was very slight. Out of the large mass of those who sought opportunity in the American colonies it is the story of relentless labor and ultimate failure that stands out. The chief beneficiaries of the system of bound white labor were not the laborers themselves but those for whom they labored.

Agricultural Communities:
North and South

Out of the combination of fertile land; a bound labor supply of white, black, and red bondsmen; and the ambition of thousands of small farmers and artisans who labored independently two variants of agricultural

[5]Richard Hofstadter, *America at 1750: A Social Portrait* (New York: Alfred A. Knopf, Inc., 1972), p. 61.
[6]Abbot E. Smith, *Colonists in Bondage: White Servitude and Convict Labor in America, 1607–1776* (Chapel Hill: University of North Carolina Press, 1947), pp. 297–300.

society emerged in eighteenth-century America. In the North, small agricultural communities, made up of a few hundred families who tilled the outlying fields or provided artisan services in the town, dotted the landscape. Slaves were relatively rare, not representing more than 2 or 3 percent of the population in most rural areas, though composing about 8 percent of the population in Boston and Philadelphia and more than twice that in New York and the surrounding area. A high percentage of men owned land, and though differences in ability and circumstances led gradually to greater social and economic stratification, the truly rich and abjectly poor were few in number and the gap between them was small in comparison to European society. Most men lived to acquire a farm of at least fifty acres. They extracted from the soil a modest income that over a lifetime's work produced no impressive wealth but allowed for security from want and provided a small inheritance for offspring.

In the Southern colonies many yeomen farmers also struggled independently although they were more frequently dispersed across the land than clustered in villages. These men have been far less noticed by historians than the thousands of landowners with slaves and indentured servants who lived on widely separated plantations along the rivers and streams that flowed from the Piedmont through the coastal plain to the ocean. But the usual picture of a Southern plantation society made up of immensely wealthy men exploiting the labor of huge gangs of black slaves is badly overdrawn. Perhaps as much as 40 percent of the Southern white males worked as tenant farmers or agricultural laborers and of the remaining men who owned land about two out of every three in the Chesapeake region worked farms of two hundred acres or less. In North Carolina farms were even smaller and men of real wealth rarer. In South Carolina the opposite was true: slaveholding was more widespread, plantations tended to be larger, and planters of substantial wealth represented a larger proportion of the population. As early as 1726 in St. George's Parish 87 of 108 families held slaves. A generation later in St. Bartholomew Parish about 250 white families owned more than 5,000 slaves.[7]

On the whole, probably not more than 5 percent of the white landowners were wealthy enough by mid-eighteenth century to possess a plantation worth £1000—not too different from the North. Similarly, those owning large numbers of slaves were not as numerous as we commonly think. Even though the number of slaves in Southern society increased rapidly in the eighteenth century, rising from about 20,000 in 1700 to 200,000 in 1750, a majority of white adult males held no slaves at all at mid-century

---

[7]Frank J. Klingberg, *An Appraisal of the Negro in Colonial South Carolina: A Study in Americanization* (Washington, D.C. The Associated Publishers, 1941), pp. 58–60; William Langhorne, "An Account of the Spiritual State of St. Bartholomew's Parish," (1752), *South Carolina Magazine of History*, 50 (1949): 200.

and the number who operated plantations with more than twenty slaves probably did not exceed 10 percent of the white taxables. Although South Carolina is a distinct exception, the South throughout the pre-Revolutionary period was numerically dominated by small landowners whose farms, if perhaps twice the size of the average New England farm, was not more than half again as large as the typical farm in Pennsylvania, New Jersey, or New York.

Nonetheless, the ideal in the South, if not the reality, was the large plantation where black slaves would make the earth yield up profits sufficient to support the leisured life. Statistically speaking, not many white colonists in the South achieved the dream. But that is what people worked for and they came to identify the quest for material comfort with the exploitation of African slave labor at a time when the Northern colonists were phasing out black and white bound labor and turning to a market economy where both goods and labor were available on a free exchange basis.

The Protestant work ethic, which purportedly propelled men upward by inculcating a life of frugality, industriousness, and highly rationalized economic activity, perhaps operated less compellingly in the psyches of Southern colonists than in their Northern counterparts. But the abundant and fertile land of the South and the wider availability of slaves after 1690 provided all the incentive necessary for an aggressive, competitive society to develop. Much folklore about Southern cavaliers reposing under magnolia trees has been handed down in the history books, but in the eighteenth century European colonizers in the South were as avid in the pursuit of wealth and material comfort as European colonizers in the North. And if the warm climate of the southern regions bred languor, it was also true that farmers in the South had no long frozen winters when there was little to do but mend harness and chop wood. The typical New England farm produced just one crop each year; but a South Carolina rice or indigo plantation produced two. Moreover the restraints of a New England community orientation and the Puritan bias against the accumulation of wealth which was not disposed of in socially useful ways never hindered entrepreneurial activity in the South. Organized religion was only shallowly rooted in most of the Southern colonies and the community orientation never took hold because communities themselves were few and far between.

Land, Ambition, and Growth

Paradoxically, one of the effects of the general growth and success of the colonies in eighteenth-century British America was the shattering of the utopian dream of the first generation. The Puritan work ethic and an atmosphere of what seemed to be limitless opportunity encouraged men to work arduously at their callings. And in the New World their labors had generally been rewarded with success. The religious impulse gradually waned and men began to look at land and the labor they invested in it not simply as a source of livelihood but as a way to wealth. Previously thought of as a means of subsistence, land now became the commodity that the wise speculator could manipulate to send his stock soaring. Puritan clergymen had long before caught scent of what was in the air and issued warnings that deterred almost nobody. "Land! land!" exclaimed Increase Mather in 1676, "hath been the Idol of many in New England."[8] As James Henretta has written recently, the concept of "limited good, the cognitive orientation often produced in peasant societies by the absence of uncultivated lands and by the general scarcity of material wealth and resources" was replaced by "a fresh perception of the possibilities afforded by the new environment."[9]

Because the ratio of people to land was so favorable compared to the societies from which they came, the most ambitious of the colonists developed a highly aggressive outlook that patterned their behavior. What was to hold a man back in these uncharted expanses of land, in these unclaimed river valleys, as soon as the Indians were gone? The new concept was of a society in which anything was possible. Thus competitive "entrepreneurial behavior made its triumphal appearance."[10]

Religion and the concept of limited gain were not dead. People still went faithfully to church and in the 1740s a religious revival swept through the colonies. But in general religious commitment, in the sense of defining one's life as a preparation for the afterlife, was on the decline. "Less of heaven and more of the earth" was the phrase that one man of the cloth used to deplore the goals of those to whom he ministered. It was Franklin's little how-to-do-it book, *The Way to Wealth*, that caught the spirit of the aggressive entrepreneurial eighteenth century, as evidenced by the fact that the book was a best seller for years. The brakes on economic ambition had been suddenly removed and with the decline of fervid Puritanism in the eighteenth century there was little left to restrain the predator instincts in those who were eager to pit themselves against their fellows in the pursuit of material gain. "Every man is for himself," lamented a prominent Philadelphian in 1706, only a generation after Penn had planted the seed of his "holy experiment."[11] Two generations later the governor of New York, who had grown up in the colony,

[8]Quoted in Perry Miller, *The New England Mind From Colony to Province* (Boston: Beacon Press, 1961), p. 37.

[9]Henretta, *Evolution of American Society*, p. 8.

[10]*Ibid.*, p. 9.

[11]Quoted in Gary B. Nash, *Quakers and Politics; Pennsylvania, 1681–1726* (Princeton: Princeton University Press, 1968), p. 303.

put it more explicitly: "The only principle of life propagated among the young people," wrote Cadwallader Colden, "is to get money and men are only esteemed according to what they are worth—that is the money they are possessed of."[12] A contemporary in Rhode Island echoed the thought when he wrote "A Man who has Money here, no matter how he came by it, he is Everything, and wanting [lacking] that he's a meer Nothing, let his Conduct be ever so ereproachable."[13]

As these acquisitive values took hold, the individual replaced the community as the conceptual unit of thought. The advice of the ancestors, such as the Puritan minister John Cotton, to "goe forth, every man that goeth, with a public spirit, looking not on your owne things only," or Winthrop's maxim that "the care of the publick must oversway all private respects," carried less and less weight in eighteenth-century society. The conquest of the wilderness and its inhabitants had proceeded far enough, men had shown enough adaptability and endurance for a hundred years, and the future possibilities seemed expansive enough that a mental set developed in which colonial Americans were eager to prove wrong the Elizabethan poet, John Donne, who counseled that no man could survive as an island unto himself. Relative self-sufficiency had been proven possible; and having gained what he had, the typical colonist wanted more. A French visitor, who took up residence in New York, described this attitudinal transformation:

> An European, when he first arrives, seems limited in his intentions, as well as in his views; but he very suddenly alters his scale. . . . He no sooner breathes our air than he forms schemes, and embarks in designs he never would have thought of in his own country. . . . He begins to feel the effects of a sort of resurrection; hitherto he had not lived, but simply vegetated; he now feels himself a man, because he is treated as such; . . . he begins to forget his former survitude and dependence. . . .[14]

The Frenchman, Hector St. John Crevecoeur, had omitted from his generalization the third of colonial society that was caught in the chains of involuntary labor, but he caught the essence of the profound psychological re-orientation that had overcome many if not most eighteenth-century colonists. The paradox was that phenomenal growth, the unleashing of economic energies, and the rise of freedom and individualism in eighteenth-century society was leading toward new and less favorable conditions. The pressure of the rapidly increasing population on the fixed

---

12Quoted in Henretta, *Evolution of American Society*, p. 99.
13Quoted in Carl Bridenbaugh, *Cities in Revolt; Urban Life in America, 1743–1776* (New York: Capricorn Books, 1964), p. 140.
14J. Hector St. John Crèvecoeur, *Letters from an American Farmer* (New York: E. P. Dutton & Co., Inc., 1957), pp. 54–56.

amount of land east of the Appalachian Mountain barrier was building up by the mid-eighteenth century. Especially in New England ungranted land in the coastal region was a thing of the past and the division and redivision of original land grants among sons and grandsons had progressed as far as it could go without splitting farms into unviably small economic units. New land—on the Maine frontier, in western Massachusetts and Connecticut, across the Appalachians in Pennsylvania, Virginia, Maryland, and the Carolinas—was the obvious solution to the problem of overcrowding. But before a westward movement could begin, hostile Indians, French, and Spanish would have to be overcome. Thus the saturation of the Eastern coastal plain made the lands of the interior tribes seem more and more attractive. Land companies began forming in the mid-eighteenth century to lay claim, however flimsy, to these valuable Western lands, which would appreciate enormously in value as the next generation came of age and sought *lebensraum* to the west.

Changing Social Structure

Population growth and economic development, carried on for a century and a half by aggressive and increasingly materialistic individuals, changed both the structure of colonial society and the attitudes of the people toward social structure—but changed them in opposite directions. Seventeenth-century European society on both sides of the Atlantic had accepted the naturalness of hierarchy in human affairs, the inevitability of poverty, and the right of those in the upper stratum of society to rule those below them. Social gradations and internal subordination were not only sanctioned by God but were thought essential to the maintenance of social stability and cohesion. Therefore care was taken to differentiate individuals by dress, by titles, in social etiquette, and even in penalties imposed in criminal proceedings. Puritans, for example, did not simply file into church on Sunday mornings and occupy the pews in random fashion. Instead, each seat was assigned according to the social rank of the person in the community. "Dooming the seats," as the assignment process was aptly called, was the responsibility of a church committee, which used every available yardstick of social respectability—age, parentage, social position, service to the community, and wealth—in drawing up a seating plan for the congregation. Puritans never entered their church without being reminded where they stood in the ranks of the community. Similarly, John Winthrop reminded the passengers of the *Arbella* on the way to Massachusetts Bay in 1630 of the conventional wisdom concerning the God-ordained nature of social hierarchy: "God Almightie in his most holy and wise providence hath soe disposed of the Condition of man-

Quakers, shown here in the meetinghouse, spoke out against slavery and the exploitation of Indians, and, unlike other Protestants, allowed women a nearly equal role in religious affairs. (Courtesy Museum of Fine Arts, Boston.)

Boston in 1764 looks prosperous, but the city has just endured a devastating fire and was in the throes of economic depression. (Courtesy Bostonian Society, Old State House.)

This eighteenth-century schoolmaster is iconographical testimony that fear and force were two key elements in European notions of childrearing and early education. (Courtesy of the Frick Art Reference Library.)

kinde, as in all times some must be rich some poore, some highe and eminent in power and dignitie; others meane and in subjeccion."[15]

In spite of the philosophical commitment to hierarchy, the early European immigrants in America were notably undifferentiated in their social makeup. Emigrant society was strongly lower-middle class in its composition and the wide availability of land, combined with the lack of opportunities to amass great fortunes when one had only his own labor and that of his wife, children, and a servant or two kept the spectrum of wealth relatively narrow throughout most of the seventeenth century. Even in the cities, where the redistribution of wealth proceeded the fastest, leading to the emergence of the genuinely wealthy and the permanently poor, the dawn of the eighteenth century witnessed a colonial society which was overwhelmingly middle class in character. In the Hudson River Valley and in the Southern colonies a handful of large plantation owners had made their mark, but the largest slaveowners in Virginia at the beginning of the eighteenth century still owned only fewer than one hundred slaves and not more than a handful of men had as much as £2000 to leave to their heirs. As late as 1722 one of Philadelphia's richest merchants died with personal possessions worth just over £1000—a sizable estate but unimpressive by European standards.

EGALITARIANISM

In the eighteenth century, and especially in the half-century before the Revolution, the ancient commitment to hierarchy and deference waned at the same time the stratification of society was increasing. Social attitudes and social structure were moving in opposite directions. For free whites (but no others) the ideal became egalitarianism, as evidenced in the remarks of one Philadelphia newspaper which reminded its readers in 1756 that the middling sort of people "enjoy and are fond of freedom, and the meanest among them thinks he has a right to civility from the greatest."[16] Such comments were common. The Frenchman, Crèvecoeur, was surprised to see hired workers who "must be at your table and feed . . . on the best you have" and the school teacher Philip Fithian wrote of "labourers at the tables and in the parlours of their betters enjoying the advantage, and honour of their society and conversation."[17]

Europeans judged what they saw against what they had known at home and thus sometimes exaggerated the degree of egalitarianism that they

15"A Modell of Christian Charity" (1630), quoted in Darrett B. Rutman, *Winthrop's Boston; A Portrait of a Puritan Town, 1630–1649* (Chapel Hill: University of North Carolina Press, 1965), pp. 7–8.

16Quoted in Hofstadter, *America at 1750*, p. 131.

17*Ibid.*, p. 141.

thought they saw. But there can be little doubt that Americans of the mid-eighteenth century, ignoring the racial oppression they were practicing, took pride in their conception of a society where a wealthy aristocracy did not dominate and no masses of poor whites were ground into the dust. The ideal was a rough economic equality where each man would have enough and a social equality "in which invidious discriminations would be abolished."[18] When Benjamin Franklin toured the English countryside in 1772 he was appalled at what he saw and raised thanks that America was different. "Landlords, great noblemen, and gentlemen, extremely opulent, living in the highest affluence and magnificence" were to be seen alongside "the bulk of the people, tenants, extremely poor, living in the most sordid wretchedness, in dirty hovels of mud and straw, and clothed only in rags." Franklin could only shake his head and take solace in the knowledge that America was different. Ignoring Indians and Africans, he wrote: "I thought often of the Happiness of New England, where every Man is a Freeholder, has a Vote in publick Affairs, lives in a tidy, warm House, has plenty of good Food and fewel, with whole cloaths from Head to Foot, the Manufacture perhaps of his own Family."[19]

Other celebrants of the unique condition of American society made similar proclamations. "You may depend upon it that this is one of the best poor man's countries in the world," a Philadelphia merchant assured his readers. "Respecting the lower classes in New England," boasted the author of *American Husbandry*, "there is scarcely any part of the world in which they are better off. . . . This great ease of gaining a farm, renders the lower class of people very industrious; which, with the high price of labour, banishes every thing that has the least appearance of begging, or that wandering, destitute state of poverty, which we see so common in England."[20] The German Mittelberger summed up the twin ideals of economic equalitarianism and democratic scorn for authorities and authoritarian institutions. Pennsylvania, he said, was "heaven for farmers, paradise for artisans, and hell for officials and preachers."[21]

It must be noted that all these commentators occupied favorable positions in society, which may account for the fact that they were describing not the reality but the dream of colonial life. The reality, in fact, was that eighteenth-century society, even for white colonists, was moving away

[18]Jackson T. Main, *The Social Structure of Revolutionary America* (Princeton: Princeton University Press, 1965), p. 236.

[19]*The Writings of Benjamin Franklin*, 10 vols., ed. Albert H. Smyth (New York: The Macmillan Co., 1907), 5: 362–63.

[20]Quoted in James T. Lemon, *The Best Poor Man's Country; A Geographical Study of Early Southeastern Pennsylvania* (Baltimore: Johns Hopkins University Press, 1972), xiii; *American Husbandry* (London, 1775), ed. Harry J. Carman (New York: Columbia University Press, 1939), pp. 52–53.

[21]Mittelberger, *Journey to Pennsylvania*, p. 48.

from the dream. As the old deferential attitudes gave way to brash, assertive, individualistic modes of thought and behavior—what would become known as "the democratic personality"—society became more stratified, wealth became less evenly distributed, and impressively rich and truly impoverished classes emerged. The tremendous influx of immigrants in the half-century after 1715 made rich men of those with sufficient capital to speculate in land, buy slaves and servants, or participate in trade. It was in the eighteenth century that the aggrandizement of wealth became clearly apparent in all sections of the country—North and South, rural and urban. In the cities of Boston, Newport, New York, Philadelphia, and Charleston stately town houses rose as testimony to the fortunes being acquired in trade, shipbuilding, and land speculation. Probably the last of these was the most profitable of all. "It is almost a proverb," wrote a Philadelphian in 1767, "that Every great fortune made here within these 50 years has been by land."[22] By the late colonial period it was not unusual to find merchant-land speculators with estates valued at £10,000–20,000. The land holdings of Israel Pemberton, a Philadelphia Quaker merchant, were valued at £60,000 just before the Revolution. Even in the rural areas of the North wealthy farmers amassed estates worth £4,000–5,000. In the South even larger fortunes had been built, for the rapid importation of African slaves after 1690, and particularly between 1720 and 1775, had accelerated the rate at which profits could be extracted from the cultivation of tobacco or rice. By the eve of the Revolution the great planters of the Chesapeake region, men such as Charles Carroll, Robert "King" Carter, and William Byrd, had achieved spectacular affluence. Their estates, valued at £100,000 or more, were equivalent in purchasing power to a fortune of two million dollars in 1970. On the large plantations of the South it was not unusual to see 300 to 400 slaves, whereas in the late seventeenth century the largest slave holder on the continent had no more than 50 bound laborers.

Waning Economic Democracy

While the rapid increase in population and the large-scale capital investment in land and slaves enabled a small number of men to accumulate fortunes that would have been noteworthy even in English society, the development of colonial society also created conditions in which a growing number of persons were finding it difficult to keep bread on the table and wood in the fireplace. This was especially true in the cities, where the differentiation of wealth proceeded most rapidly. All the major

---

[22]*Pennsylvania Magazine of History and Biography*, 1 (1877): 277.

cities built almshouses and workhouses in the second quarter of the century to provide for those who could not care for themselves—the aged, indigent, sick, insane, and orphaned. Between 1725 and 1775, however, the poor in the cities increased far more rapidly than the urban population as a whole and after about 1750 poverty was no longer confined to the old or physically depleted.

Boston, the first utopian settlement in Anglo-America, was the first to feel the pinch of economic hardship. The city had grown to about 12,000 in 1720 and increased to some 16,000 in the next two decades. But from 1740 until after the Revolution the city's population remained static as other coastal towns such as Salem, Marblehead, and Newburyport captured some of the shipbuilding industry and the New England economy in general levelled off. Expenditures for poor relief, which had stayed below £1,000 annually in the 1720s, edged upward in the next decade and were growing faster than population increases in the 1740s. By 1753 the Overseers of the Poor were reporting to the Massachusetts legislature that poor relief expenditures in Boston were double that of any town of comparable size "upon the face of the whole Earth" by the reckoning of those acquainted with such matters. Though this may or may not have been true, it was certain that a large number of people in the town were in real distress. In 1757 the Overseers reported that "the Poor supported either wholly or in part by the Town in the Alms-house and out of it will amount to the Number of about 1000 . . ." and those receiving private charity from churches and philanthropic organizations swelled the total.[23]

In the 1760s Boston became even further burdened with poverty. The city had attracted a large number of disabled veterans from the Seven Years' War and as a seaport always had its share of injured, dying, and spiritually broken mariners. The Overseers took the strictest measures to rid the town of "strangers" who wandered in looking for relief, but in spite of "warning out" 1,125 persons between 1769 and 1771, the city's alms- and workhouses in the latter year were still bulging to capacity with almost three hundred inmates, while more than five hundred other adults received outrelief. Still another eight hundred were listed as propertyless on the tax list of 1771, indicating that for the city as a whole nearly half of the white adult males were poor or unpropertied. On the eve of the Revolution, Boston, the heartbeat of the Puritan utopian dream, had become a throwback to European society.

That the growth of poverty and propertylessness in Boston was not simply the function of a stagnating economy is evident by looking at two

---

[23]*Records Relating to the Early History of Boston*, 39 vols. (Boston: Rockwell and Churchill, 1881–1909), 14: 240, 302.

rapidly growing cities during the same period—New York and Philadelphia. In New York the first pauper list of 1713 shows only two men and thirteen women, all of them aged or infirm. By 1735 the number had grown to 58 but this increase was roughly proportionate to the growth of the city's population. By 1772, however, the city was supporting 425 paupers in the workhouse and almshouse. The same upward curve is apparent in the municipal outlays for poor relief. In the decade 1725–1735 they averaged £523 annually; by 1759 they had risen to £1,200 per year; and in the years just before the Revolution they averaged about £5,000.[24]

In Philadelphia similar social patterns were emerging. The city was the main entry port for thousands of German and Scotch-Irish immigrants who crossed the Atlantic in search of greater opportunity in the eighteenth century and so it had the unenviable role of acting as a sponge for many of the sick and distressed who disembarked too sick or demoralized to make their way west to available land. But Philadelphia's poor problem was more than a reflection of a large transient population. The Overseers of the Poor reported in 1755 that in the previous decade or so the almshouse had contained about forty to sixty people per year—and this was during a period of large immigration. After that the poor rolls began to climb rapidly. By 1768 more than four hundred persons were admitted annually to the workhouse and almshouse and the number climbed dramatically to over seven hundred by 1775. Hundreds of others identified as "poor" were admitted to the Pennsylvania Hospital for the Sick Poor. Still others were provided with outrelief by the Overseers. While the population had approximately doubled between 1740 and 1775 the number of poor in the city had increased twentyfold. The expenditure of public and private monies for the distressed and disabled told the same tale. From outlays of less than £500 per year in the first quarter of the century and less than £1,000 per year in the second quarter, public expenditures rose to some £10,000 on the eve of the Revolution. Additional relief was dispensed by churches and private charitable organizations. Although the fragmentary state of the records will not permit precise calculations, a conservative estimate would place at least 10 percent of the adult members of society in these colonial cities on poor relief at the end of the colonial period. Economic democracy was waning as political democracy increased.

Inevitably the expanding economy and the democratic values incorporated in the society tended to favor the aggressive and able in their drive toward material self-aggrandizement. The greater the opportunities—one of the essential characteristics of a democratic society—the greater the gap

24Raymond Mohl, "Poverty in Early America, A Reappraisal," *New York History*, 50 (1969): 9, 13–15.

became between the rich and the poor. The growth of cultural and political egalitarianism was accompanied by, an indirectly sanctioned, the decline of economic equality. An open society with ample opportunities in the eighteenth century for entrepreneurship, and with relatively few restraints imposed by government, was leading, paradoxically, to a growing gulf between rich and poor and to a concentration of economic power in the hands of a thin upper layer of society. Culturally committed to a society in which the individual and not the community was the central concern, the white population of colonial America was transforming what they thought to be uniquely American into what was more and more resembling the European conditions that they had fled.

The differing abilities of men to manipulate their economic environment, capitalize on the freedom to exploit white and black labor, and obtain title to Indian land, was eventually recorded on the tax lists of the community where each man's wealth was set alongside that of his neighbors. In the last decade colonial historians have scrutinized those tax lists that have survived in different parts of the country. The collective result of their efforts makes one point indisputable: population growth and economic development led toward a less even distribution of wealth and an increase in propertylessness in virtually every community. The change occurred slowly in rural areas but proceeded rapidly in the seaboard centers of commercial activity.

In the rural town of Northampton, Massachusetts, for example, the upper 10 percent of property owners controlled 25 percent of the taxable wealth in 1676 and slowly increased its control of the community's assets to 34 percent in 1759. At the same time the proportion of the community's taxable property owned by the bottom third of the society remained steady at about 10 percent. In Chester County, Pennsylvania, a fertile wheat-growing region southwest of Philadelphia, the wealthiest tenth of the farmers commanded about 24 percent of the wealth in 1693 and almost 30 percent by 1760. During the same period the lowest 30 percent of the landowners saw their economic leverage decline from 17.4 to 6.3 percent of the taxable assets of the county.[25]

In the cities the rate of change was far greater. Boston's upper tenth in 1687 held 46 percent of the taxable property while the lowest 30 percent had a meagre 2.6 percent of the wealth. Four generations later, in 1771, the top tenth had 63 percent of the wealth; the lowest three tenths had virtually nothing—a mere tenth of one percent of the community's taxable resources. Economic polarization in Boston, where the population

[25]William R. Tillman, unpublished analysis of wealth distribution in Northhampton Mass.: James T. Lemon and Gary B. Nash, "The Distribution of Wealth in Eighteenth-Century America: A Century of Change in Chester County, Pennsylvania, 1693–1802," *Journal of Social History*, 2 (1968): 11–14.

was static for most of the eighteenth century and economic recession had hit hard at many elements of the community, was duplicated in vigorously expanding Philadelphia. In 1693, little more than a decade after settlement, the upper tenth laid claim to 46 percent of the city's wealth. Three-quarters of a century later, in 1772, they possessed 71 percent of the taxable wealth. As in Boston, these gains were not made at the expense of those in the bottom third of society, who possessed only a meagre 2.2 percent of the wealth in 1693, but were accomplished at the expense of those in the middling elements of society.[26]

Frontier Society

If poverty was touching the lives of a larger part of the urban population, it was the usual condition on the frontier. Here the gap between rich and poor was almost nonexistent because the rich were nowhere to be found. In its social anatomy the frontier of the mid-eighteenth century resembled rural society on the edge of the continent a century before. Whether it was in the towns of western Massachusetts and Connecticut, founded in the second and third quarters of the eighteenth century by the sons of Yankee farmers; or the lands along the Mohawk River in New York and the Susquehannah River in Pennsylvania, which represented the hopes of the German and Scotch-Irish immigrants; or the backcountry of Maryland, Virginia, and the Carolinas, which sponged up some 250,000 souls in the late colonial period, frontier society was characterized by the crude existence of farmers who all stood roughly on the same plane. They purchased land cheaply, often for as little as four shillings an acre (though this was still sufficient to allow the eastern land speculator a handsome profit), and struggled to turn a life of simple subsistence into a life of profit. Many hoped to get enough land under cultivation within a few years to produce crop surpluses for market. But with only the help of one's sons and a few farm animals this often took most of a man's life. Others struggled only to make enough improvements on a piece of land so that other settlers pushing westward on the next wave of settlement would find it attractive enough to pay a price that rewarded one's labors.

On the New England frontier, where people pushed westward in groups, founding new towns and churches as they went, the institutions of eastern society were quickly replicated. While poor, these simple villagers and farmers lived a life where institutional ligaments had not been altogether torn away. But southward from New York on the east side of the Appalachian slopes frontier society existed in what most observers

[26]Gary B. Nash, "Wealth, Poverty, and Mobility in Pre-Revolutionary American Cities," unpublished ms.

took to be a semibarbarous state. Charles Woodmason, an itinerant Anglican minister who spent three years tramping from settlement to settlement in the Carolina backcountry in the 1760s was appalled at what he found. "For thro' want of Ministers to marry and thro' the licentiousness of the People, many hundreds live in Concubinage—swopping their Wives as Cattel, and living in a State of Nature, more irregularly and unchastely than the Indians. . . ." At Beaver Creek he found "their cabbins quite open and expos'd. Little or no Bedding, or anything to cover them—Not a drop of anything, save Cold Water to drink—And all their Cloathing, a Shirt and Trousers Shift and Petticoat. Some perhaps a Linsey Woolsey. No Shoes or Stockings—Children run half naked. The Indians are better Cloathed and Lodged."[27] As an English Anglican, Woodmason carried with him all the prejudices that were usually harbored against the Presbyterian Scotch-Irish, the main inhabitants of the region; but there is little reason to doubt that the crudeness of life that he described actually existed. After preaching at Flat Creek to "a vast Body of People . . . Such a Medley! such a mixed Multitude of all Classes and Complexions," he paled at their after-service "Revelling Drinking Singing Dancing and Whoring" and threw up his hands that "most of the Company were drunk before I quitted the Spot—They were as rude in their Manners as the Common Savages, and hardly a degree removed from them." Some of what he saw made him close his eyes in horror, but he kept them open long enough to observe the young women who were "bareheaded, barelegged and barefoot with only a thin Shift and under Petticoat—Yet I cannot break them of this—for the heat of the Weather admits not of any [but] thin Cloathing." Young women, he continued "have a most uncommon Practise. . . . They draw their Shift as tight as possible to the Body, and pin it close, to shew the roundness of their Breasts, and . . . their Petticoat close to their Hips to shew the fineness of their Limbs—so that they might as well be in Puri Naturalibus—Indeed Nakedness is not censurable or indecent here, and they expose themselves often quite Naked, without Ceremony—Rubbing themselves and their Hair with Bears Oil and tying it up behind in a Bunch like the Indians —being hardly one degree removed from them."[28]

Political Individualism

Whether it was in the Carolina backcountry, virtually devoid of institutions and social stratification, or in the coastal seaports where economic

---

[27]Charles Woodmason, *The Carolina Backcountry on the Eve of the Revolution*, ed. Richard J. Hooker (Chapel Hill: University of North Carolina Press, 1953), pp. 15, 33.
[28]*Ibid.*, pp. 56, 61.

polarization was occurring alongside the growth of schools, churches, courts, and councils, the same restless individualistic energy was being released among the European colonists of eighteenth-century America. Even though opportunities may have been narrowing, reducing the life chances of poor immigrants or those born in the lower layers of society, the prevailing belief was that the environment offered boundless opportunity. In this atmosphere the "temptation to manipulate government for personal ends," as one historian has put it, became widespread.[29] Political authorities, local and provincial, found themselves beset with requests that were out of keeping with the traditional function of government. Settlers and landjobbers, locked in disputes concerning title to Indian lands, brought their causes to the legislature for settlement, and pleaded their cases with all the manipulation and oiling of wheels that we now dignify with the name of lobbying. Merchants vied for the right to supply military expeditions and greased the palms of legislators in the hope of receiving contracts. Speculators grouped together and used their influence in the colonial assemblies to gain articles of incorporation. Once incorporated, they sought further legislative favor in the form of charters for land banks—institutions that would issue paper money, backed by land— in order to enlarge the circulating medium and thus make it easier for those with frontier fever to purchase the lands they were holding. Everywhere governments found themselves in the middle of the race for riches, with the power to dispense favors and to legitimize the economic activity of one group or another.

As the Revolutionary period approached, the philosophy of individualism came to replace the philosophy of community; the commitment to self-interest prevailed over the commitment to the public interest. Social interdependence, once regarded as indispensable, crumbled beneath the pressure of individualist ambition. Though in public pronouncements political leaders continued to insist that they represented the public interest, the only true interest in an uncorrupted body politic according to traditional thinking, it was becoming recognized that political leaders were often only *defining* as the community's interest that which benefited those around them. Beginning in the 1720s more and more voices were raised that society was made up of interest groups and that the essence of politics was to make one's own interest group prevail over all others. Not until after mid-century was the old ideology of the "public interest" attacked directly. But when a writer in the *New York Gazette* asserted in 1765 that "*Self Interest* is the grand Principle of all Human Actions; it is unreasonable and vain to expect Service from a Man who must act

[29]Richard L. Bushman, *From Puritan to Yankee: Character and the Social Order in Connecticut, 1690–1765* (Cambridge: Harvard University Press, 1967), pp. 267–88.

contrary to his own Interests," he admitted explicitly what had long been in the minds of Europeans in America, though it could be admitted only with great reluctance.[30]

The argument of the private versus the public interest would continue for decades. Some regarded the triumph of individualism as a great perversion of the noble vision brought to American shores by the Puritans because they regarded the supremacy of the private interest as a formula for allowing, encouraging, and legitimizing all the most predatory instincts in men. Others argued that it was a great step forward in human history, for it put each man on his own and curbed the forces of authority necessitated by the concept of the "public interest."

In many ways the throwing off of governmental and ideological restraints, the enthronement of the concept of self-interest, was the perfect formula for the rapid development of a vast area of land blessed with abundant natural resources and peopled by ambitious, tough-minded, innovating Europeans. There can be little argument that even though opportunities may have been diminishing and the problem of urban poverty growing in the eighteenth century, the average European in America was living far better than he would have been had he remained at home. American visitors to Europe were almost correct when they argued, like Franklin, that the most wretched person in the colonies was not half as bad off as every fifth person in England.

But Franklin—and most historians writing in the century and a half after his death—have consciously or unconsciously omitted from their consideration the one-fourth of American society that was in chains or driven from the land and was thus worse off than the most wretched persons in European society. Almost 22 percent of the American population on the eve of the Revolution was black and the vast majority of them were enslaved. Countless Indians were living either in a state of semibondage within white settlements, on reservations, or were struggling to preserve their land base and their political autonomy. These were not merely the members of society who stood on the lowest rung of the ladder. More accurately, they were the basement dwellers in a house where the ladder leading to the first floor had been removed. Yet they were very much a part of the house, for without them the building could not have been constructed and could not have risen so high.

Any comparisons of European society with the society of Europeans in America must therefore take into account the fact that if Americans stood higher, it was largely because they were occupying the land of Indians

---

[30]Bernard Friedman, "The Shaping of the Radical Consciousness in Provincial New York," *Journal of American History,* 56, (1969–70): 789.

and exploiting the labor of Africans. If we take *all* the peoples of America at mid-eighteenth century and compare them with *all* the peoples of England, the contrasts in wealth, standard of living, and opportunity for advancement vanish for the most part. In America the bottom quarter of the inhabitants was enslaved or fighting for survival and thus were more miserable than those at the bottom of European society. The second and third quarters of American society, composed of indentured servants, poor frontiersmen, agricultural laborers, tenant farmers, and propertyless urban laborers and seamen were probably not much better off than those in the equivalent segments of English society. Their chief advantage was that they could hope to rise in the society where land was still relatively available and labor commanded a higher price than in the mother country. Some would realize the opportunity in their lifetime but many others, perhaps most, would fail, but pass on the promise to their children. In the top quarter of American society men were still struggling upward to the heights of power and material wealth that characterized the upper echelon of European society. Such success as they enjoyed could be attributed in large part to their ability to command the labor of a sizable number of slaves, or to speculate in land which by one means or another had been wrested from its original inhabitants. One man's release from authority was another man's captivity; one man's escape from the restraining institutions of church and government was another man's doom; one people's "city on a hill" was another people's hell.

In this sense the promise of American colonial society was intimately and unforgettably intertwined with the exploitation of African labor and Indian land. Especially in the South, the eighteenth-century shift from white indentured labor to black slave labor had greatly enhanced the profit-making potentialities for land owners and at the same time, as Edmund Morgan has pointed out, "had curbed the growth of a free, depressed lower class" that might otherwise have become a source of widespread social discontent and class conflict.[31] Freedom and slavery, white and black, material success and human exploitation were bound together in unholy covenant.

[31]Morgan, "Slavery and Freedom: The American Paradox," *Journal of American History*, 59 (1972–73): 25.

chapter 10

Wars for Empire and
Indian Strategies for Survival

Between 1675 and 1763 three European powers—France, Spain, and England—employed diplomacy and war in an ongoing struggle for trade and territory in the vast area between the Mississippi River and the Atlantic Ocean and in the waters of the Caribbean. Because both the trade and the territory they coveted in North America were in the hands of Indian tribes all three European powers were in close and continual touch with leaders of Indian society. What our history books have largely forgotten, but what was patently obvious throughout this period, was that much of the time and energy of the European authorities, whether in New Spain, New France, New England, or elsewhere in the European colonies, was spent negotiating, trading, and fighting with and against Indians of various cultures, and filing reports, requests, and complaints to the home governments concerning the state of Indian affairs. Those in charge of colonial affairs in Madrid, Paris, and London knew almost as much about the Indian inhabitants of the territories they claimed as they did of their own colonists.

In this three-cornered fight for a continent, it is easy to imagine that Indians were merely the objects of European desire, to be manipulated like pawns on a continental chessboard before finally being swept from the board altogether. This view is part of the myth of the overwhelming cultural and military force of the European colonizers and the Indians' acquiescence when confronted with this power. But the power of the Europeans has been greatly exaggerated and that of native societies underestimated. It would be more accurate to say that Indian cultures of the interior were not only reciprocally involved in the complicated maneuvers between contending European powers but played a dynamic role in the unfolding of events. They could not turn back the clock or drive the Europeans back into the sea. But unlike the less populous and weaker coastal tribes that had found no way of resisting the invaders or assimilating with them, the interior tribes were far stronger. They were therefore able to interact with the Europeans in a much different way. Throughout the eighteenth century Indians helped to shape their own history. Pitted against each other and divided among themselves, the European powers had far too few resources to overpower the inland tribes and had to rely on Indian allies to maintain themselves even in the limited areas that they occupied. Understanding the Europeans' weaknesses gave Indian nations an opportunity to exercise initiative and to gain much in exchange for their support. That they were eventually the losers should not obscure the fact that the interaction was truly a two-way process. Europeans used Indians to enhance their own power and Indians used Europeans in precisely the same way.

Only by also looking at European imperial rivalry from the Indian point of view can we understand the real nature of intercultural contact in North America. For example, while European governors and colonial bureaucrats were putting millions of words on paper, moving armies and navies across three thousand miles of water, and engaging thousands of people in the manufacture and shipment of Indian trade goods, all as a part of empire-building, the preliterate woodlands Iroquois, never numbering more than 2500 warriors and 12,000 people, were adroitly pursuing their own self-interest and shaping events in North America. The French historian La Potherie wrote in 1722: "It is a strange thing that three or four thousand souls can make tremble a whole new world. New England is very fortunate in being able to stay in their good graces. New France is often desolated by their wars, and they are feared through a space of more than fifteen hundred leagues of the country of our allies."[1] A generation later an Indian "expert" in New York warned the governor

---

[1]Quoted in Anthony F. C. Wallace, "The Origins of Iroquois Neutrality: The Grand Settlement of 1701," *Pennsylvania History*, 24 (1957): 235.

that "on whose ever side the [Iroquois] Indians fall, they will cast the balance."[2]

The strategy of France in the period after Louis XIV took the throne in 1661 was to establish an inland empire in North America that would surround the English and keep them pinned to the coast. New France was placed under royal supervision in 1663, a thousand soldiers were dispatched to the colony two years later, and an aggressive policy of territorial expansion was set in motion. By the early 1680s France had not only consolidated her hold in the St. Lawrence River Valley but had established a string of trading posts and forts along an arc that swung north and west of the English settlements like a long encircling arm. The French made exploratory trips all the way down the Illinois and Mississippi Rivers to the Gulf of Mexico and within another two decades French forts and trading posts would be rising at Mobile and Biloxi. When that occurred the deerskin and slave traders of South Carolina found themselves faced with new competitors in the vast lower Mississippi area which they had previously called their own.

The dreams of European hegemony that obsessed Louis XIV involved all the major powers in a series of global wars that occupied most of his half-century reign. Twice between 1665 and 1675 the French king cooked up a European war in order to attack his Hapsburg rivals in Europe. In the first of these he succeeded in overwhelming the Spanish Netherlands. But in the second the Protestant forces of Europe united against him, aware that the balance of power in Europe, upon which everybody depended for the preservation of peace, was in grave danger. A decade later, beginning in 1688, Louis moved again, turning first on the weakest and nearest of his neighbors, the German Rhineland, and at the same time symbolizing his determination to crush Protestant Europe by expelling all the Protestants of his country. Many of these Huguenots emigrated to England or to her colonies in America. War in Europe brought war in America and for the next quarter century with brief interruptions the armies and navies of England and France would be clashing around the world.

In the two wars from 1689 to 1697 and 1701 to 1713 the English and French in America discovered the incredible difficulties in merely bringing their military forces into contact. In a vast wilderness area the problems of weather, disease, transport, and supply were so great that only guerilla warfare was possible. The English made three attempts to strike at the centers of French power—Port Royal, Nova Scotia, which commanded the mouth of the St. Lawrence River, and Quebec, at the center

[2]Archibald Kennedy to George Clinton, 1746, Clinton Papers, vol. 3, Clements Library, University of Michigan.

EUROPEAN RIVALRY IN THE NEW WORLD, 1750

HUDSON BAY

NEWFOUNDLAND
St. Johns

CAPE BRETON
Louisbourg

NOVA SCOTIA
(*ACADIA*)

Quebec

L. Superior
Sault Ste. Marie
Ft. Frontenac
Montreal
L. Huron
L. Ontario
Albany
Boston
L. Michigan
Detroit
L. Erie
Philadelphia
New York
Ft. St. Louis
Cahokia
Kaskaskia

BERMUDAS
(British)

LOUISIANA

Charleston

Fr. Toulouse
Biloxi
Pensacola
New Orleans
St. Augustine
FLORIDA

BAHAMAS
(British)

SAN DOMINGO

ST. EUSTATIUS
(Dutch)

PORTO RICO
ANTIGUA
(Brit.)

M E X I C O

CUBA

HAITI
ST. CHRISTOPHER (Brit.)
NEVIS (Brit.)
MONTSERRAT (Brit.)
GUADELOUPE (Fr.)
MARTINIQUE (Brit.)
BARBADOS (Brit.)

YUCATAN
Belize

JAMAICA

CURAÇAO (Dutch)

HONDURAS
MOSQUITO COAST

Cartagena
Porto Bello
Panama

NEW GRANADA
VENEZUELA
Orinoco R.
GUIANA

BRITISH
FRENCH
SPANISH
DUTCH

of New France. In 1690, during the War of the League of Augsburg, they captured Port Royal but their assault on Quebec was a complete disaster. In the next war Massachusetts launched an expedition to storm Port Royal but it bogged down and failed in 1707. Even when England sent a flotilla of sixty ships and an army of five thousand men in 1709, the expeditions floundered before reaching their destinations. Boston merchants with provisioning contracts were the only real winners in these inglorious attempts.

With European-style warfare abysmally unsuccessful, both England and France attempted to subcontract military tasks to their Indian allies. This was occasionally successful, especially with the French, who were not reluctant to send their own troops into the fray with their Indian allies. Schenectady, New York, was wiped out in February 1690; Wells, Maine, and Deerfield, Massachusetts, were razed in 1704; and other towns along the New England frontier felt the force of the combined French-Indian attacks. But the English, though they pressured the Iroquois again and again to attack their enemies, went unrewarded for their efforts. The Iroquois were well aware of the internal divisions that rent the fabric of English colonial society. These were most visible in 1688–1689, at the outset of the War of the League of Augsburg, when internal rebellions in Massachusetts, New York, and Maryland set Englishman against Englishman. Even when differences within colonies were settled, animosities between colonies allowed only faint intercolonial cooperation, as a succession of royal governors and colonial administrators sent out from London were to discover. All of this was no secret to the Iroquois. When they were urged to take up arms against the French in 1692, they were quick to reply:

> You Sett us on dayly to fight & destroy your Enemies, & bidd us goe on with Courage, but wee See not that you doe anything to it yourSelfs, neither doe wee See any great Strenth you have to oppose them if the Enemy should breake out upon you; we hear of no great matter is like to be done at Sea, we hear nothing of itt; The warr must also be hottly Pursued on your Sides, what is it that our neighbors of n: England and the Rest of the English that are in Covenant with us doe, they all Stay att home & Sett us on to doe the work. . . .[3]

Iroquois Diplomacy

The English were equally unsuccessful in attempts to squeeze a recognition of English sovereignty out of their supposed allies. A succession

[3]Lawrence H. Leder, ed., *The Livingston Indian Records, 1666–1723* (Gettysburg, Pa.: Pennsylvania Historical Association, 1956), p. 165.

of royal governors in New York attempted to apply the terminology of "father" and "children" in their negotiations with the Iroquois. This linguistic device, which was a sure sign of the weakened state of an Indian nation, had been accepted by the Hudson River tribes after they had suffered devastation in wars with the Dutch and the English between 1640 and 1680. But the Iroquois had no need to accept the terminology of subordination. They "were not subjects," writes a recent historian; "although allied to New York politically, and somewhat dependent economically, they insisted constantly that they were 'free,' and they required New York's governors to call them 'brethren.' "[4] Adroit at the European game of twisting words so that appearance and reality became confused, the Iroquois would frequently make a statement such as in 1684 that "Wee have putt our selves under the great Sachim Charles that lives over the great lake" and then complete their speech with the reminder that "we are a free people uniting our selves to what sachem we please." Shortly after this declaration to the English they made it clear to the French that "We are born free, we neither depend on Yonnondio [the governor of New France] nor Corlaer [the governor of New York]. We may go where we please, and carry with us whom we please, and buy and sell what we please."[5] For the Iroquois, alliance with the English in the 1680s was only part of a game of diplomacy and no more than a temporary promise of support which could be reversed at any time.

This is not to suggest that the Iroquois were uninvolved in the Anglo-French struggle for empire. They were. But their enmeshment was not directed by the English or the French or with the goals of either European power in mind. The Iroquois calculated their own interests and made their own decisions within the councils of the Five Nations, centered at Onondaga. It was here that the representatives of the Five Nations wrestled with a problem that called for all their diplomatic skill and military strength in the last half of the seventeenth century—how to maintain the Iroquois position of middleman in the fur trade between the upper Great Lakes region and the fur markets at Albany and Montreal. It was not enough to have destroyed Huronia in the eastern Great Lakes region, for the Iroquois were still obliged to prevent the more remote tribes—Ottawas, Nippissings, and Sioux—from trading directly with the French, who were building trading posts in a vast region roughly bounded by Hudson's Bay on the north and the Ohio Valley to the south. Therefore after the end of the Huron Wars in 1656, the Iroquois block-

---

[4]Quoted in Francis Jennings, "The Constitutional Evolution of the Covenant Chain," *Proceedings of the American Philosophical Society*, 115 (1971): 90.

[5]Allen W. Trelease, *Indian Affairs in Colonial New York* (Ithaca, N.Y.: Cornell University Press, 1960), pp. 264, 267–68.

aded the rivers leading to Montreal and ambushed the canoes that came in flotillas with their annual catch of beaver and otter. Just as Spain's European enemies practiced piracy at sea in order to redirect gold and silver mined in Mexico and Peru to London or Paris, the Iroquois engaged in piracy on the waterways of the northern part of the continent to divert furs from Montreal to Albany, and thus, ultimately, from Paris to London.

The problem for France was how to protect trading links with the western tribes. Both alternative solutions, extermination of the Iroquois or alliance with them, proved impossible, though both were tried. For the Iroquois the problem was maintaining sufficient manpower to continue the interception of the western furs, while at the same time fending off enemies such as the Susquehannocks to the south or the Shawnees to the southwest. In the end, the natural alliance was between the Ottawa suppliers, the Iroquois middlemen, and the Albany buyers. The higher prices which the English were able to offer for furs, the better quality of English woolen goods, and the higher alcoholic content of English rum made trade at Albany far more desirable than trade at Montreal.

Understanding that an Ottawa-Iroquois alliance would spell disaster for New France, the French spent the last third of the seventeenth century attempting to disrupt this trading partnership. Periodic attacks were made by the French into Iroquois country and when the Indian enemy could not be engaged, his villages and food supplies were burned. Sometimes such forays were so successful, as in 1666, that the Iroquois would sue for peace and invite French missionaries into their towns to guide them, as they cleverly maintained, in "the true way." But when they calculated that the time was right, such as after defeating the Susquehannocks in 1675 and incorporating them into their fighting forces, the Iroquois would root out the Jesuit missionaries and launch devastating blows at the centers of French power. In 1680 the Five Nations invaded the Illinois country, destroying villages and French forts, and seizing French canoes and furs on the river routes leading east. They attacked again in 1684 and 1689. In the latter year the assault was not undertaken to satisfy the English, who had recently returned to war with France, but for internal Iroquois reasons, specifically in retaliation for a French offensive into Seneca country in 1687.

From time to time the French were able to enlist limited support from the Ottawas and remnants of the Hurons in their attacks on the Iroquois. But these western tribes understood clearly that their natural alliance was with those who offered the best price in trade goods. Accordingly, they gave the French enough support to keep them satisfied but never fully committed themselves to war with the Iroquois. In fact, for the most part, they gave only the appearance of hostility against the Iroquois, hewing to the policy that "we are all brothers, who ought to form only one body, and possess but one and the same spirit." The French, they reasoned, "invite us to go to war against the Iroquois; they wish to use us in order to make us their slaves. After we have aided in destroying the enemy, the French will do with us what they do with their cattle, which they put to the plow and make them cultivate the land. Let us leave them to act alone; they will not succeed in defeating the Iroquois; this is the means for being always our own masters."[6]

By the end of the seventeenth century it was becoming apparent to all parties involved that though the English vastly outnumbered the French, they could not defeat the Canadians because of disunity among the colonies and the unwillingness of the government at home to supply military forces; that the French were unable either to destroy or forge an alliance with the Iroquois because they lacked sufficient military strength for the former and suffered a competitive disadvantage in the fur trade that prohibited the latter; and that the Iroquois retained the strategic geographical position in the northern part of the continent. But in spite of their successes and the great expansion of their influence over tribes to the south and west of them, the Iroquois had suffered heavily in the quest for the middleman role in the fur trade. By the end of the seventeenth century, hard-hit by French attacks, they were seeking a new way of avoiding the costly beaver wars. It was clear to them by now that they could expect almost nothing in the way of military assistance from their Anglo-American allies since promise after promise from the New York government had gone unfulfilled.

The solution to their problem was sudden and bold. In the summer of 1701 they entered negotiations with both the English and the French and signed treaties almost simultaneously at Montreal and Albany. To the French they promised neutrality in any future war between England and France—a great gain for the French who had been plagued by the Iroquois and now could depend on their neutrality. To the English, who now lost a military ally, the Iroquois ceded their western hunting lands, conquered a half-century before from the Hurons. By this clever piece of diplomacy, the Iroquois implied that their primary allegiance was still to the English. But it was only a symbolic land cession, for the English had not the slightest ability to occupy or control this territory and in fact the lands in question had recently been reconquered by the French and their allies, the Wyandots. To complete their compromise negotiations the Iroquois made peace with the tribes to the west of them.

[6]Wallace, "Origins of Iroquois Neutrality," p. 226.

For almost half a century the Iroquois policy worked well. The Five Nations (which became the Six Nations after the addition of the Tuscaroras) disengaged from the costly beaver wars, pursued their role as fur suppliers, and increased their population by absorbing remnants of coastal tribes decimated by Europeans and elements of western tribes which they had themselves conquered. Since the early seventeenth century, when they had been struggling to assert themselves against other tribes of the Great Lakes region, the Iroquois had become the dominant power in the northeast woodlands and a force to be reckoned with by both the French and the English. Though hardly more numerous than the inhabitants of the province of New York alone at the beginning of the eighteenth century, their will to fight, their diplomatic skill, and their indispensably important position athwart the fur trading routes had raised them to a position of utmost importance. The governor of Quebec respectfully noted this position of power when he wrote home in 1711 that war with the Iroquois was to be avoided at all costs, for "the five Iroquois villages [nations] are more to be feared than the English colonies."[7]

Less than a year after the Iroquois had concluded their treaties at Albany and Montreal another Anglo-French war broke out. But while the French and their local Indian allies put the torch to towns along the New England frontier, the Iroquois remained on the sidelines, content to see the English and French trade blows. They were confirmed in their opinion that the English were unreliable military allies by New York's refusal to come to New England's aid. Afraid of jeopardizing their profitable fur trade and the black-market traffic they were conducting with the French Canadian enemy, the New Yorkers kept their minds to commerce and, according to some Massachusetts authorities, even marketed in Albany plunder from devastated New England frontier towns. The Iroquois' one act of assistance was to send three Mohawks and one Mahican to London with two prominent New Yorkers to argue for English assistance in the war against Canada. Arriving in London in 1710, they waited on Queen Anne at court, stopped the show when they attended the theatre, ran down a stag in the royal park, and were followed by throngs everywhere they went.

At the conclusion of Queen Anne's War in 1713 the Peace of Utrecht seemingly conferred substantial gains upon the English in North America. France ceded Nova Scotia, Newfoundland, and Hudson's Bay to England; recognized the sovereignty of the British over the Iroquois (the Iroquois

---

[7]Quoted in William J. Eccles, *The Canadian Frontier, 1534–1760* (New York: Holt, Rinehart and Winston, Inc., 1969), p. 133.

made no such concession); and permitted English traders to open commerce with the western tribes that had previously been linked to the French. But concessions on paper meant little if the English could not take advantage of them by occupying the areas they had gained or establishing trading posts deep in the interior. Not for another generation could the English find the strength to concern themselves with these distant regions. For now they fixed their attention on the buildup of population between the coast and the Appalachian Mountains. Only in constructing a fort and trading post at Oswego on Lake Ontario did England take advantage of her new rights. The final act of the imperial drama, and the fate of the western tribes and the Iroquois, was postponed for forty years.

Creek Diplomacy

Just as the Iroquois were able to protect their trading interests and avoid warfare by playing one European power against another, the Creek Confederation of the Southeast mastered the principles of *realpolitik* following the Yamasee War of 1715–1717. Like the Iroquois, the Creeks had been a defensive and loosely integrated confederacy before European settlement began. But they too found it possible to capitalize on the European trade to become the most formidable society in a vast region coveted by England, France, and Spain. And like the Iroquois, they not only enhanced their strength but suffered in the process through the intensification of warfare brought about by the introducion of the European trade. Less than two decades after the Iroquois perfected their "playoff system" between the English and French, the Creeks had propelled themselves into a position as "the custodians of the wilderness balance of power in the South."[8] Through a quarter-century of adroit maneuvering they extended and withdrew promises to the English, French, and Spanish in order to extract trade and military concessions. At the same time they maintained a largely autonomous position. Just as the English attempted to play Creeks and Cherokees against each other—"how to hold both as our friends, for some time, and assist them in Cutting one another's throats without offending either," as one Carolinian put it—the Creeks worked to keep French, English, and Spanish pitted against each other, with no one of the European powers gaining dominance over the other two. So skillful was their leader, Brims, in this that one Englishman in Carolina opined that he was "as great a Politician as any Governor in America."[9]

[8]Verner W. Crane, *Southern Frontier, 1670–1732* (Ann Arbor: University of Michigan Press, 1956), p. 260.
[9]*Ibid.*, pp. 263, 260–261.

For the Creeks the new policy of aggressive neutrality was a logical course to follow after the close trading alliance with the English earlier in the century had brought flagrant abuses by the English traders. In their strategy for survival, the Creeks had declared war against their exploiters, but their inability to persuade the Cherokees to join them in an all-out offensive against the English punctured the resistance movement. Now a policy of carefully limited cooperation was set in motion. Despite their defeat in war, it was far from a passive strategy. Instead it was the active response of Indian leaders who were attempting to build the strength of their people while recognizing the need and the advantages of interacting with the foreigners in their country.

The Creek politics of survival had to be devised within the context both of intra-Indian rivalries and of Anglo-French-Spanish rivalry. Ever since the English had arrived in Carolina and harassed the northern frontier of Spanish Florida, Spain had dreamed of mounting an expedition by land and sea that would wipe out English pretensions in the region. Such an attempt was made in 1702. It was an abysmal failure, however, producing only an English counterattack two years later that lay most of the Spanish missionary frontier in Florida in waste. English attacks on French trading posts on the lower Mississippi and Gulf of Mexico were planned in 1708. But a more profitable way of striking at nascent French power was found in 1711. Utilizing a military expedition primarily composed of Indian allies the English attacked the principal Indian allies of the French, the Choctaws. Yet none of these assaults on the frontier outposts of rival European nations was successful and the Peace of Utrecht, which ended hostilities between England, France, and Spain in 1713, left the English frustrated in their dream of controlling the lower South from the Atlantic to the Mississippi. It was this design of English hegemony that the Creeks hoped to prevent, while still maintaining trade connections with them.

In the aftermath of the Yamasee War the Creeks took measures to restore the balance of power by making overtures to the Spanish, whom they had fought at English instigation for many years. Chief Brims sent his son to St. Augustine in 1716 with instructions to allow the Spanish to build a fort at Coweta, the principal town of the Lower Creeks. Other Creek emissaries were sent to Mexico City to seal an alliance. During the next year Creek leaders also conferred with the Senecas, more than a thousand miles to the north, and with the English in Charleston. By 1717, the Creeks had fashioned a complicated arrangement by which some of their villages would remain within the Spanish orbit and some within the English. A formal treaty was signed with the English which left the Creeks free to trade with whomever they pleased but set fixed rates in their trade with the English, guaranteed ammunition and arms for use against tribes

not friendly to the English, and established a policy of mutual account-
ability for Creeks or Englishmen who committed crimes or injury against
each other.

Brims symbolized his balance of power strategy by commissioning one
son as his principal emissary to the English and another son as principal
emissary to the Spanish. Both English Carolinians and Spanish Florid-
ians, struggling for the upper hand with the Creeks, would attempt to
persuade Brims to name "their" son his successor in the years to come.
The English attempted to infiltrate the Creek political process in 1722
by giving a commission to Ouletta, the son of Brims who had been sent
to them, as headman of the Creek nation under his father. This attempt
to gain a recognition of English sovereignty was shattered two years later
when the Yamasees, inveterate enemies of the English and still allied to
the Spanish, murdered Ouletta. Seepeycoffey, the Spanish client son of
Brims, was now the only candidate as Brims's successor. When Seepeycoffey died in 1726, Brim's brother inherited the primary claim to head-
ship of the Creeks.

Until he died in the early 1730s Brims maintained the policy of playing
Spanish and English against each other. The Creeks continued to aid
the Yamasees, with whom the English were intermittently at war, and
they continued to attack the Cherokees with whom the English were
closely allied. The English attempted various strategies to coerce the
Creeks into an unqualified English connection—interference in Creek
political affairs, trade embargoes, and the threat of a joint Cherokee-Eng-
lish war against them. But while these tactics succeeded in bringing them
closer to the English and in convincing them to break off their traditional
support of the Yamasees, the Creeks still preserved their autonomous position and remained the pivotal force in the region. The Creeks, wrote the
Assembly of South Carolina in 1737 "have been treated with as Allies but
not as Subjects of the Crown. . . . They have maintained their own Possessions, and preserved their Independency."[10] By their strength in numbers and diplomatic skill the Creeks were able to preserve their central
position throughout the decades after the Yamasee War. Their emissaries
ranged for thousands of miles; between 1715 and 1733 they parleyed
with the Spanish in St. Augustine, Vera Cruz, and Mexico City; with the
English in Charleston and London; with the French at Fort Toulouse on
the Alabama River; and with headmen of other Indian nations from the
Florida border to the Great Lakes. At times they carried out simultaneous

10 *The Colonial Records of South Carolina, Journal of the Commons House of Assembly, Nov. 10, 1736–June 7, 1739*, ed. J. H. Easterby (Columbia: Historical Commission of South Carolina, 1951), p. 75.

negotiations with two European powers that were at swords' points, just as the Iroquois had conducted dual negotiations at Montreal and Albany in 1701.

Twice in the decades after Brims's death, the Creeks succeeded in preserving their policy of neutrality at critical junctures. In 1739, when England declared war on Spain, the Carolina government put enormous pressure on the Creeks to join General James Oglethorpe, who had founded the colony of Georgia between South Carolina and Florida only seven years before, in an assault on St. Augustine. Although a few villages of Creeks joined the English expedition, which ended in disaster, most of the Creeks remained out of the fray, convinced that the policy of trading with whomever offered the best prices, but militarily allying with no single European power, was the keystone to Creek survival and growth. The Creeks might well have congratulated themselves for adhering to their policy, for the Cherokees who joined the English brought back smallpox that spread to epidemic proportions in the Cherokee towns in 1740 and 1741. In the next year, a Creek headman gave new expression to the old strategy when he asserted that "The [Creek] land belonged to the English as well as the French and indeed to neither of them. But both had liberty to Come there to Trade."[11]

Again in the 1740s when France joined Spain in war against England, the Creeks' policy of neutrality was put to the test. James Glen, the new royal governor of South Carolina, summoned a number of headmen from the Upper Creek towns to Charleston in 1746 and in secret session confided what kinds of rewards he had in mind for the Creeks if they would join an English military assault on Fort Toulouse, the main French bastion on the lower Alabama. At a council back in their own country, however, the project was vetoed and the English were again thwarted in their efforts to obtain the Indian support they needed to drive the French from the lower South. Glen again attempted to mobilize the Creeks and Cherokees for attacks on the French in 1747, but the failure of his mission was made obvious when Malatchi, the youngest son of Brims and a pro-French chief, gained recognition as emperor of the Lower Creeks. Malatchi had been at the Charleston conference in the previous year and had refused to let the English governor browbeat him with threats of withdrawing the English trade. Instead he had returned to the principal town of the Lower Creeks, spoken against the English plan, and then personally visited St. Augustine and Fort Toulouse to inform the Spanish and French of the English proposals. The English were summarily told

---

[11]Quoted in M. Eugene Sirmans, *Colonial South Carolina; A Political History* (Chapel Hill: University of North Carolina Press, 1966). p. 198.

that they were welcome to trade in Creek country but not to build forts and could expect no Creek support for military assaults on the Spanish or French.

Transformations in Indian Society

By the middle of the eighteenth century, the interior Indian nations of North America had demonstrated their ability to adapt to the presence of Europeans and to turn their economic and political interaction with them to their own advantage. For a century and a half the culture of the Europeans had been revealed to the Indians. From it they drew selectively, adopting through the medium of the fur, skin, and slave trade European articles of clothing, weapons, metal implements, and a variety of ornamental objects. To this degree their material culture was changed. Too much, however, has been made of the extent to which this syncretizing of material objects robbed the Indians of their native skills. Agriculture, fishing, and hunting were the mainstays of Indian subsistence before the European came and they remained so thereafter. European implements such as the hoe only made Indian agriculture more efficient. The knife and fishhook enabled the natives to fish and trap with greater intensity in order to obtain the commodities needed in the barter system, but this was only an extension of ancient skills. Moreover, many of the interior tribes such as the Iroquois and the Creeks spent more of their time tranporting the furs and skins of more westerly tribes to English and French markets than they did in hunting the beaver and deer.

Interaction with European cultures brought other more important transformations in Indian society however. Not only was the method of warfare altered by the introduction of the gun, but warfare itself was greatly intensified. Not all Indian warfare was so limited in scale as to be symbolic before the arrival of the Europeans, but there was no precedent for the extermination of tribes or the slave-catching raids that characterized Creek warfare in the South in the late seventeenth and early eighteenth centuries.

ALCOHOL

A second effect, not yet fully understood, was wrought by the introduction of alcohol. There is little doubt that rum became one of the most important items in the Indian trade. It was useful to Europeans and pushed hard by traders because once Indians had acquired a taste for it, it added to the total stock of trade items that they needed. Increasing the volume of the trade was almost always the object foremost in the minds of traders and coastal merchants; thus it was the economic function of the Indians' taste for rum that mattered most to them. As for the Indians, once alcohol had been incorporated into their way of life, it became an important factor in internal Indian relations. The quality of English as opposed to French rum became a major consideration in diverting the northern fur trade from Montreal to Albany. In Carolina, though the Creek chiefs often asked for a suspension of the rum trade, the decision of the Trustees of Georgia to allow no traffic in alcohol—a part of their attempt to reform the Indian trade in the 1730s—brought only protests from the Creek headmen, who, while they understood the debilitating effects of rum on Creek culture, were unwilling to give up the power they enjoyed as distributors of rum.

Although the economic effects of the rum trade are not difficult to assess, the question of how Indian cultures were affected is far more difficult. The modern tendency has been to see Indian addiction to alcohol as a painkilling device among people caught between two cultures. Unable to maintain their traditional ways of life after becoming dependent on the material items of European culture, but equally unable to gain acceptance into white society, the Indian, it is often said, turned in despair to alcohol. Historians, anthropologists, and psychologists have thus seen drunkenness as a way of escaping internalized feelings of unworthiness that came from prolonged contact with a white society that called them "savages" and "barbarians." Drunkenness provided at least temporary flight back into a romanticized past before the white man came and thus gave momentary assistance in resolving a painful crisis of identity. The difficulty with this explanation is that whatever its value in revealing the causes of alcoholism in modern society, it will not satisfactorily explain drunkenness among either Indians or Europeans in the eighteenth century. Europeans were not known for identity crises in pre-Revolutionary society; yet their alcoholic consumption was staggering even by modern American standards and, from what can be determined from the sketchy statistics available, was far greater than among Indians of the period. If nothing else, mere availability assured this. In Philadelphia in 1772, for example, the 20,000 city dwellers could drink their fill at any of about 300 taverns and inns in the town. The amount of rum consumed on a per capita basis was far greater than that of the Indians beyond the Appalachian Mountains, who could neither obtain nor afford rum in such quantities.

When it is understood that the consumption of alcohol is given different meanings by different cultures and that drunken behavior takes many forms according to varying cultural norms, it is possible to gain some insight into the role of alcohol in the Indian societies of the interior.

Anthropologists have recently suggested that for Indians in the early periods of European contact drinking was primarily "an institutionalized 'time-out' period from ordinary canons of etiquette" and that it was only later, in the nineteenth and twentieth centuries, that it became a form of social protest and a form of release from despair. In the seventeenth and eighteenth centuries Indians imbibed rum for cultural reasons that made sense to Indians—"expansive conviviality, the letting down of customary decorum, and, in some cases, serious dignified drinking into a comatose state."[12] The consumption of alcohol was incorporated into a system of values which had earlier adopted the smoking of tobacco as a cultural habit associated not only with sociability and generosity—the "passing of the pipe"—but as a custom invested with religious functions and meanings as well.

It was one more token of the reciprocal nature of European-Indian relations that just as the drinking of European alcohol became a social habit with its own cultural functions within Indian societies, the smoking of Indian tobacco became a social habit with its own cultural meanings among Europeans. Indian smoking was adopted almost immediately by Europeans, who divested it of religious meaning and used it as a social lubricant and a mild narcotic. Once it caught on in Europe, none of the medical warnings of the most reputable doctors or even the polemics of kings, could stop the craze. By the end of the seventeenth century England was importing more than thirty million pounds of New World tobacco a year and it is probable that Europeans on both sides of the Atlantic were far more addicted to Indian tobacco than were Indians to European alcohol. This exchange of social habits, which were used for reasons relevant to each culture, was a major source of profit for the merchants in whose ships tobacco made its way from America to Europe and rum from the Caribbean to North America.

Alcohol became important in white-Indian contacts in another way. It was commonly distributed before negotiations for land or trade goods began. Many commentators in the eighteenth century observed that Indians became befuddled and were then easily swindled out of their goods. Although this may have been true among coastal Indians who came to the white settlements to barter, often staying for several days and drinking liberally at the invitation of white traders, it is unlikely that it was the typical experience. Indians did not relish being swindled any more

---

[12]Nancy Oestreich Lurie, "The World's Oldest On-Going Protest Demonstration: North American Indian Drinking Patterns," *Pacific Historical Review*, 40 (1971): 321; and Craig MacAndrew and Robert B. Edgerton, *Drunken Comportment, A Social Explanation* (Chicago: Aldine Publishing Co., 1969).

than Europeans and according to the testimony of many traders were as skillful at driving a bargain as their white trading partners. The distribution of alcohol at the beginning of negotiations was, in reality, a ritual way of initiating a beneficial contract for both sides. So long as Indians had more than one place to trade, it was not to the advantage of traders to drive them away by getting them drunk and then stealing their trade goods. This is not to say that sharp practices did not abound on both sides. On a number of occasions unauthorized traders brought quantities of rum to an Indian village, watched it eagerly consumed, and left with a winter's catch of furs and skins. But Europeans complained about being "held up" by Indians as often as Indians complained about European trickery. And when the trading was done at frontier posts or in Indian villages, which was the practice throughout the Carolina region and in the hinterlands of Virginia and Pennsylvania in the eighteenth century, the Indian, robbed of his senses through overconsumption of alcohol, was probably the exception rather than the rule. Indians took their trade where they could obtain the best prices and the amplest supply of goods they wanted. Their extraordinary mobility over land and inland waterways, often combined with the availability of barter with more than one European supplier, made it imperative for colonial traders to maintain a relationship that was to the Indians' satisfaction. When they did not, as in the case of the Carolina traders, the Indians took their trade to the French, the Spanish, or to rival traders in Georgia and Virginia. If none of the alternatives was available, their last resort was to rise up against those who abused them.

It is quite possible that when tribes lost their land, their autonomy, and their cultural integrity drinking changed from a form of social relaxation to a solvent for internalized aggressive impulses against whites that could not be outwardly expressed. This seems to have been the case among some of the remnants of the coastal tribes, which by the eighteenth century had lost their land and their power. They existed only at the pleasure of white society and the chronic and debauched drinking that was attributed to them by many observers may be indicative of the precarious inner state they were in. Almost powerless and unable to express aggression toward whites, their frustrations accumulated and were turned inward. Only drinking and in extreme cases suicide provided release from this situation. But where power was still balanced between Indians and whites, which was still the case in most parts of eighteenth-century America, the drunken Indian in our historical imagination corresponds not so much to reality as to the stereotype of the aggressive, violent "savage," who became a white cultural artifact.

POLITICAL ORGANIZATION

Besides the incorporation of material objects and use of alcohol, the primary cultural change that resulted from contact with European societies was in the realm of Indian political organization. This varied from society to society but the examples of the Creeks and Cherokees are instructive. Though they belonged to different linguistic groups and frequently warred against each other, their precontact political structures were similar and they encountered the same historical forces in the seventeenth and eighteenth centuries—trade, war, and land encroachment. Though loosely confederated, a fundamental feature of their political structures was the local autonomy of towns and clans. It was to the town, not to the "confederacy," that the mass of Creeks and Cherokees gave their primary loyalty. Any larger political agreement or action required a consensus of town opinion. Attempts were made to coordinate the policy of local towns, but no party in disagreement with the majority decision was compelled to act against its wishes. Thus towns or groups of towns often parlayed individually with Europeans, made separate agreements with traders, and acted semi-independently in military affairs. Within some sixty Cherokee and several dozen Creek towns tension between civil and military leaders increased the likelihood of factionalism. In the eighteenth century the most dominant split was between the Upper Creek towns and the Lower Creek towns, a division roughly paralleled by the split between the towns of the Overhill Cherokees and the Middle and Lower Cherokees. Such splits often revolved around geographical proximity to French or English traders.

Several important changes in Creek political structure occurred as the result of trade, war, and diplomatic contact with Europeans in the eighteenth century. The need to deal with English and Spanish traders and governments obliged the Creeks to move toward a loose "confederacy" where coordinated action would give them greater strength in their dealings with outsiders. A second political change involved a gradual move toward patrilineal dynasties among the headmen or "micos." This altered the traditional criterion for leadership, which had been membership in a leading matrilineal clan. Before contact with Europeans the chiefship of a town had resided in the dominant matrilineal clan of that village. But in the eighteenth century the tendency was to invest leadership in the son of the chief rather than in the son of the chief's sister, thus introducing a system in which matrilineality and patrilineality coexisted. One cause of this shift toward patrilineality may have been that English, Spanish, and French authorities tended to promote and support the candidacy of the chief's son, consistent with the European view of social and political organization. This was a part of the European attempt to intrude on the internal politics of Indian societies in order to influence tribal leaders in the three-cornered struggle for Indian allies and trade partners. In general, it was also true that intensified hunting, trading, and warring elevated the position of many men in Indian society and thereby contributed to a cultural climate favoring the development of patrilineal institutions.

Another way of attempting to control the political dynamics of Creek anl Cherokee societies was to support the candidacy of a particular headman's son or even to commission particular individuals in order to facilitate communication and cooperation. The English tried to establish Ouletta, the son of Brims, as their client and when he died transferred their recognition to the Spanish candidate, his brother Seepeycoffee. Annual gifts, which were an essential part of good relations, were distributed through commissioned headmen, thus enhancing their prestige within their own society. The English practice of picking particular headmen with whom to negotiate conferred power on those who had not earned their authority in the traditional way, according to matrilineage and honor, but simply through the intervention of an external authority. In time, a commission from colonial officials became an important factor in the degree of influence wielded by a particular chief.

Intermarriage with an Indian woman was another way of gaining influence in a tribe, particularly if the woman was from an influential clan. Mary Musgrove Bosomworth, a niece of Brims, married three Englishmen in succession, and though she was fiercely anti-English on occasion, her husbands attained positions of great importance within the Creek confederation. Thus through commissioning client headmen and intermarrying with Indian women the Carolinians worked to strengthen the pro-English faction in the Creek confederacy and to wield some influence in political decisions.

Although this kind of interventionism can be seen as a way of upsetting traditional lines of political authority and customs for recruiting headman in a way that benefited the English, it can also be regarded as a purposeful adjustment of traditional political methods by Indian peoples who faced new and powerful invaders and desired a continuous flow of trade goods. By modifying the customary criteria of kinship the Creeks selected leaders better equipped to act in their interest. Access to the English or Spanish was gained by marrying one's sister to a European, by accepting a commission, or by having a European father. But in any of these cases the Creeks were not simply passive and helpless objects responding to white initiative. In a period of shifting power among the

European groups present in the region, the Creeks were "coping creatively in a variety of ways with the different situations in which they found themselves."[13]

Like the Creeks, the Cherokees changed their political practices in the eighteenth century in response to new needs related to war and trade with Europeans. Before about 1730 the nearly autonomous village was the basic unit of Cherokee political authority. There was little need for larger political unification. But tension with their Creek neighbors, encouraged by the English whose strategy of survival was to keep their allies divided against each other, and intermittent hostilities with the English created a need for political centralization. By mid-century the Cherokees had formed a supravillage political organization. Civil chiefs or "priests," under the leadership of Old Hop, gathered together the fragmented authority of the earlier period and formed a tribal "priest state" in which the Cherokee towns coordinated decision making.

When this proved inadequate to the tasks at hand in the difficult years after mid-century, warriors began to assume the dominant role in tribal councils. Whereas before the warrior had been greatly respected but outranked by the civil chiefs, by the 1760s the Cherokees adapted to a new era of strife by making "warring and warriors an unambiguous part of the good life" and by giving the war chiefs new and coercive political authority over the nation.[14] By this process, initiated within Cherokee society, political changes were made that enabled dozens of villages to unify and amalgamate their strength.

While the interior tribes blended a wide variety of European trade goods into their material culture and adapted their political structures to meet new situations, other aspects of their life were characterized by a high degree of social identity and cultural persistency. Iroquois, Creeks, Cherokees, and other tribes were singularly unimpressed with most of the institutions of European life and saw no reason to replace what they valued in their own culture with what they disdained in the culture of others. This applied to the newcomers' political institutions and practices, system of law and justice, religion, education, family organization, and child-rearing practices. In all these areas the Indians carefully observed European customs but saw little that they regarded as worthy of emulation. Confident of their own beliefs and politically autonomous, they refused to incorporate alien ideas, values, and institutions into their way

[13]Robert F. Berkhofer, Jr., "The Political Context of a New Indian History," *Pacific Historical Review*, 40 (1971): 364.

[14]Fred Gearing, "Priests and Warriors; Social Structures for Cherokee Politics in the 18th Century," American Anthropological Association *Memoir* 93 (1962): 102.

of life. Indeed, so far as the Indians could ascertain, these institutions often failed to work successfully in the Europeans' own cultural system.

The Anglican missionaries of the Society for the Propagation of the Gospel were continually plagued by this paradox in their efforts to convert Indians to Christianity. Why, asked Indians, should they convert to a system that, despite its claims of superiority, was ridden with crime, social disorder, and political factionalism? "[The Indians] are for the most part great lovers of Justice & Equity in their dealings," wrote Robert Maule, an Anglican missionary in Carolina in 1709, "and I have asked some of them whether they would learn to be or had any desire to become of the white men's religion. They have plainly told me no: what's the matter sayd I, why so? Because, replys they, Backarara [the white man] no good; Backarara Cheat; Backarara Lye, Backarara Drink Brandy, me no Love that."[15] Itinerant clergymen in the Carolinas repeated the same message over and over again in their reports to superiors in London. Most of the settlers, wrote a plaintive Charles Woodmason at the end of the colonial period, lived "after a loose and lascivious manner. . . . The Manners of the North Carolinians in General, are Vile and Corrupt—the whole Country is a Stage of Debauchery Dissoluteness and Corruption. . . . Polygamy is very Common, . . . bastardly, no Disrepute—Concubinage General."[16] Could it be any wonder then that he was unable to convince the Indians of the superiority of the white way of life?

The Carolinas were still in a frontier stage, of course, but throughout the colonies Anglican missionaries complained of the same problem— attempting to indoctrinate "savages" in Christian ways when most of the Christians with whom they came in contact were more "savage" than the Indians themselves. Drunkenness, dishonesty, and noncooperation were among the most visible characteristics of white society, thus rendering it illogical in the minds of Indians to regard as superior the white Christian culture to which they were so incessantly urged to aspire. John Lawson, a proprietary official in the Carolinas in the early eighteenth century, captured the essence of the reason for the lack of cultural borrowing outside the realm of material objects. "They are really better to us," he wrote in 1708, "than we are to them; they always give us Victuals at their Quarters, and take care we are arm'd against Hunger and Thirst: We do not

---

[15]Robert Maule to Society for the Propagation of the Gospel, [June 3, 1710], SPG Mss, A5, No. 133 (microfilm of Library of Congress transcripts), UCLA Research Library.

[16]Charles Woodmason, *Carolina Backcountry on the Eve of the Revolution: The Journal and Other Writings of Charles Woodmason, Anglican Itinerant*, ed. Richard J. Hooker (Chapel Hill: University of North Carolina Press, 1969), pp. 80–81.

so by them (generally speaking) but let them walk by our Doors Hungry, and do not often relieve them. We look upon them with Scorn and Disdain, and think them little better than Beasts in Humane Shape, though if well examined, we shall find that, for all our Religion and Education, we possess more Moral Deformities, and Evils than these Savages do, or are acquainted withal."[17] Indians were not secretive in their disdain of white culture. When it was suggested to the Iroquois in 1744 that they send some of their young men to Virginia for a white education, they counterproposed that "if the English Gentlemen would send a Dozen or two of their children to Onondaga, the great Council would take care of their Education, bring them up in really what was the best Manner and make men of them."[18]

In marriage and social relations it was much the same. Although Europeans often disparaged Indian customs of companionate marriage or serial monogamy and accused them of "licentiousness," "debauchery," and "faithlessness" in their sexual practices, domestic relations among the Indians, as a few European observers admitted, were entirely satisfactory to them and seemed infinitely better than those of their European critics. Shortly after his arrival in the colonies, Thomas Paine reported the opinion of an "American savage" concerning Christian marriages. "Either the Christian's God was not so good and wise as he was represented," the Indian reportedly avowed,

> or he never meddled with the marriages of his people; since not one in a hundred of them had anything to do either with happiness or common sense. Hence as soon as ever you meet, you long to part; and not having this relief in your power, by way of revenge, double each other's misery. Whereas in ours [Indian marriages] which have no other ceremony than mutual affection, and last no longer than they bestow mutual pleasures, we make it our business to oblige the heart we are afraid to lose; and being at liberty to separate, seldom or never feel the inclination. But if any should be found so wretched among us, as to hate where the only commerce ought to be love, we instantly dissolve the band. God made us all in pairs; each has his mate somewhere or other; and it is our duty to find each other out, since no creature was ever intended to be miserable.[19]

In sum, while the material aspects of Indian culture were changed im-

[17]Lawson, *A New Voyage of Carolina,* . . . ed. Hugh T. Lefler (Chapel Hill: University of North Carolina Press, 1967), p. 243.

[18]Quoted in A. Irving Hallowell, "The Backwash of the Frontier: The Impact of the Indian in American Culture," in Paul Bohannan and Fred Plog, eds., *Beyond the Frontier: Social Process and Cultural Change* (Garden City, N.Y.: The Natural History Press, 1967), p. 325.

[19]*The Complete Writings of Thomas Paine*, 2 vols., Philip S. Foner, ed. (New York: Citadel Press, 1945), 2: 1119–20.

portantly and political structures were altered to a lesser degree, most aspects of Indian life were marked by cultural persistency rather than change in the long period of interaction with Europeans. Indian societies were as selective as European societies in borrowing from the cultures with which they came into contact. They syncretized what served them well and rejected what promised no improvement within the framework of their own values and modes of existence. They wished to interact not merge with Europeans.

For the first half of the eighteenth century interior tribes such as the Creeks, Cherokees, and Iroquois maintained a state of equipoise with the European colonial societies by artfully playing one European power against another and serving periodic reminders to the Europeans that Indian trade and military assistance were as valuable to them as the European trade goods were to native societies. "To preserve the Ballance between us & the French," wrote New York's Indian secretary, "is the great ruling Principle of Modern Indian Politics,"[20] Indians were useful to Europeans, Europeans were useful to Indians, and power was roughly divided between them. But in the third quarter of the eighteenth century two great changes, occurring on opposite sides of the Atlantic, all but ended the existing equilibrium between Indian and European peoples.

Population Increase

On the American side of the ocean, it was the tremendous population buildup, especially in the English colonies, that by the 1750s had created a shortage of land on the coastal plain and sent thousands of land-hungry settlers spilling toward and through the mountain gaps in the Appalachians in search of new territory. From a population of a quarter million in 1700, the English colonies grew to 1.2 million in 1750 and increased another .4 million in the next decade. Three-quarters of this increase came in the colonies south of New York. The advance agents of this enormous westward rush were eastern land speculators. They had only to watch the German and Scotch-Irish immigrants disembarking daily at Baltimore, Philadelphia, and New York to understand that fortunes were to be made by those who could lay claim to land west of the existing settlements.

With capital provided by London investors, Virginia tobacco planters, and northern merchants, land companies were formed in the 1740s and 1750s to capitalize on this demographic explosion. The Ohio Land Com-

<hr>

[20]Peter Wraxall, *An Abridgment of the Indian Affairs* . . ., Charles H. McIlwain, ed. (Cambridge: Harvard University Press, 1915), p. 219.

pany, organized in 1747, acquired half a million acres in the Ohio Valley. The Susquehanna Land Company, organized five years later, acquired rights to hundreds of thousands of acres in Pennsylvania. The Delaware Company, the Miami Company, the Indiana Company, and other private syndicates all raced to establish claims in the next decade. Though some, like the Susquehanna Company, advertised that their purpose was to "open the most effectual Door for carrying the Light of the glorious Gospel of Christ among the numerous tribes of Indians that inhabit those inland Parts," there was little doubt of the principal object in mind.[21] Inexorably, the agents of English society began to exert pressure on Indian leaders to cede and sell their lands in order to pave the way for new white settlements. Moreover the farther west settlement moved, the closer it came to the western trading empire of the French and the Indian nations allied to them.

Indian Strategy in the Seven Years' War

On the opposite side of the Atlantic the revival of international rivalries worked to hasten this showdown west of the Allegheny Mountains. In 1748 France and England had composed the differences that had led them to war in 1743, but even as the ink was drying on the articles of conciliation the way was being prepared for a renewal of hostilities. The powerful merchant element in England, supported by American clients, was calling for a destruction of French overseas trade. Even before events in Europe brought formal declarations of war, fighting had begun in the North American wilderness. By the time it was over, in the mid-1760s, France would have vacated her North Atlantic claims and the precious system of balancing off European powers, the key to Indian autonomy, would be shattered.

During the 1740s English fur traders from Virginia and Pennsylvania pushed deep into the Ohio Valley, establishing outposts on the Ohio River and its tributaries. By 1749 the French commander at Fort Miami, south of Detroit, reported that about three hundred English traders were operating in the Ohio country and successfully luring the Indians into their trade orbit. Men with a sense of geopolitics had realized for decades that the struggle for the continent would hinge on control of the trans-Allegheny west. For more than a century the English had been content to populate the narrow coastal plain, leaving the continental heartlands to

[21]Petition of Subscribers to the Susquehannah Company, 1755, in Julian P. Boyd, ed., *The Susquehannah Company Papers* (Wilkes-Barre, Pa.: Wyoming Historical & Genealogical Society, 1930), 1: 255.

their rivals and obtaining their share of the Indian trade through trade connections centered at Albany and Charleston. Now they were challenging the French where the French interest was vital. In addition, it was obvious that trailing just behind the fur traders were the land speculators, themselves the advance guard of a population growing by geometric proportions.

France's choices were to resist or surrender the continent to the English and Spanish. They chose the former, attempting to block further English expansion by establishing forts throughout the Ohio Valley and by prying the Indians loose from their English connections. Attempts were made to convince the Iroquois, Shawnees, and Delawares of the Ohio region that only an alliance with the French would guarantee their survival. "The English," warned one French emissary in the early 1750s, "are much less anxious to take away your peltries than to become masters of your lands . . . and your blindness is so great, that you do not perceive that the very hand that caresses you, will scourge you, like negroes and slaves, so soon as it will have got possession of those lands."[22]

Though the Indians were fully aware of the westward surging population, they were unwilling in the short run to break the connections with English traders that brought them European commodities which the French could not match in cost and quality. Moreover, English strength in the area was a reality and French talk of trade south of the Great Lakes was only a promise. In 1752 France began a four-year campaign to alter this situation, attacking English trading posts and building forts of their own. By 1755, they had driven the English traders out of the Ohio Valley, established themselves as far east as the forks of the Ohio River, near the present Pittsburgh, Pennsylvania, and smartly rebuffed the ambitious young Colonel George Washington, who attempted to expel them from Fort Duquesne.

English attempts to respond to this bold French campaign were fatally crippled by internal division, which was starkly revealed at the Albany Congress of 1754. This was the first attempt of the colonies to unify for military purposes and through united action to woo the all-important Iroquois out of their position of neutrality. One of the main purposes of the Congress was to demonstrate to the Iroquois that fighting resolve and cohesion prevailed in the English colonies. But while representatives of the colonies were attempting to work out a plan of confederation, land agents from Connecticut and Pennsylvania were deep in intrigue concerning the purchase of Iroquois lands west of the Susquehannah River. In the end the attempt at intercolonial cooperation fell to pieces and the

[22]Quoted in Eccles, *Canadian Frontier*, p. 158.

Iroquois left the conference convinced that the English, as they said, were "like women: bare and open and without fortifications."[23]

It was decided in the capitals of Europe, not America, to force a showdown. In London, two regiments under the command of General James Braddock were dispatched. In Paris, four thousand regulars were ordered to the French strongholds at Louisbourg on Cape Breton Island, guarding the St. Lawrence seaway, and at Quebec. The year which it took Braddock to make his way across the Atlantic and then lead his army, reinforced by American enlistees, across Pennsylvania and into the western wilderness was the last of his life. Less than twenty miles from Fort Duquesne the French and their Indian allies ambushed the British-Americans and Braddock's reputedly invincible army of 2,200 was routed by an attacking force one third as large. Two-thirds of the English force was killed and wounded and the survivors fled, leaving artillery, horses, cattle, and supplies behind.

For the rest of the summer of 1755 the Virginia and Pennsylvania backcountry was terrorized by Indian raiders who for years had silently nursed grudges against white land encroachers and ungenerous traders. Now was their opportunity to attach themselves to French military power and to even scores that went back decades. Among the first to strike at the English, Scotch-Irish, and German communities were the Delawares, who a generation before had been cheated out of their tribal lands in eastern Pennsylvania. Just as they had streamed westward as refugees from colonial oppression, now they sent thousands of European refugees fleeing eastward as they burned, killed, and pillaged all along the Pennsylvania frontier. "Almost all the women & children over Sasquehannah have left their habitations, & the roads are full of starved, naked, indigent multitudes," cried one colonist.[24]

In 1756 and 1757 one French victory after another threw the English colonies into panic. The English post at Oswego, on Lake Erie, fell in August 1756. Two thousand troops at Fort William Henry, at the foot of Lake George, surrendered in August 1757. So desperate was the English situation that it was reported in Quebec that the governor of Pennsylvania, terrified at Indian attacks that had carried within thirty miles of Philadelphia, was willing to allow hostile Indians free passage through his colony if they would concentrate their attacks on the Virginia frontier. Other raids on the New England border, in the Mohawk Valley of New York, and along the entire frontier from New York to Georgia led to gloomy speculations in the English settlements that the continent would fall to the French and their Indian allies. Never was disunity within the

[23]E. B. O'Callaghan, ed., *Documents Relative to the Colonial History of the State of New-York* (Albany: Weed, Parsons & Co., 1855), 6: 870.

[24]Quoted in Douglas E. Leach, *The Northern Colonial Frontier, 1607–1763* (New York: Holt, Rinehart and Winston, 1966), p. 200.

English colonies and the triumph of the private good over the community interest so painfully felt. Seventy thousand French Canadians and their Indian allies had taken on a million and a half Englishmen, supported by the British army, and whipped them hollow.

In these circumstances, English hopes rested with obtaining the support, or, at the very least, pledges of neutrality from the four main Indian confederacies of the interior—the Iroquois, Cherokees, Creeks, and Choctaws. If they should be drawn into the French camp, even the massive reinforcements of British troops and supplies being mobilized under the direction of William Pitt, who assumed the English prime ministership in the dark days of 1756, might not be able to stanch the French tide. Perhaps never since the initial band of settlers had been obliged to rely upon the coastal Indians to supply them with food and teach them agricultural techniques that would see them through the "starving time" were the English colonists so dependent on the Indians' goodwill.

Nor was it clear how Indian support or neutrality could be secured. A century of intermittent hostility and the frantic hungering after the Indians' western lands that had occurred during the previous decade seemed to suggest that the allegiance of the populous interior tribes would be difficult to obtain. The words written in 1754 by Edmond Atkin, Charleston Indian trader and soon to become English Superintendent of the Southern Indians, seemed prophetic. "The Importance of Indians," wrote Atkin, "is now generally known and understood. A Doubt remains not, that the prosperity of our Colonies on the Continent, will stand or fall with our Interest and favour among them. While they are our Friends, they are the Cheapest and Strongest Barrier for the Protection of our Settlements; when Enemies, they are capable by ravaging in their method of War, in spite of all we can do, to render those Possessions almost useless."[25]

IROQUOIS

The case of the Iroquois is illustrative of the English vulnerability to which Atkin pointed. In negotiations with the French the English pretended that Iroquois support was a certainty and bluntly informed the governor of Canada that all members of the Iroquois tribes were indisputably subjects of the King of England.[26] But the English knew that the allegiance of the Iroquois and their dependents, the eastern Delawares, could be secured in only two ways: through purchase or through a demon-

---

[25]Wilbur R. Jacobs, ed., *Indians of the Southern Colonial Frontier; the Edmond Atkin Report and Plan of 1755* (Columbia: University of South Carolina Press, 1954), pp. 3–4.

[26]Governor Clinton to Governor of Canada, Oct. 10, 1748, in O'Callaghan, ed., *Documents Relating to Hist. of New-York*, 6: 492.

stration of power so great that the Iroquois would be convinced that the English would prevail with or without their support and would accordingly find it politic to choose the winning side at the outset. The first strategem proved a failure in 1754 when representatives of the Six Nations left the Albany Congress with thirty wagonloads of gifts, but gave in return only tantalizing half-promises of support against the French, who continued to score major victories in the next three years. Only when paid as mercenaries, such as in 1757 when about five hundred Mohawks collected £33,602 for services rendered to the English forces in New York, would the Iroquois support the Anglo-Americans.[27]

Further attempts were made during the next two years to get the Iroquois to subdue the attacking Delawares, who had driven the settlement line in Pennsylvania back to the eastern counties. Pennsylvania itself was badly divided between pacifistic Quakers, who believed that their Scotch-Irish frontiersmen were only reaping what they had sowed through years of abusing and defrauding Indians, and militant Anglicans and Presbyterians, who wanted taxes passed for a stern counteroffensive against the attackers. "The Indians learned our Weakness, by being informed of our Divisions," wrote the colony's official interpreter in 1757 after a conference convened for the purpose of buying off the Delawares' wrath.[28]

Not for another year, however, until October 1758, were the English able to get a promise from the Iroquois to control the Delaware and halt the attacks on the Pennsylvania settlements. Agreement was reached at Easton, Pennsylvania, and the Indians left the conference with a wagon train of "gifts." It is easy to suppose that these Indian concessions were simply a response to white stimuli. From the Indian point of view, however, the Easton Treaty had a different meaning. No military commitment was made to the English. The Iroquois, in exchange for their pledge of neutrality and their assurance that the hostile Delawares would be quieted, resecured the vast tract of land west of the Susquehanna River that they had ceded to Pennsylvania four years before at the Albany Congress. Territorial security west of the Alleghenies was thus reassured.

Except for the halfhearted support of the Mohawks, the easternmost of the Six Nations, the Iroquois either maintained their neutrality or, as in the case of the Senecas, fought with the French in the campaigns of 1757 and 1758. As for the Mohawks, their allegiance to the English can be explained not only by their proximity to the English trading center at

[27]Wilbur R. Jacobs, *Diplomacy and Indian Gifts: Anglo-French Rivalry Along the Ohio and Northwest Frontiers, 1748–1763* (Stanford: Stanford University Press, 1950), p. 178.

[28]Lawrence H. Gipson, *The British Empire Before the American Revolution*, 14 vols. (New York: Alfred A. Knopf, 1936–69), 7:58.

Albany but by the huge amounts they were paid for their services and by the fact that William Johnson, appointed British Superintendent of the Northern Indians, had married a Mohawk woman and lived among them for years following his arrival in America in 1739. As all the English who attempted to woo the Iroquois in the dark years from 1754 to 1758 found out, the Six Nations were bent on pursuing their traditional policy of disengagement from European wars and the protection of their tribal homelands. For these reasons they opposed any military expeditions that sought to pass through their lands. As late as May 1758, Johnson, the most influential Englishman with the Six Nations, was specifically invited to stay away from a grand council of the Iroquois at Onondaga where he had hoped to recruit their support for the summer campaign against the French at Fort Ticonderoga. Though the Mohawks promised some support, they were careful to join the English forces only after the main battle had been fought.

In 1759, however, the Iroquois reversed their position. Feelers by Johnson in February led him to report optimistically that if the English mounted an expedition against the French stronghold at Fort Niagara "or elsewhere, thro' the Country of the Six Nations, I shou'd be able to prevail upon the greater Part if not the whole of them, to join His Majesty's Arms."[29] It was not Johnson who was able to "prevail," however, but the Iroquois, who in their own councils assessed the Anglo-French military situation and then reformulated their own polity. After four years of defeat, the tide had turned in the British favor in July 1758 when Louisbourg and Fort Frontenac, the strategic centers of French power at opposite ends of the St. Lawrence, fell before Anglo-American assaults. In November 1758 the French, abandoned by the Delaware, who had been satisfied by the Easton Treaty promises, abandoned Fort Duquesne at the forks of the Ohio River. By the end of the year the upper Ohio Valley was in English hands for the first time in four years. William Pitt had mobilized the fighting power of the English nation—more men were put in the field than existed in all of New France—and the colonists had put aside their intramural squabbling long enough to stem the French tide.

These English victories helped to move the Iroquois away from their long-held position of neutrality. Adding to the incentive to join cause with the English was the capture of French ships bringing trade goods for the year to Montreal—an unexpected turn of fortune that vastly improved the English position in wooing the Six Nations. By April 1759, the Iroquois chiefs, consistent with the change of policy negotiated at the Treaty of Easton, came to the Mohawk town of Canajoharie and prom-

[29] *Ibid.*, p. 342.

ised eight hundred warriors for an attack on Fort Niagara, the strategic French fur trading depot on Lake Ontario. The Iroquois had calculated correctly: the French were going down to defeat in North America.

For the Iroquois, this precipitous reversal of events called for a rapid realignment of allegiances. This had been accomplished by July 1759 when the Iroquois drove the French from Fort Niagara and thereby laid open to the English the strategic gateway to the western tribes. The capture of Niagara, wrote an English officer, was "of the utmost consequence to the English, as it gives us the happy opportunity of commencing & cultivating a friendship with those numerous tribes of Indians who inhabit the Borders of Lake Erie, Huron, Michigan & even Lake Superiour; And the Fur trade which is carried on by these tribes, which all centers at Niagara, is so very considerable, that I am told by very able judges that the French look upon Canada [as] of very little importance without the possession of this important Pass."[30] The French empire in North America was now all but shattered.

It is important to note that throughout the war the Six Nations were able to assess accurately the shifting military balance between the rival European powers and formulate their own policy accordingly. Though they wrote no field memoranda and moved no troops or supplies through the field, their communication network extended across the entire region in which the French and English were fighting. In their councils they demonstrated a keen understanding of when the strategic balance was tipping in the British direction. Most histories of the "Great War for Empire" applaud William Johnson's skill in "winning over" the Iroquois of "persuading" them to join the English side. But the evidence is much more compelling that the Iroquois were continually reassessing their own position and calculating how their self-interest could best be served. Despite English blandishments, presents, and even the return of previously acquired territory, the Iroquois refused to join the English side through the first four years of war or even to allow the English passage through their territory. But when the military superiority of the English began to show itself in 1759, the Iroquois quickly adjusted their policy of neutrality and joined in reaping the benefits of victory. If their policy of *realpolitik* failed at all, it was in not perceiving that the maintenance of French power in North America was essential to their long range interests.

CHEROKEES

In the South the Creeks and Cherokees were involved in similar calculations of self-interest. The Cherokees were even larger in number than the Iroquois and Creeks, probably totalling about 12,000 at mid-eight-

---

[30]Quoted in Leach, *Northern Colonial Frontier*, p. 204.

eenth century. The English regarded their allegiance or neutrality as indispensable to colonial existence in the region from Virginia to Georgia. Settled in the Appalachian Mountains to the west of the Carolina and Georgia settlers, and known for the valor of their warriors, they had been allied to the English in trade and war since the late seventeenth century. Faced with other Indian enemies, the Carolinians came to regard Cherokee support as a cornerstone of their Indian policy. The Cherokees were not unaware of this. They understood that they had played the decisive role in the Yamasee War of 1715, maneuvering, as the Carolinians admitted, in the best tradition of European power politics. "The last time they were here [in Charleston] they insulted us to the last degree," Carolina leaders complained in 1717, "and indeed by their demands (with which we were forced to comply) made us their tributaries."[31]

The support of the Cherokees wavered at various points after the Yamasee War, especially in the 1730s. Trade abuses during that decade had aroused their ire and when the German mystic, Gottlieb Priber, reached them in 1736, he found them ripe for his message. Priber's genuine respect for Indian culture and his disaffection from European society, which he regarded as hopelessly corrupt, made him welcome in the Cherokee towns. Historians have been fascinated with the utopian communal state based on Plato's Republic which Priber preached wherever he went and which made him so subversive in white settlements. But for the Cherokees Priber's importance was in his efforts to teach them the use of weights and measures so they could protect themselves against dishonest traders. Priber also cautioned them to maintain their freedom by trusting no Europeans and encouraged them to cultivate trade connections with the French at New Orleans as a way of diminishing the English influence. His plan for Indian survival in the South included a confederacy of all the major tribes of the region, a city of refuge for escaped slaves and debtors within Cherokee territory, and an iron resolve among the Indians to surrender no territory, to make no concessions to any European power, and to continue the balance-of-power game in relations with the French, English, and Spanish. That the Cherokees regarded him as "a great beloved man" is a clear indication of how vibrantly anti-European, especially anti-English, ideas resonated in the Cherokee mind, even while close relations with the Carolinians were carried on.

When the South Carolina government ordered Priber's arrest in 1739 the Cherokees refused to surrender him to colonial authorities. But in 1743 he was captured by the Creeks on his way to the French in New Orleans and turned over to the English in Georgia. He died after a few

---

[31]Quoted in David D. Wallace, *South Carolina: A Short History, 1520–1948* (Chapel Hill: University of North Carolina Press, 1951), p. 90.

years of imprisonment in Frederica, Georgia. In 1748 the Carolina government further antagonized the Cherokees by refusing to honor a treaty of mutual support when the Cherokees were attacked by the Upper Creeks. In response the Cherokees attacked white Carolina traders, demonstrating that they did not regard themselves as English dependents but possessed enough power to control their own destiny. Overtures to the French were periodically made to keep the English off balance.

That the dependency of the English upon the Cherokee was as least as great as Cherokee dependence upon the Carolinians was plainly admitted at the end of the Cherokee uprising of 1750 when the governor of South Carolina reminded the legislative assembly that "it is absolutely necessary for us to be in friendship with the Cherokees in particular," for "they are reckoned to be about three thousand gunmen, the greatest nation we know of in America except the Choctaws. . . ."[32] Because the Choctaws had long been tied to the French in the trans-Mississippi area the Cherokees provided an indispensable buffer between the English and their French enemies. That the Crown was willing to commit some £6000 for presents to the Creeks and Cherokees in 1749 and 1750 was sterling testimony to the English regard for maintaining the alliance. South Carolina expenditures for Indian presents doubled between 1750 and 1758, reaching £14,837 in the latter year—further proof of the ability of the Indians to play on the Carolinians' dependence on them.[33]

The Cherokee policy of maintaining an apparent alliance with the English, while in actuality attempting to retain independence of action, was never better demonstrated than from 1753 to 1755. In late 1753 and in 1754, the governor of Virginia worked assiduously to gain Cherokee support for Washington's attempt to dislodge the French at the forks of the Ohio. Only with Indian support could the larger French forces be overcome. The Cherokee chiefs responded by promising the Virginians a thousand warriors, while at the same time pressing the government of Carolina for better trading prices and consulting with the French at Fort Toulouse on the Alabama River. To the governor of Virginia, they expressed interest in a revival of the old Virginia-Cherokee trade, which in the past had been employed by the Cherokees to remind the Carolinians that their trade was desirable but not irreplaceable. But in the end their promise to send warriors to join Washington on his foray into the wilderness disappeared like smoke.

In the following year, when the Virginians came again, seeking support

[32]David H. Corkran, *The Cherokee Frontier: Conflict and Survival, 1740–1762* (Norman: University of Oklahoma Press, 1962), p. 15.

[33]Sirmans, *Colonial South Carolina*, p. 275; Jacobs, ed., *Atkin Report and Plan*, pp. 27n, 31n.

for Braddock's campaign, the Cherokees skillfully used promises of hundreds of warriors, who were never to join Braddock's expedition, in order to gain a trade with Virginia on more favorable terms than the Carolinians offered. They were well aware that South Carolina and Virginia were close to blows in their struggle for control of the Cherokee trade and they used this intercolonial feud to their own advantage. When Braddock suffered his disastrous defeat, he had only eight Indians with his army.

In May 1755 the Carolinians met the Cherokee headmen deep in the backcountry for treaty making. When the Cherokees agreed to recognize the English king as their sovereign and to cede some of their lands to the Crown, the Carolinians believed they had accomplished a major breakthrough in luring the Indians out of their neutrality. In exchange they pledged to supply more trade goods at lower prices and to build a fort in Cherokee country that would offer protection against French and Creek enemies.

How badly the English could misapprehend Indian uses of diplomacy was clearly revealed in the next five years. Although the governor of South Carolina would celebrate the treaty of 1755 and boast about the "adding of near 10,000 people to his Majesty's subjects and above 40,000,000 acres to his territories," the Cherokees regarded themselves and their territory as subject to British authority only so long as it served mutually satisfactory goals.[34] About 250 Cherokees fought with the Virginia militia on the western frontier in 1757, but they agreed to serve not as allies but as mercenaries. When they were not paid according to agreement, they promptly plundered Virginia frontier settlements in order to collect by force what the white government failed to give them. The process was repeated in the next year, but this time the Virginia frontiersmen, for whom the Indians were presumably fighting, began ambushing Cherokees who were returning from battle and living off the land as they made their way home. Thirty Cherokees lost their lives at the hands of their allies in the summer and fall of 1758. Adding to the incentive of Indian-hating Virginians was the colony's £50 scalp bounty, meant to apply to enemy Indians such as the Shawnees. To avaricious Virginians scalps were scalps, whether Cherokee or Shawnee. Each earned its bearer the equivalent of a year's income as a frontier farmer.

Nothing more than a few incidents of this sort were required to fan into a roaring blaze the anti-English embers that had been kept alive in the Cherokee towns by the pro-French factions. Messengers went out to the Creeks and Chickasaws and by the winter of 1758–1759 talk of a pan-Indian uprising had spread across the southern frontier. English agents

34Quoted in Corkran, *Cherokee Frontier*, p. 61.

worked hard to convince the tribes that a blockade of French shipping in North America would make it impossible for the Indians to obtain guns, ammunition, and even normal trade goods from the French. It was the greatest weapon the English possessed.

Though the ability of the English to cut the French supply lines kept the Creeks out of the anti-English rebellion, the Cherokees had the deaths of several dozen of their tribesmen to account for. Border warfare broke out throughout the Carolina and Virginia backcountry and though a number of conciliatory Cherokee headmen made their way to Charleston for peace talks in September 1759, South Carolina's governor, William Henry Lyttelton, was by this time as eager for war as the angry Cherokees. With 1,700 men he mounted an expedition into Cherokee territory, perhaps the largest English force ever assembled in the South for an Indian war. The peace treaty which Lyttelton extracted from the Cherokees with this force blamed the Indians for all that had transpired. In effect, it was no peace treaty at all. The Cherokee chiefs signed it under duress but it served only to inflame them more.

By 1760 the war had erupted again at an even higher level of intensity and this time the Cherokees were far more united in opposition to the English. The new governor of South Carolina, William Bull, soon recognized that the united Cherokees were more than a match for the largest force of militiamen which he could put in the field. Bowing to circumstances, he agreed to a treaty which made concessions to the Cherokees on "terms that perhaps may not be thought suitable, according to the Rules of Honour, observed among Europeans," as the governor delicately put it.[35] The arrival of 1,300 of Sir Jeffrey Amherst's crack troops in April 1760 and their subsequent expedition against the Cherokees proved the difficulties of fighting Indians in their own territory. Bogging down in the hilly terrain, ambushed at every turn, the expedition, as one historian has concluded, "accomplished little, except possibly to boost Cherokee morale."[36] Badly mauled, the force returned to Charleston. Shortly thereafter the main English garrison in Cherokee country surrendered to a Cherokee siege. The next summer 1,800 British regulars, joined by 700 provincial militiamen, tried again and this time, by burning Cherokee villages and crops, they were more successful. With supplies from the French virtually cut off, the Cherokees submitted to a peace treaty that acknowledged English sovereignty and established the eastern boundary of the Cherokee territory.

Throughout the Rebellion of 1759–1761, the Cherokees made attempts to enlist the support of the Creeks. Two generations before, the refusal

[35]Quoted in Sirmans, *Colonial South Carolina*, p. 335.
[36]*Ibid.*, p. 336.

of the Cherokees to join the Creeks in the Yamasee War against the Carolinians had cost the Creeks their victory. Now the Creek decision to remain neutral cost the Cherokees decisively. Although a few Creeks killed
unscrupulous English traders in 1760, most of them recognized that the
French could not provide trade goods and ammunition and therefore
maintained a position of neutrality. Left to fight the English themselves,
the Cherokees struggled against food shortages, lack of ammunition, and
a smallpox epidemic. The only trade goods reaching them from the
French, ironically, were provided by New England ship captains, who
brought contraband supplies to the French forts on the Gulf of Mexico.
The desperate shortage of trade goods forced the Cherokees back to ancient customs—fashioning clothes from deer and bear skins and tipping
their arrows with bone points instead of trader's brass. But cut off from an
alternate supply of trade goods and unable to organize a pan-Indian offensive, they joined the French as losers in the Great War for Empire.

CREEKS

Whereas the Iroquois made common cause with the English once French
invincibility had been shattered and the Cherokees alternately allied with
and fought against the English during the Seven Years' War, the Creeks
remained steady to the policy of neutrality that had been the hallmark
of their diplomacy since the Yamasee War. Their major concerns were
trade and the maintenance of their political sovereignty. Throughout the
1750s and early 1760s the Creeks ranged from the Cherokee country to
the French trading posts at Fort Toulouse and Mobile, accepting presents
from both English and French and driving hard bargains for more favorable terms in the deerskin trade. Pro-French, pro-English, and neutralist
factions argued bitterly in the Creek towns. But by 1757, British naval
superiority had all but blockaded French shipping and this struck a near-
fatal blow at the Creek headmen who were advocating a pan-Indian anti-
English rebellion of Shawnees, Cherokees, Creeks, Chickasaws, and
Catawbas. The English solidified their hold on the Creeks in 1758 and
1759 by showering them with presents. Sensitive to the possibility that
the Cherokee insurgency might spread, Governor Henry Ellis of Georgia
spent the spring of 1760 trying to "set every Person of Influence upon
endeavouring to create a Rupture between those two Nations"—the
Creeks and Cherokees.[37]

Though they refused to join the Cherokees, the Creeks used the rebellion of their neighbors for their own benefit. When English trade goods

[37]Quoted in W. W. Abbot, *The Royal Governors of Georgia, 1754–1775* (Chapel
Hill: University of North Carolina Press, 1959), p. 80.

became scarce or when prices rose, they dropped the word to English traders that the arguments of the Cherokees and French, with whom they were in constant communication, had taken on a new attractiveness. But the fact of the matter was that the outbreak of the Cherokee rebellion had badly divided the Creeks. The pro-French faction continued to urge the Cherokees on to greater efforts against the English and even murdered eleven English settlers in an attempt to precipitate an English attack which would galvanize the Creek nation behind the Cherokees. The Carolina and Georgia governments failed to rise to the bait, however. The decision not to respond to the murder of the traders or even to demand that the Creeks put the murderers to death was dramatic evidence of the precarious position of the Southern colonists and their vital need to keep the Creeks neutral. Had the balance of power lay with the English, strenuous measures would have been taken to make the Creeks accountable for such killings.

In spite of Cherokee victories in 1760 and 1761, including the setback they administered to an expedition of 1,600 British and American soldiers, the Creek effort to check English expansionism was ultimately undermined by the inability of the French to supply an alternate flow of vital weapons and trade goods. At a grand meeting of the French, Cherokees, and Creeks at Fort Toulouse in March 1761 it became transparently clear that the French had no munitions, presents, or trade goods to back up their talk of expelling the English from the continent. English victories in the North had all but sealed the fate of the French on the continent. For the Creeks the years of internal division and external negotiating were over. For a half-century they had maintained their neutrality and kept open a profitable trade with both the French and English. But in the process they had become dependent on the European trade connection.

Anglo-American victories in the North, beginning in 1759 with the capture of Fort Niagara, continuing with Wolfe's dramatic victory at Quebec, and culminating in the following year with the fall of Montreal, all but ended almost two centuries of French presence in North America. Peace was not formally recognized until 1763 but hostilities ended two years before.

For the Indian nations which had demonstrated such independence of action and such impressive power during the Seven Years' War the Peace of Paris was a severe blow. Unlike the coastal tribes, which had watched their numbers and autonomy ebb through contact with European civilization, the interior tribes had grown stronger, more militarily awesome, and more technologically developed as a result of their political and economic connections with the English, French, and Spanish. Although they had become dependent on the European trade, they had been able to turn this dependency to their own advantage so long as more than one source of trade goods existed. They had mastered the European style of diplomatic intrigue, used it to serve their own self-interests, and proved their ability to evade or defeat numerically superior European forces.

But though they might play a controlling role on land, the Indian nations possessed not a shred of power to control the ocean separating Europe and North America or the trade goods that flowed across it. In the end it was this factor that undermined their strength. Control of the Atlantic by the British navy dealt a near-fatal blow to the playoff system, for the French in America without trade goods were hardly better than no Frenchmen at all. This inability to obtain French trade goods not only diminished their room for maneuver but rendered futile the nascent pan-Indian movements against the English which might have extended from Seneca country on the shores of the eastern Great Lakes to Yamasee territory in Florida and included the Miamis, Shawnees, Delawares, Cherokees, Catawbas, Creeks, Choctaws, and Chickasaws to name only the larger tribes. A mere fraction of these peoples had driven back the Anglo-American frontier to within one hundred miles of the coast in the early stages of the Seven Years' War. Had they been unified under French arms and supplies, the designs of the French imperialists to rule the continent might have materialized.

By the terms of the Peace of Paris, signed by England, France, and Spain in 1763, Canada and all of North America east of the Mississippi River was recognized as English territory. France ceded the territory west of the Mississippi to Spain. Spain ceded Florida to England. And from that year onward English sway in the eastern half of North America was unchallenged in the courts of Europe. No longer could the Creeks, Cherokees, or Iroquois employ the playoff system to gain advantages in trade since only one source of trade goods remained. Even hostilities between the colonies, which Indian groups had often exploited, were less visible, for the wartime effort had unified the thirteen English provinces to an unprecedented degree. Two centuries of European rivalry for possession and control of eastern North America had come to a dramatically swift end. To this reality Iroquois, Cherokees, Creeks, and other interior tribes and nations were now forced to adjust, even though most of them regarded English political and territorial claims as invalid until agreed upon or altered in bilateral negotiations.

chapter 11

The Mixing of Peoples

While Indians, Africans, and Europeans, each embracing a diversity of people, were working out their destinies in a complicated setting of tribal and imperial rivalry, economic growth, population change, and social and political transformation, they were also interacting with each other at the most intimate and personal levels. This sexual and social mixing of individuals of different genetic stocks, usually called miscegenation, is in itself of little interest unless one is concerned with pseudoscientific attempts to specify the relative size of various "racial" groups in a society, an exercise usually conducted with propagandistic and political purposes in mind. Miscegenation is, however, important in another way. By measuring the extent of it we can develop insights into the process of acculturation and assimilation—the mixing of cultural elements and the absorption of one culture into another. Miscegenation is usually an important element in both these processes.

Most thinking on the subject of miscegenation in North America starts with the arresting notion that Europeans on this continent simply did not intermix with Africans and Indians with anywhere near the same frequency as in colonial Latin American societies. Nor did Africans and Indians mix to the same degree. Latin America is known as the area of the world where the most extensive intermingling of the races in human history has taken place; and North America, where Europeans, Indians, and Africans also converged during roughly the same period of time, is noted for the general absence of any such genetic intermixture. The census figures of modern North and South America seem to confirm this belief. They show, for example, that only 20 percent of the Venezuelans are classified as white, that only 11 percent of Panamanians are white, that mulattoes in Brazil make up a much larger portion of the population than in the United States, and so forth. Although the criteria for defining membership in a particular racial group vary greatly from place to place and are never very exact, it is not necessary to be precise about the exact racial composition of any of the New World societies since the principal point is not in dispute—that widely practiced interracial sexual liaisons produced a dramatically larger proportion of mestizos (European-Indian), mulattoes (European-African), and mustees (African-Indian) in the population of the southern half of the New World than in the northern half.

Two explanations are commonly advanced to explain this. The first is that before the European rediscovery of the New World the Spanish and Portuguese had far greater experience in interacting with people of different cultures, particularly with darkskinned people, than did the English. Through centuries of war and trade with the Berbers, Moors, and other peoples of the Middle East and North Africa, Iberian culture had already absorbed new cultural and genetic elements and developed flexible attitudes about the mixing of peoples in sexual congress. The English, by contrast, had largely remained within their island fortress, sheltered from other cultures and therefore predisposed toward viewing interracial contacts with suspicion and even alarm.

A corollary to this argument is that, once in the New World, the permissive attitudes of the Catholic church toward non-Christian people, the Roman system of law, which preserved a place of dignity and semiautonomy for the slave, and the paternalistic attitudes of the authoritarian Iberian governments combined to make racial intermixture acceptable and therefore common in the areas of the world where Spain and Portugal were confronting Indians and Africans in large numbers. By contrast, it is argued that English Protestantism was unusually rigid in considering admittance of "savage" people to the covenant of the faith; English law had nothing to say on the subject of enslavement, leaving colonists free to elaborate the most rigid institutions to contain their bound laborers; and the English government was uninterested in exercising very much authority in its colonies, especially in the matter of the treatment of subordinate non-English groups. Given these differences in prior experience, in institutions and attitudes, and in governmental policy, it was therefore not surprising that the history of interracial mixing should be so different in the colonies of Spain and Portugal and the colonies of England.

Such arguments have lost much of their explanatory force in recent years as historians have looked more carefully at the social and demographic conditions underlying the history of cultural interaction in various parts of the New World. Although material and ideological factors are admitted by almost all historians to be interrelated, the differences in the degree and nature of interracial mixing in North and South America now seem to be fundamentally related to conditions encountered in the New World rather than attitudes developed in the Old World. The availability of white women; the ratio of Europeans, Africans, and Indians in a given area; the extent to which Indians could be pressed into forced labor systems; and the need to employ non-Europeans in positions of importance—all of these seem to have had a role in shaping the pattern of intercultural mixing. Thus it is no surprise to discover that in areas where European women were in short supply white men put aside whatever racial prejudices they might have brought to the New World and consorted with women of another race. Their alternatives were sexual abstinence, homosexuality, or bestiality. All three attracted some males; but the vast majority of men seem to have preferred heterosexual relations with women of a different cultural group. Nor should we be surprised to find that where Indians or Africans were relatively numerous, intermixture was far more common than where they were relatively scarce. In New England, where Indians were only sparsely settled and had been devastated by epidemics in the early years of European settlement, little red-white mixing occurred. In Mexico, where Spanish men were engulfed by the densely settled Indians, a great deal of mixing occurred throughout the colonial period.

Such common-sense explanations are overly simplistic, of course, and must be subjected to far more detailed study. Only in the area of black-white relations has enough research been undertaken to allow for firm generalizations. Indian-white and African-Indian relations remain largely unstudied. Since this is the work of the next generation of scholars only tentative suggestions can be offered in these areas.

Indian-European Contact

Because contact between Indians and Europeans preceded all other contacts and may have had some influence on what later occurred, it is best to begin with them. In New England, and later in the Mid-Atlantic colonies of New York, New Jersey, Pennsylvania, and Delaware, miscegenation between Europeans and Indians was extremely limited. Englishmen had emigrated to these parts of the emerging English empire with their families, or, if they were single men, found a sufficient number of single women to satisfy their needs for marriage partners. Parity between the sexes was established very quickly and continued throughout the colonial period, except following periods of war when women sometimes outnumbered men by a small margin. Reinforcing this demographic situation was a strong cultural factor. Emigration by family insured the rerooting of an entire cultural superstructure to which miscegenation was highly threatening, especially given the view, almost universal among whites, that their culture was far superior to that of red and black "savages."

The second demographic factor operating was the relatively small number of Indians in these areas and the relative inaccessibility of those who escaped epidemics or the periodic conflict which rapidly reduced the coastal Indian societies during the initial period of contact. Intercultural marriage was a rarity. A number of fur traders operating on the frontier took Indian wives and almost all of them had frequent sexual contact with Indian women. But the one notable case of intermarriage in the settled regions involved William Johnson, the northern superintendent of Indian affairs, who took a Mohawk wife. Later knighted for his military exploits, Johnson gained great influence with the Mohawk, who renamed him Warraghiyagey, meaning "man who undertakes great things." This high tribute was conferred in large part because Johnson had deviated so radically from the white norm in accepting Mohawk customs and learning their language, as few white men cared to do. Johnson was not born or raised in the colonies and few cared to follow the example of even a high imperial official when it came to matrimony so long as there were plenty of European women in the Northern colonies. It was said that Johnson's precedent-shattering marriage, noteworthy enough to attract the attention of the London newspapers, led to eighteen other red-white unions, but even so the number is insignificant.

Farther south in the Chesapeake colonies a different demographic pattern prevailed in the first few decades. With few exceptions, white women were unavailable in Virginia until about 1620. Yet white men do not seem to have had much recourse to Indian women. This could be explained either by the conscious decision of the Powhatan-affiliated tribes to prevent their women from mixing with the European intruders, who seemed hostile from the outset, or by an English aversion to Indian women strong enough to overcome heterosexual desires. Several early eighteenth-century Virginia commentators believed the latter to have been the case. They were advocating intermarriage with Indians even at this late date and advising that if such a "modern policy" had been followed from the outset, the costly hostilities of the early years might have been avoided. William Byrd, no stranger to the pleasures of the flesh with women of different skin colors, claimed the English were imbued with a "false delicacy" in the early years and thus could not bring themselves to sleep with Indian women. Byrd believed that the Chesapeake tribes had been offended by this rejection and could never "perswade themselves that the English were heartily their Friends, so long as they disdained to intermarry with them." Robert Beverley, author of *The History and Present State of Virginia,* took a similar view, regretting that intermarriage had never occurred and convinced that the Indians had been eager for it.[1]

The limited evidence bearing on this question does not support such views however. A large part of the predominantly male Virginia colony was composed of representatives of the English lower class, including many who had military experience in Ireland, the Spanish Netherlands, and other parts of the world. Squeamishness was not notable in their makeup and their later willingness to consort with African women suggests that the real cause of infrequent sexual contact with Indian women is to be found in Indian rather than European desires. The English did not establish themselves as conquerors in the early years, as had the Spanish and Portuguese, and therefore the Chesapeake tribes were under no constraints to yield up their women. Indian women were not denied to Virginians who stole away from oppressive conditions in their own community to live among Powhatan's people, and their numbers became large enough to bring about laws imposing severe penalties on such renegade behavior. But the one case of intermarriage within the white community involved vows taken between John Rolfe and Pocahontas. That the marriage was political, regardless of whatever love the two may have felt for each other, has already been pointed out. Some historians have claimed that the King's council, by deliberating whether Rolfe had not committed high treason in marrying an Indian princess, discouraged any further intermarriage. But the charge under consideration was high treason, for marrying the daughter of a quasi-enemy, and the fact is that Pocahontas and Rolfe were feted in London wherever they went, including the royal court. By the early eighteenth century the Board of Trade was pushing an official policy of intermarriage in the American colonies,

---

[1]William Byrd, *Histories of the Dividing Line Betwixt Virginia and North Carolina,* ed. William K. Boyd (Raleigh: North Carolina Historical Commission, 1929), p. 3; Robert Beverley, *History and Present State of Virginia,* ed. Louis B. Wright, (Chapel Hill: University of North Carolina Press, 1960), pp. 38–39.

a clear indication that moral scruples were not offended in England by thoughts of the commingling of red and white blood.

After the first few decades of English settlement on the Chesapeake, the imbalance of white males and females was redressed. Moreover, by the end of the second Indian war in 1644 the native population in the tidewater area was only a small fraction of the white population and by the conclusion of Bacon's Rebellion in 1675 only a few Indians remained within the areas of white settlement. That Governor Spotswood could claim in 1717 that the "inclinations of our people are not the same with those of [the French] Nation" regarding intermarriage, as evidenced by the fact that not one such marriage was known in Virginia at that time, cannot be taken as evidence that racial prejudice prohibited such partnerships.[2] Neither the need nor the opportunity for Indian-white marriages remained. That French "inclinations" in New France were different is not so much a reflection on variations in national character as on differential needs. And even along the St. Lawrence, where Frenchmen commonly took Indian wives and mistresses, it was admitted that European women were preferred. But Indian women remained far preferable to no women at all.

The only English area in which demographic characteristics even roughly paralleled those in the Spanish and Portuguese colonies was the Southeast—the Carolinas and Georgia. It was here in the early years that white women were relatively unavailable but Indian women could easily be found. The result was a considerable contact between Englishmen and Indian women. Conspicuously absent from the records are any indications of "squeamishness" when it came to intercultural sexual liaisons. Instead, contemporary accounts and records are filled with references to unembarrassed sexual relations between the two peoples. This was especially true of the fur traders who operated in the interior regions and would not give up the satisfactions of Indian "She-Bed-Fellows," as the early eighteenth-century commentator John Lawson called them. Women were specifically designated by the Indian tribes as "Trading Girls," according to Lawson, and were given special haircuts to denote that their role was to satisfy the traders while getting money "by their Natural Parts." Only these women were available to white men, however, for Indian males, wrote Lawson, "are desirous (if possible) to keep their Wives to themselves, as well as those in other Parts of the World."[3]

While traders consorted with Indian women in the interior, white Car-

---

[2] R. A. Brock, ed., *The Official Letters of Alexander Spotswood . . .* Virginia Historical Society *Collections*, N.S., 2: (Richmond: Virginia Historical Society, 1885), 227.

[3] Lawson, *Voyage to Carolina*, ed., Lefler, pp. 189–90.

olinians confronted Indian women sold into slavery in the coastal settlements. After the Yamasee War of 1715, in which slave raiding figured as an important cause, the enslavement of Indians in Carolina diminished. But during the first half-century of the colony's history, the large number of children of Indian mothers and white fathers in Charleston testified to the extensive miscegenation practiced there. White men outnumbered white women in South Carolina by more than 13 to 9 as late as 1708 and womanless men were not reluctant to avail themselves of Indian women. In Georgia no less a figure than Thomas Bosomworth, chaplain of Oglethorpe's utopian colony, found it respectable to marry a Creek woman in the early years of settlement and many others followed his example. Both John McDonald and Alexander Cameron, Deputy Indian Commissioners to the Cherokees in the late colonial period, married Cherokee women and the postrevolutionary Cherokee leaders, Sequoyah and George Lowrey, were both born of interracial marriages during this era.

Interracial mixing between Indians and Europeans, then, was limited more by demographic considerations than by prior attitudes. It is also clear in the miscegenation laws passed by all the colonies during the colonial period that attitudes differed toward black-skinned Africans and tawny-skinned Indians. Miscegenation laws were aimed almost exclusively at white-black mating. Only North Carolina and Virginia forbade marriage between Indians and whites (though Massachusetts debated such a law) and no colonies applied special penalties for red-white fornication as they often did for cases involving blacks and whites. In fact, many transplanted Europeans, applying their own standards of beauty, described Indian women as beautiful, whereas no such descriptions can be found of African women. Indian women, wrote Robert Beverley in 1705, were "generally Beautiful, possessing uncommon delicacy of Shape and Features, and wanting no Charm but that of a fair complexion."[4] Many other colonial commenators spoke in a similar vein.

The general lack of red-white sexual intermingling forecast the overall failure of the two cultures to assimilate. The amalgamation of Indians and whites never proceeded very far in eighteenth-century America because Indians were seldom eager to trade their culture for one which they found inferior and because the colonists found the Indians useful only as trappers of furs, consumers of European trade goods, and military allies. All these functions were best performed outside the white communities. This is in striking contrast to the Latin American colonies where the lack of white women and the subjugation of Indian laborers had brought the two peoples into close contact and thus created a large mestizo population. Even the most conservative estimates of the mestizo

---

[4] Beverley, *History and Present State of Virginia*, ed. Wright, p. 159.

population show that it had reached 25 percent of the population in early nineteenth-century Spanish America and many of these individuals rose to the position of artisan, foreman on the encomiendas, militiaman, and even collector of tithes and taxes. But in colonial America the half-Indian, half-white person, usually the product of a liaison between a white fur trader and an Indian women, remained in almost all cases within Indian society. A number of the male offspring became fur traders themselves or intermediaries between English and Indian society. Others, such as Joseph Brant of the Mohawks and Alexander McGillivray of the Creeks, became noted leaders of Indian resistance in the second half of the eighteenth century. Although historians have not yet systematically studied the American mestizo, who revealingly was called by the derogatory term "half-breed," there are some indications that these persons, whom white colonists recognized only as Indians, were the most alienated of all people from white society. One Virginian gave explicit expression to this in 1757 when he wrote that traders who consorted with Indian "squaws" left their offspring "like bulls or bears to be provided for at random by their mothers. . . . As might be expected," he pointed out, "some of these bastards have been the leading men or war captains that have done us so much mischief."[5]

The one case in which transculturation between Indians and Europeans did occur involved the Indianization of whites rather than the Europeanization of Indians. Throughout the colonial period, much to the horror of the guardians of white culture, colonists in eastern North America ran away to Indian settlements, or, when they were captured in war and had lived with a tribe for a few years, frequently showed great reluctance to return to white society. This "reversion to savagery," as those who insisted on the superiority of white culture regarded it, has attracted the attention of American novelists since the late eighteenth century. For white colonists, of course, the prospect of their own people preferring the Indian way of life to their own was a disturbing anomaly. "None can imagine what it is to be captivated, and enslaved to such atheistical, proud, wild, cruel, barbarous, brutish (in one word) diabolical creatures as these, the worst of the heathen," wrote a seventeenth-century Puritan.[6]

But in spite of such fantasy characterizations, colonists were obliged to live with the notion that many of their own kind found Indian society more fulfilling to their needs than Anglo-American culture. To make matters worse, virtually no Indians took the reverse route, choosing to

[5]James Hugo Johnston, *Race Relations in Virginia and Miscegenation in the South, 1776–1860* (Amherst: University of Massachusetts Press, 1970), p. 169.

[6]Quoted in Roy Harvey Pearce, "The 'Ruines of Mankind': The Indian and the Puritan Mind," *Journal of the History of Ideas*, 13 (1952): 205.

remain in white society after exposure to it. Hector St. Jean Crevecoeur, the famous Frenchmen who lived in America for more than a decade in the late colonial period, wrote in his celebrated *Letters from an American Farmer*:

> "By what power does it come to pass, that children who have been adopted when young among these people, can never be prevailed on to readopt European manners? Many an anxious parent I have seen after the last war [Seven Years War], who at the return of peace, went to the Indian villages where they knew their children had been carried in captivity; when to their inexpressible sorrow, they found them so perfectly Indianised, that many knew them no longer, and those whose more advanced ages permitted them to recollect their fathers and mothers, absolutely refused to follow them, and ran to their adopted parents for protection against the effusions of love their unhappy real parents lavished on them! Incredible as this may appear, I have heard it asserted in a thousand instances, among persons of credit. . . . There must be in their social bond," Crevecoeur speculated, "something singularly capitivating, and far superior to anything to be boasted of among us; for thousands of Europeans are Indians, and we have no examples of even one of those Aborigines having from choice become Europeans."[7]

Crevecoeur's testimony, an elaboration of a phenomenon earlier observed by Cadwallader Colden, governor of New York, and Benjamin Franklin, has been amply corroborated by historical research, leaving little doubt that this transculturation operated basically in only one direction and that it became extremely difficult to convince "white Indians" to return to their native culture once they had experienced Indian life. The reason for this provides a piercing insight into the differences between the two cultures. Even before the arrival of Europeans, Indian cultures had customarily adopted into their society as full-fledged members any persons captured in war. On some occasions a captive was even taken into a particular family to replace a lost child or other relative. This integration of newcomers into the kinship system and into the community at large, without judgmental comparisons of the superiority of the captor culture, made it easy for the captured "outsider" to make a rapid personal adjustment. A white child taken into Indian society was treated on equal terms and prepared for any role open to others of his or her age. That a number of whites and Negroes who had fled to Indian communities or had been captured by them became chiefs is the most dramatic evidence of the nearly complete receptiveness of Indian cultures to "outsiders."

White society contrasted sharply in this regard. Though a number of

[7] J. Hector St. John Crevecoeur, *Letters from an American Farmer* (New York: E. P. Dutton & Co., Inc., 1957), pp. 208–09.

Indian children were adopted into white families, the general pattern was to socially isolate the newcomer. "It was not that the Indian could not be raised 'up' to the level of civilization," writes one student of the subject, "but rather, the lack of an equivalent desire on the part of whites to welcome and assimilate the Indian, and the absence of any established cultural means that would mediate the transition from one culture to the other in a manner that was psychologically sound."[8] Even Christianized Indians trained in white schools, such as the Mohegan Samson Occum, were expected to return to Indian society rather than occupy a place of dignity in white culture. Indians were always regarded as aliens and were rarely allowed to live within white society except on its periphery. The colonists, operating from their small communities and surrounded by a culture they chose to regard as not only inferior but as "barbaric" and "savage," "erected a defensive wall of heightened consciousness of superiority" in order to keep out those who seemed so threatening.[9] This inability to develop the mentality or social mechanisms for incorporating Indians into their midst betrayed a sense of personal and cultural insecurity among a people who never tired of proclaiming the superiority of their way of life.

White-Black Intermixture

The extent of white-black intermixture in colonial America is a more complicated phenomenon because whites and blacks were always in close proximity, both in areas where white women were plentiful and in areas where they were scarce. This proximity led to widespread sexual contact, although it rarely involved intermarriage. At first glance, one might imagine that the rarity of racial intermarriage stemmed from a deep-seated white aversion to blackness itself, but if this was the case it would be impossible to explain what almost every observer of eighteenth-century society claimed to see—that "the country swarms with mulatto bastards," in the words of one Virginian.[10] Though such comments do nothing to define miscegenation with statistical precision, eighteenth-century censuses help to clarify the point. In Maryland in 1755 a special census showed that 8 percent of the Negroes in the colony were mulatto. A generation later in Rhode Island the census of 1783 revealed that 16.5 percent of the colony's 2,806 Negroes were of mixed blood. A register of slaves for

[8]A. Irving Hallowell, "American Indians, White and Black: The Phenomenon of Transculturation," *Current Anthropology*, 4 (1963): 527.
[9]*Ibid.*, p. 528.
[10]Quoted in Johnston, *Race Relations in Virginia*, p. 170.

Chester County, Pennsylvania, in 1780 listed 20 percent of the Negroes as mulattoes.[11] In all three areas white women were almost as numerous as white men, indicating that even when white women were available, white men frequently had sexual relations with black women.

That these contacts were not even more extensive can be explained primarily by the fact that in the period when white women were in short supply, black women were also unavailable. Slaves did not begin to enter the English colonies in significant numbers until the end of the seventeenth century and by that time the number of white women in all but the infant colony of South Carolina nearly equalled the number of white men. In the Southern plantations in 1720, the slave population was about 50,000; not more than about 10,000 of these could have been black women. At the same time some 70,000 adult white colonists inhabited the Southern colonies of whom almost half were women. This is in stark contrast to the situation in Portuguese Brazil, Spanish Peru, or even the English islands in the West Indies. In all of these zones of contact European women were relatively unavailable for much longer periods of time.

It is the example of the English Caribbean colonies that provides the clinching evidence for the case against prior attitudes determining the nature and degree of racial intermixture. With white women not present in roughly equal numbers with white men until the second century of settlement, black women were unhesitantly exploited to fill the gap. Even married white plantation owners "keep a Mulatto or Black Girl in the house or at lodgings for certain purposes," reported one traveler, and a famous eighteenth-century historian of the English sugar islands colorfully pronounced that "He who should presume to shew any displeasure against such a thing as simple fornication, would for his pains be accounted a simple blockhead; since not one in twenty can be persuaded, that there is either sin; or shame in cohabiting with his slave."[12]

In the mainland colonies, however, interracial sex brought private pleasure but public condemnation. But this was mainly an eighteenth- rather than a seventeenth-century development. Historians have worked assiduously to show that Africans in North America were being separated from whites shortly after their arrival in the second decade of the seventeenth century. But not until 1662, when Virginia passed a law imposing a fine for fornication between white and black partners that was twice the usual amount, did an unambiguous law appear on the books that ex-

[11]Edward B. Reuter, *The Mulatto in the United States* (rpr. New York: Negro Universities Press, 1969), pp. 112–14; Evarts B. Greene and Virginia D. Harrington, *American Population before the Federal Census of 1790* (New York: Columbia University Press, 1932), pp. 69–70.

[12]Jordan, *White Over Black: American Attitudes Toward the Negro, 1550–1812* (Chapel Hill: University of North Carolina Press, 1968), p. 140.

pressed public distaste for racial intermixture. Interracial marriage was banned in Virginia in 1691, in Massachusetts in 1705, in Maryland in 1715, and thereafter in Delaware, Pennsylvania, North and South Carolina, and Georgia.

The key change in the eighteenth century was not a marked increase or decrease in miscegenation, reflecting changes in private urges, but a shifting of public attitudes toward it. "By the turn of the century," writes Winthrop Jordan, "it was clear in many continental colonies that the English settlers felt genuine revulsion for interracial sexual union, at least in principle."[13] The grand jury in Charleston, South Carolina, for example, inveighed against "The Too Common Practice of Criminal Conversation with Negro and other Slave Wenches in this Province" in 1743.[14] Similar comments can be found in all of the colonies. But with the black population growing rapidly and slavery becoming a basic institution in colonial society, lawmakers were discovering that while they could not manage biology they could at least keep the legitimate offspring of the dominant group purebred by laws prohibiting interracial marriage.

In a society where slavery was touching the lives of a great proportion of the inhabitants, it was becoming necessary to contain the black population in a tight web of authority and to reassert again and again the dominance of whites. One way of accomplishing this was to emphasize the heathen or "savage" condition of the slave, which justified slavery on the one hand and made sexual contact publicly impermissible on the other. In a variety of public statements and in laws, the offspring of white-black copulation were being described as "spurious" or "mongrel." That the mulatto was given no higher standing than the pureblood black, and that he was in law regarded as fully black, not only contrasted starkly with the situation of the mulatto in almost every other part of the New World but was profoundly revelatory of the frame of mind that was overtaking eighteenth-century Americans. Black women were not needed by white males in a demographic sense. But sexual relations with them went on and on. Desire could not be legislated out of the white psyche and if the laws and public pronouncements did not correspond with private urges, there was little harm done so long as the domination of whites was preserved by disowning children of mixed racial inheritance.

As the eighteenth century wore on, racial attitudes towards Indians and Afro-Americans began to diverge sharply. This divergence was closely tied to striking differences in the nature and degree of sexual contact that characterized red-white and black-white relationships. White attitudes toward the black man cannot be dissociated from the fact that sexual

[13]*Ibid.*, p. 139.
[14]Quoted in *ibid.*, p. 140.

relations, especially between white men and black women, were frequent and usually coercive throughout the eighteenth century. White men might ban interracial marriage as a way of stating with legal finality that the Negro, even when free, was not the equal of the white man. But white power was also served by sexually exploiting black women outside of marriage—a way of acting out the concept of white domination. Racial intermingling, so long as it involved free white men and slave black women, was a way of intimately and brutally proclaiming the superior rights and strength of white society.

Contact of this character had no parallel in the case of the Indian woman. When she was accessible, for example, to fur traders, she was not in the hapless position of a slave woman, nearly defenseless to resist the advances of a master with power of life and death over her. If an Indian woman chose to submit to a white man, it was usually on mutually agreeable terms. Furthermore, it was widely known that Indian men rarely molested female prisoners. In these differences we can find the source and meaning of a fear which has preoccupied white America for three hundred years—the fear of the black male lusting after the white woman. This vision of the "black rapist," so enduring in contemporary attitudes and literature, runs through the accounts of slave uprisings which occurred in the eighteenth and nineteenth centuries. In large part this fear of black men, who are seen rising not in quest of their freedom but in pursuit of white women, seems to stem from feelings of guilt originating in the sexual exploitation of black women and an associated fear of the black avenger, presumably filled with anger and poised to retaliate against those who first enslaved him and then plundered his women. This element of sexual fear is only rarely expressed in the literature concerning the Indian. Since little guilt could have been aroused by the occasional and noncoercive contacts with Indian women, white men, when they encountered hostile Indian males, rarely pictured them as sexual avengers. In the eighteenth century the Indian was almost never caricatured as the frenzied rapist, lurking in the bush or stalking white women. Indeed, the Indian was sometimes viewed as a peculiarly asexual creature; this in turn created a confused image in the white mind of a hostile, and yet sexually passive, "savage." His hostility was not doubted; but the hostile Indian, it was commonly regarded, was a man with knife in hand, bent on obtaining the scalp of the white encroacher. It was imagined, however, that hostile black men had focused on a different part of the anatomy in their quest for revenge.

The most striking fact about miscegenation in pre-Revolutionary America is that it did not result in widespread acculturation or assimilation, at least in comparison to other New World societies. In the Spanish and Portuguese colonies Indian women had been seized as a part of the general enslavement of the indigenous populations and thereafter Spanish men lived surrounded by them. Through concubinage and intermarriage these women were incorporated into Spanish and Portuguese life and the mestizo offspring of such matches were recognized by their Spanish fathers. Mestizos, in fact, were to play a large role in later stages of Spanish colonization and conquest. Though Spaniards and Portuguese men would quickly reject their Indian women when Iberian women became available and, according to a recent study, "preferred to marry a white prostitute rather than a native woman," there is little doubt that the extent of intermixture was far greater than in North America and led to the assimilation of a sizable part of the Indian population.

The case of the African was somewhat similar. Slaves arrived earlier in the Spanish and Portuguese colonization process than in English North America; they came in larger numbers proportionate to their European masters; and their services as artisans and supervisors of Indian slaves gave many of them a status far above that of the common field laborer. As the Conquest period ended, the Iberian colonies evolved their own form of racism, with individuals classified according to skin color—a "pigmentocratic system" as it has been called.[15] But because all the caste groups in the racial hierarchy were regarded as natural parts of a multiracial society, the prohibitions against interracial contact and racial intermarriage did not take root. As the degrees of intermixture between the three cultural groups became more and more elaborate, passage from one group to another became relatively easy until finally the system of trying to distinguish between *mestizo, castizo, mulatto, morisco, albino, torna atras, lobo, zambaigo, cambujo, albarazado, barcono, chamiso,* and so forth broke down.

In the North American colonies, however, assimilation was rejected by Englishmen, who had strong objections not to sexual relations with black-skinned women but to conferring status on blacks by accepting such intermingling as legitimate or by admitting its product to white society. Though skin color came to assume importance through generations of association with slavery, white colonists developed few qualms about intimate contact with black women. But raising the social status of those who labored at the bottom of society and who were defined as abysmally inferior was a matter of serious concern. It was resolved by insuring that that mulatto would not occupy a position midway between white and black. Any black blood classified a person as black; and to be black was almost always to be a slave. The "mulatto escape hatch" that Carl Degler has described in Latin American society did not exist in British North

---

[15]Magnus Mörner, *Race Mixture in the History of Latin America* (Boston: Little, Brown and Company, 1967), pp. 54–60.

America, for there was relatively little need to call upon Negroes or mulattoes for important, status-conferring services and the extremely well-rooted institution of the white family, an outgrowth of a family pattern of settlement and a generous supply of white women, gave special reasons for excluding the living evidence of a sexual congress that threatened the purity of white culture.

In the American colonies, then, the need was for plantation labor and the urge was for occasional sex partners with whom one could act out all one's sexual fantasies, since black women were defined as lascivious by nature. By prohibiting racial intermarriage, winking at interracial sex, and defining all mixed offspring as black, white society found the ideal answer to its labor needs, its extracurricular and inadmissible sexual desires, its compulsion to maintain its culture purebred, and the problem of maintaining, at least in theory, absolute social control.

That this system of sexual politics was linked not so much to the national prejudices of Englishmen as to the historical circumstances of English settlement in North America becomes clearer by looking at the status of the mulatto in English Jamaica. By the mid-eighteenth century more than 90 percent of the Jamaica population was black and white men greatly outnumbered white women. Such distorted demographic features called for a system in which black women would be available without scruple to white men and where mulatto offspring would rise to places of importance in the island society. This is precisely what happened. Miscegenation occurred on a massive scale and by 1733 the practice of conferring privileges and property on mulattoes was written into law. The Jamaican example, writes Degler, "strongly suggests that under certain circumstances even the quite different cultural attitudes of Englishmen could be changed, and in a direction remarkably like that taken by the Portuguese in Brazil."[16]

African-Indian Contact

The convergence of African and Indian cultures is the least studied and least understood chapter in the history of race relations in early America. Naturally it is useless to look for this kind of acculturation in places where Indians and Africans did not meet in substantial numbers. Thus in New England, where the coastal tribes had been killed off before more than a trickle of Africans had arrived, little cross-fertilization was possible. It is notable, however, that in the few places such as Cape Cod

[16]Carl N. Degler, *Neither Black Nor White: Slavery and Race Relations in Brazil and the United States* (New York: The Macmillan Company, 1971), p. 240.

where Indians did survive, their mixture with a small number of free Negroes was pronounced by the late eighteenth century. This also occurred in a number of New England towns, especially along the coast, where Indian slaves from South Carolina had been imported in substantial numbers in the early eighteenth century. A census in South Kingston, Rhode Island, in 1730 showed 333 Negro slaves and 223 Indians slaves; the resulting intermixture of blood was not to be wondered at. A report in Massachusetts in 1795 stated that the blacks of Massachusetts "have generally . . . left the country and resorted to the maritime towns. Some are incorporated, and their breed is mixed with the Indians of Cape-Cod and Martha's Vineyard."[17] In New York, which contained the largest slave population north of the Chesapeake, intermixture of slaves and Indians, though unquantifiable, seems to have been far from unusual. Negro and Indian slaves had formed a blood bond in 1712 when they joined hands in an insurrection in New York City. Thereafter, provincial officials knew that the best places to look for escaped slaves were among the small local tribes that remained on Long Island and in the Hudson River Valley. It was in the cities of the North, however, that black slaves were concentrated and these were precisely the places where Indians in the second half of the eighteenth century were only occasionally to be found.

In the Chesapeake colonies, the possibility of African-Indian amalgamation was also reduced by the sheer force of circumstances. When Indians were relatively numerous in the tidewater region of Maryland and Virginia, slaves were present only in small numbers. In 1670, less than two thousand slaves inhabited the Chesapeake region and by the end of Bacon's Rebellion in 1676 the Indian population in the regions settled by whites was insignificant. Nonetheless, a considerable number of runaway slaves were given refuge among several of the coastal tribes, and their descendants, mixed with whites as well, exist today in isolated tri-ethnic communities in Delaware, Maryland, Virginia, and North Carolina.

Only in South Carolina and Georgia did Indians and Africans in substantial numbers find themselves confronting Europeans simultaneously. Here was the one area in English America where the situation that prevailed in most of the areas of Portuguese and Spanish colonization was duplicated. Historians have not examined this Afro-Indian acculturative process in any detail and most of those who have inquired into it have accepted the reports of eighteenth-century publicists who claimed that "a natural antipathy subsisted between Indians and negroes, and prevented the two from uniting and conspiring the destruction of the colony"

[17]Quoted in Kenneth W. Porter, "Relations between Negroes and Indians within the Present Limits of the United States," *Journal of Negro History*, 17 (1932): 311.

or stated baldly, for example, that "we have read nowhere of any alliance, intercourse or sympathy between the two races."[18]

More careful consideration will reveal that these allegations were attempts to hide the gnawing fear that Indians and slaves would combine forces and drive their white exploiters back into the sea. Such fears were well grounded, for during the pre-Revolutionary period the Indians of the Southeast remained numerous in the white areas of settlement and, combined with the black slaves, greatly outnumbered the white population. White South Carolinians, for example, were outnumbered by their black and Indian slaves and by free Indians surrounding them by ratios of three and four to one throughout most of the early period of colonization. Even by the mid-eighteenth century, there were only about 25,000 whites in the colony along with some 40,000 black slaves and perhaps 60,000 Indians gathered in the Creek, Cherokee, Choctaw, Chickasaw, and subsidiary tribes. Twenty years later, on the eve of the Revolution, the white population had increased to some 50,000 but the slave population had increased even faster—to about 75,000. South Carolinians lived surrounded by those who, if they could find a means for concerted action, might overwhelm them at any moment. Indian uprisings that punctuated the colonial period and a succession of slave uprisings and insurrectionary plots that were nipped in the bud kept South Carolinians sickeningly aware that only through the greatest vigilance and through policies designed to keep their enemies divided could they hope to remain in control of the situation.

That the white Carolinians were able to retain a precarious hold on the situation is a testimony to their ability to play one Indian tribe against another and to their partial success in keeping Indians and Negro slaves divided. The policy, as one Carolinian put it, was "to make Indians & Negro's a checque upon each other least by their Vastly Superior Numbers we should be crushed by one or the other."[19] Various methods were devised to accomplish this. Laws were passed prohibiting Afro-Americans, whether slave or free, from traveling in Indian country as traders or traders' helpers. Indian tribes were persistently asked to return fugitive slaves, and treaties signed with Creeks, Cherokees, and other tribes almost always included a clause stipulating that escaped slaves must be turned over to the Carolina government. Bounties were offered to Indians for the capture and return of escaped slaves. Patrols were used in frontier areas to prevent slaves from reaching Indian country. And suspicion of blacks

[18]Quoted in Chapman J. Milling, *Red Carolinians* (Chapel Hill: University of North Carolina Press, 1940), p. 63.

[19]Quoted in William S. Willis, Jr., "Divide and Rule: Red, White, and Black in the Southeast," *Journal of Negro History*, 48 (1963): 165.

among the Indians was fostered as a way of keeping mutual aid between them to a minimum. "It has been allways the policy of this government," wrote Governor Lyttelton in 1738, "to create an aversion in them [Indians] to Negroes."[20]

A double purpose was served by incorporating black slaves into the South Carolina militia during Indian wars. Without them, the Carolinians would have been hard pressed to defeat their Tuscarora, Yamasee, or Cherokee enemies; secondly, the use of black soldiers helped to remind the Indians that Africans were not their friends. Half the Carolinian force which Governor Craven led against the Yamasee in 1715 was black and another black company marched with Captain Pight in the same campaign. When these forces proved incapable of defeating the Yamasees the Assembly called for a "standing army" of 1200 men, including "400 negroes or other slaves."[21] This was merely an implementation of the policy begun in 1708 to compose the militia of equal numbers of blacks and whites. In the 1740 expedition against St. Augustine seventy-three slaves were included. By 1747 the militia law was changed to allow for no more than one-third black soldiers, a sign of a growing fear of black insurgency, but in the campaigns against the Cherokee in 1760 a small number of black Carolinians again fought against Indian enemies of the white government. How precariously the Carolinians were suspended between red revolt and black insurrection was indicated in the Cherokee War. More blacks were needed to fight against the Indian enemy, but in an era of large slave importations the anxiety concerning black rebellion was also great. Thus a motion to equip 500 slaves "to serve against the savages" failed by a single vote in the Carolina assembly.

Just as slaves were used to quash Indian uprisings, Indians were employed to put down black rebellions. In the most spectacular black insurrection in South Carolina, the Stono revolt of 1739, "settlement" Indians were called in to pursue the slaves who had eluded white militiamen and were on their way to Spanish Florida. The South Carolina assembly requisitioned clothes, guns, and ammunition for each Indian and promised £50 for each slave brought back alive or £25 for each slave returned dead. More than £2,000 was finally paid for the services of the Indians. What the white militia was unable to do, Indians were employed to accomplish. Other attempts were made at warding off black rebellions by relocating Indian tribes in areas where large numbers of slaves were developing the rice and indigo plantations that became the foundation of the South Carolina economy in the eighteenth century. This policy orig-

20*Ibid.*

21David D. Wallace, *South Carolina: A Short History, 1520–1948* (Chapel Hill: University of North Carolina Press, 1951), p. 88.

inated in the early eighteenth century and was pursued with special vigor in the 1730s when the buildup of the slave population kept Carolina vibrating with fears of black rebellion. In 1737 Cherokee warriors were requested "to come down to the settlements to be an awe to the negroes,"[22] and though there is no record of whether or not they responded, the request reflects the white policy of pitting Indians against black slaves.

In spite of these strenuous efforts at promoting hatred between Indians and Africans, a surprising number of slaves were harbored within the Indian communities throughout the colonial period. It is impossible to measure this phenomenon with statistical precision but the persistent inclusion in Indian treaties of a clause providing for the return of escaped slaves demonstrates that the bounties offered Indians for slave catching often evoked little response. The Tuscarora tribe, for example, gave refuge to a large number of slaves in the period before the outbreak of war in 1711. When war came, these Africans fought with the Tuscaroras and one of them, named Harry, was said to have designed the Tuscarora fortress on a tributary of the Neuse River. Four years later, during the Yamasee uprising, fugitive slaves were also active in the raids on white settlements. Even after the Yamasee had given up their struggle, they refused to return their black allies which, according to one Carolina official, "has encouraged a great many more [slaves] lately to run away to that Place."[23]

Because the Yamasees were located along the coast between the English settlements and the Spanish outposts in Florida, slaves had additional reason to flee in this direction. As early as 1699 the Spanish issued a royal decree promising protection to all fugitive English slaves and this offer was repeated periodically during the first half of the eighteenth century. Even after the Yamasee War ended, the Indians not only encouraged Carolina slaves to join them but engaged in slave-stealing raids on outlying plantations. In 1738, twenty-three slaves escaped from Port Royal and made their way to St. Augustine. They soon joined an enclave of free Negroes where thirty-eight escaped slave men, many with families, were already settled. In a sense this was simply the advance guard of the fifty to a hundred slaves who rose at Stono in 1739 in a mass attempt to kill whites and flee to Spanish Florida. When Governor Oglethorpe of Georgia launched his attack on St. Augustine in 1740 as a part of the Anglo-Spanish war that had broken out, he was met with the combined resistance of Spanish, Indians, and ex-Carolina slaves, who had no difficulty repulsing the expedition in which the Carolinians invested more

22Willis, "Divide and Rule," p. 175.
23Quoted in Milling, *Red Carolinians*, p. 153.

than £7,000. Two years later the Spaniards retaliated with an attack on Georgia; among the invasionary forces was a regiment whose Negro commanders "were clothed in lace, bore the same rank as the white officers, and with equal freedom and familiarity walked and conversed with their comrades and chief."[24] An eighteenth-century historian of South Carolina revealed how precarious the hold of white slave masters was on their slaves when he conjectured that if the Spanish expedition had attacked South Carolina rather than Georgia the English would have been lost, for in South Carolina there were "such numbers of negroes, they would soon have acquired such a force, as must have rendered all opposition fruitless and ineffectual."[25]

Slaves in the South fled not only to Spanish Florida and the Yamasee. As early as 1725 a prominent South Carolina slave holder reported with concern that the slaves had become well acquainted with the hill country of the Cherokees and were becoming fluent not only in English but in the Cherokee language. The Creeks also harbored runaway slaves in their towns. In the same year that concern for slave proficiency in the Cherokee language was expressed a Spanish delegation arrived at Coweta, the principal town of the Lower Creeks, with an ex-Carolina slave who served as interpreter between the Creeks and Spanish. Still another ex-slave was active as an interpreter between the French and the Creeks during this period, testifying to the linguistic ability of some of the escaped slaves and their ability to assimilate into the frontier cultures of the other European nations as well as into Creek, Cherokee, or Yamasee societies. Runaway slaves, concludes one student of red-black contacts in the Southeast, "operated to an unknown extent, but evidently with considerable effectiveness, as French and Spanish agents among Indian tribes bordering on the English settlements."[26] The threat of losing slaves to the Creeks was great enough in 1722 for the governor of South Carolina to issue a proclamation prohibiting Creeks from entering the white settlements of the colony, since their visits, purportedly for the purpose of trade, were encouraging large numbers of slaves to follow them back into the interior. As late as the 1760s the Carolinians were pressing the Creeks hard for the return of runaway slaves, and although blacks were occasionally handed over, hundreds remained in the Indian territory, blending their cultural attributes with those of the Creeks, Cherokees, and others.

By fashioning the harshest slave code of any of the colonies, by paying dearly for Indian support at critical moments, and by militarizing their

---

[24]Kenneth W. Porter, "Negroes on the Southern Frontier, 1670–1763," *Journal of Negro History*, 33 (1948): 68.

[25]*Ibid.*

[26]*Ibid.*, p. 77.

society, white Carolinians were able to restrict the flow of black slaves into the backcountry. The Cherokee hill country never became the equivalent of the Maroon mountain hideaways in Jamaica or the Brazilian *quilombos* as a refuge for runaway slaves as many Carolinians feared. But neither was the policy of fostering hatred between the two groups entirely successful. Throughout the eighteenth century slaves ran away in substantial numbers and joined Indian settlements. On occasion, when the price was high enough or the need to propitiate the Carolinians great enough, some of these would be returned to their white masters. But in most cases they seemed to have disappeared into Indian society where they took Indian wives, produced children of mixed blood, and contributed to Afro-Indian acculturation in the same fashion as those slaves who lived with settlement Indians in the coastal region. So common was Afro-Indian contact in the Southern colonies that the term *mustee* was added to the Southern vocabulary in order to categorize the offspring of African and Indian parents.

In spite of the evidence of considerable contact between Indians and Africans, it would be historically inaccurate and politically simplistic to assume that their relations can be explained by a natural affinity of oppressed peoples to unite against their oppressors. At no time in the colonial period did Creeks, Cherokees, and other Southern tribes work in a concerted way to unite with slaves. The problems of communications, language, and cultural differences would have made this difficult enough; but more importantly, Indian groups, especially after the Yamasee War of 1715, were far more intent on using white society for their own ends than eliminating it altogther. Thus, in their steadfast adherence to self-interest they acted variously towards Africans. Sometimes they held them as slaves; sometimes they gave them refuge and adopted them into their villages; sometimes, when white pressure became intense, they returned enough of them to satisfy white demands; and sometimes they hunted them down for pay. Only when an Indian tribe had a firm trading connection outside the English orbit, such as the Apalachees of Spanish Florida, were the slaves of English colonists welcomed without qualification.

In the final analysis the mixture of peoples in eighteenth-century America was the combined product of demographic ratios and the historical circumstances of English settlement. By 1770 there were some 2.3 million persons living east of the Allegheny Mountains but of these, 1.7 million were white, .5 million were black, and only .1 million or less were red. Such a preponderance of whites stood in stark contrast to almost every other part of the New World where Europeans had settled and, all other factors aside, would have guaranteed a fairly low level of miscegenation. Where people of different colors did live in close proximity, interracial

contact occurred to a considerable extent. That interracial liaisons were
not socially legitimized, as in other European colonies, reflected not only
a difference in settlement patterns but the special concern for the preservation of "civilized society" in English North America, centering around
the family. Whatever prior attitudes may have been among the Portuguese in Brazil, the French in Canada, or the English in the West Indies,
these colonists represented a small minority of the population in their New
World environments and, short of defeating their own purposes, could
hardly have adopted the kind of strict ethnocentric social attitudes and
laws that the English legislated in their North American colonies, where
they stood forth as such an overwhelming part of the total population.

To be sure, what is most surprising is the degree of crossing of color
lines that occurred within a society where the dominant group was making such strenuous claims for keeping its bloodstream pure. The gap between public pronouncements, as expressed in laws prohibiting miscegenation, and actual social practice, as visible in the large mixed blood
population, can only be explained in terms of the white desire to maintain rigid social control while at the same time indulging in sexual grati-
fication, which partners with different skin color heightened rather than
threatened.

chapter 12

Red, White, and Black
on the Eve of Revolution

"It is just and reasonable, and essential to our Interest, and the Security of our Colonies," stated the proclamation of George III in 1763, "that the several Nations or tribes of Indians with whom We are connected, and who live under our Protection, should not be molested or disturbed in the Possession of such Parts of our Dominions and Territories as, not having been ceded to or purchased by Us, are reserved to them, or any of them, as their Hunting Grounds."[1] Thus at the conclusion of seven years of international war the English government attempted to coordinate a continental Indian policy in North America where for a century and a half each colony had been left to conduct its own Indian affairs. Stung by the fact that most of the North American tribes had given their allegiance to the French in the Seven Years' War, the English government attempted to launch a new policy which would separate red men and

[1]Quoted in Francis Paul Prucha, *American Indian Policy in the Formative Years; The Indian Trade and Intercourse Acts, 1790–1834* (Lincoln: University of Nebraska Press, 1970 rpr.), p. 5.

white men and keep them separate. No more resounding declaration of the failure of assimilation, for which many in the past had spoken but few had done anything to foster, could have been made.

Red-White Relations After 1763

By the terms of the Proclamation of 1763, a line was to be drawn, roughly following the crestline of the Appalachian Mountains, from Maine to Georgia. The various colonial governors were charged with forbidding "for the present and until our further Pleasure be known" any surveys or land grants beyond the Appalachian watershed. "All the Lands and Territories lying to the Westward of the Sources of the Rivers which fall into the Sea from the West and North West" were specifically reserved for Indian nations. All white settlers already beyond the Appalachian divide were to withdraw east of the line.

The Proclamation of 1763 is one of the most poignant documents in American history. Historians who are fond of the "frontier thesis" of Frederick Jackson Turner have argued that this attempt to dam up the energy of restless westward-looking Americans alienated the colonists and provided a major impetus for throwing off the restraining yoke of the mother country. Less idealistic historians have agreed that the proclamation was a major irritant leading to Revolution but have pointed out that those most irritated by it were the large land speculators of the Eastern seaboard, who boiled at seeing the greatest potential source of profit in North America put beyond their grasp at the very moment that the French "menace" had been cleared from the continent. But what has rarely been noted is that for several years before the colonial bureaucrats in London drew the 1763 boundary the Indian tribes of the interior, from the Senecas, Ottawas, Illinois, Miamis, and Sioux of the North to the Cherokees, Creeks, and Choctaws of the South, had themselves been attempting to fix a territorial line that would limit white expansion. Their attempts were inspired by their certainty that, contrary to the language of the Proclamation of 1763, they did not live under English "protection" but in fact could protect their own interests and insure their survival only by throwing off English "protection" and fighting to preserve their land.

Though the Indian tribes of the interior had no way of counting the population increase in the Thirteen Colonies, they were keenly aware that settlers in unprecedented numbers were moving into their tribal hunting grounds almost on the heels of the Anglo-American armies that had been pushing the French out of the Ohio Valley beginning in 1759. The population rise between 1750 and 1765, in fact, had equalled that which occurred during the entire first half of the eighteenth century and more than half of the increase was concentrated in the colonies of New

York, Pennsylvania, and Virginia. It was through the western parts of
these colonies that land-hungry speculators and immigrants began pouring as soon as the French were expelled. Both before and after the Proclamation Line of 1763 had been set, land poachers were busily staking
out claims to lands for which the English, by the terms of their own
treaties with Indian tribes, had no claim. Creek lands, for example, were
guaranteed by a treaty signed in 1733 and the limits of white settlement
in Cherokee territory had been set at the end of the Cherokee War in
1761 in a treaty with the government of Virginia. But neither of these
treaties had any effect on white land speculators or settlers who swarmed
into Indian territory, secure in the knowledge that their provincial governments had neither the desire nor the power to do much about it.

The Indian response, even without the possibility of French aid, was
to meet force with force. The entire Southern frontier was marked with
bloody clashes in the early 1760s, as Indians and settlers fought over Indian lands which the provincial governments had guaranteed to the
tribes. Attempts were made to form another pan-Indian defensive league,
even at the risk that the English would cut off the supply of trade goods,
while the English did their best at a series of conferences to wheedle land
cessions from the Creeks and Cherokees and to fan enmity between the
major tribes. It was obvious from the determination of the Southern
tribes to resist English encroachments that the defeat of the Cherokees in
1761 "had not dampened the martial ardor of the southern Indians."[2]
Even with the French removed from the continent, power was still
roughly in balance. This was vividly symbolized in 1763 by the refusal of
the Creeks to surrender their tribesmen who had murdered fourteen
white land poachers and by the decision of the English, who tried unsuc-
cessfully to obtain the support of the Cherokees and Choctaws for a war
against the Creeks, to let the murders go unavenged. The Creeks, on the
other hand, were unable to forge a Southern Indian alliance in 1763 when
such a unified Indian movement might have joined a major Indian uprising in the Northwest to give the native peoples their best advantage of
the eighteenth century.

If the Indian reaction to the English victory over France was not one
of cowed submission in the South, it was even more aggressive in the
North. In June 1761 the Senecas, always the most pro-French of the Six
Nations, carried a red wampum belt (signifying an intention to go to war)
to Detroit where the British army was garrisoned among the various tribes
that had formally fought with the French—the Delawares, Shawnees, Ot-

[2]John R. Alden, *John Stuart and the Southern Colonial Frontier: A Study of Indian
Relations, War, Trade, and Land Problems in the Southern Wilderness, 1754–1775*
(Ann Arbor: University of Michigan Press, 1944), p. 177.

tawas, Hurons, Chippewas, and Potawatomies. The Seneca mission represented an attempt to take the lead in resisting the new English Indian policy, which curtailed trade, required the Indians to bring their furs to the British forts, ended the system of annual "presents," prohibited trade in rum, and in general instituted trading terms that were far less satisfactory to the Indians than those which had existed before the war. The Senecas had an additional incentive for taking to the warpath. General Amherst, the commander-in-chief of the Anglo-American forces during the Seven Years' War, had seen fit to reward some of his officers with Seneca lands near Niagara in violation of a treaty between the Iroquois and the New York government. Such generosity at the expense of the Senecas was not lightly regarded in the Indian towns.

What the Senecas proposed to other northern tribes was a coordinated attack on all the English outposts which ranged along the Great Lakes and as far south as Pittsburgh. The English were to be driven out of the Ohio Valley, out of Iroquois country, and back across the mountains to the coastal plain. Whether this "nativistic" plan included a resolve to give up the English trade altogether is not certain, although it is possible that after many years of trade difficulties they considered no trade at all preferable to a restricted trade at pinched prices. Although the western tribes rejected the Seneca plan after long discussion, they were far from pleased by what they heard from Sir William Johnson, the Northern Indian superintendent, when he arrived at Detroit three months later. Johnson claimed he came to brighten "the chain of friendship," and spoke glowingly of the King's concern for the welfare "of all his subjects." But he had nothing to promise in regard to the high price of trade goods, the unavailability of rum, the stoppage of annual presents, and the inadequate supplies of ammunition that were now allotted to the tribes. These, he said, were matters of official policy beyond his control.

Although Johnson reported optimistically to General Amherst at the conclusion of the conference, averring that he left Detroit with matters "settled on so stable a foundation there that unless greatly irritated thereto, they will never break the peace," the brute fact of the matter was that the Indians, for all their show of amity, were deeply embittered.[3] The most experienced English trader in the Ohio Valley, George Croghan, accurately perceived the situation. "The Indians . . . ," he wrote, "had great expectations of being very generally supplied by us, and from their poverty and mercenary disposition they can't bear such a disappointment. Undoubtedly the general [Amherst] has his own reason for not allowing any present or ammunition to be given them, and I wish it may

[3]Quoted in Howard H. Peckham, *Pontiac and the Indian Uprising* (Chicago: University of Chicago Press, 1961), p. 86.

have its desired effect, but I take this opportunity to acquaint you that I dread the event as I know Indians can't long persevere. . . . Their success at the beginning of this war on our frontiers is too recent in their memory to suffer them to consider their present inability to make war with us, and if the Senecas, Delawares and Shawnees should break with us, it will end in a general war with all western nations. . . ."[4]

Adding to the inflammatory state of affairs were the preachings of a charismatic Delaware prophet named Neolin. At the moment when the English were cutting off trade goods to which the Indians had become accustomed, Neolin began an odyssey through the Indian territories, preaching that Indians must either return to "their original state that they were in before the white people found out their country" or face slow extinction at the hands of the swarming settlers crossing the mountains. Several traders described in detail the renaissance of Indian culture that the Delaware Prophet preached. Neolin's vision, which he related had been conveyed to him in dreams by the Master of Life, made clear that the Indians' salvation lay not in adopting Christianity and European culture but in returning to ancient customs. Rum must be forsworn. The material objects of white culture must be forsworn. Population increase must be curbed through abstinence so that the difficult return to the old ways could be accomplished. "Such is the sad condition to which we are reduced," preached Neolin.

> What is now to be done, and what remedy is to be applied? I will tell you, my friends. Hear what the Great Spirit has ordered me to tell you! You are to make sacrifices, in the manner that I shall direct; to put off entirely from yourselves the customs which you have adopted since the white people came among us; you are to return to that former happy state, in which we lived in peace and plenty, before these strangers came to disturb us, and above all, you must abstain from drinking their deadly beson [liquor], which they have forced upon us for the sake of increasing their gains and diminishing our numbers.[5]

Neolin's message, which resonated with tremendous force not only in Delaware country but also among other western Indian nations, called not only for cultural renaissance but in addition for revolutionary resistance. "Wherefore do you suffer the whites to dwell upon your lands?" he asked. "Drive them away; wage war against them. I love them not. They know me not. They are my enemies, they are your brothers' enemies. Send them back to the lands I have made for them. Let them remain there."[6]

---

[4]*Ibid.*, pp. 97–98.

[5]Anthony F. C. Wallace, *The Death and Rebirth of the Seneca* (New York: Alfred A. Knopf, Inc., 1970), p. 120.

[6]*Ibid.*, p. 118.

Such were the words that Neolin reported were revealed to him by the Master of Life. Throughout 1762 they were passed by word of mouth and on inscribed deerskin parchment from one Indian settlement to another.

As Anthony Wallace has pointed out, Neolin's formula for cultural revitalization was not a complete return to the traditional elements of Indian culture but represented a blend of native and European elements. Some of the old customs, such as war rituals and polygamy were not to be revived and some Christian concepts, such as written prayers and a written "Bible" or "Great Book," were to be retained. But the significance of Neolin's appeal for the de-Europeanization of Indian culture was that it demonstrated how autonomously and creatively the western tribes could respond to the new situation that confronted them after the defeat of the French. His disciples carried his message throughout the western territories; large numbers of Indians, acting on his advice to boycott European trade goods, began hunting only to supply their own needs; and, most spectacularly, an Ottawa leader named Pontiac became a convert to Neolin's doctrine and made it the spiritual underpinning of the uprising he led against the English beginning in May 1763.[7]

According to a French account, Pontiac inspired his warriors with a speech that reflected Neolin's nativism. "It is important for us, my brothers," he exhorted, "that we exterminate from our lands this nation which seeks only to destroy us."[8] Under this banner Pontiac led an assault on Fort Detroit, the strongest of the British garrisons in the Great Lakes region. While the Ottawas lay siege to the fort, other tribes rubbed out the British outposts in the western Great Lakes region and as far east as Pittsburgh. In rapid succession the forts at Michilimachinac, St. Joseph, Sandusky, Presqu' Isle, Le Boeuf, and Venango fell as Shawnees, Delawares, Chippewas, Hurons, Miamis, Potawatomis, and Senecas joined the fray. But the Indians were unable to overwhelm the three major British forts at Detroit, Niagara, and Pittsburgh. The war dragged on through the summer and when news of it reached London the government hurriedly issued the Proclamation Act. Military reinforcements were sent from the East and by summer's end a standoff had been reached. Pontiac went on fighting sporadically for another two years and the English colonies hummed with rumors that he was conspiring with Creek and Choctaw chiefs to organize a grand alliance of eighteen Indian nations. But the tribes lacked vital supplies of powder, shot, and guns and in the end were forced to sue for peace. Without the presence in North America of another European power their supply problems could not be overcome.

Though Pontiac's resistance movement collapsed, the major interior

[7]*Ibid.*, pp. 120–21.
[8]Quoted in Peckham, *Pontiac and the Indian Uprising*, p. 119.

tribes continued to preserve their political autonomy in the decade prior to the outbreak of the American Revolution. "The Six Nations, Western Indians, etc.," wrote William Johnson to London in 1764, "having never been conquered, either by the English or French, nor subject to the[ir] Laws, consider themselves as a free people."[9] But the preservation of political autonomy did little to stem the tide of westward-looking land speculators and farmers. This demographic pressure alone was enough to overcome all efforts of the English government to fashion a policy of governing the interior parts of the continent in such a way that the Indian trade would be fairly conducted and the tribes upheld in their possession of land.

Two factors operated decisively in the fate of the trans-Appalachian territories after 1763. The first was that the English government, staggering under the immense debt accumulated in the course of the Seven Years' War, was unwilling to commit resources for maintaining garrisons in the interior to enforce the provisions of the Proclamation Act of 1763. Economizing in colonial government took precedence over the protection of Indian land. Consequently the interior garrisons were abandoned after Pontiac's Revolt and the plan to coordinate and control the Indian trade and Indian affairs of the various colonies, never successfully implemented, was scrapped. Reliance was placed on drawing lines on maps—lines that theoretically separated Indians and Englishmen—and in issuing stern commands to royal governors and colonial officials to uphold what was printed on the maps.

The second controlling factor in the trans-Appalachian West was that English officials had not a shred of power to enforce any kind of regulation in the interior, particularly after 1764, when a whole cluster of issues concerned with imperial authority in the colonies threw the colonists into a quasirevolutionary state. The Proclamation Line of 1763 existed only on paper and nobody, neither colonists nor Indians, took it seriously. Colonial governors, who were often closely connected with land speculators, bombarded London colonial administrators with reasons why exceptions must be made to the Proclamation Act. These included scores of false assertions that interior tribes had abandoned their claims to various parcels of land west of the Appalachians. When such requests were turned down, the governors turned their heads and permittted land grants, surveys, and private purchases of land from Indian tribes such as the Creeks and Cherokees, who did not recognize the right of the English government to demarcate boundaries. When settlers moved onto land still claimed by the Indians, they were usually left to fight it out among themselves.

[9]Quoted in Prucha, *American Indian Policy*, p. 19.

Most of the energy of colonial governors and their appointees was spent not in enforcing the Proclamation Act but assisting expanionist-minded speculators and settlers through a policy of promoting and perpetuating intertribal Indian hostility. Thus the main points of English Indian policy—prevention of encroachment on Indian lands and order and equity in the Indian trade—were reduced to a shambles in the decade before the Revolution. Nobody in the colonies could discover any reason to abstain from exploiting the dynamic combination of a ballooning population and vast tracts of Western land occupied only by Indians bereft of a European ally or an alternate supply of trade goods. Nor could anybody in England discover a means of compelling the Americans in the West to obey Crown commands at a time when even along the Atlantic seaboard the King's authority was being challenged at every turn.

For the interior tribes, who were the beneficiaries of an unenforceable English policy designed to guarantee them the land between the Appalachians and the Mississippi, the alternatives were limited after Pontiac's Revolt. They could seek other Indian allies in another attempt to forge a pan-Indian uprising, as did one faction of the Creeks, led by The Mortar, who had been staunchly anti-English for decades. They could seek private revenge for white depredations and land grabbing, as did Logan, a displaced Cayuga living on the Virginia frontier, whose family was wiped out by outlaw frontiersmen and who led a party of warriors in retaliatory raids that set off the brief but bloody Lord Dunmore's War in 1774. They could continue to seek French support in New Orleans while hoping for a French renaissance on the continent, as did the Choctaws. Or they could bow to the white tidal wave and sell off their land, tract by tract, at the best price possible to private individuals and land companies who were confident that they could safely ignore both the Proclamation of 1763 and colonial statutes forbidding such purchases.

Abolitionism

For Afro-Americans the decade ending the colonial period was one of both hope and despair. In the Northern colonies the banner of abolitionism was being raised sufficiently high to make the question of slavery a public issue for the first time since Africans had arrived in Jamestown in 1619. Led by Quaker humanitarians such as John Woolman and Anthony Benezet, and joined by a score of New England ministers and emerging revolutionary leaders, the cry went up that the institution of slavery was a contradiction of the principles of liberty and opportunity which demarcated the American experience from that of postfeudal Europe.

In developing a rationale for revolution in the decade after the Seven Years' War and in mounting propaganda attacks on mother England, colonial leaders found themselves asking questions not only about the nature of English authority and its legitimate limits in the colonies, but about the nature of the colonial society they had built. The revolutionary arguments about the natural rights of man, the consent of the governed, the nature of tyranny and the naturalness of equality contained intellectual dynamite. These stirring phrases led toward regions where even the most radical patriot leaders had not intended to go. They were primarily concerned with the threatening actions of Parliament and the King's ministers. But when they spoke of inalienable rights or the dignity of all men or abuses of power they unconsciously pointed a finger at themselves. The more they used catchwords like "slavery" and "tyranny" to describe English imperial reforms, the more difficult it became to ignore domestic slavery, which by the 1760s embraced about 20 percent of the population in the colonies. Men who wrote about inalienable rights and human dignity, about the natural equality of man, could no longer overlook the anomalous plight of the Afro-American, even though it had little to do with the issues dividing the colonies and England.

Men on both sides of the Atlantic and on both sides of the Anglo-American argument pointed out the contradiction. How could Americans treat Negroes "as a better kind of Cattle . . . while they are bawling about the Rights of human Nature?" asked one English official.[10] An American patriot chided his countrymen: "Blush ye pretended votaries for freedom! ye trifling patriots! who are making a vain parade of being advocates for the liberties of mankind, who are thus making a mockery of your profession by trampling on the sacred natural rights and privileges of Africans; for while you are fasting, praying, nonimporting, nonexporting, remonstrating, resolving, and pleading for a restoration of your charter rights, you at the same time are continuing this lawless, cruel, inhuman, and abominable practice of enslaving your fellow creatures."[11]

The very values and ideologies being invoked in the defense of colonial freedom were thus used to indict the system of labor undergirding the colonial economy of the South and to a lesser degree supporting economic enterprise in the North. Slavery was an insult to the principles for which the revolutionaries were preparing to fight. "Oh, the shocking, the intolerable inconsistence! . . . This gross, barefaced, practiced inconsistence,!"

[10]Quoted in Jordan, *White Over Black: American Attitudes Toward the Negro, 1550–1812* (Chapel Hill: University of North Carolina Press, 1968), p. 291.

[11][John Allen], *The Watchman's Alarm to Lord N_____h* (1774), in Bernard Bailyn, *The Ideological Origins of the American Revolution* (Cambridge: Harvard University Press, 1967), p. 240.

cried Samuel Hopkins, a Congregationalist minister of Rhode Island on the eve of war.[12]

Not only the degradation of blacks under slavery, but the accompanying degradation of whites, concerned many of those who declared their opposition to slavery in the pre-Revolutionary decade. Quaker John Woolman, whose abolitionist efforts of the 1750s were widely ignored, was convinced that slave holding, even by the kindliest of masters, did "yet deprave the mind in like manner and with as great certainty as prevailing cold congeals water." The absolute authority exercised by the master over the slave established "ideas of things and modes of conduct" that inexorably molded the attitudes of children, neighbors, and friends of slave holders.[13] As Woolman traveled through the colonies he became convinced that slavery was indelibly printing the notion of white superiority on the white mind. Such an idea was incompatible both with the Christian concept of the brotherhood of all men and rationalist thought of the eighteenth century, which stressed natural equality. Because slaves were always employed in servile labour and lived in abject conditions, most people grew from childhood to look upon them "as a contemptible, ignorant Part of Mankind."[14] Thus the outward condition of the slave, the result of white exploitation and desire for material gain, was taken to correspond with the inward condition of the displaced African. But for Woolman, the slave's outer degradation was a function of the white man's "inner corruption." White men had enslaved themselves in the process of enslaving the African, he said, and were as chained to the institution as were their slaves. The imprisonment of blacks was external and physical, while for the whites it was internal and spiritual. In either case the implications for the health of American society were fearful to contemplate.

These thoughts were raised not only in the North. Writing on the eve of the Revolution in Virginia, Jefferson warned his countrymen of the psychological and spiritual prison they had constructed for themselves through building their country on the backs of black slaves. "There must doubtless be an unhappy influence on the manners of our people produced by the existence of slavery among us," he wrote.

> The whole commerce between master and slave is a perpetual exercise of the most boisterous passions, the most unremitting despotism on the one part, and degrading submissions on the other. Our children see this, and

[12]Quoted in *ibid.*, p. 244.

[13]Quoted in Gary B. Nash, "Slaves and Slaveholders in Colonial Philadelphia," *William and Mary Quarterly*, 3d ser., 29 (1973): 243.

[14]Quoted in Jordan, *White Over Black*, p. 273.

learn to imitate it; for man is an imitative animal. . . . From his cradle to his grave he is learning to do what he sees others do. . . . The parent storms, the child looks on, catches the lineaments of wrath, puts on the same airs in the circle of smaller slaves, gives a loose to the worst of passions, and thus nursed, educated, and daily exercised in tyranny, cannot but be stamped by it with odious peculiarities. The man must be a prodigy who can retain his manners and morals undepraved by such circumstances.[15]

From this increasing awareness of white racial prejudice and its effects came a movement to end slavery. For the first time the incompatibility of enslaving Africans with the principles which white colonial society took to be the foundation of its uniqueness gained wide recognition. In response, a number of Northern colonies abolished the slave trade or taxed it out of existence before the Declaration of Independence was signed. Slavery, however, was not abolished, so while a small number of Yankee merchants were forced to reroute their ships, it cost other colonial whites little or nothing.

In the South the ideological war against slavery got nowhere. The 1760s, in fact, saw the largest slave importations of any decade in the colonial period. In South Carolina, for example, slaves imported between 1760 and 1770 exceeded those brought in during the previous quarter century and in the early 1770s the influx increased again. After the Seven Years' War more than 85 percent of all American slaves were concentrated in the plantation colonies of Maryland, Virginia, North Carolina, and South Carolina with the number in Virginia almost equalling those of the other Southern provinces. Virginia had never had more than half as many slaves as the sugar island of Jamaica between 1670 and 1730 but she overtook the West Indian plantation by 1760 and a decade later counted almost 200,000 slaves in the colony.

This kind of massive capital investment in black labor made the question of abolishing slavery almost academic in the parts of the country where it counted the most. For example, in Virginia, which had a white population equivalent to that of Sacramento, California, or Jersey City, New Jersey, today, the capital investment in slaves was about £5.5 million or, in terms of today's money, $145,000,000. Who would compensate slave holders for this property? Thus, while Afro-Americans heard of pamphlets advocating abolition and even pondered reports that the legislatures of Virginia and other colonies were debating the issue, those slave holders with large sums invested in the institution were organizing to turn back the campaign which sought to eliminate what had become the

---

[15]Thomas Jefferson, *Notes on the State of Virginia*, ed. Thomas P. Abernethy (New York: Harper & Row, Publishers, 1964), p. 155.

primary source of wealth, power, and prestige in the colonial South. The abolitionist critique of American society resounded loudly where only one of every ten American slaves lived; it was barely heard, or listened to, where the other nine of ten toiled.

As the colonial period drew to a close, Afro-American culture in the plantation South was in a state of flux. The importation of large numbers of Africans, at an all-time high in the South in the early 1770s, kept alive African cultural traditions and the spark of militancy. In South Carolina, for example, where the number imported relative to the American-born slave population was the greatest, a wave of insurrectionary activity coursed through the province. Once before, following a period of heavy slave importations in the 1730s, Carolinians had been terrified by a series of uprisings that started at Stono, where several hundred slaves escaped in 1739, and killed a number of whites on their way to Florida. Even the execution of 44 blacks had not prevented another plot in Charleston and still another in the interior in the the next year. So great was white fear that slave importations were forbidden for three years. Now in the 1760s the process was repeated. In 1761 a wave of poisoning swept over the colony. Four years later more than one hundred slaves made a concerted attempt to establish a colony in the interior. And in 1766 black men took literally the white rhetoric concerning liberty and equality by parading through the streets of Charleston chanting "Liberty, Liberty!" The words were so frightening that the city was under arms for a week, as rumors of insurrection spread like a brushfire through the colony.[16] A nervous legislature quickly passed a three-year prohibitive tariff on slaves in order to reduce importations to a trickle. More than seven thousand slaves had been imported in 1765 but in the next year a mere 101 entered the colony.

Even in Virginia, where the burgeoning slave population primarily reflected natural increase rather than new importations, blacks were far from reconciled to plantation slavery. When opportunities arose to throw off the shackles of perpetual servitude, they moved with speed and determination. In 1775, when hostilities had already begun without a formal declaration of war, Governor Dunmore of Virginia issued a proclamation offering freedom to any Virginia slave who escaped his or her master and reached the British garrisons. The effect of the proclamation on white society was to galvanize the South against England, for Dunmore had hit a sensitive nerve by conjuring up the vision of a large body of free Negroes, armed by the British, abroad in the land. The proclamation, wrote one prominent Southerner, tended "more effectually to work an eternal

[16]Pauline Maier, "The Charleston Mob and the Evolution of Popular Politics in Revolutionary South Carolina, 1765–1784," *Perspectives in American History*, 4 (1970): 176–77.

separation between Great Britain and the Colonies—than any other ex-
pedient, which could possibly have been thought of." Another put it more
graphically: "Hell itself could not have vomitted anything more black
than this design of emancipating our slaves."[17]

Thousands of black Virginians, perhaps as many as one-third of the
adult males, made an attempt to reach the British garrisons. Making
personal declarations of independence, they achieved liberty by joining
those who were called enemies of freedom by white American patriots.
In general, the appraisal of Joseph Galloway, a Philadelphia loyalist,
would seem to characterize the Afro-American population on the eve of
the Revolution. "The Negroes," wrote Galloway, "may all be deemed so
many Intestine [internal] Enemies, being all slaves and desirous of Freedom, and would, was an opportunity offered them, Take up Arms against
their Masters."[18] Docility and dependency were by no means the dominant characteristics of the Afro-American personality in the third quarter
of the eighteenth century. Slave masters continued to fear their black
slaves and slaves continued to seek ways to ameliorate their condition,
while devising cultural forms which made slave life bearable.

Cultural Interaction of
Red, White, and Black

At the end of the colonial period, American society, some 2.5 million
strong, was far from a homogeneous culture. Almost two hundred years
of European colonization and the continuous interaction of three large
and internally diverse cultural groups had left a conglomeration of cultural entities. Each had its own goals and to a large extent its own values. Two of the groups, European and Indian, retained a considerable
degree of autonomy, although both were somewhat limited in what they
could do by the presence of the other and by the political and economic
relationships that they had contracted during the colonial epoch. The
third group, the Afro-Americans, was necessarily limited by the fact that
most of its members were enslaved. But Afro-Americans also retained a
measure of autonomy, though it appeared in more subtle forms.

The complex interaction of the three cultural groups was filled with
paradoxes. Europeans in America claimed that they wished to assimilate
Indians and Africans but they found that the most effective way to exploit

[17]Quoted in Benjamin Quarles, *The Negro in the American Revolution* (Chapel
Hill: University of North Carolina Press, 1961), p. 20n.

[18]Benjamin F. Stevens, ed., *Facsimiles of Manuscripts in European Archives Relating to America, 1773–1783* (London, 1889–1895), 24, No. 2079.

the land of one and the labor of the other was to follow a nonassimilationist policy. Bringing Christianity to non-Christians was an expensive and time-consuming enterprise, useful only to the extent that it better enabled Europeans to make use of the resources of those they sought to dominate. Since it often gave little promise of accomplishing that—and in fact frequently threatened to make the utilization of Indian land and African labor more difficult—it was given a low priority. Only minimal efforts were made to instruct Indian tribes in Christian doctrine and most of the efforts were inspired by the hope that conversion would go hand in hand with pacification and political control. Southern slaves were widely exposed to Christian doctrine in the upper South where the threat of slave revolt was not so keenly felt, but were carefully shielded from the potentially radical message of Christianity in South Carolina and Georgia. That slaves in the North were broadly inculcated with Protestantism only reflected the belief that where slaves were vastly outnumbered by whites instruction in the precepts of Protestantism, with emphasis on dutiful work in one's present station, would act as a damper on rebelliousness. In education it was the same: slaves were educated in those things that enabled them to function in their work more effectively; but education as a concept, as a process of inquiry, was shunned for it promised only to cultivate aspirations that were inappropriate to those whose servitude was lifelong.

A handful of reformers and churchmen kept alive the humanitarian impulse, based on the theory that Africans and Indians should be assimilated into Anglo-American society. But though hardly admissible in public discussion, most colonists regarded the two cultural minorities in their midst as most useful when unassimilated or semiassimilated. Indeed, a large majority of the colonists came to regard slaves as unassimilable, as was to be clearly revealed when the emancipation of slaves in the Revolutionary era brought cries for their repatriation to Africa. So far as the assimilation of Indians was concerned, nothing could have been less desirable to European settlers, who coveted Indian land but not land with Indians on it. Nor did Indians seek entry into white society, for there was little they wanted from Europeans that they could not obtain through bartering skins and furs. Thus the problem for European colonists was how to obtain Indian land and exploit the presence of these "obstacles" to colonial expansion. Because they were almost as internally divided as the Indian nations and rarely in the colonial period had enough power to force the interior tribes to give up their land or political autonomy, the colonists based their Indian policy on the principle of keeping tribes divided against each other. "If we cannot destroy one nation of Indians by another, our country must be lost," wrote the governor of South Carolina in 1717, and the statement stood as an accurate characterization of colonial policy for the rest of the century.[19]

Also working against assimilation was the inner need of white colonists to justify their exploitation of Africans and Indians by an insistence on the wide gap that separated "barbarian savages" from "civilized" Europeans. By definition, assimilation would narrow this gap, making Africans and Europeans or Indians and Europeans more alike. But when mighty master and lowly slave, or reasonable European and pagan savage, were admitted to be alike, either in outward customs and manners or in inner capacity, then the entire rationale of domination and exploitation would come crashing down. This positive need to deny alikeness and to oppose any measures that would increase the similarity of peoples in colonial society was an important reason for resisting the Christianization of slaves. It also worked to convince white colonists that Indians were unassimilable. One of the mistaken notions about colonial Americans that endured in England was that the settlers would happily receive the missionaries of the Anglican Society for the Propagation of the Gospel, which hoped to convert both slaves and Indians to the word of Christ. As Winthrop Jordan has pointed out, the Bishop of London summed up this misconception of the colonial desire for assimilation when he "referred to Negroes as 'truly a Part of our own Nation'—which was just what the colonists were sure Negroes were not."[20] The same was true for Indians.

A second paradox was that white American culture developed the most pervasively negative attitudes toward the cultural minority in its midst that was indispensably valuable to it—the Afro-Americans—and held the more positive attitudes toward the cultural minority which stood only as an obstacle to white society once their military assistance was no longer needed—the Indians. Colonial society grew in size and strength in direct relationship to an increase in slaves and a decrease in "land-cluttering" Indians. Yet it was the black man upon whom the colonists fastened the most indelibly negative images. The key to this irony was that the colonist almost always encountered the black man as a slave and thus came to think of him as an abject and less than human creature; but the English settler met the Indian as an adversary or a half-trusted ally. The Indian maintained the freedom and power to come and go, to attack and kill, to give and withhold support, and to retain his political sovereignty. Though he was hated for many of these things, they earned him a grudging respect. The Anglo-Indian relationship in the eighteenth century was

[19]Quoted in David D. Wallace, *South Carolina: A Short History, 1520–1948* (Chapel Hill: University of North Carolina Press, 1951), pp. 91–92.
[20]Jordan, *White Over Black*, p. 208.

rarely that of master and slave with all rights and power concentrated on one side. Instead, when Indian and Englishmen met, they were involved in a set of power relationships in which each side, with something to offer the other, maneuvered for the superior position. That the Indian was the ultimate loser in most of these interchanges cannot obscure the fact that for several hundred years Anglo-Americans confronted Indians as formidable adversaries rather than as chattels. Though they were exploited, excluded, and sometimes decimated in their contacts with European civilization, Indians always maneuvered from a position of strength.

Africans in America, by contrast, were rarely a part of any political or economic equation. They had only their labor to offer and even that was not subject to contractual agreement. African slaves were not entirely powerless in their dealings with white society but they were relatively powerless as compared with Indians. This maldistribution of power in the black-white context could not help but affect attitudes. Unlike the Indian, the African was rarely able to win the respect of the white man because his situation was rarely one where respect was required or even possible. Tightly trapped in an authoritarian relationship where virtually all power was on the other side, Africans, as they became more and more important to the white man's economy, could only sink lower and lower in the white man's estimation. Meanwhile, the Indian, though hated, was often held in awe for his fighting ability, his dignity, and even his oratorical skill. American colonists may have scoffed at the efforts of the Enlightenment philosophers to depict the American native as a "noble savage," the archetype of natural beauty and virtue, uncorrupted by materialistic Western civilization; but their image of the Indian came to have a positive side. The sociology of red-white and black-white relations had differed greatly over six generations. From these variations evolved distinct white attitudes, in both cases adverse, but in significantly different ways.

A third paradox in the convergence of cultures was that the cultural group that was enslaved, degraded, and despised survived and flourished demographically in America, while the group that maintained its freedom, much of its power, and a considerable amount of European respect suffered depopulation and gradual decline. It is in no way to minimize the pain, humiliation, and brutality of slavery to point out that Africans in America were remarkably successful in a demographic sense, particularly in contrast to most other areas of the New World. Probably not more than 250,000 slaves were imported into the mainland colonies in the colonial period and yet on the eve of the Revolution the black population stood at close to .5 million. Although careful studies of slave fertility and mortality have not yet been made, the limited data we have suggest that while black mortality was far higher than white mortality, black fertility may have been rather close to the white norm. It can be stated with greater certainty that slave mortality in eighteenth-century America was far lower than almost anywhere else in the New World. This is not necessarily explained by more humane treatment on American plantations. More important was the more favorable epidemic environment of North America in general. The Caribbean islands were known as graveyards for white and black alike and in the Latin America countries tropical diseases swept away African slaves like leaves in a windstorm.

A comparison of Virginia and Jamaica slave imports and slave populations illustrates the point. The slave populations of the two colonies were almost equal in 1775, with Virginians owning about 200,000 slaves and the Jamaicans about 193,000. But between 1700 and 1775, Virginia had imported not more than 100,000 slaves by the most liberal estimates, while in Jamaica net importations were more than three and a half times as great. It is probable that life for African slaves on eighteenth-century Southern plantations was healthier than in other parts of the New World and that because of a more favorable sex ratio than in other plantation areas the chances of family life were much greater.

By contrast, the Indian tribes east of the Appalachian Mountains suffered major population declines in the first two centuries of contact with Europeans. Although they were not struck down in the same catastrophic proportions as the indigenous people of Mexico and most parts of Latin America, their mortality rates and natural decline stood in stark contrast to the natural increase of the enslaved Africans. Particularly in areas of white settlement, along the coastal plain from Maine to Georgia, only remnants of the Indian population remained on the eve of the Revolution. Connecticut, for example, counted 930 Indians in a census in 1762; Massachusetts found 1,681 in 1764; Virginia listed only 130 in 1774; and Rhode Island tabulated 1,482 in the same year. At the same time the black population, even setting aside increases through importation, was growing rapidly. This was due to a number of factors. First, Africans were far more resistant to European epidemic diseases and by the mid-eighteenth century were being immunized, like whites, against the biggest killer of all—smallpox. Hardly an Indian tribe or nation in the eastern part of the continent escaped the dread killer. The eastern Massachusetts tribes had been decimated even before the Puritans arrived and were again struck down in substantial numbers in the early years of white settlement. The Iroquois were scourged several times in the seventeenth and eighteenth centuries. The Catawba population of North Carolina was reduced by half during a single epidemic in 1759 and a raging smallpox epidemic hit the Cherokees so severely in 1738 that according to several estimates they lost nearly half their population. The disease swept the Creeks in the last years of the seventeenth century and continued to diminish their numbers in the following decades. Far less important as a killer were the wars which tribes fought with European settlers and with each other at the instigation of their trading partners. But these too took a toll on life that was not duplicated in the slave experience. Still another cause of depopulation was alcohol, which though it killed slowly in contrast to smallpox and other epidemic diseases, also took its toll.

All the lethal factors that decimated Indian villages throughout eastern North America, while touching slaves only incidentally, were linked to white calculations of the usefulness of blacks as opposed to Indians. White colonists did not, of course, possess direct control over bacteriological and demographic factors. But they eagerly sought to increase the black slave population while reducing the Indian population. To this end they instituted policies which influenced, if they did not control, population curves. Blacks, for example, were inoculated against smallpox and given medical treatment in case of sickness. For a plantation owner to do this was only to preserve his property, just as he would attempt to maintain the health of his horses and farm animals. If Indians, however, contracted an epidemic disease, the colonist could only give thanks that God had seen fit to diminish their numbers in order to make more room for "civilized" men. European colonists only occasionally waged bacteriological warfare in a conscious way, such as by spreading smallpox through infested trade goods, but they were uninterested in arresting epidemic disease among the Indians in contrast to their slaves. With alcohol it was the same. It was rationed out to slaves at holiday time and sometimes at week's end as a reward for compliance or in order to increase their willingness to accept the labor system. But alcohol was distributed among Indian tribes in order to create not only dependency but addiction. Rum was a liquid form of control for white colonists in their dealings with both Africans and Indians. But it was intended to sustain life among blacks while destroying life among Indians.

The third killer, war, was also controlled to some extent by whites. Black rebellion was, of course, quelled as quickly as possible, for it was a direct threat to the labor system and to social dominance by whites. But war with Indians and war among Indians was often a carefully calculated objective in white minds. No sooner had they determined that they could outmatch local tribes than colonists in the seventeenth century invoked any pretext, however flimsy, to make war on coastal tribes. Thus, Emanuel Downing, the brother-in-law of John Winthrop, wrote the leader of the Massachusetts colony in 1645 that he thought a war with the Narragansett Indians would be of "verie considerable" advantage to the colony.

Downing, a lawyer, argued that it would be a sin in God's eyes for the Puritans, "having power in our hands, to suffer them to maynteyne the worship of the devill which their paw wawes often doe," and then predicted the history of the next century by pointing out that "If upon a Just warre the Lord should deliver them [the Narragansetts] into our hands, wee might easily have men, woemen, and children enough to exchange for Moores, which wilbe more gaynefull pilladge for us than wee conceive, for I doe not see how wee can thrive untill wee gett into a stock of slaves sufficient to doe all our buisines, for our children's children will hardly see this great Continent filled with people, soe that our servants will still desire freedome to plant for them selves, and not stay but for verie great wages. And I suppose you know verie well how wee shall mainteyne 20 Moores cheaper than one Englishe servant."[21]

Downing's willingness to please God while serving the colonists' material needs was a typical seventeenth-century mode of justifying war against local tribes. But in the eighteenth century such arguments were couched in purely secular language and then applied to strong interior tribes rather than to small coastal societies. In this changed context, the policy became to create animosities between Indian groups. This was not only the most effective deterrent to pan-Indian uprisings against the Europeans but contributed to the general population decline of Indians.

Thus, while escaping slavery in most cases, native Americans found themselves confronting a mushrooming European population that sought the land they occupied and could conceive of no way that Indians could be useful to white society except to aid in the process of their own collective decimation and dispossession of land. This had not been true for most of the colonial period, for when the European population was small, while it had been divided among Spanish, French, and English contenders for continental supremacy, and while the fur and skin trade had been a major factor in the colonial economy, the Indian had been a functional part of the process of building a new society in the New World. By the mid-eighteenth century, however, the Indian trade had become a minor part of the colonial economy. Fishing and ship building in New England, grain and livestock production in the Middle Colonies, and tobacco, rice, and indigo production on Southern plantations had become the principal forms of economic activity. By 1763 the elimination of France as an imperial rival eliminated the need for Indian military support. Finally, the tremendous growth of population in the two generations before the Revolution made acquisition of the interior river valleys of the continent the preoccupation of both eastern entrepreneurs, for whom population

---

21Quoted in Almon W. Lauber, *Indian Slavery in Colonial Times Within the Present Limits of the United States* (New York: Columbia University Press, 1913), p. 311.

growth had created a new source of wealth far greater than the fur trade, and the swarming settlers who poured through the mountain gaps into the Trans-Appalachian region.

A final paradox was that many Indian societies embodied what Englishmen and other Europeans had come to find in the New World but were destroyed or driven westward while daring to be what Europeans could not. It is true that many colonists came venturing across the Atlantic for nothing more than material gain; but many others saw the "wilderness" of North America as a place where tired, corrupt, materialistic, self-seeking Europeans might begin a new life centered around the long-lost but ever-valuable concepts of reciprocity, spirituality, and community. From John Winthrop to William Penn to John Adams the notion of transplanted Europeans building a virtuous society in cities on the hill coursed through the dreamlife of the newcomers. Yet as time passed and Europeans became more numerous, it became more and more evident that the people in North America who were best upholding these values and organizing their society around them were the people who were being driven from the land.

It was not simply the romantic side of eighteenth-century Enlightenment thinking that caricatured the Indians as the possessors of a better formula for living. As early as the 1660s Thomas Traherne, an English poet, was writing that

> Earth was better than Gold, and . . . Water was, every Drop of it, a Precious Jewel. And that these were Great and Living Treasures: and that all Riches whatsoever els was Dross in Comparison . . . The Sun is Glorious. A Man is a Beautifull Creature . . . The Stars Minister unto us, the World was Made for you . . . But to say This Hous is yours, and these Lands are another Mans and this Bauble is a Jewel and this Gugaw a fine Thing . . . is deadly Barbarous and uncouth . . . becaus the Nature of the Thing contradicts your Words. . . . By this you may see who are the Rude and Barbarous Indians. For verily there is no Salvage Nation under the Cope of Heaven that is more absurdly Barbarous than the Christian World.[22]

These thoughts would echo down the corridors of seventeenth- and eighteenth-century history. Even hard-bitten, unsentimental colonists often recognized that Indian society, though by no means without its problems and its own disreputable characters, put white society to shame. The English Commissioners investigating Bacon's Rebellion in 1676 wrote a scorching letter to the governor and legislative assembly of Virginia asking them to stop the land grabbing of settlers who already had

---

[22]Thomas Traherne, *Centuries, Poems and Thanksgivings*, ed. H. M. Margoliouth (London: Oxford at the Clarendon Press, 1958), 1: 115, 117.

title to all the land they could use but "still Covett & seek to deprive them [the Indians] of more, out of meer Itch of Luxurie rather than any reall lack of it, which shames us and makes us become a Reproach and a by-word to those more Morall heathens."[23] Three-quarters of a century later Thomas Pownall, governor of Massachusetts, excoriated the colonists for violating their own principles and wrote that "the frauds, abuses, and deceits that these poor people have been treated with and suffered under have had no bounds."[24] Edmond Atkin, an Indian trader of South Carolina, and a man who knew Indians not from drawing-room accounts but from years of intimate contact, wrote in 1755 that

> No people in the World understand and pursue their true National Interest, better than the Indians. . . . Yet in their publick Treaties no People on earth are more open, explicit, and Direct. Nor are they excelled by any in the observance of them. . . . It were easy to make appear, with respect to . . . all Ruptures of Consequence between the Indians & the white People, and the Massacres that ensued, which have created such a Horror of the former, That the latter were first the Aggressors; the Indians being driven thereto under Oppressions and Abuses, and to vindicate their Natural Rights.[25]

Throughout the colonial period European observers stood in awe of the central Indian traits of hospitality, generosity, bravery, and the spirit of mutual caring. Indians seemed to embody these Christian virtues almost without effort in a corner of the earth where Europeans, attempting to build a society with similar characteristics, were being pulled in the opposite direction by the natural abundance around them—toward individualism, disputatiousness, aggrandizement of wealth, and the exploitation of other humans. The Pennsylvania Moravian missionary John Heckewelder was one of a long succession of colonists, beginning with Roger Williams in 1643, who invited his white countrymen to compare their own behavior with that of the Indians he knew. For them, he wrote:

> Whatever liveth on the land, whatsoever groweth out of the earth, and all that is in the rivers and waters flowing through the same, was given jointly to all, and everyone is entitled to his share. From this principle, hospitality flows as from its source. With them it is not a virtue but a strict duty. Hence they are never in search of excuses to avoid giving, but freely supply their neighbour's wants from the stock prepared for their own use. They give and are hospitable to all, without exception, and will always

[23]*Virginia Magazine of History and Biography*, 14 (1906–7): 274.

[24]Quoted in Georgiana C. Nammack, *Fraud, Politics, and the Dispossession of the Indians; The Iroquois Land Frontier in the Colonial Period* (Norman: University of Oklahoma Press, 1969), p. 31.

[25]Jacobs, ed., *Atkin Report and Plan*, p. 38.

share with other and often with the stranger, even to their last morsel. They rather would lie down themselves on an empty stomach, than have it laid to their charge that they had neglected their duty, by not satisfying the wants of the stranger, the sick or the needy.[26]

Heckewelder did not need to belabor the point—that these Indian virtues came far closer to the precepts of Christianity that most colonists found it comfortable to admit.

This was a kind of innocence that beckoned destruction. By embodying some of the virtues around which Europeans had hoped to reorganize their cultural system, but could not, the Indian was a disturbing reminder of the retrogression rather than the progress of European man in his New World setting. Englishmen, Germans, Scotch-Irish, Swedes, Finns, Dutch, French Huguenots, and others might congratulate themselves on the eve of the American Revolution for "taming the Wilderness"; for building thriving seaports where none had previously existed; for raising towns, churches, schools, and governments along a thousand miles of coastal plain from Maine to Georgia. They had chosen productivity and acquisitiveness, both of which proceeded far. But it was obvious from looking in any direction that this had been accomplished at a terrible price in exploitation and human suffering, enslavement and alienation.

---

[26]Heckewelder, *Account of the History, Manners, and Customs of the Indian Nations, Who Once Inhabited Pennsylvania* . . . (Philadelphia: American Philosophical Society, 1819), p. 85.

Bibliographical Essay

Students who wish to deepen their understanding of the interaction among ethnic and cultural groups in early America will soon learn that many of the books and journals they need to consult are not shelved in the American history section of their library but in the sections devoted to anthropology, ethnography, African history, and even music and folklore. In the bibliography that follows particular attention is given to identifying these less familiar works of scholarship and relatively little attention is given to the immense historical literature concerning Englishmen and other Europeans in North America during the colonial period. Comprehensive guides to this more traditional approach to the history of early America can be found in Alden T. Vaughan, *The American Colonies in the Seventeenth Century* (New York, 1971) and Jack P. Greene, *The American Colonies in the Eighteenth Century, 1689–1763* (New York, 1969).

Indian Culture

A few general histories of Indian culture in North America are worth consulting by those who are making their first acquaintance with "the first Americans." Among the best are Harold E. Driver, *Indians of North America* (Chicago, 1961); Fred Eggan, *The American Indian: Perspectives for the Study of Social Change* (Chicago, 1967); Harold Fey and D'Arcy McNickle, *Indians and Other Americans; Two Ways of Life Meet* (New York, 1959); Frederick Hodge, ed., *Handbook of American Indians North of Mexico* (New York, 1960); Wilbur R. Jacobs, *Dispossessing the American Indian* (New York, 1972); Alvin M. Josephy, Jr., *The Indian Heritage of America* (New York, 1968); William Christie MacLeod, *The American Indian Frontier* (New York, 1928); D'Arcy McNickle, *They Came Here First; The Epic of the American Indians* (New York, 1949); Robert Spencer and Jesse Jennings, *The Native Americans; Prehistory and Ethnology of the North American Indians* (New York, 1965); Edward H. Spicer, ed., *Perspectives in American Indian Culture Change* (Chicago, 1961); Ruth M. Underhill, *Red Man's America; A History of Indians in the United States* (Chicago, 1953); Deward E. Walker, Jr., *The Emergent Native Americans; A Reader in Culture Contact* (Boston, 1972); Jennings C. Wise, *The Red Man in the New World Drama* (Washington, D.C., 1931); and Clark Wissler, *Indians of the United States; Four Centuries of Their History and Culture* (New York, 1940).

More detailed accounts of Indian life in North America before the arrival of Europeans are numerous, but students should be aware that new findings by archaeologists and new conceptual approaches by anthropologists are continually changing our understanding of how long human life has existed in North America, how societies changed, and how cultural diffusion took place. Some general works on the "prehistory" of North America are Jesse Jennings, *Prehistory of North America* (New York, 1968); Jesse Jennings and Edward Norbeck, eds., *Prehistoric Man in the New World* (Chicago, 1964); Paul S. Martin, George I. Quimby, and Donald Collier, *Indians Before Columbus; Twenty Thousand Years of North American History Revealed by Archaeology* (Chicago, 1947); Kenneth Macgowan and Joseph A. Hester, Jr., *Early Man in the New World* (Garden City, N.Y., 1962); William T. Sanders and Joseph Marino, *New World Prehistory; Archaeology of the American Indian* (Englewood Cliffs, N.J., 1970); and Gordon Willey, ed., *Prehistoric Settlement Patterns in the New World* (New York, 1956). The volumes edited by Jennings and Norbeck and by Willey include references to almost all the important literature in this area.

Several special topics concerning Indian life before European colonization deserve special attention. The development of agriculture, which is of critical importance in the evolution of all societies, is discussed in Richard S. MacNeish, "The Origins of New World Agriculture," *Scien-entfic American*, 211 (1964), 29–37. As to the population of the Americas before European arrival—a question fraught with implications for the study of later European-Indian contacts—students should consult the long-standard work of James Mooney, *The Aboriginal Population of America North of Mexico* (Washington, D.C., 1928) and then read the revisionist article by Henry F. Dobyns, "Estimating Aboriginal American Population; An Appraisal of Techniques with a New Hemispheric Estimate," *Current Anthropology*, 7 (1966), 395–416, along with the appended comments of several dozen anthropologists and demographers.

European-Indian Contact

After gaining some understanding of the peoples of North America before Europeans "discovered" the ancient "New World," students will be better able to comprehend the early stages of European-Indian contact. Books are legion on the early voyages of discovery, but a good place to start is with Carlo M. Cipolla, *Guns, Sails and Empires; Technological Innovation and the Early Phases of European Expansion, 1400–1700* (New York, 1966); John B. Brebner, *The Explorers of North America, 1492–1806* (New York, 1933); and Samuel E. Morison, *The European Discovery of America; The Northern Voyages A.D. 500–1600* (New York, 1971).

For Europeans, the exploration of North America was not only geographical but psychic as well, for the native inhabitants had a profound impact on the European mind—an impact that was later to play an important role in the character of intercultural relations. Only an interdisciplinary approach will fully reveal what Europeans thought about who and what these inhabitants of North America were. Thus the following books represent the work of scholars in a half-dozen disciplines: Henri Baudet, *Paradise on Earth: Thoughts on European Images of Non-European Man*, trans. Elizabeth Wentholt (New Haven, 1965); David Bidney, "The Idea of the Savage in North American Ethnohistory," *Journal of the History of Ideas*, 15 (1954) 322–27; Edward Dudley and Maximillian E. Novak, eds., *The Wild Man Within: An Image in Western Thought from the Renaissance to Romanticism* (Pittsburgh, 1972); Leslie A. Fiedler, *The Return of the Vanishing American* (New York, 1968); Carolyn T. Foreman, *Indians Abroad, 1493–1938* (Norman, Okla., 1943); Lee E. Huddleston, *Origins of the American Indians; European Concepts, 1492–1729* (Austin, Texas, 1967); G. K. Hunter, "Elizabethans and Foreigners," in Allardyce Nicoll, ed., *Shakespeare in His Own Age* (Cambridge, 1964); Sidney Lee, "The American Indians in Elizabethan England," in Frederick S. Boas, ed., *Elizabethan and Other Essays* (Oxford, 1929); Gary B. Nash, "The Image of the Indian in the Southern Colonial Mind," *William and Mary Quarterly*, 29 (1972), 197–230; Roy H. Pearce, *The Savages of America; A Study of the Indian and the Idea of Civilization* (Baltimore, 1953); and "The Metaphysics of Indian-Hating," *Ethnohistory*, 4 (1957), 27–40; Edmundo O'Gorman, *The Invention of America* (Bloomington, Ind., 1961); Carl O. Sauer, *Sixteenth Century North America; The Land and the People as Seen by Europeans* (Berkeley, 1971); and Wilcomb E. Washburn, "The Moral and Legal Justification for Dispossessing the Indians," in James M. Smith, ed., *Seventeenth-Century America; Essays in Colonial History* (Chapel Hill, N.C., 1959).

The study of early European-Indian relations in North America begins not with English colonists and native peoples but with the arrival of the Spanish, Dutch, and the French on the continent. It is important to study this interaction of non-English people with Indian tribes because it allows for a comparative perspective on the later English experience. A general introduction to a comparative study of European-Indian relations is provided in a group of essays in Howard Peckham and Charles Gibson, eds., *Attitudes of Colonial Powers Toward the American Indian* (Salt Lake City, 1969). More detailed analyses of French-Indian relations in Canada by both historians and anthropologists are: Alfred G. Bailey, *The Conflict of European and Eastern Algonkian Cultures, 1504–1700* (St. John, New Brunswick, 1937); William J. Eccles, *The Canadian Frontier, 1534–1760* (New York, 1969); Robert Goldstein, *French-Iroquois Diplomatic and Military Relations, 1609–1701* (The Hague, 1969); John H. Kennedy, *Jesuit and Savage in New France* (New Haven, 1950); Mary Ross, "French Intrusions and Indian Uprisings in Georgia and South Carolina, 1577–1580," *Georgia Historical Quarterly*, 7 (1923), 251–81; Bruce G. Trigger, "Trade and Tribal Warfare on the St. Lawrence in the Sixteenth Century," *Ethnohistory*, 9 (1962), 240–56; and Bruce G. Trigger, "The Destruction of Huronia; A Study in Economic and Cultural Change, 1609–1650," *Transactions of the Royal Canadian Institute*, 33 (1960), 14–45. For French relations with Indian tribes on the Lower Mississippi, a case of culture contact that stands in vivid contrast to the Canadian experience, consult Andrew C. Albrecht, "Indian-French Relations at Natchez," *American Anthropologist*, 48 (1946), 321–54; Jean Delanglez, "The Natchez Massacre and Governor Perier," *Louisiana Historical Quarterly*, 17 (1934), 631–41; Jean Delanglez, *The French Jesuits in Lower Louisiana, 1700–63* (New Orleans, 1935); and Charles E. O'Neill, *Church and State in French Colonial Louisiana; Policy and Politics to 1732* (New Haven, 1966).

Spanish-Indian acculturation in North America, which was partly determinative of what followed in the English period of settlement, can be

followed in Charles Gibson, *Spain in America* (New York, 1966); Wood-
bury Lowrey, *The Spanish Settlements within the Present Limits of the
United States*, vol. 1, *1513–1561*; vol. 2, *1562–1574* (New York, 1901–
1905); William C. Sturtevant, "Spanish-Indian Relations in Southeastern
North America," *Ethnohistory*, 9 (1962), 41–94; and in further works
cited by these authors. For the Dutch record in New Netherland the
student is well advised to begin with Allen W. Trelease, *Indian Affairs
in Colonial New York; The Seventeenth Century* (Ithaca, N.Y., 1960).

Extending the scope of European-Indian relations to other parts of the
New World is a valuable way of establishing the special character of cultural interaction in North America. Magnus Mörner's *Race Mixture in
the History of Latin America* (Boston, 1967) is an excellent place to begin.
Regarding Spanish colonization see Lewis Hanke, *Aristotle and the American Indian; A Study in Race Prejudice in the Modern World* (London,
1959); Lewis Hanke, *The Spanish Struggle for Justice in the Conquest
of America* (Philadelphia, 1949); Murdo J. MacLeod, *Spanish Central
America; A Socio-economic History, 1420–1720* (Berkeley, 1973); and
James M. Lockhart, *Spanish Peru, 1532–1560; A Colonial Society* (Mad-
ison, Wis., 1968). The Portuguese case is carefully examined in Charles
R. Boxer, *Race Relations in the Portuguese Colonial Empire, 1415–1825*
(Oxford, 1963); Mathias C. Kiemen, *The Indian Policy of Portugal in the
Amazon Region, 1614–1693* (Washington, D.C., 1954); and Alexander N.
Marchant, *From Barter to Slavery; The Economic Relations of Portu-
guese and Indians in the Settlement of Brazil, 1500–1580* (Baltimore,
1942). Charles R. Boxer's *The Dutch Seaborne Empire, 1600–1800* (New
York, 1965) includes material on Dutch relations with Indian peoples.

Before embarking on more detailed investigations of English-Indian
interaction in early America, students can profit by assaying the ideas of
various historians on how this subject can—and ought to be—approached.
In the order of their publication the most important of these are: William N. Fenton, *American Indian and White Relations to 1830; Needs
and Opportunities for Study* (Chapel Hill, N.C., 1957); Stanley Pargellis,
"The Problem of American Indian History," *Ethnohistory*, 4 (1957),
113–24; Wilcomb E. Washburn, "A Moral History of Indian-White Relations; Needs and Opportunities for Study," *Ethnohistory*, 4 (1957–58),
47–61; Bernard W. Sheehan, "Indian-White Relations in Early America;
A Review Essay," *William and Mary Quarterly*, 26 (1969), 267–86; Robert F. Berkhofer, Jr., "The Political Context of a New Indian History,"
Pacific Historical Review, 40 (1971), 357–82; and Wilcomb E. Washburn,
"The Writing of American Indian History; A Status Report," *Pacific
Historical Review*, 40 (1971), 261–81.

Another prerequisite for studying English-Indian relations is the acquisition of a broad understanding of tribal cultures at the time of contact.

A few articles that will start the student along this path by dealing with culture groups rather than specific tribes are: I. Pablovna Averkieva, *Slavery Among the Indians of North America*, trans. G. R. Elliott (Victoria, B.C., 1966); John M. Cooper, "Land Tenure among the Indians of Eastern and Northern North America," *Pennsylvania Archaeologist,* 8 (1938), 55–59; and "Is the Algonquian Family Ground System Pre-Columbian," *American Anthropologist,* n.s. 41 (1939), 66–90; William N. Fenton, "Factionalism in American Indian Society," in *Tirage a part: Actes du IVᵉ Congres International des Sciences Anthropologiques et Ethnologiques,* II (Vienna, 1952), 330–40; Carolyn T. Foreman, *Indian Women Chiefs* (Muskogee, Okla., 1954); Wendell S. Hadlock, "War Among the Northeastern Woodland Indians," *American Anthropologist,* n.s. 49 (1947), 204–21; A. Irving Hallowell, "The Nature and Function of Property as a Social Institution," in Hallowell, *Culture and Experience* (Philadelphia, 1955), 236–49; Bernard G. Hoffman, "Ancient Tribes Revisited; A Summary of Indian Distribution and Movement in the Northeastern United States from 1534 to 1779," *Ethnohistory,* 14 (1967), 1–46; Nathaniel Knowles, "The Torture of Captives by the Indians of Eastern North America," *Proceedings of the American Philosophical Society,* 82 (1940), 151–225; Ralph M. Linton, "Land Tenure in Aboriginal America," in Oliver La Farge, ed., *The Changing Indian* (Norman, Okla., 1942), 42–54; George S. Snyderman, "Concepts of Land Ownership among the Iroquois and Their Neighbors," in William N. Fenton, ed., *Symposium on Local Diversity in Iroquois Culture* (Washington, D.C., 1951), 13–34; and "The Functions of Wampum," *Proceedings of the American Philosophical Society,* 98 (1954), 469–94; Frank G. Speck, "The Family Hunting Band as the Basis of Algonkian Social Organization," *American Anthropologist,* n.s. 17 (1915), 289–305; and "Culture Problems in Northeastern North America," *Proceedings of the American Philosophical Society,* 65 (1926), 272–311; John R. Swanton, *Social Organization and Social Usages in the Southeast* (Washington, D.C., 1928); Ruth M. Underhill, *Red Man's Religion; Beliefs and Practices of the Indians North of Mexico* (Chicago, 1965); Anthony F. C. Wallace, "Political Organization and Land Tenure among the Northeastern Indians, 1600–1830," *Southwest Journal of Anthropology,* 13 (1957), 301–21; and William S. Willis, Jr., "Patrilineal Institutions in Southeastern North America," *Ethnohistory,* 10 (1963), 250–69. In reading these materials students will quickly find that anthropologists, like historians, have fundamental disagreements concerning the conceptualization and interpretation of data recovered from the past. And like historians, they are susceptible to cultural bias.

From studying broad culture groups, one must turn to examining individual cases of contact. Because colonial historians have written primarily about early colonists and anthropologists primarily about native groups, one is obliged to consult the relevant literature from several disciplines. In some cases the approaches have been combined in what is called ethnohistorical analysis. Thus in studying the first major Indian-English confrontation—in the Chesapeake area of Virginia—students must fathom a maze of articles written from a variety of approaches. From the historians have come important works such as Wesley Frank Craven, *The Southern Colonies in the Seventeenth Century, 1607–1689* (Baton Rouge, 1949); "Indian Policy in Early Virginia," *William and Mary Quarterly*, 1 (1944), 65–82; and *White, Red and Black; The Seventeenth-Century Virginian* (Charlottesville, Va., 1971); Edmund S. Morgan, "The Labor Problem at Jamestown, 1607–1618," *American Historical Review*, 76 (1971), 595–611; and "The First American Boom; Virginia 1618 to 1630," *William and Mary Quarterly*, 28 (1971), 169–98; Keith Glenn, "Captain John Smith and the Indians," *Virginia Magazine of History and Biography*, 52 (1944), 228–48; W. Stitt Robinson, Jr., "The Legal Status of the Indian in Colonial Virginia," *Virginia Magazine of History and Biography*, 61 (1953), 249–59; "Tributory Indians in Colonial Virginia," *Virginia Magazine of History and Biography*, 67 (1959), 49–64; and "Virginia and the Cherokees; Indian Policy from Spotswood to Dinwiddie," in Darrett B. Rutman, ed., *The Old Dominion; Essays for Thomas Perkins Abernethy* (Charlottesville, Va., 1964); Wilcomb E. Washburn, *The Governor and the Rebel; A History of Bacon's Rebellion in Virginia* (Chapel Hill, N.C., 1957); and two biographies of Pocahontas whose acceptance of the English colonists and marriage to one of them suggests why she, rather than her father Powhatan, has captured the American imagination: Philip L. Barbour, *Pocahontas and Her World* (Boston, 1969) and Grace Woodward, *Pocahontas* (Norman, Okla., 1969). From the anthropologists and ethnohistorians of early Virginia the following are particularly worthy of attention: Lewis R. Binford, "An Ethnohistory of the Nottoway, Meherran and Weanock Indians of Southeastern Virginia," *Ethnohistory*, 14 (1967), 104–218; David I. Bushnell, Jr., "Virginia before Jamestown," in *Essays in Historical Anthropology of North America* (Washington, D.C., 1940); Christian F. Feest, "Powhatan; A Study in Political Organization," *Wiener Volkerkundlicher Mitteilungen*, 8 (1966), 69–83; Nancy O. Lurie, "Indian Cultural Adjustment to European Civilization," in James M. Smith, ed., *Seventeenth-Century America; Essays in Colonial History* (Chapel Hill, N.C., 1959); Ben C. McCary, *Indians in Seventeenth-Century Virginia* (Williamsburg, Va., 1957); Maurice Mook, "The Anthropological Position of the Indian Tribes of Tidewater Virginia," *William and Mary Quarterly*, 2nd series, 23 (1943), 27–40; and "Algonkian Ethnohistory of the Carolina Sound," *Washington Academy of Sciences Journal*, 34 (1944), 181–97, 213–28; James Mooney, "The-

Powhatan Confederacy, Past and Present," *American Anthropologist*, n.s. 9 (1907), 129–152; Frank G. Speck, *Chapters on the Ethnology of the Powhatan Tribes of Virginia* (New York, 1928); *The Rappahonnock Indians of Virginia* (New York, 1925); and "The Ethnic Position of the Southeastern Algonkian," *American Anthropologist*, n.s. 26, (1924), 184–200; and Theodore Stern, "Chickahominy; The Changing Culture of a Virginia Indian Community," *Proceedings of the American Philosophical Society*, 96 (1952), 152–225.

To the north and south of the Virginian-Powhatan encounter the story of Anglo-Indian relations can be followed in Raphael Semmes, "Aboriginal Maryland, 1608–89," *Maryland Historical Magazine*, 24 (1929), 157–72, 195–209; Francis Jennings, "Glory, Death, and Transfiguration; The Susquehannock Indians in the Seventeenth Century," *Proceedings of the American Philosophical Society*, 112 (1968), 15–53; Jane Henry, "The Choptank Indians of Maryland Under the Proprietary Government," *Maryland Historical Magazine*, 65 (1970), 171–80; Charles M. Hudson, *The Catawba Nation* (Athens, Ga., 1970); and Douglas Rights, *The American Indian in North Carolina* (Durham, N.C., 1947).

The second major case of culture contact between Englishmen and native North Americans in the seventeenth century came in New England. Students can learn much about the English colonists in the Puritan studies listed in Alden T. Vaughan's *The American Colonies in the Seventeenth Century* and in the works discussed in Michael McGiffert's "Puritan Studies in the 1960's," *William and Mary Quarterly*, 27 (1970), 36–67. Of special importance in understanding cultural interaction are three works which probe the Puritan mind for characteristics that imparted a special quality to the Puritan approach to Indian affairs: James Axtell, "The Scholastic Philosophy of the Wilderness," *William and Mary Quarterly*, 29 (1972), 335–66; Peter N. Carroll, *Puritanism and the Wilderness; The Intellectual Significance of the New England Frontier, 1629–1700* (New York, 1969); and Roy H. Pearce, "The 'Ruines of Mankind'; The Indian and the Puritan Mind," *Journal of the History of Ideas*, 13 (1952), 200–17.

Widely divergent opinions are held by historians on how the Puritans intended to conduct their relations with people of a different culture. The labels "coexistence" and "coercion" can stand for the two approaches that historians have discerned. Both interpretations are well amplified in the following works: Leonard A. Adolf, "Squanto's Role in Pilgrim Diplomacy," *Ethnohistory*, 11 (1964), 247–61; David Bushnell, "The Treatment of the Indians in Plymouth Colony," *New England Quarterly*, 26 (1953), 193–218; Jack L. Davis, "Roger Williams among the Narragansett Indians," *New England Quarterly*, 43 (1970), 593–604; Gordon M. Day, "English-Indian Contacts in New England," *Ethnohistory*, 9

(1962), 24–40; Chester E. Eisinger, "The Puritans' Justification for Taking the Land," *Essex Institute Historical Collections,* 84 (1948), 131–43; Francis Jennings, "Virgin Land and Savage People," *American Quarterly,* 23 (1971), 519–41; Yasu Kawashima, "Legal Origins of the Indian Reservation in Colonial Massachusetts," *American Journal of Legal History,* 13 (1969), 42–56; and "Jurisdiction of the Colonial Courts over the Indians in Massachusetts, 1689–1763," *New England Quarterly,* 42 (1969), 532–50; Douglas E. Leach, *Flintlock and Tomahawk; New England in King Philip's War* (New York, 1958); John Sainsbury, "Miantonomo's Death and New England Politics, 1630–1645," *Rhode Island History,* 30 (1971), 111–23; Alden T. Vaughan, *New England Frontier; Puritans and Indians, 1620–1675* (Boston, 1965); Wilcomb E. Washburn, "Governor Berkeley and King Philip's War," *New England Quarterly,* 30 (1957), 363–77; Alvin G. Weeks, *Massasoit of the Wampanoags* (Fall River, Mass., 1920); George F. Willison, *Saints and Strangers* (New York, 1945); and Harry A. Wright, "The Technique of Seventeenth-Century Indian-Land Purchases," *Essex Institute Historical Collections,* 77 (1941), 185–97. Anthropological contributions have been made by M. K. Bennett, "The Food Economy of the New England Indians, 1605–75," *Journal of Political Economy,* 63 (1955), 369–97; Regina Flannery, *An Analysis of Coastal Algonquian Culture* (Washington, D.C., 1939); and Froelich G. Rainey, *A Compilation of Historical Data Contributing to the Ethnography of Connecticut and Southern New England Indians* (New Haven, 1936).

No Indian group in eastern North America has been more studied by historians and anthropologists than the Iroquois, whose geographical position placed them in close contact for two centuries with European settlers from France, Holland, and England. Both anthropologists and historians are represented in the following selection, which represents only an introduction to Iroquois studies: William N. Fenton, "Problems Arising from the Historic Northeastern Position of the Iroquois," in *Essays in Historical Anthropology of North America* (Washington, D.C., 1940); James T. Flexner, *Mohawk Baronet: Sir William Johnson of New York* (New York, 1959); Barbara Graymont, *The Iroquois in the American Revolution* (Syracuse, N.Y., 1972); Thomas Robert Henry, *Wilderness Messiah: The Story of Hiawatha and the Iroquois* (New York, 1955); George T. Hunt, *The Wars of the Iroquois; A Study in Intertribal Relations* (Madison, Wis., 1940); Francis Jennings, "The Constitutional Evolution of the Covenant Chain," *Proceedings of the American Philosophical Society,* 115 (1971), 88–96; Georgiana C. Nammack, *Fraud, Politics, and the Dispossession of the Indians; The Iroquois Land Frontier in the Colonial Period* (Norman, Okla., 1969); Arthur C. Parker, *History of the*

Seneca Indians (Port Washington, N.Y., 1967); Cara B. Richards, "Matriarchy or Mistake; The Role of Iroquois Women through Time," in Verne F. Ray, ed., *Cultural Stability and Cultural Change, Proceedings of the 1957 . . . Meeting of the American Ethnological Society* (Seattle, 1957), 36–45; George S. Snyderman, "Behind the Tree of Peace; A Sociological Analysis of Iroquois Warfare," *Pennsylvania Archaeologist*, 18 (1948), 2–93; Allen W. Trelease, *Indian Affairs in Colonial New York; The Seventeenth Century* (Ithaca, N.Y., 1960); Anthony F. C. Wallace, "The Dekanawidah Myth Analysed as the Record of a Revitalization Myth," *Ethnohistory*, 5 (1958), 118–30; "Dreams and the Wishes of the Soul; A Type of Psychoanalytic Theory among the Seventeeth-Century Iroquois," *American Anthropologist*, 60 (1958), 234–48; "Origins of Iroquois Neutrality; The Grand Settlement of 1701," *Pennsylvania History*, 24 (1957), 223–35; and *The Death and Rebirth of the Seneca* (New York, 1969).

Of special interest to students of Indian-European relations, because it casts grave doubts on the thesis so widely enunciated by white historians that conflict was inevitable between cultural groups as widely separated as Algonquians and Europeans, is the interaction of the Pennsylvania Quakers and the Delaware (Lenni Lenape) Indians. Both the early Quaker contacts with the Delawares and the subsequent breakdown of amicable relations are detailed in the following selections: Thomas E. Drake, "Penn's Experiment in Race Relations," *Pennsylvania Magazine of History and Biography*, 68 (1944), 372–87; Francis Jennings, "The Delaware Interregnum," *Pennsylvania Magazine of History and Biography*, 89 (1965), 174–98; Rayner W. Kelsey, *Friends and the Indians, 1655–1917* (Philadelphia, 1917); W. W. Newcomb, Jr., *The Culture and Acculturation of the Delaware Indians* (Ann Arbor, Mich., 1956); Theodore G. Thayer, "The Friendly Association," *Pennsylvania Magazine of History and Biography*, 67 (1943), 356–76; Frederick B. Tolles, "Nonviolent Contact; the Quakers and the Indians," *Proceedings of the American Philosophical Society*, 107 (1963), 93–101; Sherman P. Uhler, *Pennsylvania's Indian Relations to 1754* (Allentown, Pa., 1951); Anthony F. C. Wallace, *King of the Delawares; Teedyuscung, 1700–1763* (Philadelphia, 1949); Paul A. W. Wallace, *Indians in Pennsylvania* (Harrisburg, Pa., 1961); and C. A. Weslager, *The Delaware Indians; A History* (New Brunswick, N.J., 1972).

Because it was not settled until the last third of the seventeenth century the southeast was the last zone of Anglo-Indian contact in the colonization of North America. But interaction between the English settlers of the Carolinas and Georgia with the Creeks and Cherokees, the two most powerful tribes of this region, is among the most instructive examples of culture contact because these powerful tribes, like the Iroquois, maintained their political power and cultural integrity long after the smaller coastal tribes had been decimated or made subordinate. This complex confrontation, which involved shifting alliances between the three European powers contending for advantage in the area and the two Indian powers seeking preeminency must be followed in both historical and anthropological accounts. The best of them are: John P. Brown, *Old Frontiers; The Story of the Cherokee Indians from Earliest Times to the Date of Their Removal to the West* (Kingsport, Tenn., 1938); David H. Corkran, *The Cherokee Frontier; Conflict and Survival, 1740–62* (Norman, Okla., 1962); and *The Creek Frontier, 1540–1783* (Norman, Okla., 1967); John P. Corry, *Indian Affairs in Georgia, 1732–56* (Philadelphia, 1936); R. S. Cotterill, *The Southern Indians; The Story of the Civilized Tribes before Removal* (Norman, Okla., 1954); E. Merton Coulter, "Mary Musgrove, 'Queen of the Creeks'; A Chapter of Early Georgia Troubles," *Georgia Historical Quarterly*, 11 (1927), 1–30; Verner W. Crane, *The Southern Frontier, 1670–1732* (Ann Arbor, Mich., 1929); Frederick Gearing, *Priests and Warriors; Social Structures for Cherokee Politics in the 18th Century* (Menasha, Wis., 1962); Mary R. Haas, "Creek Inter-town Relations," *American Anthropologist*, 42 (1940), 479–89; Charles M. Hudson, ed., *Red, White and Black; Symposium on Indians in the Old South* (Athens, Ga., 1971); Robert L. Meriwether, *The Expansion of South Carolina, 1729–1765* (Kingsport, Tenn., 1940); Chapman J. Milling, *Red Carolinians* (Chapel Hill, N.C., 1940); James Mooney, *Myths of the Cherokee* (Washington, D.C., 1900); Morris E. Opler, "The Creek 'Town' and the Problem of Creek Indian Political Reorganization," in Edward H. Spicer, ed., *Human Problems in Technological Change; A Casebook* (New York, 1952); Hale G. Smith, *The European and the Indian; European-Indian Contacts in Georgia and Florida* (Gainesville, Fla., 1956); Alexander Spoehr, *Changing Kinship Systems; A Study in the Acculturation of the Creeks, Cherokees, and Choctaws* (Chicago, 1947); John R. Swanton, *The Indians of the Southeastern United States* (Washington, D.C., 1946); *Indian Tribes of Lower Mississippi Valley and Adjacent Coast of the Gulf of Mexico* (Washington, D.C., 1911); and *Early History of the Creek Indians and Their Neighbors* (Washington, D.C., 1922); and Grace Steele Woodward, *The Cherokees* (Norman, Okla., 1963). Two valuable accounts of smaller coastal tribes in the southeast are John T. Juricek, "The Westo Indians," *Ethnohistory*, 11 (1964), 134–73, and James W. Covington, "Apalachee Indians 1704–1763," *Florida Historical Quarterly*, 50 (1972), 366–84.

In the national imagination and in the more popular forms of historical literature warfare has always stood out as the crucial element in Indian-white relations. But three aspects of the acculturative process—disease, trade, and religion—deserve much greater emphasis. Of the three, trade is especially important, for along the trade routes went not only material goods but microorganisms and ideology as well. For various aspects of the Indian trade and for different assessments of its conduct and importance the following contributions are among the most significant in the last generation of scholarship: W. Neil Franklin, "Pennsylvania-Virginia Rivalry for the Indian Trade of the Ohio Valley," *Mississippi Valley Historical Review*, 20 (1934), 463–80; "Virginia and the Cherokee Indian Trade, 1673–1752," *East Tennessee Historical Society Publications*, 4 (1932), 3–21; and "Virginia and the Cherokee Indian Trade, 1753–1775," *East Tennessee Historical Society Publications*, 5 (1933), 22–38; H. B. Fant, "The Indian Trade Policy of the Trustees for Establishing the Colony of Georgia in America," *Georgia Historical Quarterly*, 15 (1931), 207–22; Harold A. Innis, *The Fur Trade in Canada* (New Haven, 1930); Philip M. Hamer, "Anglo-French Rivalry in the Cherokee Country, 1754–1757," *North Carolina Historical Review*, 2 (1925), 303–22; Charles A. Hanna, *The Wilderness Trail, or The Ventures and Adventures of the Pennsylvania Traders on the Allegheny Path*, 2 vols. (New York, 1911); Wilbur R. Jacobs, "Unsavory Sidelights on the Colonial Fur Trade," *New York History*, 34 (1953), 135–48; Francis Jennings, "The Indian Trade of the Susquehanna Valley," *Proceedings of the American Philosophical Society*, 110 (1966), 406–24; Jean Lunn, *The Illegal Fur Trade out of New France, 1713–60* (Toronto, 1939); John McManus, "An Economic Analysis of Indian Behavior in the North American Fur Trade," *Journal of Economic History*, 32 (1972), 36–53; Francis X. Moloney, *The Fur Trade in New England, 1620–1676* (Cambridge, 1931); Walter O'Meara, *Daughters of the Country; The Women of the Fur Traders and Mountain Men* (New York, 1959); Mary Rothroch, "Carolina Traders among the Overhill Cherokees, 1690 to 1760," *East Tennessee Historical Society Publications*, 1 (1929), 3–18; Lewis O. Saum, *The Fur Trader and the Indian* (Seattle, 1965); Allen W. Trelease, "The Iroquois and the Western Fur Trade," *Mississippi Valley Historical Review*, 49 (1962), 32–51; and the previously mentioned works by Eccles and Trelease.

On the role of disease in Indian-European relations see P. M. Ashburn, *The Ranks of Death; A Medical History of the Conquest of America*, ed. Frank D. Ashburn (New York, 1947); Alfred W. Crosby, Jr., *The Columbian Exchange; Biological and Cultural Consequences of 1492* (Westport, Conn., 1972); John Duffy, "Smallpox and the Indians of the American Colonies," *Bulletin of the History of Medicine*, 25 (1951), 324–41; and E. Wagner and Allen E. Stearn, *The Effect of Smallpox on the*

Destiny of the Amerindian (Boston, 1945). Alcohol, another form of disease brought by Europeans to Indian societies in the view of many historians and anthropologists, is reexamined in Nancy Oestreich Lurie, "The World's Oldest On-Going Protest Demonstration; North American Indian Drinking Patterns," *Pacific Historical Review*, 40 (1971), 311–32 and Craig MacAndrew and Robert B. Edgerton, *Drunken Comportment; A Social Explanation* (Chicago, 1969).

English missionary activity, which must be seen in a political as well as religious context, is analyzed in G. Gordon Brown, "Missions and Cultural Diffusion," *American Journal of Sociology*, 50 (1944), 214–19; R. Pierce Beaver, "Methods in American Missions to the Indians in the Seventeenth and Eighteenth Centuries; Calvinist Models for Protestant Foreign Missions," *Journal of Presbyterian History*, 47 (1969), 124–48; Elma Gray, *Wilderness Christians; The Moravian Mission to the Delaware Indians* (Ithaca, N.Y., 1956); H. Ward Jackson, "The Seventeenth-Century Mission to the Iroquois," *Historical Magazine of the Protestant-Episcopal Church*, 29 (1960), 240–55; Francis Jennings, "Goals and Functions of the Puritan Missions to the Indians," *Ethnohistory*, 18 (1971), 197–212; Frank J. Klingberg, *Anglican Humanitarianism in Colonial New York* (Philadelphia, 1940); Juan A. Ortega y Medina, "An Analysis of the Missionary Methods of the Puritans," *The Americas*, 14 (1957–58), 125–34; Sidney H. Rooy, *The Theology of Missions in the Puritan Tradition* (Delft, 1965); Norman E. Tanis, "Education in John Eliot's Indian Utopias, 1646–1675," *History of Education Quarterly*, 10 (1970), 308–23; Ola E. Winslow, *John Eliot; "Apostle to the Indians"* (Boston, 1968); W. Stitt Robinson, "Indian Education and Missions in Colonial Virginia," *Journal of Southern History*, 18 (1952): 152–68, and in the previously mentioned work by Vaughan. Fruitful comparisons can be made with French and Spanish Catholic missionary efforts by reading these works conjunctively with the earlier mentioned books by O'Neill, Kennedy, Eccles, and Hanke.

Acculturation, of course, was a two-way process. On "Indianization" of European colonists some especially valuable works are: Erwin H. Ackerknecht, "White Indians," *Bulletin of the History of Medicine*, 15 (1944), 18–35; Marius Barbeau, "Indian Captivities," *Proceedings of the American Philosophical Society*, 94 (1950), 522–48; Thomas A. Boyd, *Simon Girty; The White Savage* (New York, 1928); Felix S. Cohen, "Americanizing the White Man," in Lucy Kramer Cohen, ed., *The Legal Conscience; Selected Papers of Felix S. Cohen* (New Haven, 1960); A. Irving Hallowell, "The Backwash of the Frontier; The Impact of the Indian on American Culture," in Walker D. Wyman and Clifton B. Kroeber, eds., *The Frontier in Perspective* (Madison, Wis., 1957); and "American Indians, White and Black; The Phenomenon of Transculturalization," *Current Anthropology*, 4 (1963), 519–31; J. Norman Heard, *White into Red; A Study of the Assimilation of White Persons Captured by Indians* (Metuchen, N.J., 1973); Alvin M. Josephy, Jr., *The Indian Heritage of America* (New York, 1968); Roy H. Pearce, "The Significance of the Captivity Narrative," *American Literature*, 19 (1947), 1–20; and *Savagism and Civilization; A Study of the Indian and the American Mind* (Baltimore, 1965).

Afro-American History

Afro-American history begins in Africa and students who wish to learn more about the Atlantic slave trade and the initial phases of the enslavement process should first gain a basic understanding of African cultures at the time of initial contact with Europeans. A good place to begin is with Basil Davidson, *The Africans Genius; An Introduction to African Social and Cultural History* (Boston, 1969). Davidson's valuable bibliography will lead students to other important works.

The slave trade should be considered in an international context. Among the many contributions to the literature of this commerce, which was to play such a crucial role in the development of colonial societies in the New World, the following are especially important: Basil Davidson, *The African Slave Trade; Pre-Colonial History, 1450–1850* (Boston, 1961); Philip D. Curtin, *The Atlantic Slave Trade; A Census* (Madison, Wis., 1969); K. G. Davies, *The Royal African Company* (London, 1957); Elizabeth Donnan, "The Slave Trade into South Carolina before the Revolution," *American Historical Review*, 33 (1927–28), 804–28; Peter Duignan and Clarence Clendenen, *The United States and the African Slave Trade, 1619–1862* (Stanford, 1963); J. D. Fage, "Slavery and the Slave Trade in the Context of West African History," *Journal of African History*, 10 (1969), 393–404; Daniel P. Mannix and Malcolm Cowley, *Black Cargoes; A History of the Atlantic Slave Trade, 1518–1865* (New York, 1962); James Pope-Hennessy, *Sins of the Fathers; A Study of the Atlantic Slave Traders, 1441–1807* (New York, 1968); Walter Rodney, *West Africa and the Atlantic Slave Trade* (Nairobi, 1969); "Upper Guinea and the Significance of the Origins of Africans Enslaved in the New World," *Journal of Negro History*, 54 (1969), 327–45; and "African Slavery and Other Forms of Social Oppression on the Upper Guinea Coast in the Context of the Atlantic Slave Trade," *Journal of African History*, 7 (1966), 431–43; and A. P. Thornton, "The Organization of the Slave Trade in the English West Indies, 1660–1685," *William and Mary Quarterly*, 12 (1955), 399–409.

Some general works on slavery which deal with the origins of the labor system in the New World are Roger T. Anstey, "Capitalism and Slavery;

A Critique," *Economic History Review*, 21 (1968), 307–20; David Brion Davis, *The Problem of Slavery in Western Culture* (Ithaca, N.Y., 1966); Stanley M. Elkins, *Slavery; A Problem in American Institutional and Intellectual Life* (Chicago, 1959); Oscar and Mary F. Handlin, "Origins of the Southern Labor System," *William and Mary Quarterly*, 7 (1950), 199–222; Robert C. Haywood, "Mercantilism and Colonial Slave Labor, 1700–1763," *Journal of Southern History*, 23 (1957), 454–69; C. L. R. James, "The Atlantic Slave Trade and Slavery; Some Interpretations of Their Significance in the Development of the United States and the Western World," *Amistad*, 1 (1970), 119–64; Wilbert E. Moore, "Slave Law and the Social Structure," *Journal of Negro History*, 26 (1941), 171–202; Edmund S. Morgan, "Slavery and Freedom; An American Paradox," *Journal of American History*, 59 (1972), 3–21; and Eric Williams, *Capitalism and Slavery* (Chapel Hill, N.C., 1944).

More specialized studies of slavery in the southern colonies in the colonial period are Jonathan L. Alpert, "The Origin of Slavery in the United States; The Maryland Precedent," *American Journal of Legal History*, 14 (1970), 189–221; John S. Bassett, *Slavery and Servitude in the Colony of North Carolina* (Baltimore, 1896); James Curtis Ballagh, *A History of Slavery in Virginia* (Baltimore, 1902); Jeffrey R. Brackett, *The Negro in Maryland; A Study in the Institution of Slavery* (Baltimore, 1889); James M. Clifton, "A Half-Century of a Georgia Rice Plantation," *North Carolina Historical Review*, 47 (1970), 368–415; Wesley Frank Craven, *White, Red and Black; The Seventeenth-Century Virginian* (Charlottesville, Va., 1971); Adele Hast, "The Legal Status of the Negro in Virginia, 1705–1765," *Journal of Negro History*, 54 (1969), 217–39; Alice R. Huger Smith, *A Carolina Rice Plantation of the Fifties* (New York, 1936); Edward McCrady, "Slavery in the Province of South Carolina, 1670–1770," *American Historical Association Report* (Washington, D.C., 1895), 631–73; James A. Padgett, "The Status of Slaves in Colonial North Carolina," *Journal of Negro History*, 14 (1929), 300–27; Paul C. Palmer, "Servant into Slave; The Evolution of the Legal Status of the Negro Laborer in Colonial Virginia," *South Atlantic Quarterly*, 65 (1966), 355–70; Wilbur H. Siebert, "Slavery and White Servitude in East Florida, 1726–1776," *Florida Historical Quarterly*, 10 (1931), 3–23; M. Eugene Sirmans, "The Legal Status of the Slave in South Carolina, 1670–1740," *Journal of Southern History*, 28 (1962), 426–73; Thad W. Tate, Jr., *The Negro in Eighteenth-Century Williamsburg* (Williamsburg, Va., 1965); Rosser H. Taylor, *Slaveholding in North Carolina; An Economic View* (Chapel Hill, N.C., 1926); Darold D. Wax, "Georgia and the Negro Before the American Revolution," *Georgia Historical Quarterly*, 51 (1967), 63–77; and Thomas Jackson Woofter, *Black Yeomanry; Life on St. Helena Island* (New York, 1930).

Among the studies of northern slavery in the colonial period, the most important are Henry S. Cooley, *A Study of Slavery in New Jersey* (Baltimore, 1896); Lorenzo J. Greene, *The Negro in Colonial New England, 1620–1776* (New York, 1942); Winthrop D. Jordan, "The Influence of the West Indies on the Origins of New England Slavery," *William and Mary Quarterly*, 18 (1961), 243–50; Edgar J. McManus, *Black Bondage in the North* (Syracuse, N.Y., 1973); and *Negro Slavery in New York* (Syracuse, N.Y., 1966); Simeon F. Moss, "The Persistence of Slavery and Involuntary Servitude in a Free State (1685–1866)," *Journal of Negro History*, 35 (1950), 289–314; Gary B. Nash, "Slaves and Slaveholders in Colonial Philadelphia," *William and Mary Quarterly*, 30 (1973), 223–56; Edward R. Turner, *The Negro in Pennsylvania; Slavery, Servitude, Freedom, 1639–1861* (Washington, D.C. 1911); Richard C. Twombly and Robert H. Moore, "Black Puritan; The Negro in Seventeenth-Century Massachusetts," *William and Mary Quarterly*, 24 (1967), 224–42; Darold D. Wax, "Quaker Merchants and the Slave Trade in Colonial Pennsylvania," *Pennsylvania Magazine of History and Biography*, 86 (1962), 143–59.

Comparative studies of slavery in the last generation have done more to increase our understanding of American slavery than almost any other conceptual approach to the history of this institution. Thus students will want to examine slavery outside of North America, both in English colonies in the West Indies and in the colonies of Spain, Portugal, France, and Holland. The field of comparative slave studies is growing enormously and only a fraction of the many studies can be mentioned here. But of special importance are studies that compare two or more slave societies, such as Carl N. Degler, *Neither Black Nor White; Slavery and Race Relations in Brazil and the United States* (New York, 1971); Marvin Harris, *Patterns of Race in the Americas* (New York, 1964); Herbert S. Klein, *Slavery in the Americas; A Comparative Study of Virginia and Cuba* (Chicago, 1967); and Frank Tannenbaum, *Slave and Citizen; The Negro in the Americas* (New York, 1946). Further insights into this literature can be gained by consulting Eugene D. Genovese and Laura Foner, eds., *Slavery in the New World; A Reader in Comparative History* (Englewood Cliffs, N.J., 1969) and Genovese, "Materialism and Idealism in the History of Negro Slavery in the Americas," *Journal of Social History*, 1 (1967–68), 371–94. Valuable studies of seventeenth- and eighteenth-century slavery in individual colonies outside of North America are Ronald H. Chilcote, ed., *Protest and Resistance in Angola and Brazil* (Berkeley, Calif., 1972); Harry J. Bennett, *Bondsmen and Bishops; Slavery and Apprenticeship on the Codrington Plantations of Barbados, 1710–1838* (Berkeley, Calif., 1958); Richard S. Dunn, *Sugar and Slaves; The Rise of the Planter Class in the British West Indies, 1624–1713* (Chapel Hill, N.C., 1972); Florestan Fernandes, *The Negro in Brazilian*

Society (New York, 1969); Elsa V. Goveia, *Slave Society in the British Leeward Islands at the End of the Eighteenth Century* (New Haven, 1965); Gwendolyn M. Hall, *Social Control in Slave Plantation Societies* (Baltimore, 1972); Orlando Patterson, *The Sociology of Slavery; An Analysis of the Origins, Development and Structure of Negro Slave Society in Jamaica* (London, 1967); and Frank W. Pitman, "Slavery on the British West India Plantations in the Eighteenth Century," *Journal of Negro History*, 11 (1926), 584–668.

The connections between racism and slavery are intimate. The major work in this area is Winthrop D. Jordan, *White Over Black; American Attitudes Toward the Negro, 1550–1812* (Chapel Hill, N.C., 1968). Jordan's book can be supplemented by Milton Cantor, "The Image of the Negro in Colonial Literature," *New England Quarterly*, 36 (1963), 452–77; Carl N. Degler, "Slavery and the Genesis of American Race Prejudice," *Comparative Studies in History and Society*, 2 (1959), 49–66; and Lawrence Lerner, "The Machiavel and the Moor," *Essays in Criticism*, 9 (1959), 339–60. Also profitable are the psychoanalytical and anthropological approaches of Erik H. Erikson, "The Concept of Identity in Race Relations," *Daedalus*, 95 (1966), 145–71 and John R. Swanton, "Notes on the Mental Assimilation of Races," *Journal of the Washington Academy of Sciences*, 16 (1926), 493–502.

A number of special topics concerning the evolution of Afro-American society in colonial America deserve attention. Miscegenation and the status of the mulatto is of great importance. It is dealt with comprehensively in the previously mentioned work of Winthrop Jordan and Carl Degler and also in Carter G. Woodson, "The Beginnings of Miscegenation of the Whites and Blacks," *Journal of Negro History*, 3 (1918), 335–53; Winthrop D. Jordan, "American Chiaroscuro; The Status and Definition of Mulattoes in the British Colonies," *William and Mary Quarterly*, 19 (1962), 183–200; and Edward B. Reuter, *The Mulatto in the United States* (Boston, 1918).

Slave resistance is studied in many of the works already mentioned but is the special concern of the following studies: Raymond A. Bauer and Alice H. Bauer, "Day to Day Resistance to Slavery," *Journal of Negro History*, 27 (1942), 388–419; Thomas J. Davis, "The New York Slave Conspiracy of 1741 as Black Protest," *Journal of Negro History*, 56 (1971), 17–30; Marion D. duB. Kilson, "Towards Freedom; An Analysis of Slave Revolts in the United States," *Phylon*, 25 (1964), 175–87; Gerald W. Mullin, *Flight and Rebellion; Slave Resistance in Eighteenth-Century Virginia* (New York, 1972); Ferenc M. Szasz, "The New York Slave Revolt of 1741; A Re-Examination," *New York History*, 48 (1967), 215–30; and Darold D. Wax, "Negro Resistance to the Early American Slave Trade," *Journal of Negro History*, 51 (1966), 1–15.

Important works on the manumission of slaves and the role of the free Negro in colonial society, also studied in many of the more general histories mentioned above, include James H. Brewer, "Negro Property Owners in Seventeenth-Century Virginia," *William and Mary Quarterly*, 12 (1955), 575–80; David W. Cohen and Jack P. Greene, eds., *Neither Slave Nor Free; The Freedman of African Descent in the Slave Societies of the New World* (Baltimore, 1972); John D. Duncan, "Slave Emancipation in Colonial South Carolina," *American Chronicle: A Magazine of History*, 1 (1972), 64–66; C. Ashley Ellefson, "Free Jupiter and the Rest of the World; The Problems of a Free Negro in Colonial Maryland," *Maryland Historical Magazine*, 66 (1971), 1–13; John H. Russell, *The Free Negro in Virginia, 1619–1865* (Baltimore, 1913); Elaine MacEacheren, "Emancipation and Slavery in Massachusetts; A Re-examination, 1770–1790," *Journal of Negro History*, 55 (1970), 289–306; and James W. Wright, *The Free Negro in Maryland, 1634–1860* (New York, 1921).

The best study of early abolitionist thought is David B. Davis, *The Problem of Slavery in Western Culture*. Also see Thomas E. Drake, *Quakers and Slavery in America* (New Haven, 1950); W. E. B. DuBois, *The Suppression of the African Slave Trade* (New York, 1896); Wylie Sypher, *Guinea's Captive Kings; British Anti-Slavery Literature of the Eighteenth Century* (Chapel Hill, N.C., 1942); and Arthur Zilversmit, *The First Emancipation; The Abolition of Slavery in the North* (Chicago, 1967).

The conversion of the African slave to the Christian religion, an important element in the acculturative experience, is studied in Denzil T. Clifton, "Anglicanism and Negro Slavery in Colonial America," *Historical Magazine of the Protestant-Episcopal Church*, 39 (1970), 29–70; Mary F. Goodwin, "Christianizing and Educating the Negro in Colonial Virginia," *Historical Magazine of the Protestant-Episcopal Church*, 1 (1932), 143–52; Marcus W. Jernegan, "Slavery and Conversion in the American Colonies," *American Historical Review*, 21 (1915–16), 504–27; Jerome W. Jones, "The Established Virginia Church and the Conversion of Negroes and Indians, 1620–1760," *Journal of Negro History*, 46 (1961), 12–23; Frank J. Klingberg, "The African Immigrant in Colonial Pennsylvania and Delaware," *Historical Magazine of the Protestant-Episcopal Church*, 11 (1942), 126–53; James B. Lawrence, "The Religious Education of the Negro in the Colony of Georgia," *Georgia Historical Quarterly*, 14 (1930), 41–57; Edgar L. Pennington, "The Work of the Bray Associates in Pennsylvania," *Pennsylvania Magazine of History and Biography*, 58 (1934), 1–25; and "Thomas Bray's Associates and Their Work Among the Negroes," *American Antiquarian Society Proceedings*, n.s., 48 (1938), 311–403; and Douglas C. Strange, " 'A Compassionate Mother to Her Poor Negro Slaves': The Lutheran Church and Negro Slavery in Early America," *Phylon*, 29 (1968), 272–81. But these studies should be considered not only from the viewpoint of white religious effort, as all too often has been the case, but from the vantage point of the black response to white European culture. This requires studying cultural characteristics as they existed in the African societies from which slaves were taken and the adaptation of these characteristics in a new physical and cultural environment. Among the work of anthropologists, ethnomusicologists, and historians which students may profitably consult are William R. Bascom, "Acculturation Among the Gullah Negroes," *American Anthropologist*, 43 (1941), 43–50; Roger Bastide, *African Civilizations in the New World* (New York, 1971); John W. Blassingame, *The Slave Community; Plantation Life in the Ante-Bellum South* (New York, 1972); Melville J. Herskovits, *The Myth of the Negro Past* (Boston, 1941); W. Robert Higgins, "The Geographical Origins of Negro Slaves in Colonial South Carolina," *South Atlantic Quarterly*, 70 (1971), 34–47; Lawrence W. Levine, "Slave Songs and Slave Consciousness; An Exploration in Neglected Sources," in Tamara K. Hareven, ed., *Anonymous Americans; Explorations in Nineteenth-Century Social History* (Englewood Cliffs, N.J., 1971); John Lovell, Jr., *Black Song: The Forge and the Flame* (New York, 1972); John S. Mbiti, *African Religions and Philosophy* (New York, 1969); Sidney W. Mintz, "Toward an Afro-American History," *Journal of World History*, 13 (1971), 317–31; John Rublowsky, *Black Music in America* (New York, 1971); Eileen Southern, *The Music of Black Americans; A History* (New York, 1971); Lorenzo D. Turner, "African Survivals in the New World with Special Emphasis on the Arts," in John A. Davis, ed., *Africa from the Point of View of American Negro Scholars* (Paris, 1958); Norman E. Whitten, Jr. and John F. Szwed, eds., *Afro-American Anthropology; Contemporary Perspectives* (New York, 1970); and William S. Willis, Jr., "Anthropology and Negroes on the Southern Colonial Frontier," in James C. Curtis and Lewis L. Gould, eds., *The Black Experience in America* (Austin, Tex., 1970).

Indian slavery, widely practiced by English colonists for several generations, is conspicuous for its absence in the historical literature. But see Almon W. Lauber, *Indian Slavery in Colonial Times Within the Present Limits of the United States* (New York, 1913) and Sanford Winston, "Indian Slavery in the Carolina Region," *Journal of Negro History*, 19 (1934), 431–40.

Another aspect of intercultural contact in early America was that between African and Indians. Much remains to be done in this area but some glimpses into the problem can be gained by consulting Laurence Foster, *Negro-Indian Relationships in the Southeast* (Philadelphia, 1935); Peter B. Hammond, "Afro-Americans, Indians, and Afro-Asians; Cultural Contacts Between Africa and the Peoples of Asia and Aboriginal America," in Gwendolan M. Carter and Ann Paden, eds., *Expanding Horizons in African Studies* (Evanston, Ill., 1969); John M. Lofton, Jr., "White, Indian, and Negro Contacts in Colonial South Carolina," *Southern Indian Studies*, 1 (1949), 3–12; Kenneth W. Porter, "Relations between Negroes and Indians within the Present Limits of the United States," *Journal of Negro History*, 17 (1932), 287–367; and "Negroes on the Southern Frontier, 1670–1763," *Journal of Negro History*, 33 (1948), 53–78; and William S. Willis, Jr., "Divide and Rule; Red, White and Black in the Southeast," *Journal of Negro History*, 48 (1963), 157–76.

Rivalry for North America

International rivalry for the North American continent has been the subject of a vast literature, mostly cast in the genre of political or military history. Almost every item of importance is listed in the bibliography by Jack P. Greene listed earlier and, for the period just before the American Revolution, in John Shy, *The American Revolution* (Northbrook, Ill., 1973). Works that deal primarily with the role of Indian societies in this struggle for the eastern half of the continent, and which have importance for social and cultural as well as political and military history, are John R. Alden, *John Stuart and the Southern Colonial Frontier; A Study of Indian Relations, War, Trade, and Land Problems in the Southern Wilderness, 1754–1775* (Ann Arbor, Mich., 1944); Richmond P. Bond, *Queen Anne's American Kings* (Oxford, 1952); Julian P. Boyd, ed., *Indian Treaties Printed by Benjamin Franklin, 1736–1762* (Philadelphia, 1938); Kenneth Coleman, "The Southern Frontier; Georgia's Founding and the Expansion of South Carolina," *Georgia Historical Quarterly*, 56 (1972), 163–74; Louis DeVorsey, Jr., *The Indian Boundary in the Southern Colonies, 1763–75* (Chapel Hill, N.C., 1966); Randolph C. Downes, *Council Fires on the Upper Ohio; A Narrative of Indian Affairs in the Upper Ohio Valley Until 1795* (Pittsburgh, 1940); Lawrence Henry Gipson, *The British Empire Before the American Revolution*, 14 vols., (New York, 1958–69); Charles S. Grant, "Pontiac's Rebellion and the British Troop Moves of 1763," *Mississippi Valley Historical Review*, 40 (1953), 75–88; Wilbur R. Jacobs, *Diplomacy and Indian Gifts; Anglo-French Rivalry along the Ohio and Northwest Frontiers, 1748–1763* (Stanford, 1950); *Indians of the Southern Colonial Frontier; The Edmond Atkin Report and Plan of 1755* (Columbia, S.C., 1954); and "Wampum; The Protocol of Indian Diplomacy," *William and Mary Quarterly*, 6 (1949), 596–604; Douglas E. Leach, *The Northern Colonial Frontier, 1607–1763* (New York, 1966); Charles H. McIlwain, ed., Introduction to *An Abridgement of the Indian Affairs . . . Transacted in the Colony of New York, from the Year 1678 to the Year 1751, by Peter*

Wraxall (Cambridge, 1915); John K. Mahon, "Anglo-American Methods of Indian Warfare, 1676–1794," *Mississippi Valley Historical Review*, 45 (1958), 254–75; Ronald D. Martin, "Confrontation at the Monongahela; Climax of the French Drive into the Upper Ohio Region," *Pennsylvania History*, 37 (1970), 133–50; William T. Morgan, "The Five Nations and Queen Anne," *Mississippi Valley Historical Review*, 13 (1926), 167–89; Howard H. Peckham, *Pontiac and the Indian Uprising* (Princeton, N.J., 1947); Dawson A. Phelps, "The Chickasaw, the English, and the French, 1699–1744," *Tennessee Historical Quarterly*, 16 (1957), 117–33; Helen L. Shaw, *British Administration of the Southern Indians, 1756–1783* (Lancaster, Pa., 1931); Jack M. Sosin, *Whitehall and the Wilderness; The Middle West in British Colonial Policy, 1760–1775* (Lincoln, Neb., 1961); Paul A. W. Wallace, *Conrad Weiser, 1696–1760; Friend of Colonist and Mohawk* (Philadelphia, 1945); and Nicholas B. Wainwright, *George Croghan; Wilderness Diplomat* (Chapel Hill, N.C., 1959). For nativistic movements, which were an important part of the eighteenth-century Indian response to changing conditions of contact with European colonizers, see Ralph Linton, "Nativistic Movements," *American Anthropologist*, 45 (1943), 230–40; Anthony F. C. Wallace, "Revitalization Movements; Some Theoretical Considerations for Their Comparative Study," *American Anthropologist*, 58 (1956), 264–81; and Charles E. Hunter, "The Delaware Nativist Revival of the Mid-Eighteenth Century," *Ethnohistory*, 18 (1971), 39–50.

Social and Political Change

For social and political change in the eighteenth-century colonies students should consult the essays and bibliographies in Stanley N. Katz, ed., *Colonial America: Essays in Social and Political Development* (Boston, 1970) and Gary B. Nash, *Class and Society in Early America* (Englewood Cliffs, N.J., 1970). A few important books and articles which have appeared more recently are: J. M. Bumsted, "Religion, Finance, and Democracy in Massachusetts; The Town of Norton as a Case Study," *Journal of American History*, 57 (1970–71), 817–31; Edward M. Cook, Jr., "Social Behavior and Changing Values in Dedham, Massachusetts, 1700 to 1775," *William and Mary Quarterly*, 27 (1970), 546–80; Jack P. Greene, "Search for Identity; An Interpretation of the Meaning of Selected Patterns of Social Response in Eighteenth-Century America," *Journal of Social History*, 3 (1970), 189–224; James A. Henretta, *The Evolution of American Society, 1700–1815* (Lexington, Mass., 1973); Richard Hofstadter, *America at 1750; A Social Portrait* (New York, 1971); Rhys Isaac, "Problems of the Anglican Establishment in Virginia in the Era of the Great Awakening and the Parsons' Cause," *William and*

Mary Quarterly, 30 (1973), 3–32; Sung Bok Kim, "A New Look at the Great Landlords of Eighteenth-Century New York," *William and Mary Quarterly*, 27 (1970), 581–614; James T. Lemon, *The Best Poor Man's Country; A Geographical Study of Early Southeastern Pennsylvania* (Baltimore, 1972); Kenneth Lockridge, "Social Change and the Meaning of the American Revolution," *Journal of Social History*, 6 (1973), 403–39; Pauline Maier, "Popular Uprisings and Civil Authority in Eighteenth-Century Massachusetts," *William and Mary Quarterly*, 27 (1970), 3–35; Susan Norton, "Population Growth in Colonial America; A Study of Ipswich, Massachusetts," *Population Studies*, 25 (1971), 433–52; John C. Rainbolt, "The Alteration in the Relationship Between Leadership and Constituents in Virginia, 1660 to 1720," *William and Mary Quarterly*, 27 (1970), 411–34; Daniel Scott Smith, "The Demographic History of Colonial New England," *Journal of Economic History*, 32 (1972), 165–83; and G. B. Warden, *Boston, 1689–1776* (Boston, 1970).

index